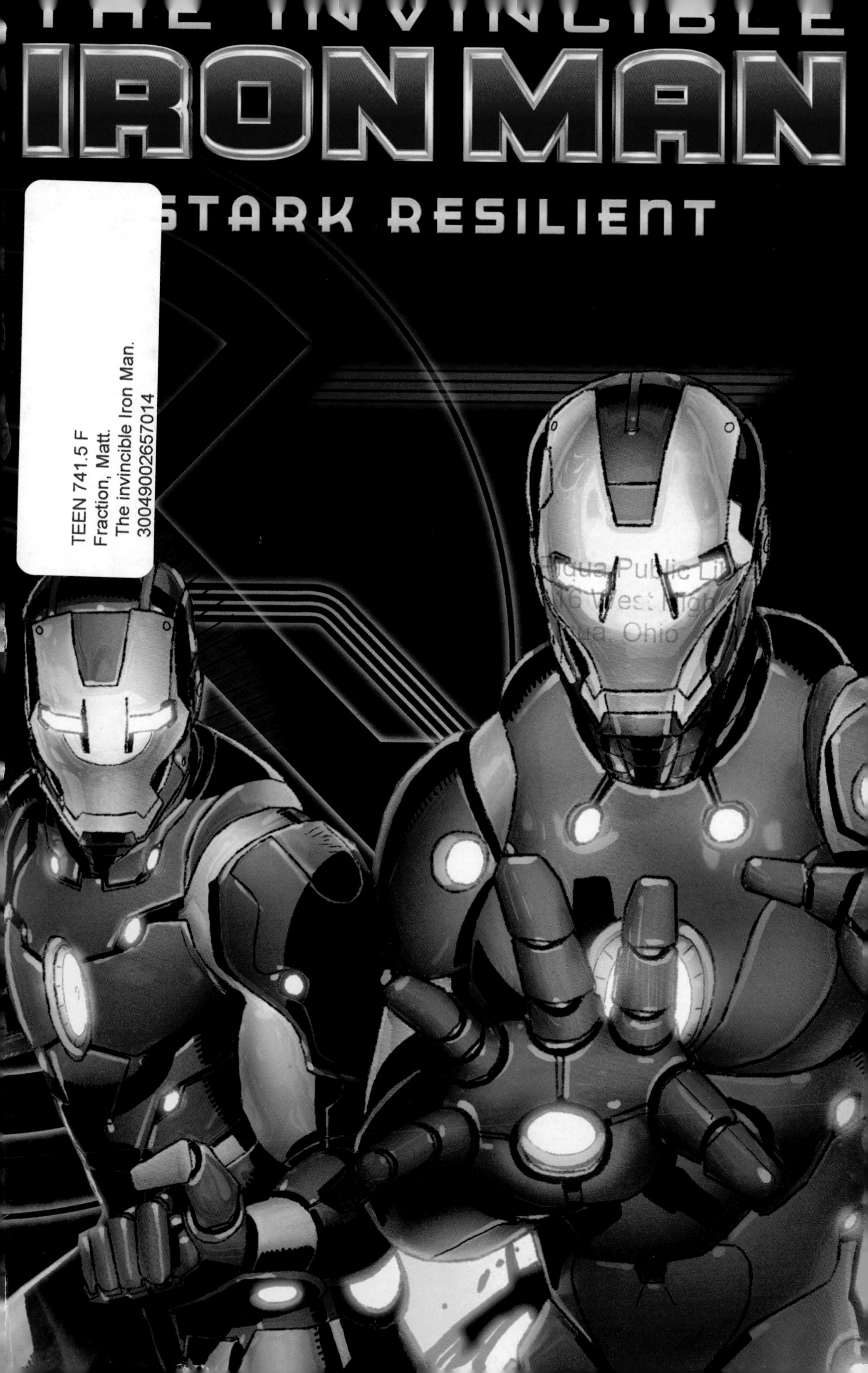
THE INVINCIBLE
IRON MAN
STARK RESILIENT

THE INVINCIBLE IRON MAN

STARK RESILIENT

WRITER: **MATT FRACTION**
ARTIST: **SALVADOR LARROCA**
COLORS: **FRANK D'ARMATA**

"AGAIN AT THE END OF THE WORLD WITH YOUR PAL PEPPER POTTS" & "GOOD MORNING, TONY"
ARTIST: **JAMIE MCKELVIE**
COLORS: **MATTHEW WILSON**

LETTERS: **VC'S JOE CARAMAGNA**
COVER ART: **SALVADOR LARROCA** & **FRANK D'ARMATA**
ASSISTANT EDITOR: **ALEJANDRO ARBONA**
EDITORS: **RALPH MACCHIO** & **STEPHEN WACKER**

COLLECTION EDITOR: **JENNIFER GRÜNWALD**
EDITORIAL ASSISTANTS: **JAMES EMMETT** & **JOE HOCHSTEIN**
ASSISTANT EDITORS: **ALEX STARBUCK** & **NELSON RIBEIRO**
EDITOR, SPECIAL PROJECTS: **MARK D. BEAZLEY**
SENIOR EDITOR, SPECIAL PROJECTS: **JEFF YOUNGQUIST**
SENIOR VICE PRESIDENT OF SALES: **DAVID GABRIEL**
BOOK DESIGNER: **RODOLFO MURAGUCHI**

EDITOR IN CHIEF: **JOE QUESADA**
PUBLISHER: **DAN BUCKLEY**
EXECUTIVE PRODUCER: **ALAN FINE**

INVINCIBLE IRON MAN VOL. 6: STARK RESILIENT BOOK 2. Contains material originally published in magazine form as INVINCIBLE IRON MAN #29-33. First printing 2011. Hardcover ISBN# 978-0-7851-4834-0. Softcover ISBN# 978-0-7851-4835-7. Published by MARVEL WORLDWIDE, INC., a subsidiary of MARVEL ENTERTAINMENT, LLC. OFFICE OF PUBLICATION: 135 West 50th Street, New York, NY 10020. Copyright © 2010 and 2011 Marvel Characters, Inc. All rights reserved. Hardcover: $19.99 per copy in the U.S. and $22.50 in Canada (GST #R127032852). Softcover: $15.99 per copy in the U.S. and $17.99 in Canada (GST #R127032852). Canadian Agreement #40668537. All characters featured in this issue and the distinctive names and likenesses thereof, and all related indicia are trademarks of Marvel Characters, Inc. No similarity between any of the names, characters, persons, and/or institutions in this magazine with those of any living or dead person or institution is intended, and any such similarity which may exist is purely coincidental. **Printed in the U.S.A.** ALAN FINE, EVP - Office of the President, Marvel Worldwide, Inc. and EVP & CMO Marvel Characters B.V.; DAN BUCKLEY, Chief Executive Officer and Publisher - Print, Animation & Digital Media; JIM SOKOLOWSKI, Chief Operating Officer; DAVID GABRIEL, SVP of Publishing Sales & Circulation; DAVID BOGART, SVP of Business Affairs & Talent Management; MICHAEL PASCIULLO, VP Merchandising & Communications; JIM O'KEEFE, VP of Operations & Logistics; DAN CARR, Executive Director of Publishing Technology; JUSTIN F. GABRIE, Director of Publishing & Editorial Operations; SUSAN CRESPI, Editorial Operations Manager; ALEX MORALES, Publishing Operations Manager; STAN LEE, Chairman Emeritus. For information regarding advertising in Marvel Comics or on Marvel.com, please contact Ron Stern, VP of Business Development, at rstern@marvel.com. For Marvel subscription inquiries, please call 800-217-9158. Manufactured between 1/3/2011 and 1/31/2011 (hardcover), and 1/3/2011 and

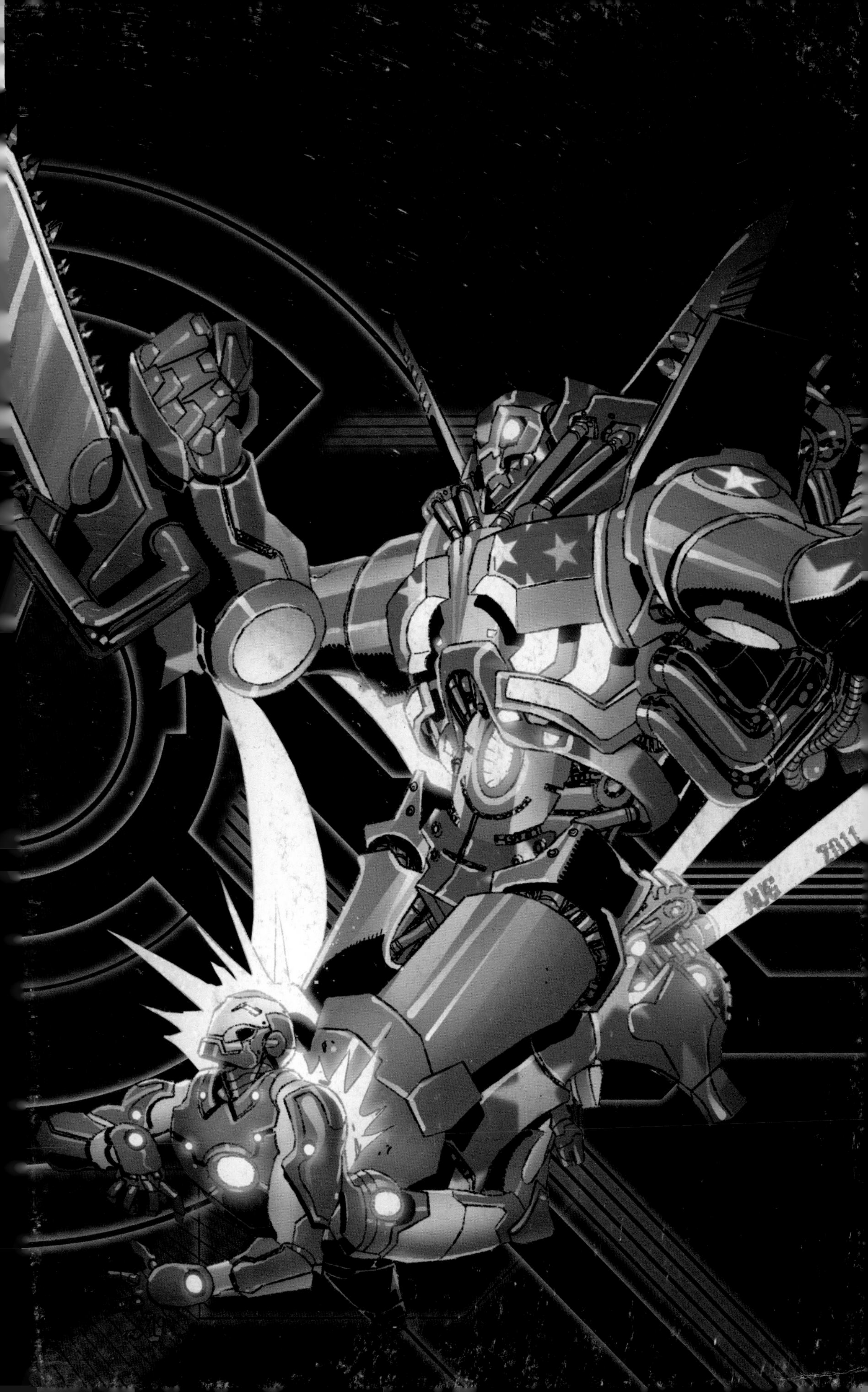
MG 2011

PREVIOUSLY:

To protect everything, Tony Stark destroyed everything. He drove his corporation into the ground, went on the run, incinerated his armory of Iron Man suits...even deleted the contents of his brain like a faulty hard drive.

Now Tony's back and fighting to get on his feet. His mind is restored...but he's missing his memories of the recent past. With his C.O.O. Pepper Potts and a small but dedicated staff, he's building a new repulsor technology company from the ground up — Stark Resilient. His goal: free energy for the world...starting with a high-performance RT-powered car. And with a new vision of what he has to do, he's built a revolutionary new suit of armor. But Pepper, who was once the armored hero Rescue, wants a new suit of armor of her own, as well. She's persuaded Tony to surgically implant a new repulsor like his in her chest.

Threats are on the horizon for Tony as well. Justine and Sasha Hammer, the daughter and granddaughter of Stark's late corporate rival Justin Hammer, are vying to take Stark's place at the top of the military-industrial food chain. They're peddling their own suit of armor to the highest bidder — the mecha-soldier of fortune, Detroit Steel — and selling surplus weaponry from the defunct law enforcement agency H.A.M.M.E.R. Not coincidentally, just as the Hammers are in Tokyo to license Detroit Steel to the Japanese military, an extremist cell carries out a destructive terror attack...with weapons made by Stark Industries. There are casualties, but Detroit Steel is in time to stop it heroically — and in front of the press. Hoping to investigate the perpetrators, Iron Man and his fellow armored hero War Machine take off for Tokyo, where they're upstaged and embarrassed by Detroit Steel and the Hammers.

But Tony encounters a familiar face...Sasha Hammer, Tony believes, is the girlfriend and partner in crime of his recent enemy Ezekiel Stane...who successfully crippled Stark Industries and nearly killed Tony...

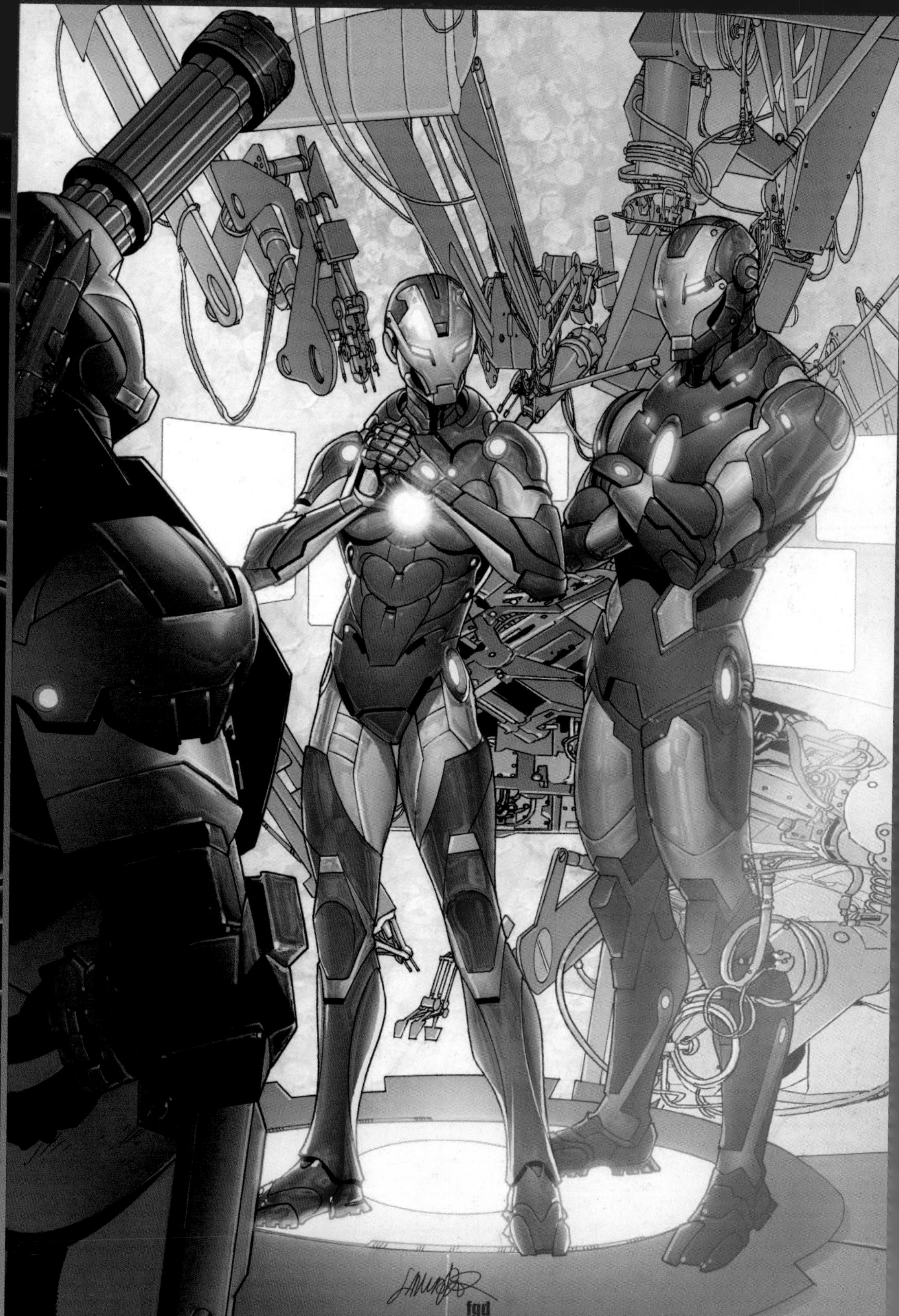
fgd

PREDATORS AND PREY IN THEIR

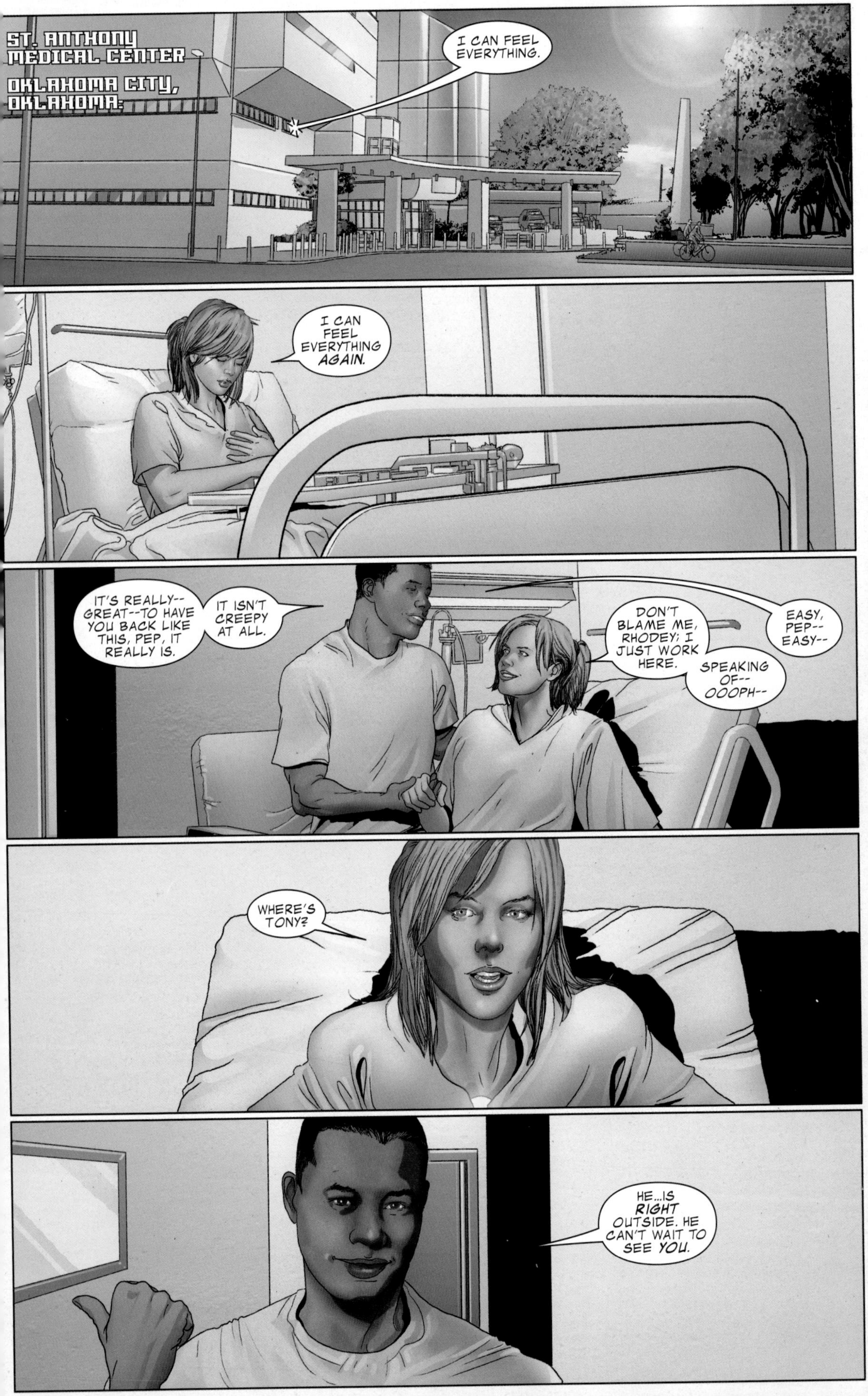
ST. ANTHONY MEDICAL CENTER
OKLAHOMA CITY, OKLAHOMA:
I CAN FEEL EVERYTHING.
I CAN FEEL EVERYTHING AGAIN.
IT'S REALLY--GREAT--TO HAVE YOU BACK LIKE THIS, PEP, IT REALLY IS.
IT ISN'T CREEPY AT ALL.
DON'T BLAME ME, RHODEY; I JUST WORK HERE.
EASY, PEP--EASY--
SPEAKING OF--OOOPH--
WHERE'S TONY?
HE...IS RIGHT OUTSIDE. HE CAN'T WAIT TO SEE YOU.

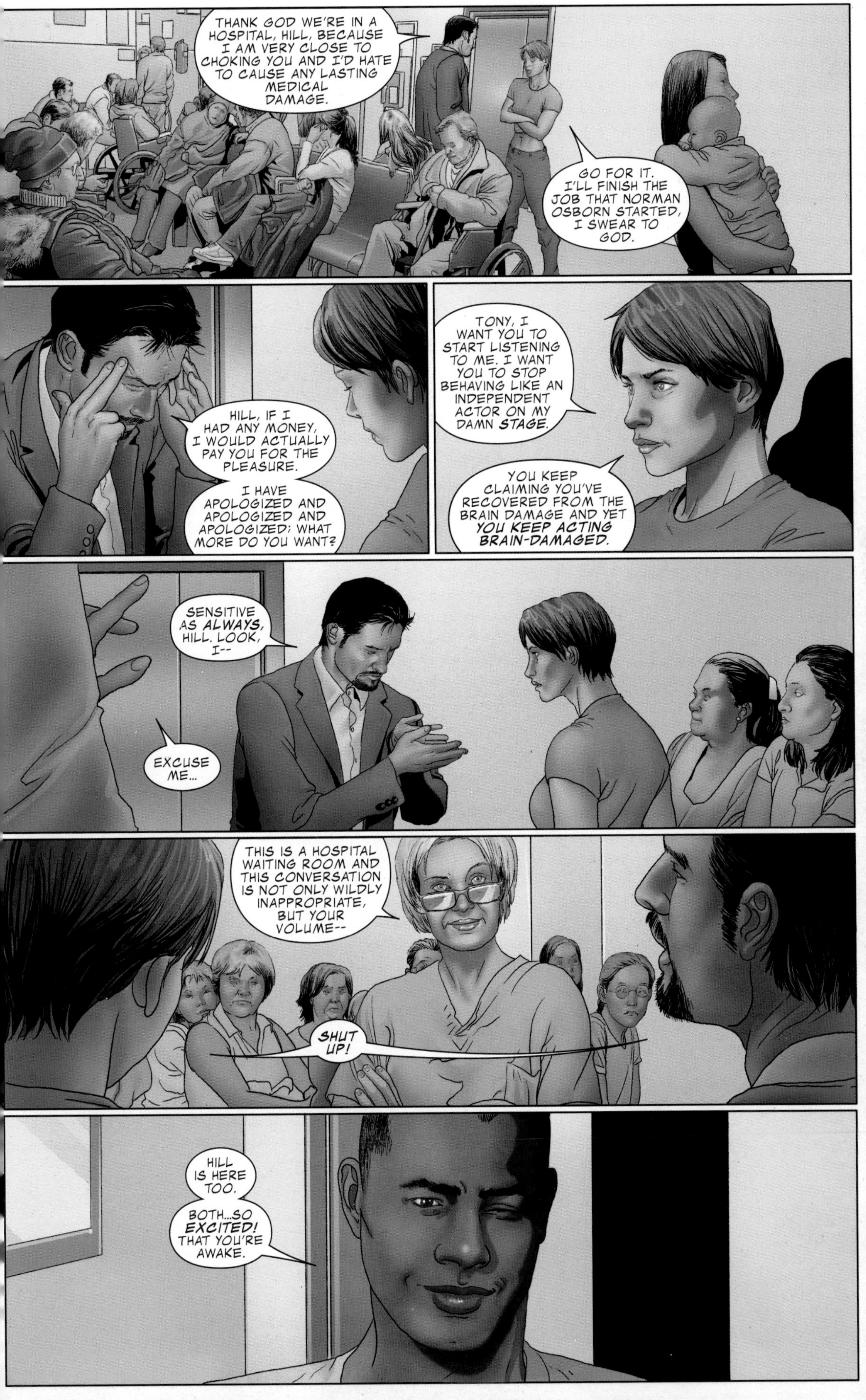
THANK GOD WE'RE IN A HOSPITAL, HILL, BECAUSE I AM VERY CLOSE TO CHOKING YOU AND I'D HATE TO CAUSE ANY LASTING MEDICAL DAMAGE.
GO FOR IT. I'LL FINISH THE JOB THAT NORMAN OSBORN STARTED, I SWEAR TO GOD.
HILL, IF I HAD ANY MONEY, I WOULD ACTUALLY PAY YOU FOR THE PLEASURE.
I HAVE APOLOGIZED AND APOLOGIZED AND APOLOGIZED; WHAT MORE DO YOU WANT?
TONY, I WANT YOU TO START LISTENING TO ME. I WANT YOU TO STOP BEHAVING LIKE AN INDEPENDENT ACTOR ON MY DAMN **STAGE**.
YOU KEEP CLAIMING YOU'VE RECOVERED FROM THE BRAIN DAMAGE AND YET ***YOU KEEP ACTING BRAIN-DAMAGED.***
SENSITIVE AS ***ALWAYS,*** HILL. LOOK, I--
EXCUSE ME...
THIS IS A HOSPITAL WAITING ROOM AND THIS CONVERSATION IS NOT ONLY WILDLY INAPPROPRIATE, BUT YOUR VOLUME--
SHUT UP!
HILL IS HERE TOO.
BOTH...SO ***EXCITED!*** THAT YOU'RE AWAKE.

HAMMER INDUSTRIES FACILITY
ELY, NEVADA:

WE CAN'T WAIT FOR YOU TO SEE THIS, LT. JOHNSON.

THE *TECHS* HAVE BEEN WORKING AROUND THE CLOCK ON THESE.

SAY HELLO TO YOUR BACKUP.

JUSTINE HAMMER. AS I LIVE AND BREATHE.

AND HERE I WAS THINKING YOU WERE GOING TO DROP THE BALL.

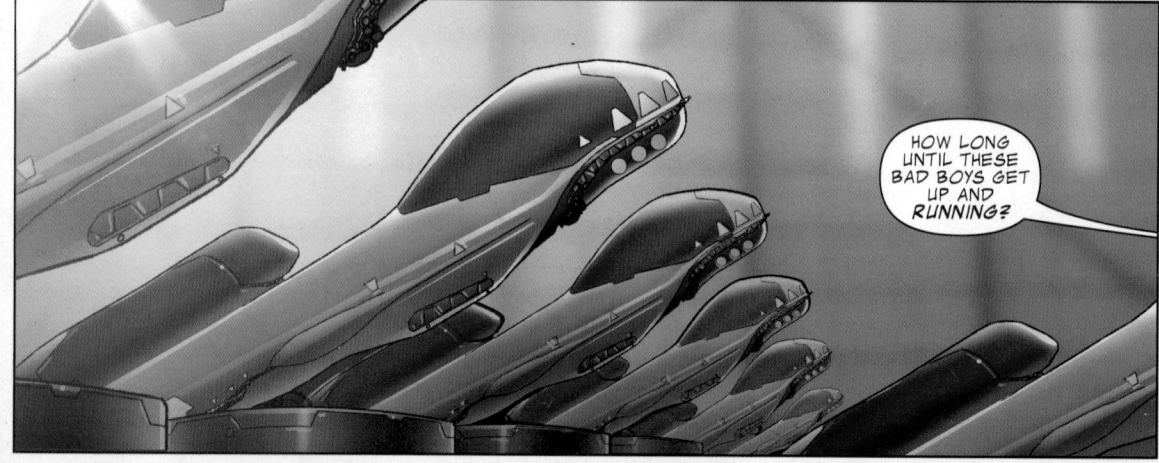

HOW LONG UNTIL THESE BAD BOYS GET UP AND *RUNNING?*

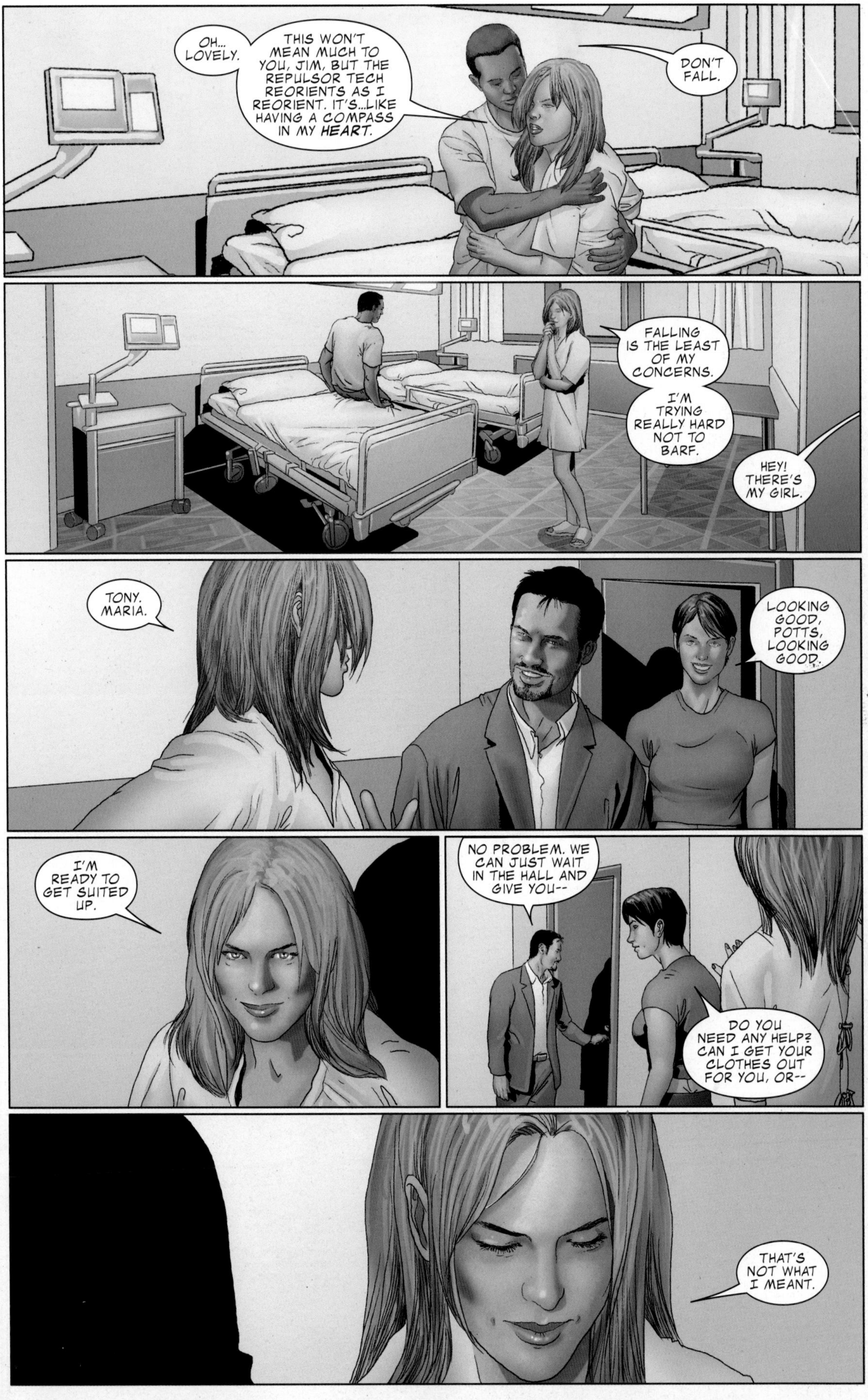
OH... LOVELY.
THIS WON'T MEAN MUCH TO YOU, JIM, BUT THE REPULSOR TECH REORIENTS AS I REORIENT. IT'S...LIKE HAVING A COMPASS IN MY HEART.
DON'T FALL.
FALLING IS THE LEAST OF MY CONCERNS.
I'M TRYING REALLY HARD NOT TO BARF.
HEY! THERE'S MY GIRL.
TONY. MARIA.
LOOKING GOOD, POTTS, LOOKING GOOD.
I'M READY TO GET SUITED UP.
NO PROBLEM. WE CAN JUST WAIT IN THE HALL AND GIVE YOU--
DO YOU NEED ANY HELP? CAN I GET YOUR CLOTHES OUT FOR YOU, OR--
THAT'S NOT WHAT I MEANT.

SASHA?
IT'S MOM.

WE'RE READY WHENEVER YOUR NERDS ARE READY.

BE RESPECTFUL, MOTHER DARLING.

I'M GOING TO MURDER YOU FOR MAKING ME DRESS LIKE THIS.

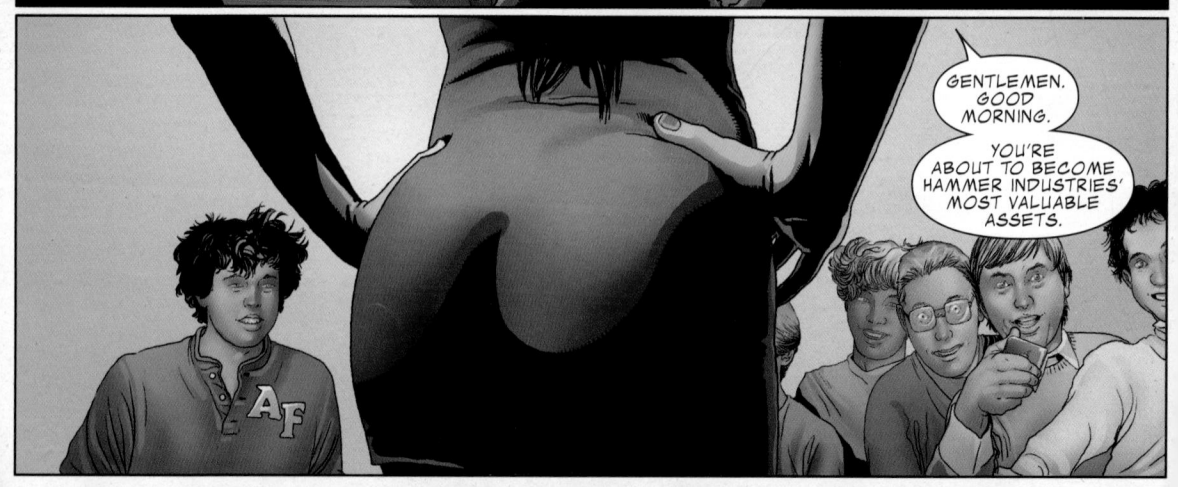

GENTLEMEN. GOOD MORNING.

YOU'RE ABOUT TO BECOME HAMMER INDUSTRIES' MOST VALUABLE ASSETS.

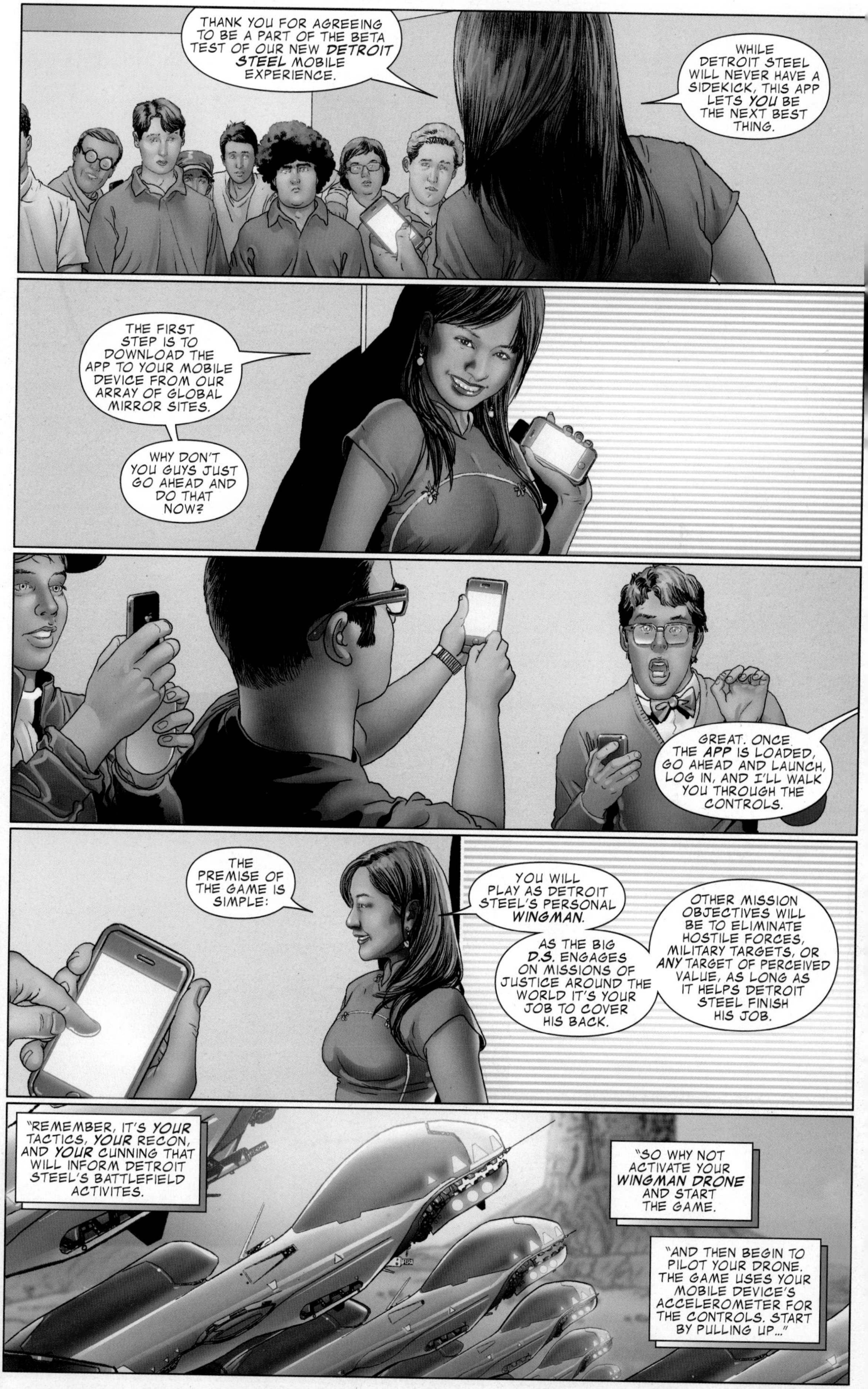

THANK YOU FOR AGREEING TO BE A PART OF THE BETA TEST OF OUR NEW *DETROIT STEEL* MOBILE EXPERIENCE.
WHILE DETROIT STEEL WILL NEVER HAVE A SIDEKICK, THIS APP LETS *YOU* BE THE NEXT BEST THING.
THE FIRST STEP IS TO DOWNLOAD THE APP TO YOUR MOBILE DEVICE FROM OUR ARRAY OF GLOBAL MIRROR SITES.
WHY DON'T YOU GUYS JUST GO AHEAD AND DO THAT NOW?
GREAT. ONCE THE *APP* IS LOADED, GO AHEAD AND LAUNCH, LOG IN, AND I'LL WALK YOU THROUGH THE CONTROLS.
THE PREMISE OF THE GAME IS SIMPLE:
YOU WILL PLAY AS DETROIT STEEL'S PERSONAL *WINGMAN*.
AS THE BIG *D.S.* ENGAGES ON MISSIONS OF JUSTICE AROUND THE WORLD IT'S YOUR JOB TO COVER HIS BACK.
OTHER MISSION OBJECTIVES WILL BE TO ELIMINATE HOSTILE FORCES, MILITARY TARGETS, OR *ANY* TARGET OF PERCEIVED VALUE, AS LONG AS IT HELPS DETROIT STEEL FINISH HIS JOB.
"REMEMBER, IT'S *YOUR* TACTICS, *YOUR* RECON, AND *YOUR* CUNNING THAT WILL INFORM DETROIT STEEL'S BATTLEFIELD ACTIVITES.
"SO WHY NOT ACTIVATE YOUR *WINGMAN DRONE* AND START THE GAME.
"AND THEN BEGIN TO PILOT YOUR DRONE. THE GAME USES YOUR MOBILE DEVICE'S ACCELEROMETER FOR THE CONTROLS. START BY PULLING UP..."

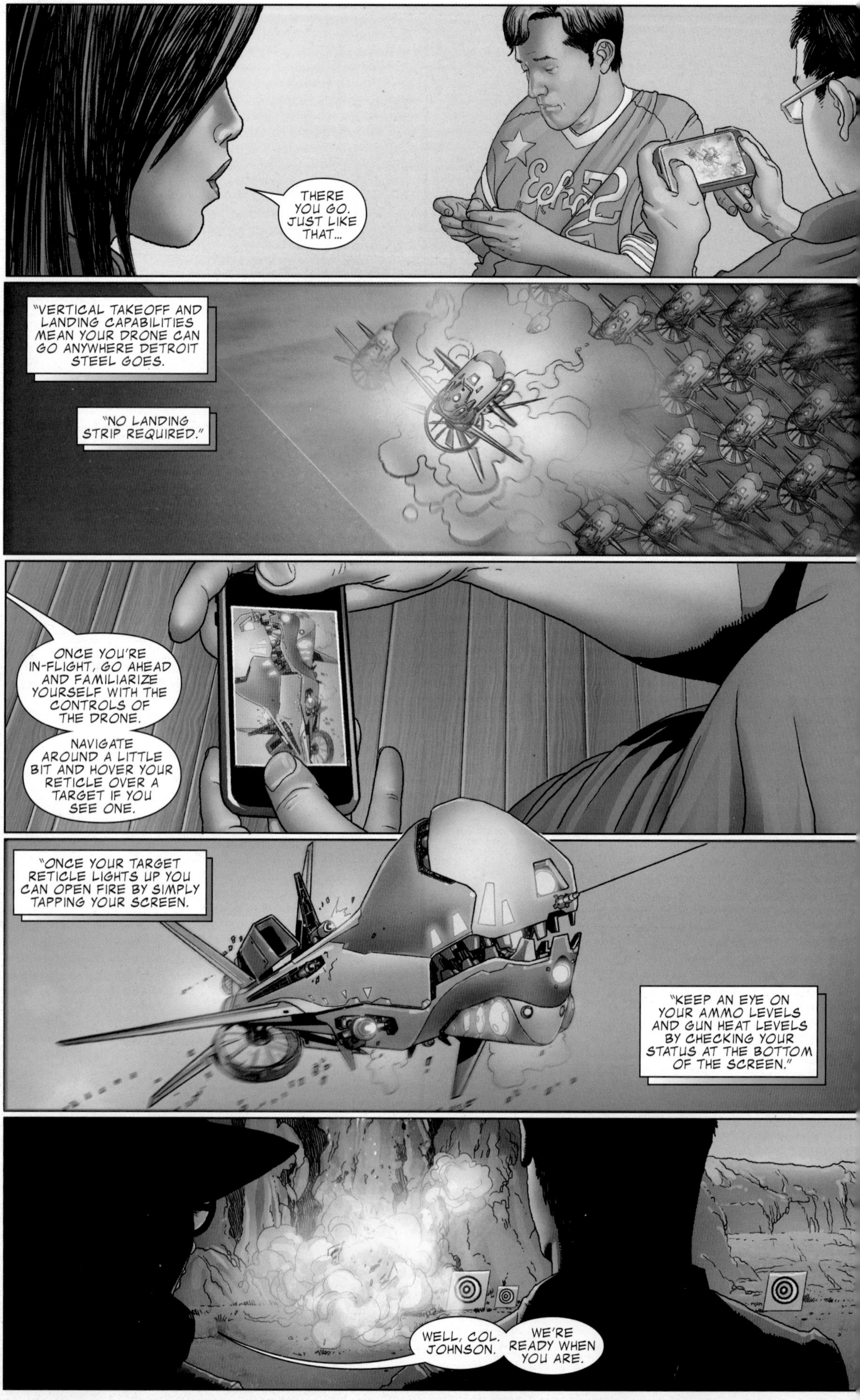
THERE YOU GO. JUST LIKE THAT...
"VERTICAL TAKEOFF AND LANDING CAPABILITIES MEAN YOUR DRONE CAN GO ANYWHERE DETROIT STEEL GOES.
"NO LANDING STRIP REQUIRED."
ONCE YOU'RE IN-FLIGHT, GO AHEAD AND FAMILIARIZE YOURSELF WITH THE CONTROLS OF THE DRONE.
NAVIGATE AROUND A LITTLE BIT AND HOVER YOUR RETICLE OVER A TARGET IF YOU SEE ONE.
"ONCE YOUR TARGET RETICLE LIGHTS UP YOU CAN OPEN FIRE BY SIMPLY TAPPING YOUR SCREEN.
"KEEP AN EYE ON YOUR AMMO LEVELS AND GUN HEAT LEVELS BY CHECKING YOUR STATUS AT THE BOTTOM OF THE SCREEN."
WELL, COL. JOHNSON.
WE'RE READY WHEN YOU ARE.

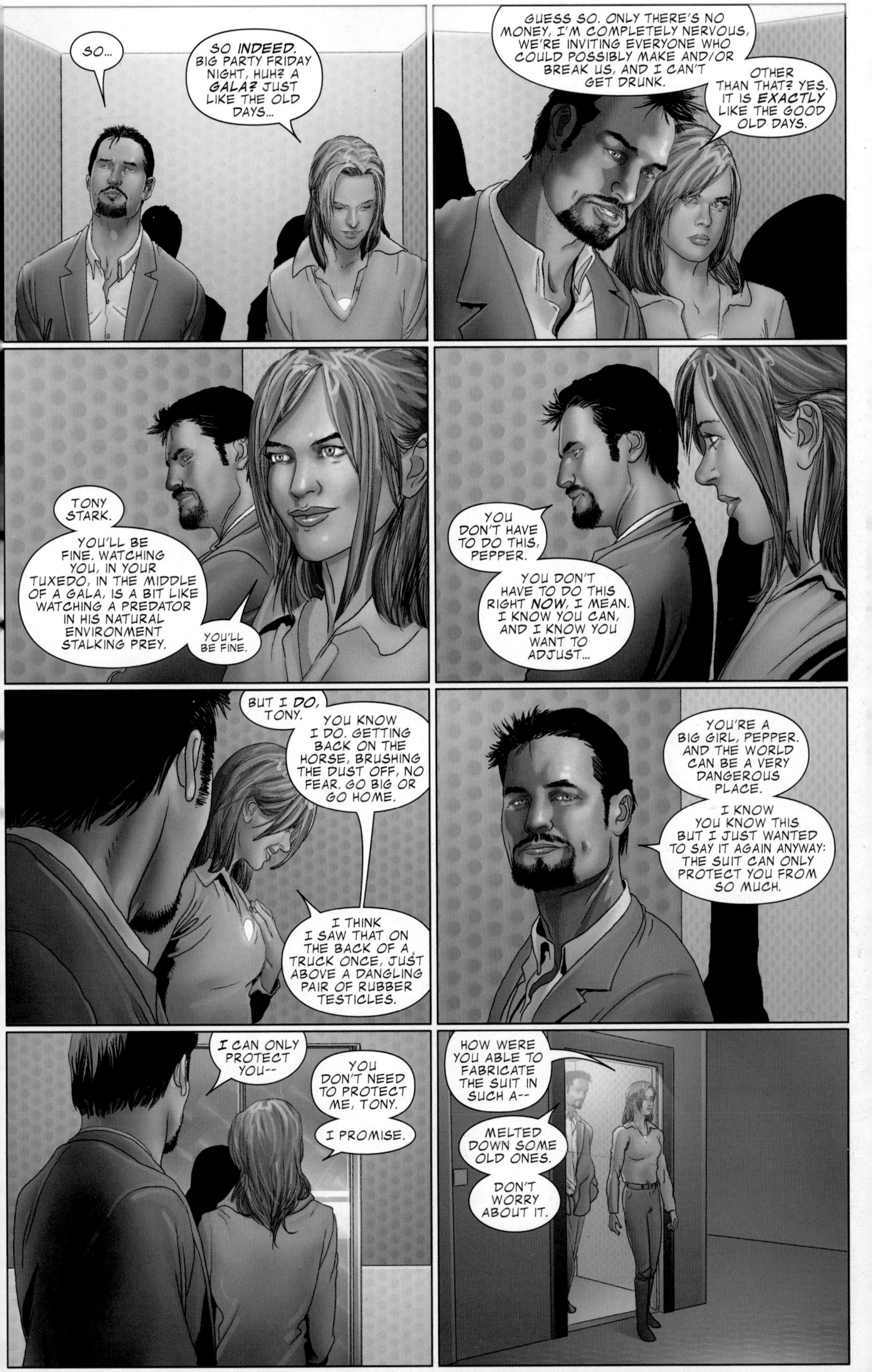
SO...
SO INDEED. BIG PARTY FRIDAY NIGHT, HUH? A GALA? JUST LIKE THE OLD DAYS...
GUESS SO. ONLY THERE'S NO MONEY, I'M COMPLETELY NERVOUS, WE'RE INVITING EVERYONE WHO COULD POSSIBLY MAKE AND/OR BREAK US, AND I CAN'T GET DRUNK.
OTHER THAN THAT? YES. IT IS EXACTLY LIKE THE GOOD OLD DAYS.
TONY STARK.
YOU'LL BE FINE. WATCHING YOU, IN YOUR TUXEDO, IN THE MIDDLE OF A GALA, IS A BIT LIKE WATCHING A PREDATOR IN HIS NATURAL ENVIRONMENT STALKING PREY.
YOU'LL BE FINE.
YOU DON'T HAVE TO DO THIS, PEPPER.
YOU DON'T HAVE TO DO THIS RIGHT NOW, I MEAN. I KNOW YOU CAN, AND I KNOW YOU WANT TO ADJUST...
BUT I DO, TONY.
YOU KNOW I DO. GETTING BACK ON THE HORSE, BRUSHING THE DUST OFF, NO FEAR. GO BIG OR GO HOME.
I THINK I SAW THAT ON THE BACK OF A TRUCK ONCE, JUST ABOVE A DANGLING PAIR OF RUBBER TESTICLES.
YOU'RE A BIG GIRL, PEPPER. AND THE WORLD CAN BE A VERY DANGEROUS PLACE.
I KNOW YOU KNOW THIS BUT I JUST WANTED TO SAY IT AGAIN ANYWAY: THE SUIT CAN ONLY PROTECT YOU FROM SO MUCH.
I CAN ONLY PROTECT YOU--
YOU DON'T NEED TO PROTECT ME, TONY.
I PROMISE.
HOW WERE YOU ABLE TO FABRICATE THE SUIT IN SUCH A--
MELTED DOWN SOME OLD ONES.
DON'T WORRY ABOUT IT.

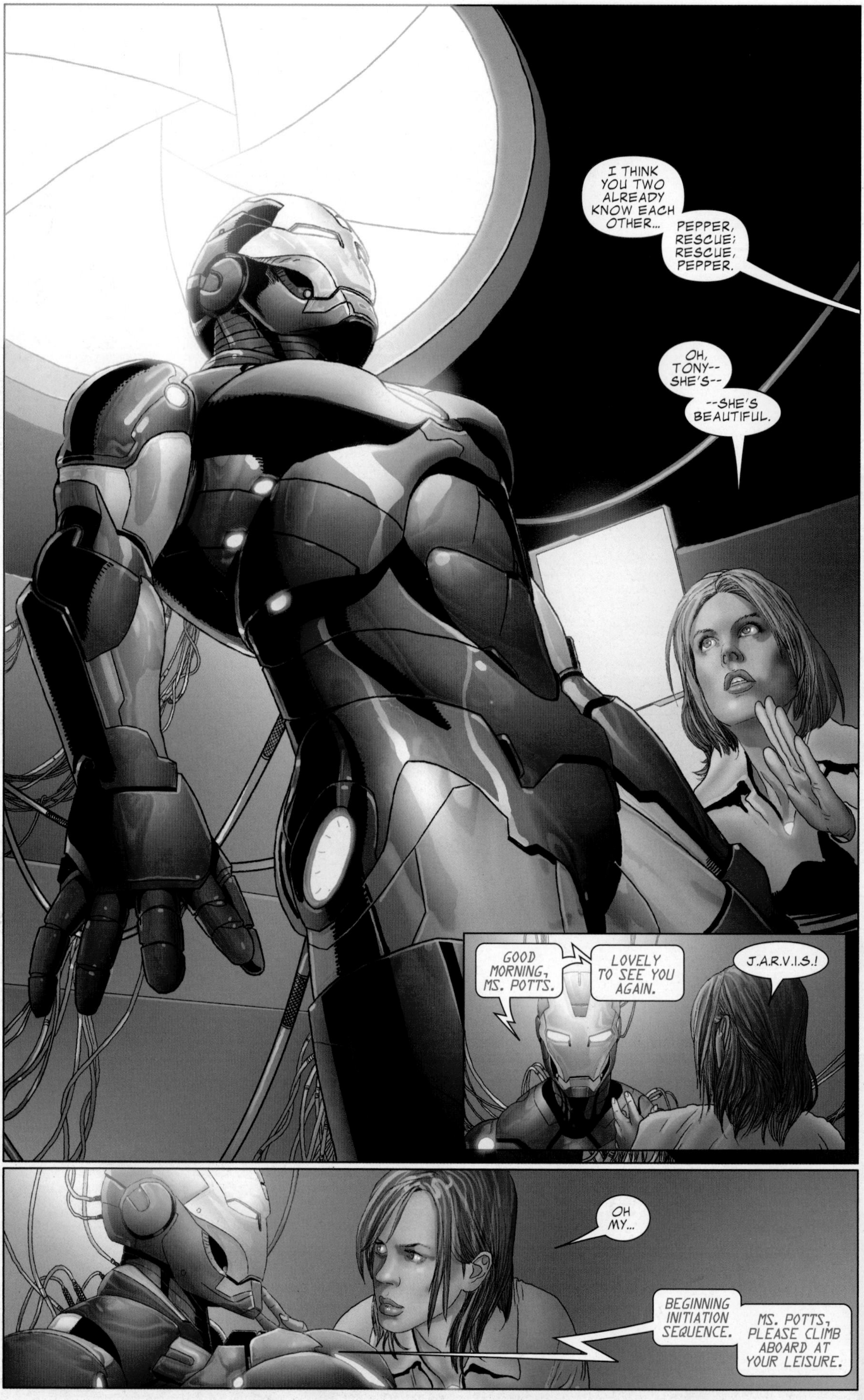
I THINK YOU TWO ALREADY KNOW EACH OTHER...
PEPPER, RESCUE; RESCUE, PEPPER.
OH, TONY-- SHE'S--
--SHE'S BEAUTIFUL.
GOOD MORNING, MS. POTTS.
LOVELY TO SEE YOU AGAIN.
J.A.R.V.I.S.!
OH MY...
BEGINNING INITIATION SEQUENCE.
MS. POTTS, PLEASE CLIMB ABOARD AT YOUR LEISURE.

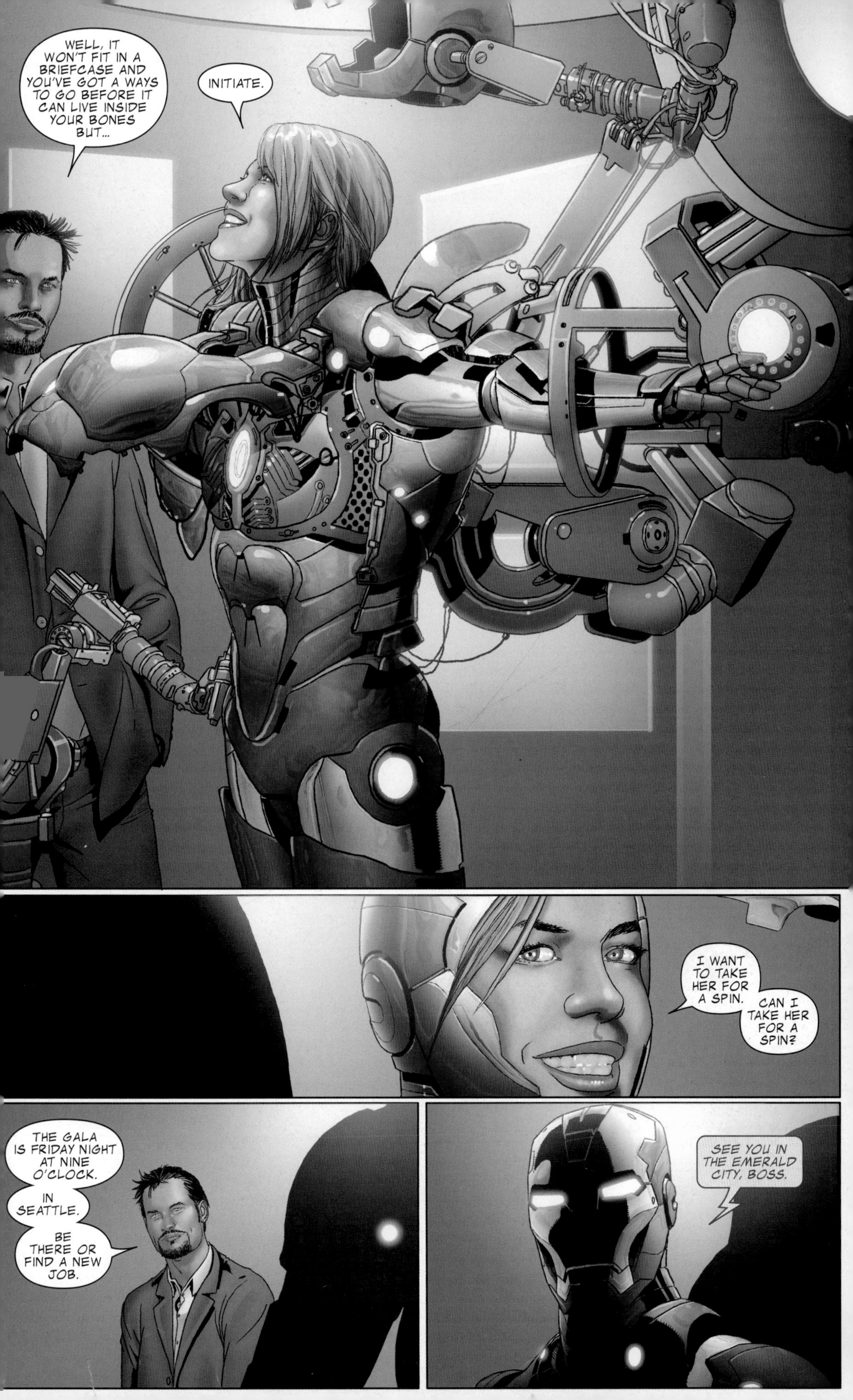
WELL, IT WON'T FIT IN A BRIEFCASE AND YOU'VE GOT A WAYS TO GO BEFORE IT CAN LIVE INSIDE YOUR BONES BUT...
INITIATE.
I WANT TO TAKE HER FOR A SPIN.
CAN I TAKE HER FOR A SPIN?
THE GALA IS FRIDAY NIGHT AT NINE O'CLOCK.
IN SEATTLE.
BE THERE OR FIND A NEW JOB.
SEE YOU IN THE EMERALD CITY, BOSS.

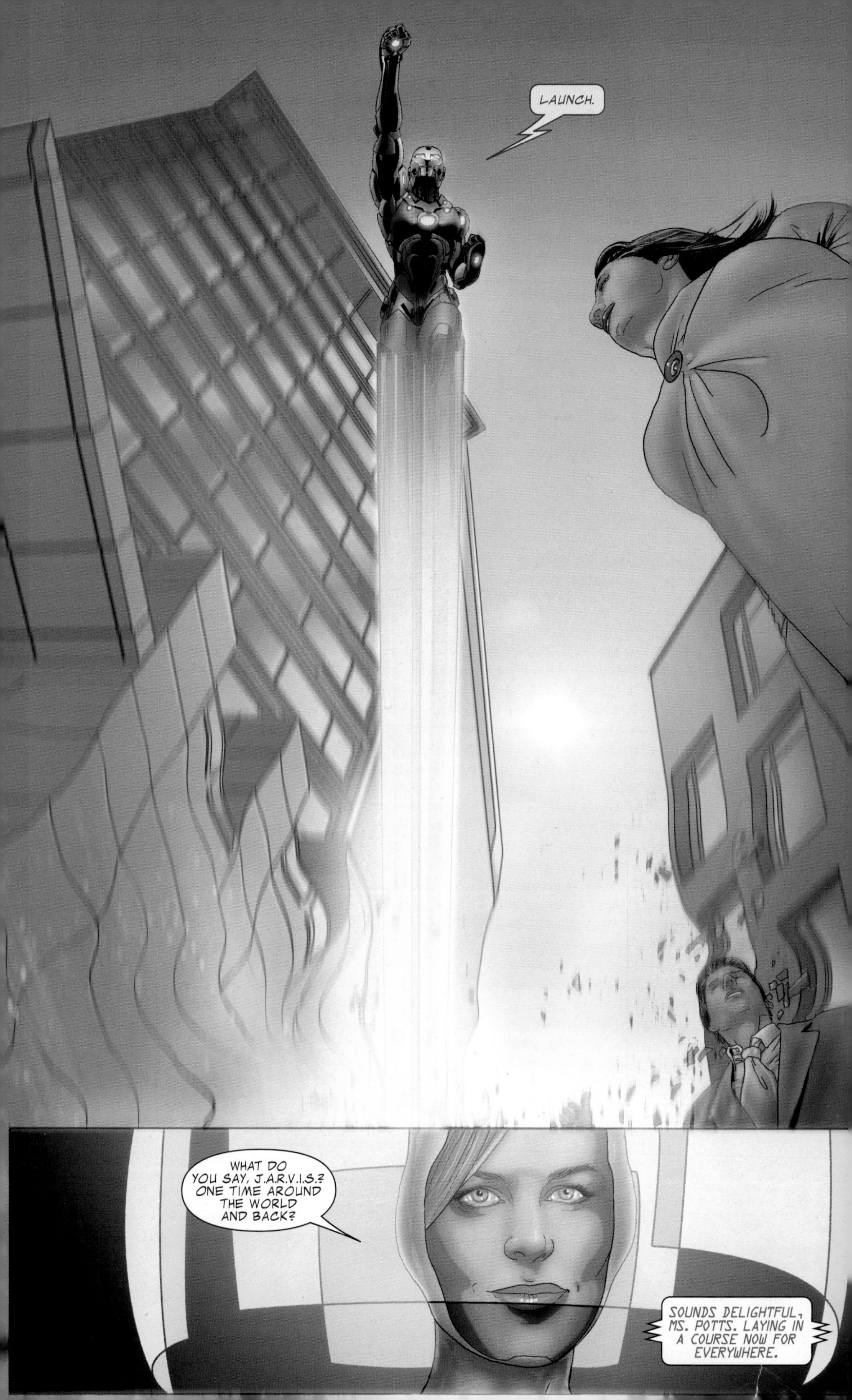
LAUNCH.
WHAT DO YOU SAY, J.A.R.V.I.S.? ONE TIME AROUND THE WORLD AND BACK?
SOUNDS DELIGHTFUL, MS. POTTS. LAYING IN A COURSE NOW FOR EVERYWHERE.

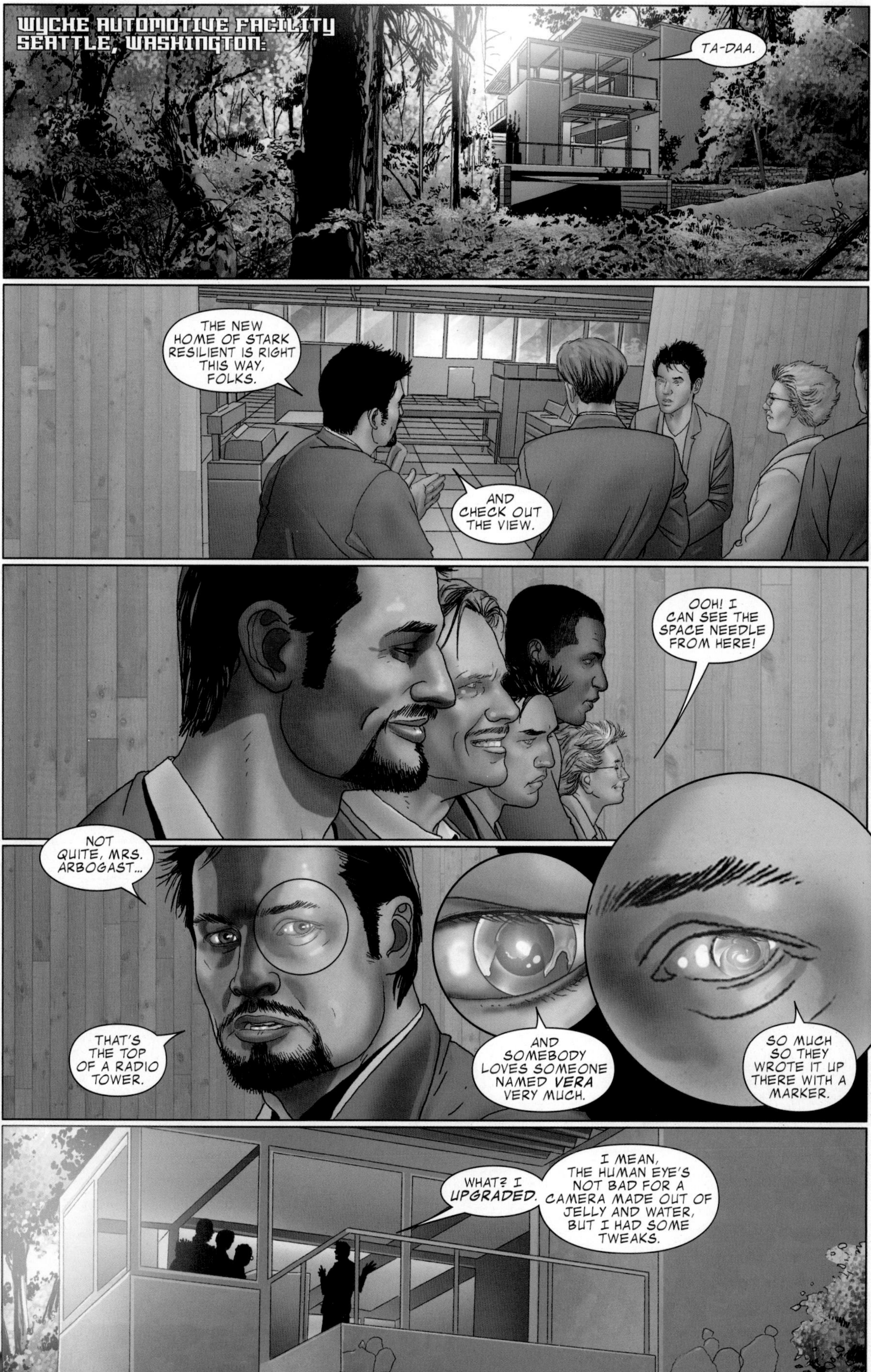

WYCKE AUTOMOTIVE FACILITY
SEATTLE, WASHINGTON:
TA-DAA.
THE NEW HOME OF STARK RESILIENT IS RIGHT THIS WAY, FOLKS.
AND CHECK OUT THE VIEW.
OOH! I CAN SEE THE SPACE NEEDLE FROM HERE!
NOT QUITE, MRS. ARBOGAST...
THAT'S THE TOP OF A RADIO TOWER.
AND SOMEBODY LOVES SOMEONE NAMED VERA VERY MUCH.
SO MUCH SO THEY WROTE IT UP THERE WITH A MARKER.
WHAT? I UPGRADED.
I MEAN, THE HUMAN EYE'S NOT BAD FOR A CAMERA MADE OUT OF JELLY AND WATER, BUT I HAD SOME TWEAKS.

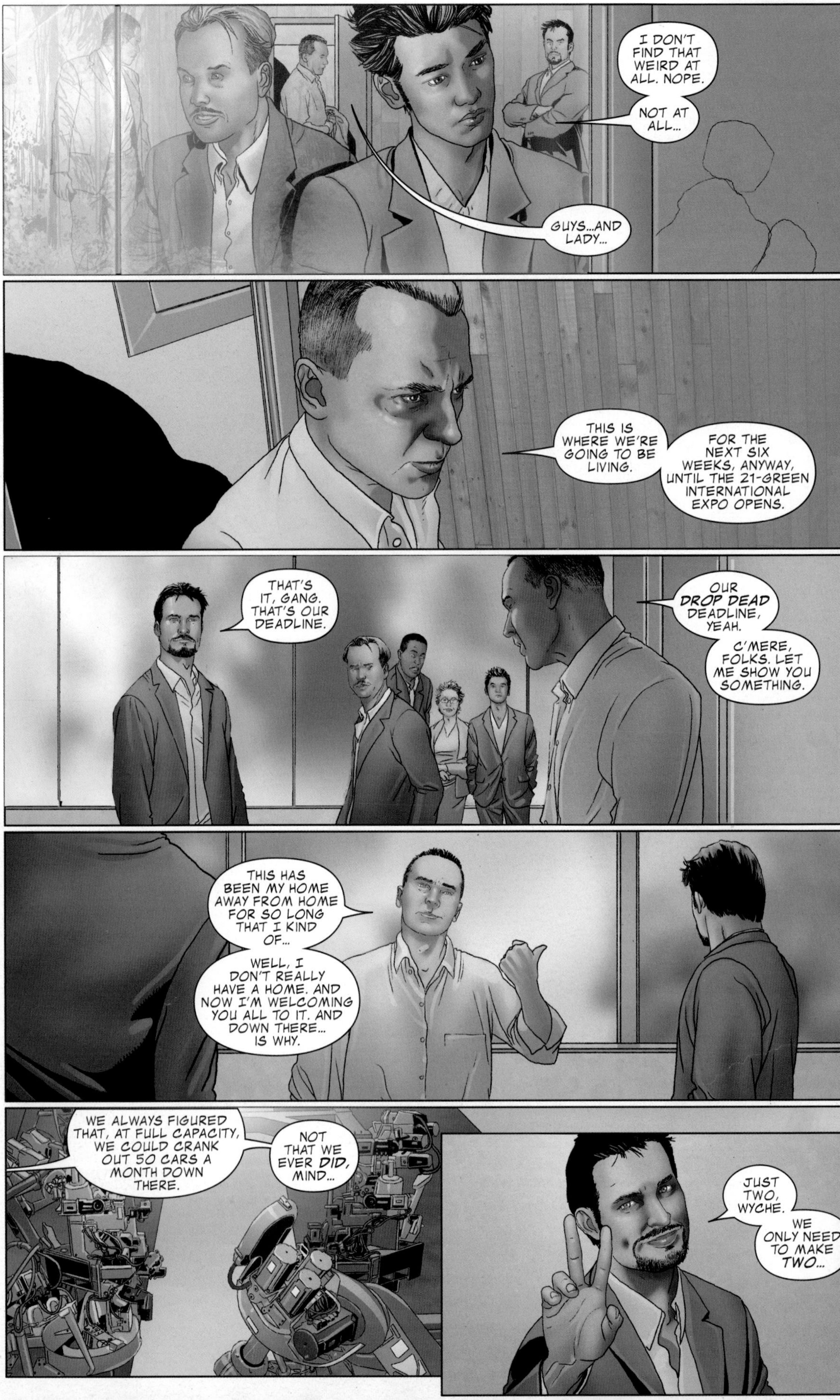
I DON'T FIND THAT WEIRD AT ALL. NOPE.
NOT AT ALL...
GUYS...AND LADY...
THIS IS WHERE WE'RE GOING TO BE LIVING.
FOR THE NEXT SIX WEEKS, ANYWAY, UNTIL THE 21-GREEN INTERNATIONAL EXPO OPENS.
THAT'S IT, GANG. THAT'S OUR DEADLINE.
OUR ***DROP DEAD*** DEADLINE, YEAH.
C'MERE, FOLKS. LET ME SHOW YOU SOMETHING.
THIS HAS BEEN MY HOME AWAY FROM HOME FOR SO LONG THAT I KIND OF...
WELL, I DON'T REALLY HAVE A HOME. AND NOW I'M WELCOMING YOU ALL TO IT. AND DOWN THERE... IS WHY.
WE ALWAYS FIGURED THAT, AT FULL CAPACITY, WE COULD CRANK OUT 50 CARS A MONTH DOWN THERE.
NOT THAT WE EVER ***DID,*** MIND...
JUST TWO, WYCHE.
WE ONLY NEED TO MAKE ***TWO...***

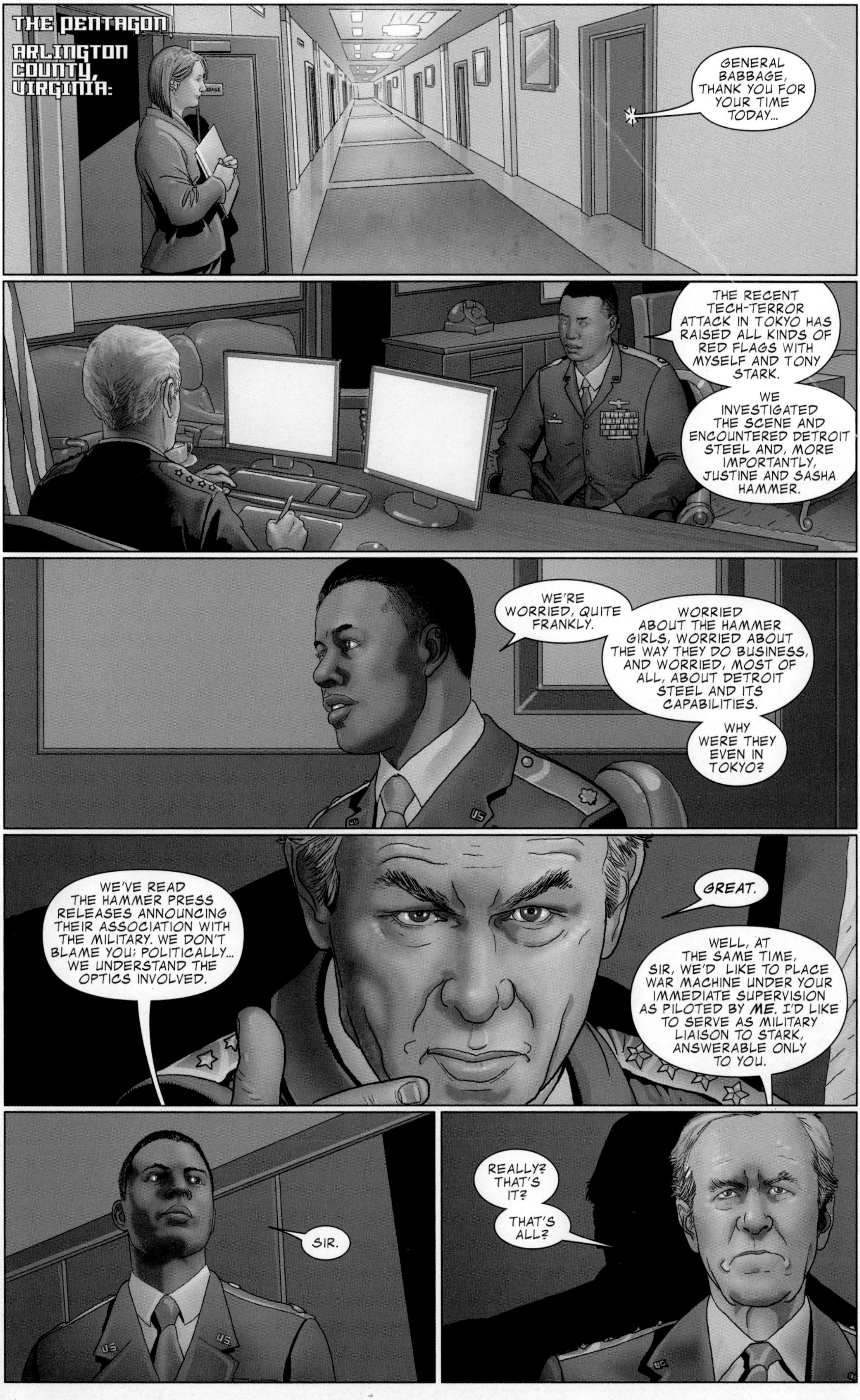
THE PENTAGON
ARLINGTON COUNTY, VIRGINIA:
GENERAL BABBAGE, THANK YOU FOR YOUR TIME TODAY...
THE RECENT TECH-TERROR ATTACK IN TOKYO HAS RAISED ALL KINDS OF RED FLAGS WITH MYSELF AND TONY STARK.
WE INVESTIGATED THE SCENE AND ENCOUNTERED DETROIT STEEL AND, MORE IMPORTANTLY, JUSTINE AND SASHA HAMMER.
WE'RE WORRIED, QUITE FRANKLY.
WORRIED ABOUT THE HAMMER GIRLS, WORRIED ABOUT THE WAY THEY DO BUSINESS, AND WORRIED, MOST OF ALL, ABOUT DETROIT STEEL AND ITS CAPABILITIES.
WHY WERE THEY EVEN IN TOKYO?
WE'VE READ THE HAMMER PRESS RELEASES ANNOUNCING THEIR ASSOCIATION WITH THE MILITARY. WE DON'T BLAME YOU; POLITICALLY... WE UNDERSTAND THE OPTICS INVOLVED.
GREAT.
WELL, AT THE SAME TIME, SIR, WE'D LIKE TO PLACE WAR MACHINE UNDER YOUR IMMEDIATE SUPERVISION AS PILOTED BY ME. I'D LIKE TO SERVE AS MILITARY LIAISON TO STARK, ANSWERABLE ONLY TO YOU.
SIR.
REALLY? THAT'S IT?
THAT'S ALL?

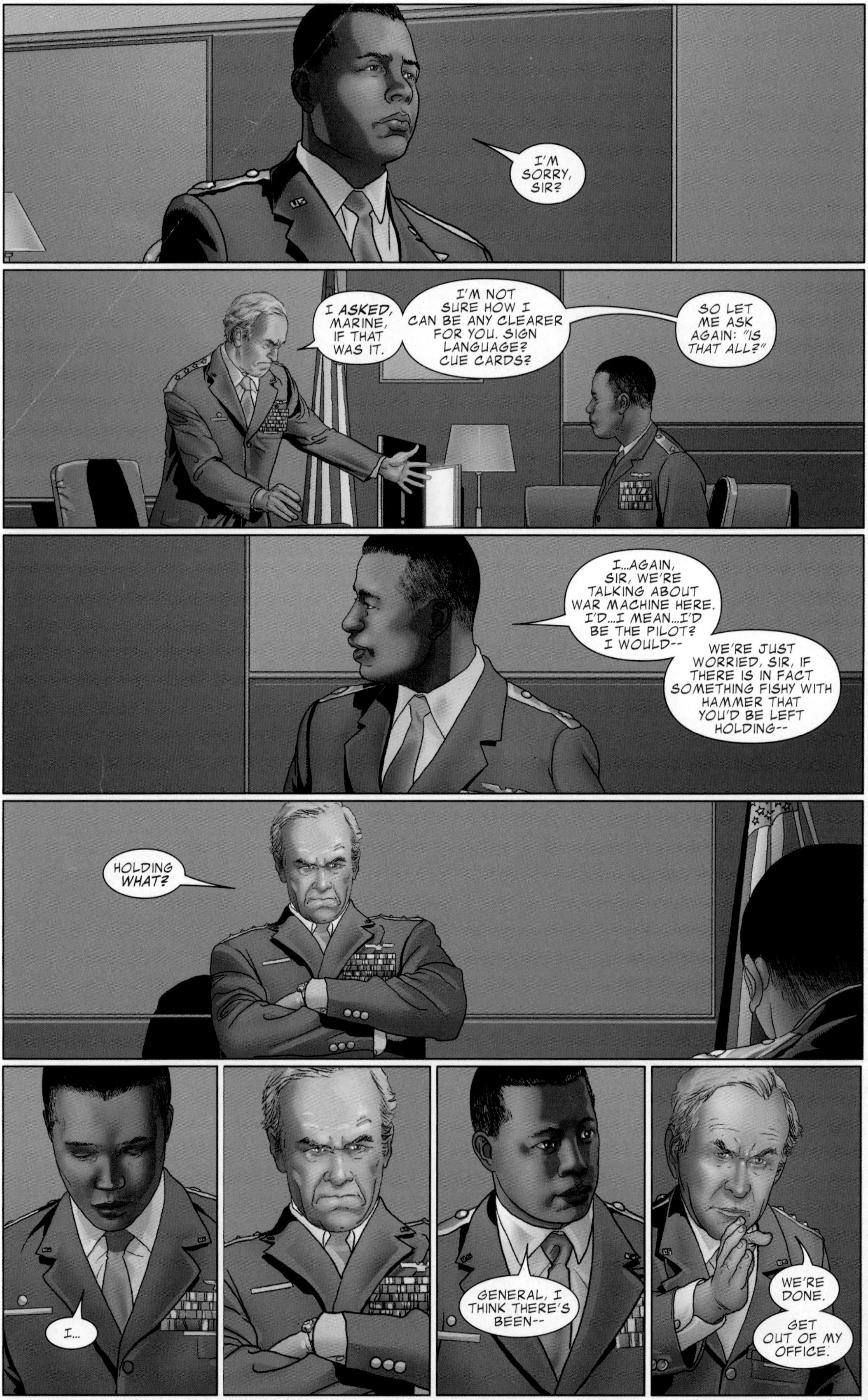
I'M SORRY, SIR?
I ASKED, MARINE, IF THAT WAS IT.
I'M NOT SURE HOW I CAN BE ANY CLEARER FOR YOU. SIGN LANGUAGE? CUE CARDS?
SO LET ME ASK AGAIN: "IS THAT ALL?"
I...AGAIN, SIR, WE'RE TALKING ABOUT WAR MACHINE HERE. I'D...I MEAN...I'D BE THE PILOT? I WOULD--
WE'RE JUST WORRIED, SIR, IF THERE IS IN FACT SOMETHING FISHY WITH HAMMER THAT YOU'D BE LEFT HOLDING--
HOLDING WHAT?
I...
GENERAL, I THINK THERE'S BEEN--
WE'RE DONE.
GET OUT OF MY OFFICE.

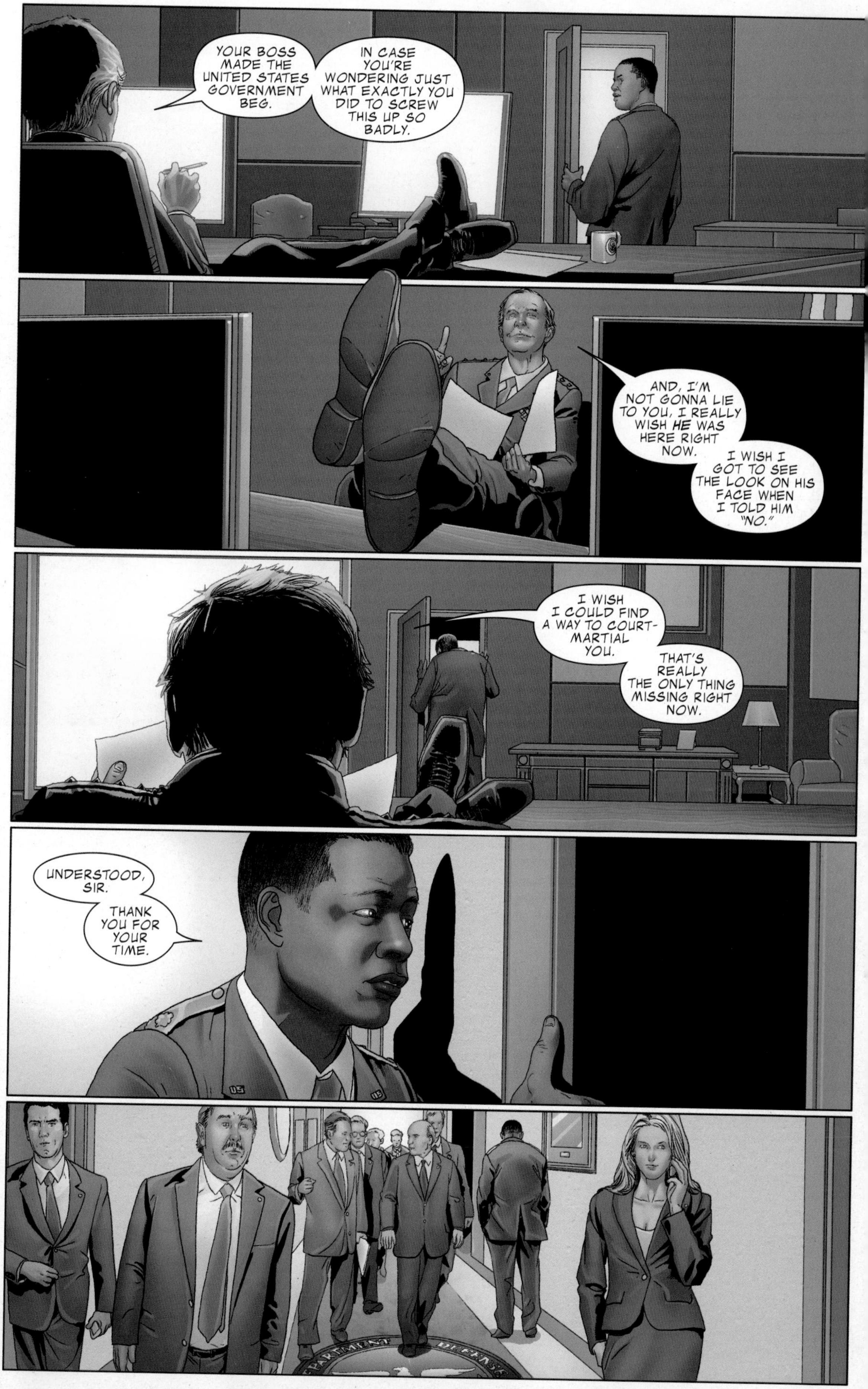
YOUR BOSS MADE THE UNITED STATES GOVERNMENT BEG.
IN CASE YOU'RE WONDERING JUST WHAT EXACTLY YOU DID TO SCREW THIS UP SO BADLY.
AND, I'M NOT GONNA LIE TO YOU, I REALLY WISH *HE* WAS HERE RIGHT NOW.
I WISH I GOT TO SEE THE LOOK ON HIS FACE WHEN I TOLD HIM "NO."
I WISH I COULD FIND A WAY TO COURT-MARTIAL YOU.
THAT'S REALLY THE ONLY THING MISSING RIGHT NOW.
UNDERSTOOD, SIR.
THANK YOU FOR YOUR TIME.

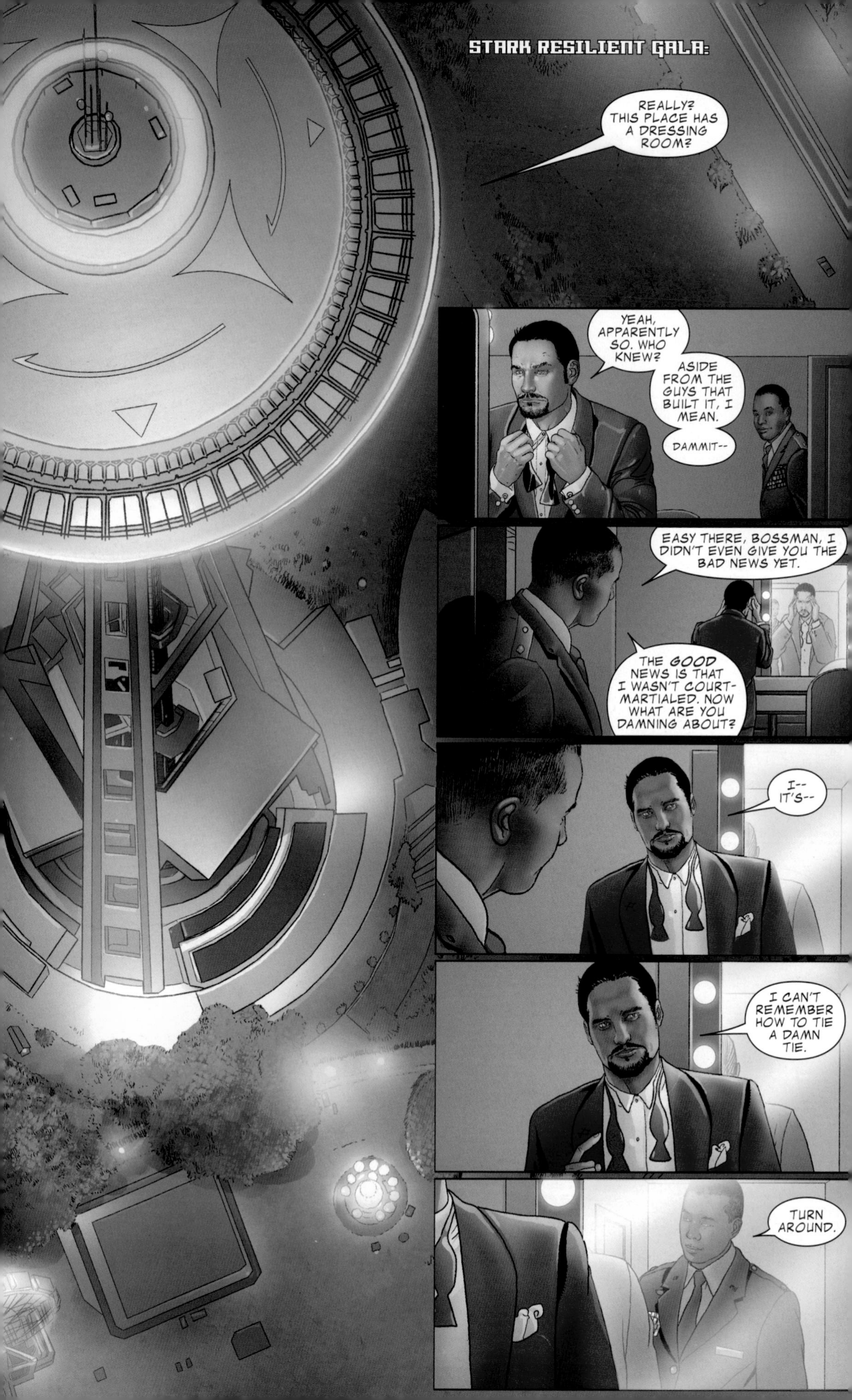
STARK RESILIENT GALA:
REALLY? THIS PLACE HAS A DRESSING ROOM?
YEAH, APPARENTLY SO. WHO KNEW?
ASIDE FROM THE GUYS THAT BUILT IT, I MEAN.
DAMMIT--
EASY THERE, BOSSMAN, I DIDN'T EVEN GIVE YOU THE BAD NEWS YET.
THE GOOD NEWS IS THAT I WASN'T COURT-MARTIALED. NOW WHAT ARE YOU DAMNING ABOUT?
I-- IT'S--
I CAN'T REMEMBER HOW TO TIE A DAMN TIE.
TURN AROUND.

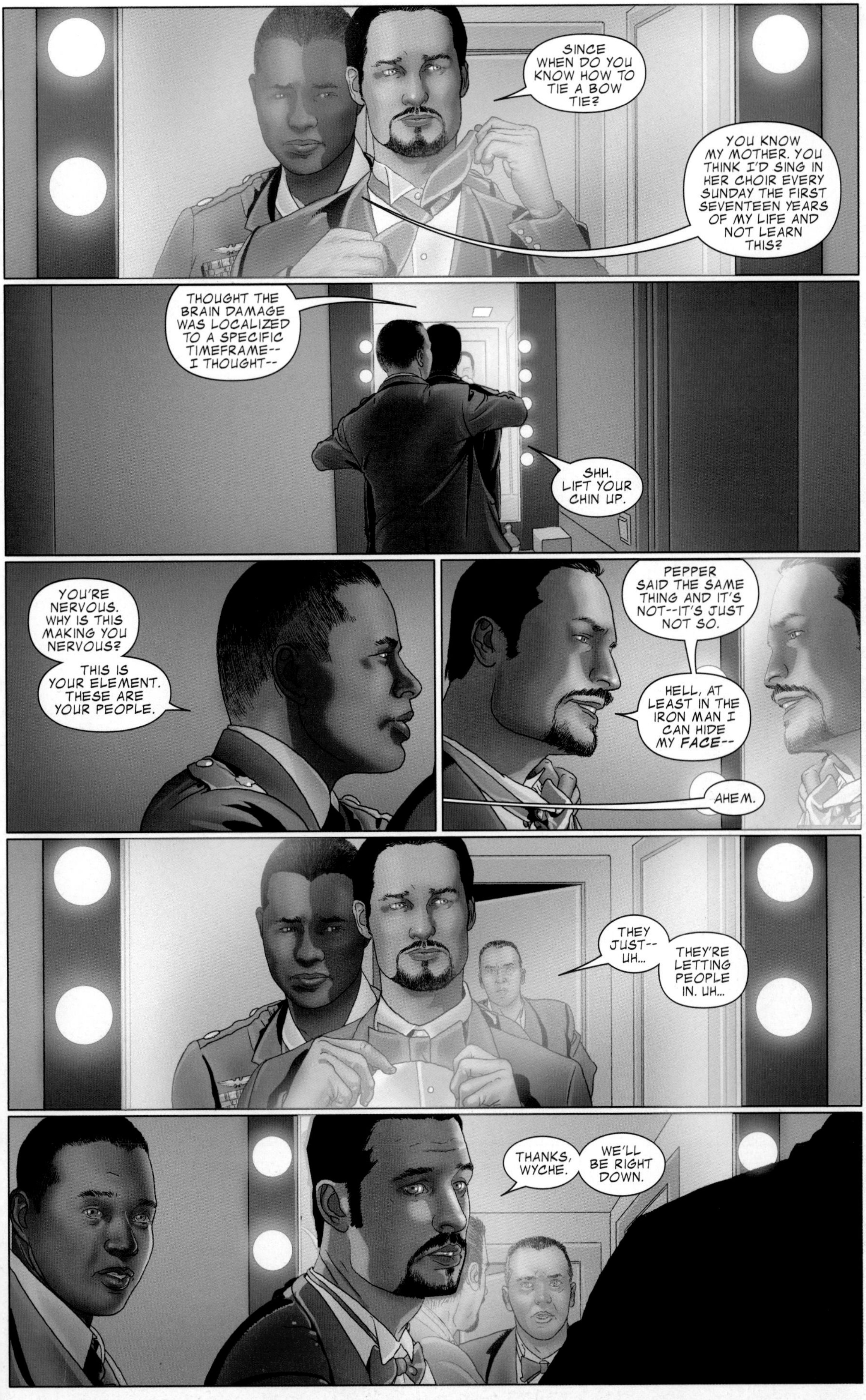
SINCE WHEN DO YOU KNOW HOW TO TIE A BOW TIE?
YOU KNOW MY MOTHER. YOU THINK I'D SING IN HER CHOIR EVERY SUNDAY THE FIRST SEVENTEEN YEARS OF MY LIFE AND NOT LEARN THIS?
THOUGHT THE BRAIN DAMAGE WAS LOCALIZED TO A SPECIFIC TIMEFRAME-- I THOUGHT--
SHH. LIFT YOUR CHIN UP.
YOU'RE NERVOUS. WHY IS THIS MAKING YOU NERVOUS?
THIS IS YOUR ELEMENT. THESE ARE YOUR PEOPLE.
PEPPER SAID THE SAME THING AND IT'S NOT--IT'S JUST NOT SO.
HELL, AT LEAST IN THE IRON MAN I CAN HIDE MY FACE--
AHEM.
THEY JUST-- UH...
THEY'RE LETTING PEOPLE IN. UH...
THANKS, WYCHE.
WE'LL BE RIGHT DOWN.

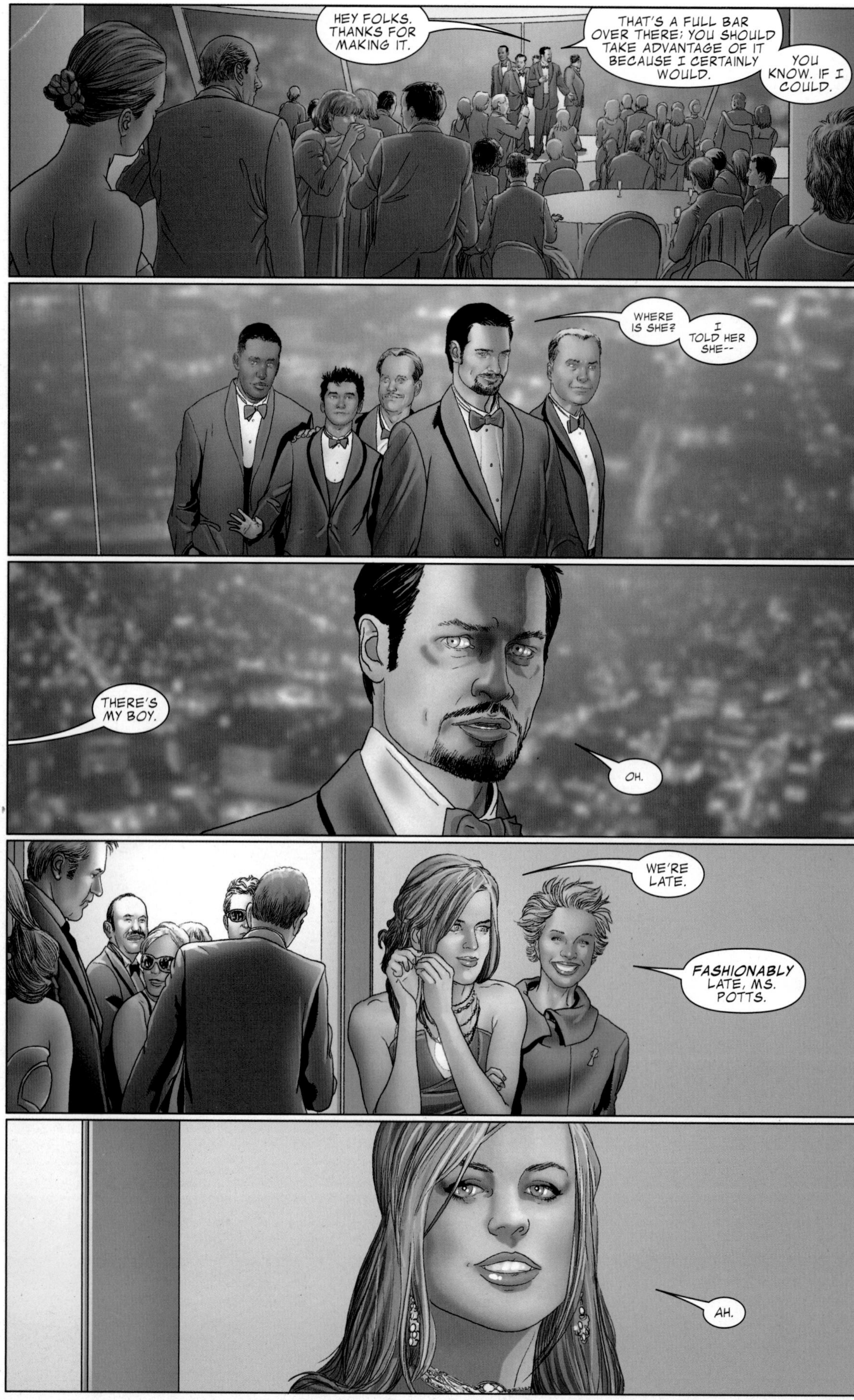
HEY FOLKS. THANKS FOR MAKING IT.
THAT'S A FULL BAR OVER THERE; YOU SHOULD TAKE ADVANTAGE OF IT BECAUSE I CERTAINLY WOULD.
YOU KNOW. IF I COULD.
WHERE IS SHE?
I TOLD HER SHE--
THERE'S MY BOY.
OH.
WE'RE LATE.
FASHIONABLY LATE, MS. POTTS.
AH.

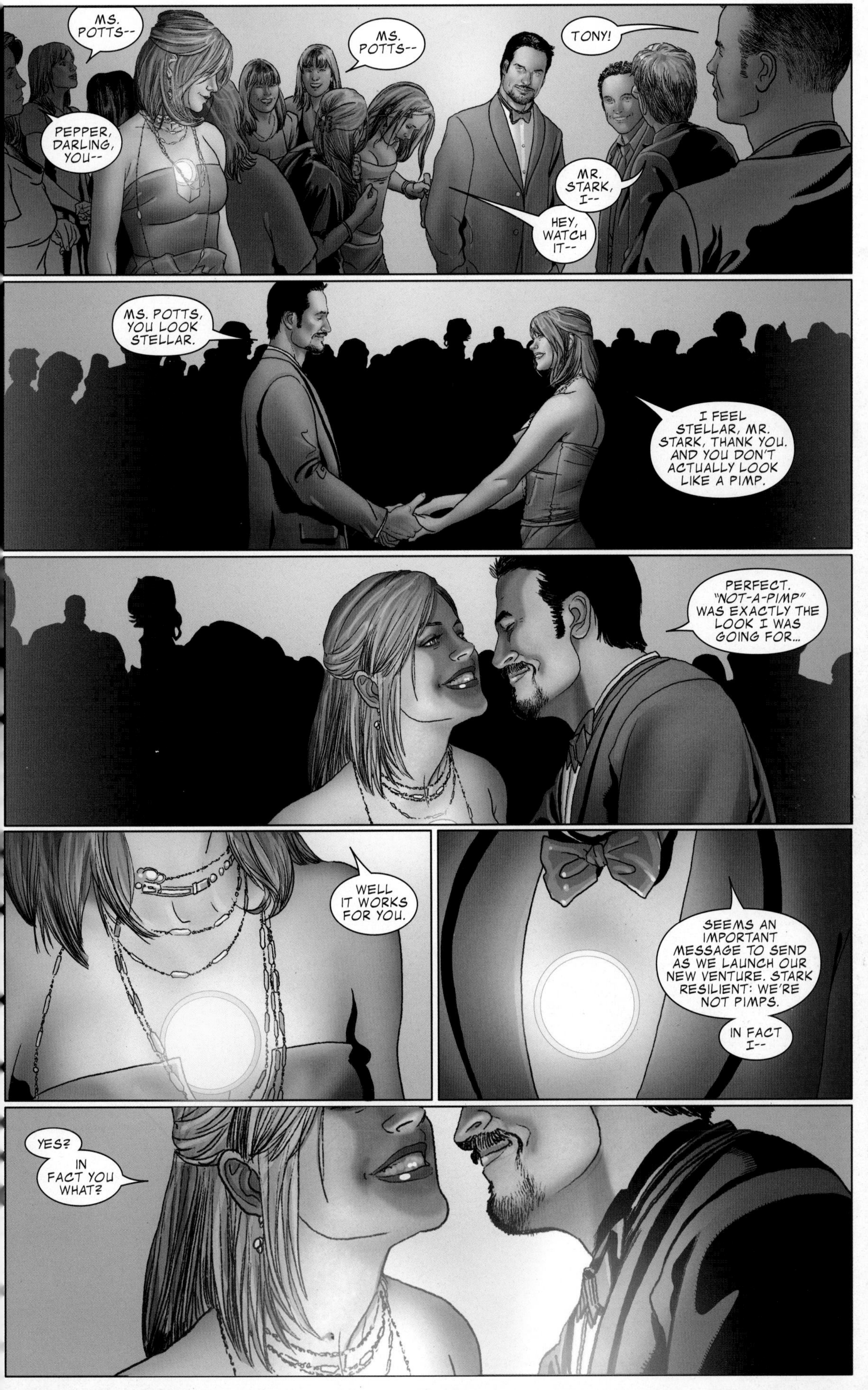
MS. POTTS--
PEPPER, DARLING, YOU--
MS. POTTS--
TONY!
MR. STARK, I--
HEY, WATCH IT--
MS. POTTS, YOU LOOK STELLAR.
I FEEL STELLAR, MR. STARK, THANK YOU. AND YOU DON'T ACTUALLY LOOK LIKE A PIMP.
PERFECT. "NOT-A-PIMP" WAS EXACTLY THE LOOK I WAS GOING FOR...
WELL IT WORKS FOR YOU.
SEEMS AN IMPORTANT MESSAGE TO SEND AS WE LAUNCH OUR NEW VENTURE. STARK RESILIENT: WE'RE NOT PIMPS.
IN FACT I--
YES?
IN FACT YOU WHAT?

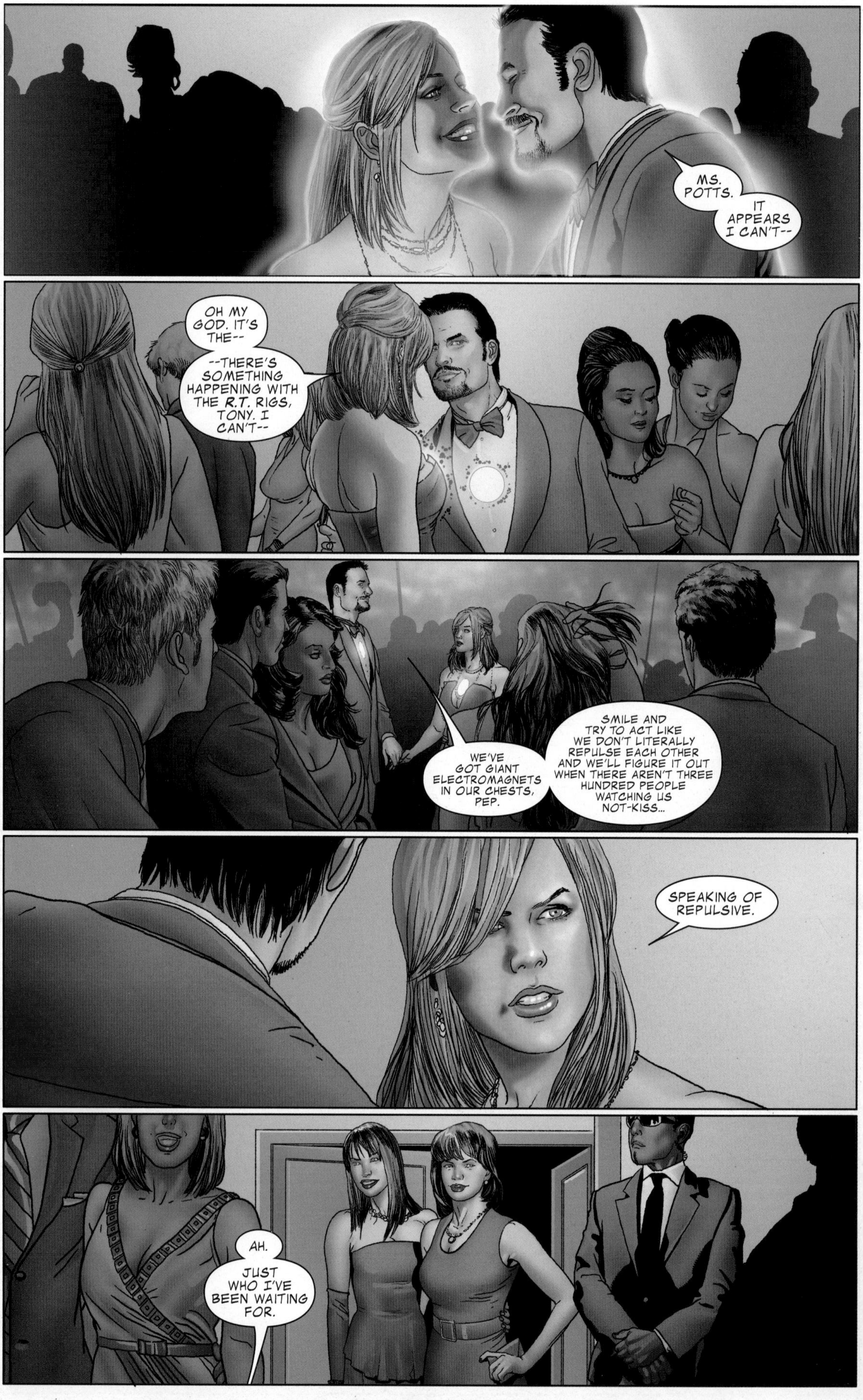
MS. POTTS.
IT APPEARS I CAN'T--
OH MY GOD. IT'S THE--
--THERE'S SOMETHING HAPPENING WITH THE R.T. RIGS, TONY. I CAN'T--
WE'VE GOT GIANT ELECTROMAGNETS IN OUR CHESTS, PEP.
SMILE AND TRY TO ACT LIKE WE DON'T LITERALLY REPULSE EACH OTHER AND WE'LL FIGURE IT OUT WHEN THERE AREN'T THREE HUNDRED PEOPLE WATCHING US NOT-KISS...
SPEAKING OF REPULSIVE.
AH.
JUST WHO I'VE BEEN WAITING FOR.

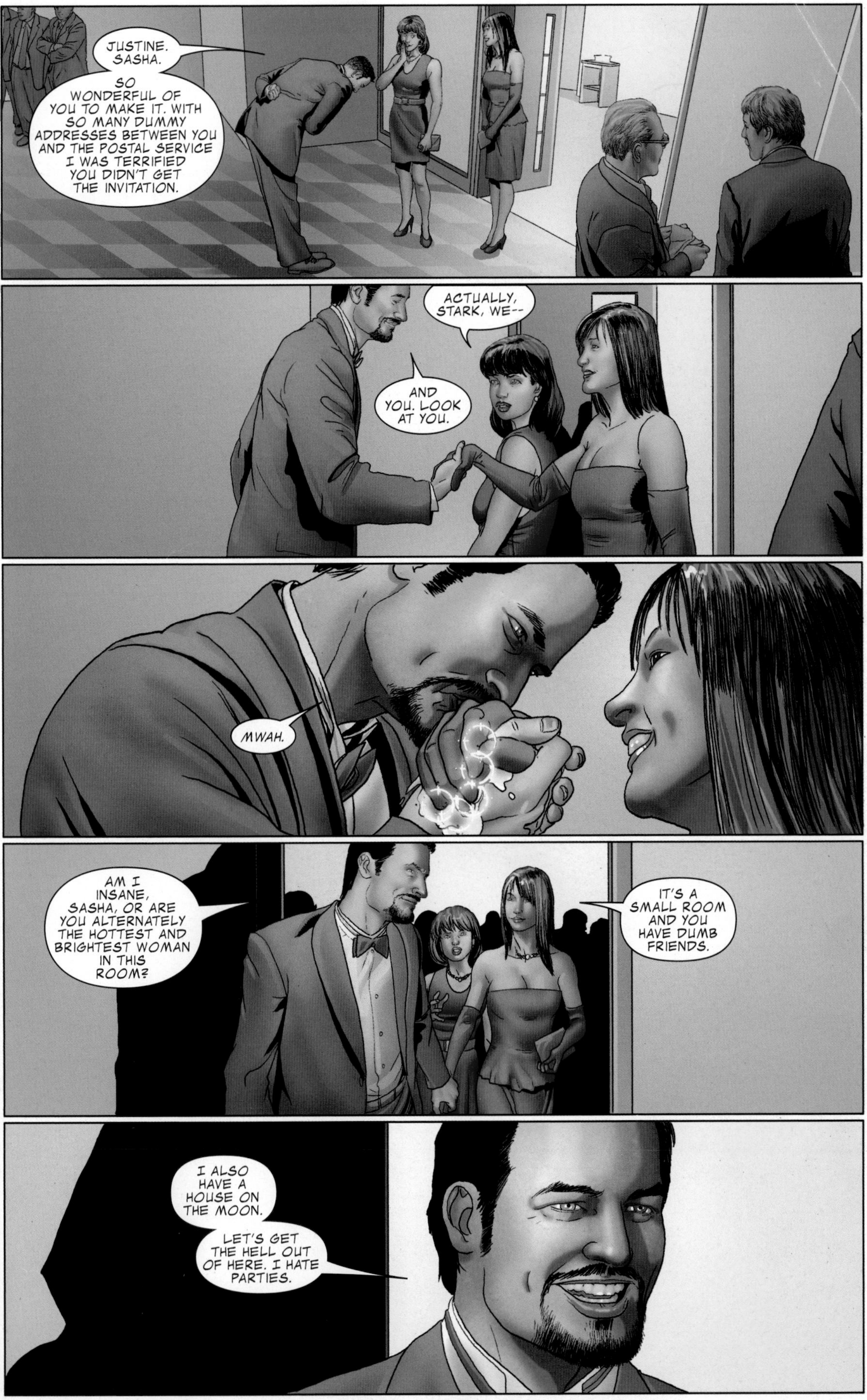
JUSTINE. SASHA.
SO WONDERFUL OF YOU TO MAKE IT. WITH SO MANY DUMMY ADDRESSES BETWEEN YOU AND THE POSTAL SERVICE I WAS TERRIFIED YOU DIDN'T GET THE INVITATION.
ACTUALLY, STARK, WE--
AND YOU. LOOK AT YOU.
MWAH.
AM I INSANE, SASHA, OR ARE YOU ALTERNATELY THE HOTTEST AND BRIGHTEST WOMAN IN THIS ROOM?
IT'S A SMALL ROOM AND YOU HAVE DUMB FRIENDS.
I ALSO HAVE A HOUSE ON THE MOON.
LET'S GET THE HELL OUT OF HERE. I HATE PARTIES.

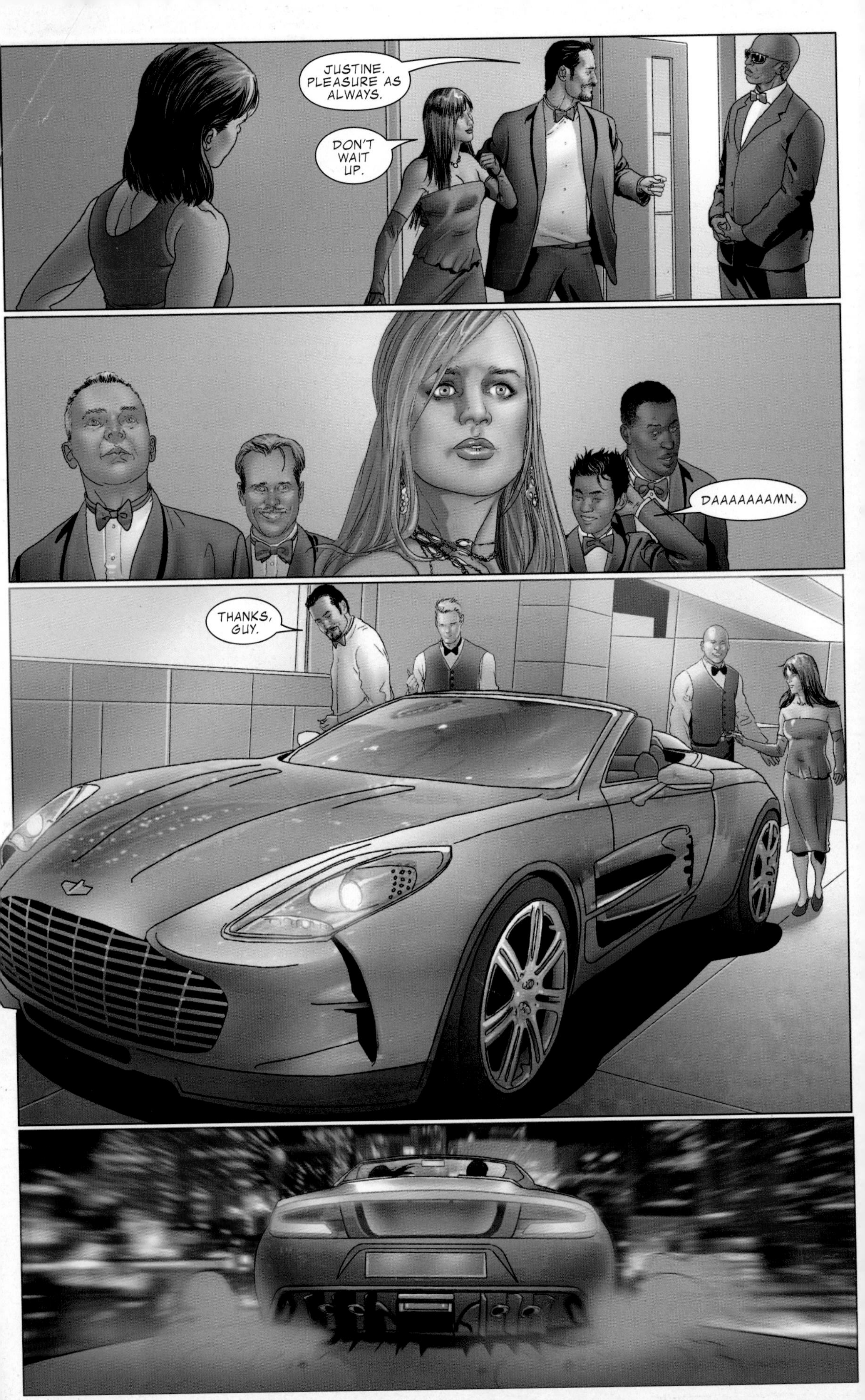
JUSTINE. PLEASURE AS ALWAYS.
DON'T WAIT UP.
DAAAAAAAMN.
THANKS, GUY.

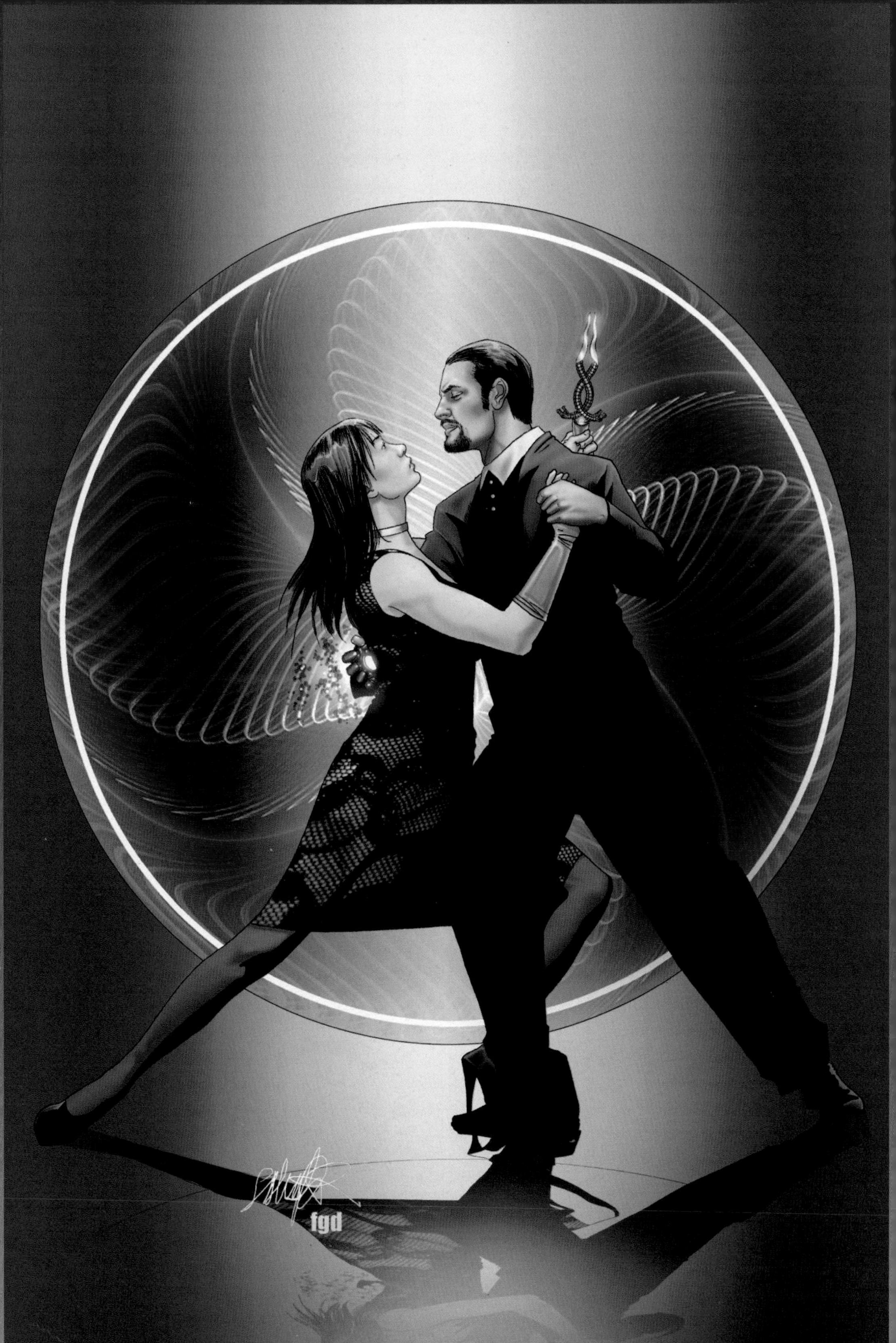
fgd

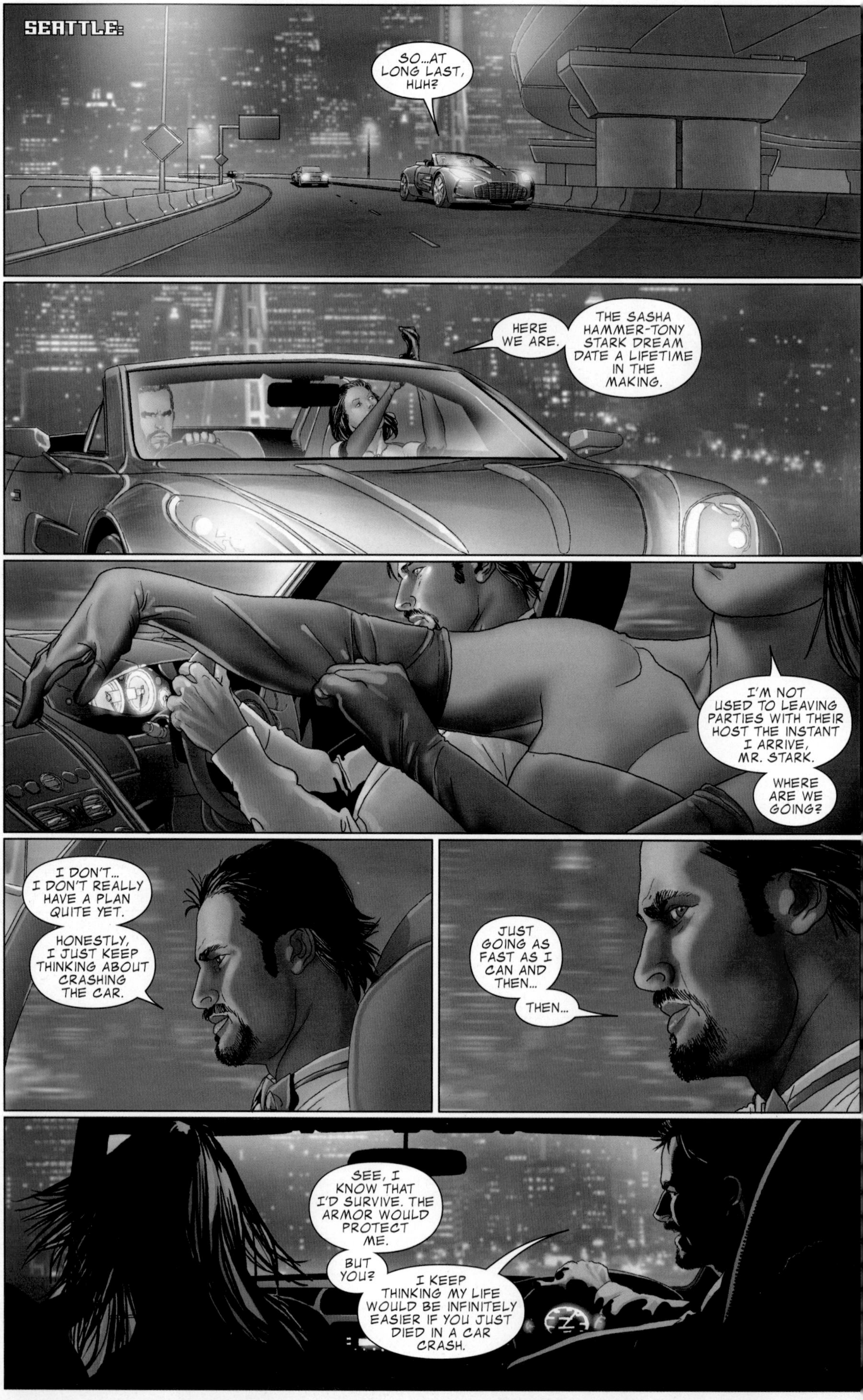
SEATTLE:
SO...AT LONG LAST, HUH?
HERE WE ARE.
THE SASHA HAMMER-TONY STARK DREAM DATE A LIFETIME IN THE MAKING.
I'M NOT USED TO LEAVING PARTIES WITH THEIR HOST THE INSTANT I ARRIVE, MR. STARK.
WHERE ARE WE GOING?
I DON'T... I DON'T REALLY HAVE A PLAN QUITE YET.
HONESTLY, I JUST KEEP THINKING ABOUT CRASHING THE CAR.
JUST GOING AS FAST AS I CAN AND THEN...
THEN...
SEE, I KNOW THAT I'D SURVIVE. THE ARMOR WOULD PROTECT ME.
BUT YOU?
I KEEP THINKING MY LIFE WOULD BE INFINITELY EASIER IF YOU JUST DIED IN A CAR CRASH.

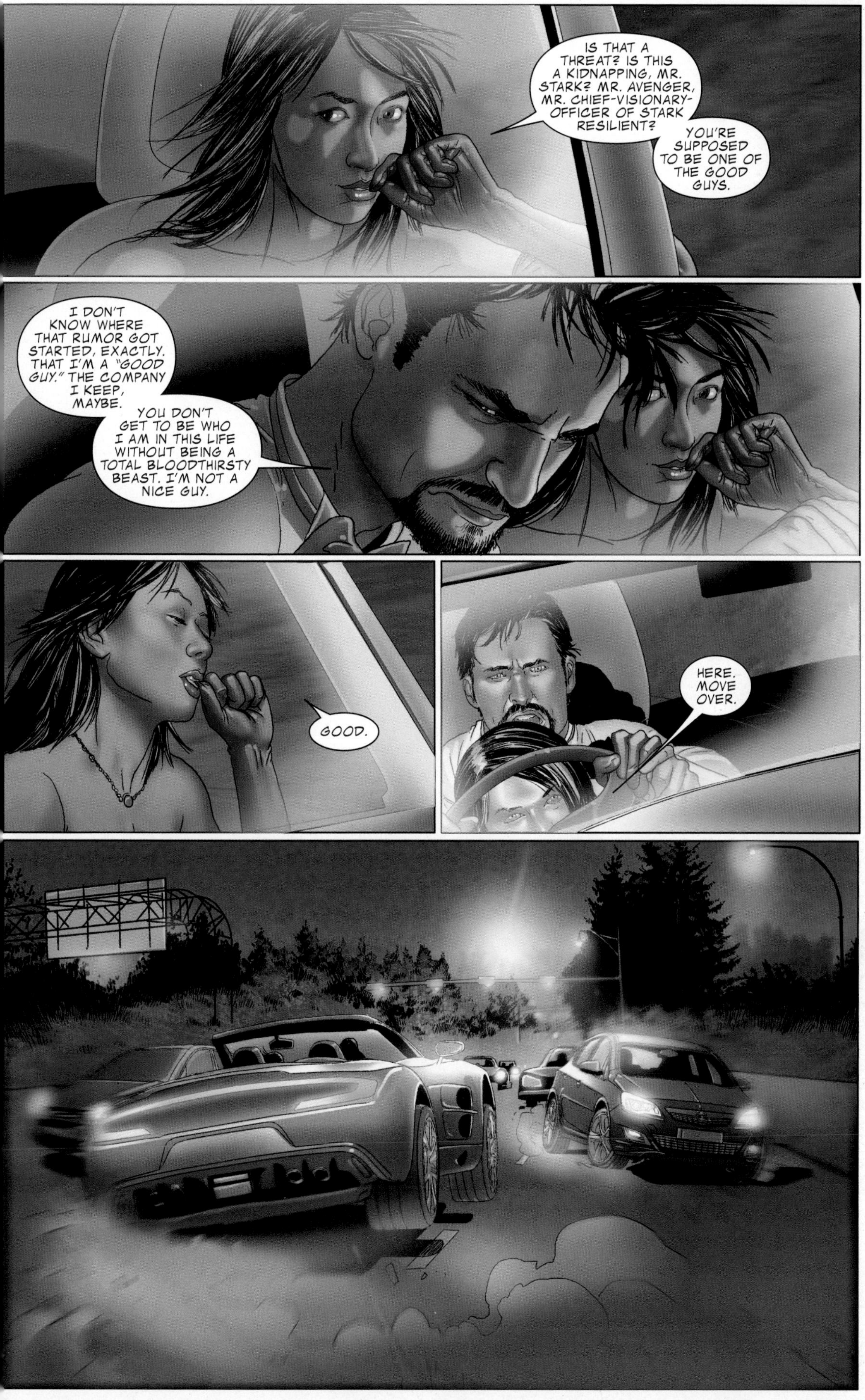
IS THAT A THREAT? IS THIS A KIDNAPPING, MR. STARK? MR. AVENGER, MR. CHIEF-VISIONARY-OFFICER OF STARK RESILIENT?
YOU'RE SUPPOSED TO BE ONE OF THE GOOD GUYS.
I DON'T KNOW WHERE THAT RUMOR GOT STARTED, EXACTLY. THAT I'M A "GOOD GUY." THE COMPANY I KEEP, MAYBE.
YOU DON'T GET TO BE WHO I AM IN THIS LIFE WITHOUT BEING A TOTAL BLOODTHIRSTY BEAST. I'M NOT A NICE GUY.
GOOD.
HERE. MOVE OVER.

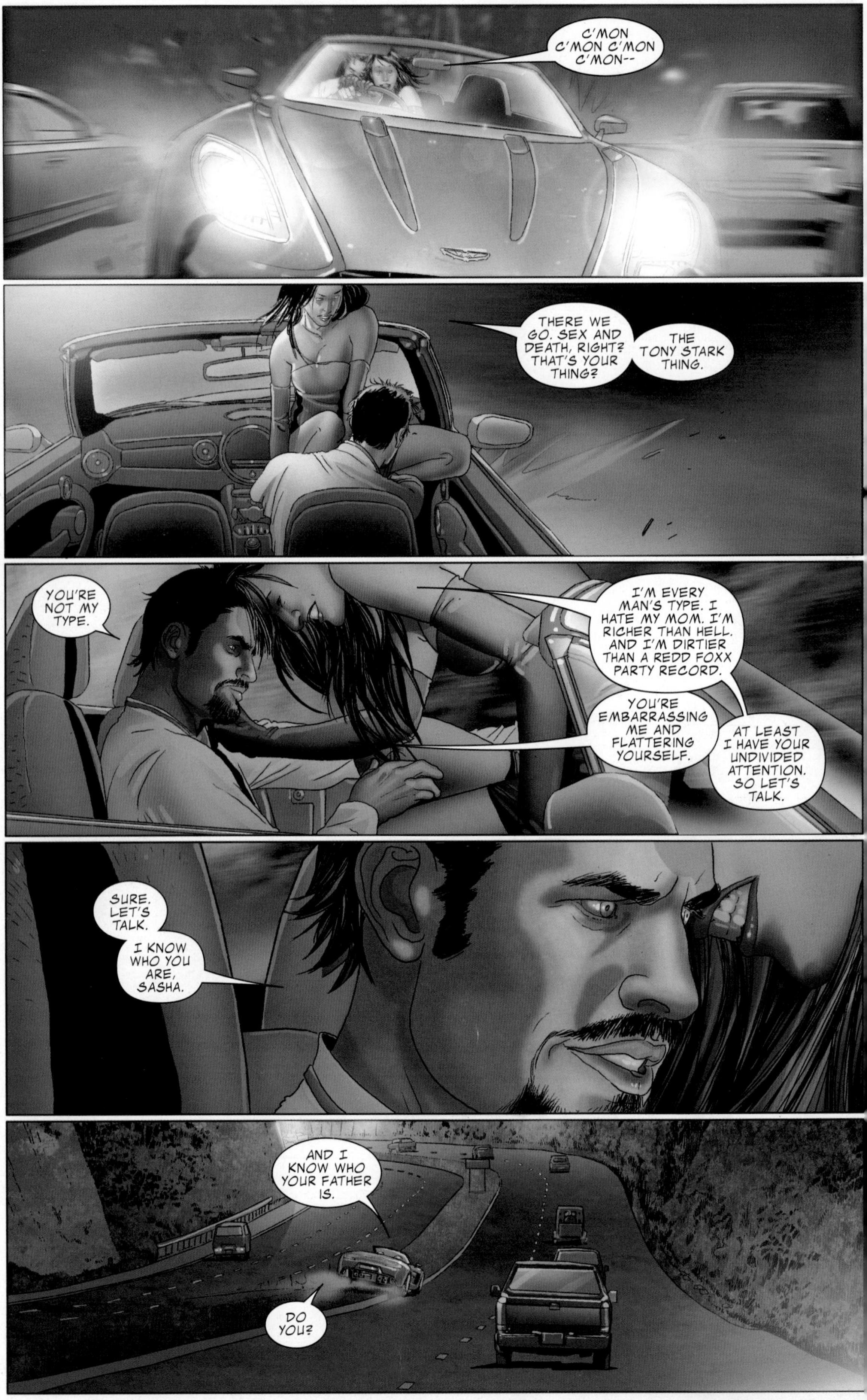
C'MON C'MON C'MON C'MON--
THERE WE GO. SEX AND DEATH, RIGHT? THAT'S YOUR THING?
THE TONY STARK THING.
YOU'RE NOT MY TYPE.
I'M EVERY MAN'S TYPE. I HATE MY MOM. I'M RICHER THAN HELL. AND I'M DIRTIER THAN A REDD FOXX PARTY RECORD.
YOU'RE EMBARRASSING ME AND FLATTERING YOURSELF.
AT LEAST I HAVE YOUR UNDIVIDED ATTENTION. SO LET'S TALK.
SURE. LET'S TALK.
I KNOW WHO YOU ARE, SASHA.
AND I KNOW WHO YOUR FATHER IS.
DO YOU?

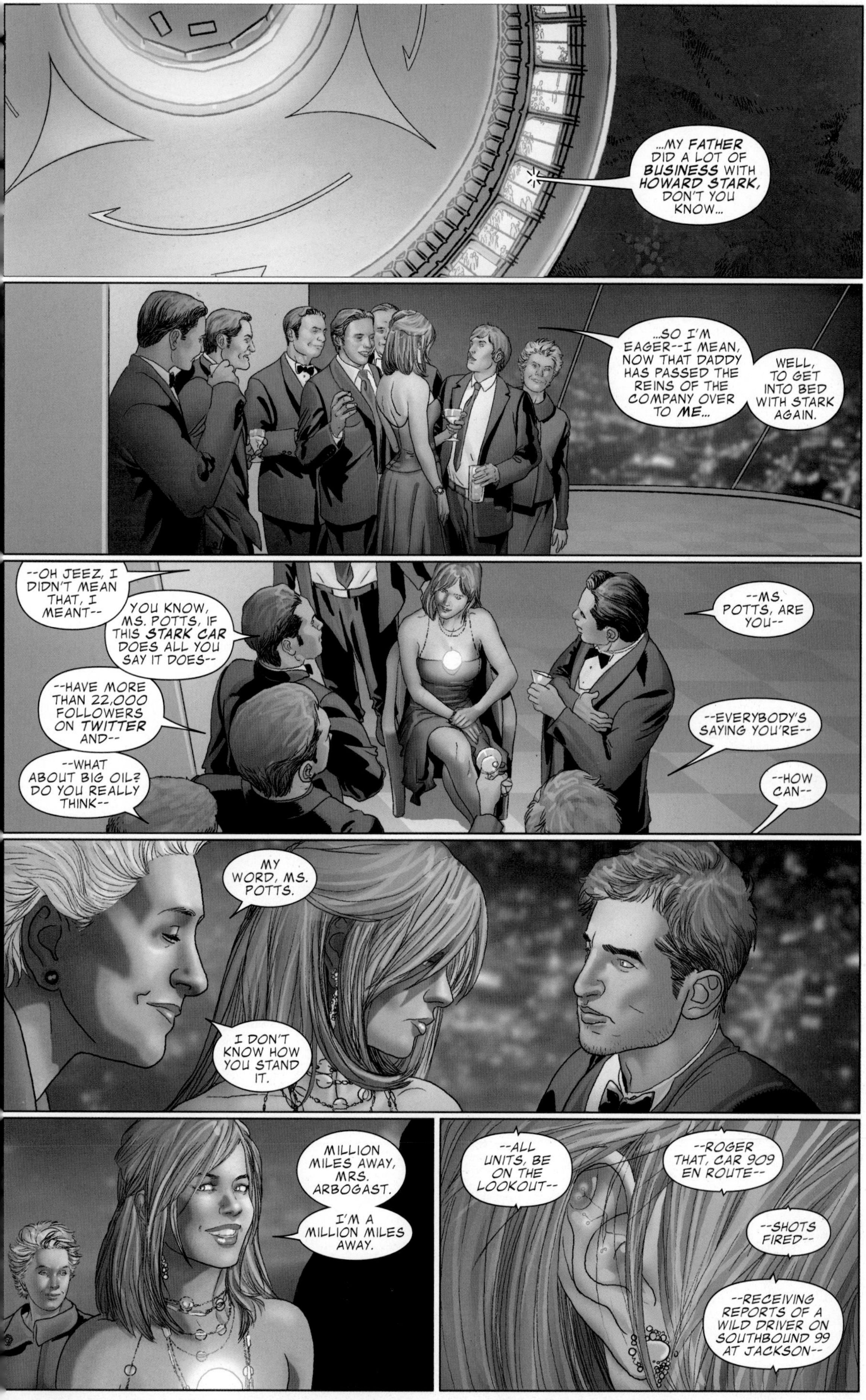
...MY FATHER DID A LOT OF BUSINESS WITH HOWARD STARK, DON'T YOU KNOW...
...SO I'M EAGER--I MEAN, NOW THAT DADDY HAS PASSED THE REINS OF THE COMPANY OVER TO ME...
WELL, TO GET INTO BED WITH STARK AGAIN.
--OH JEEZ, I DIDN'T MEAN THAT, I MEANT--
YOU KNOW, MS. POTTS, IF THIS STARK CAR DOES ALL YOU SAY IT DOES--
--HAVE MORE THAN 22,000 FOLLOWERS ON TWITTER AND--
--WHAT ABOUT BIG OIL? DO YOU REALLY THINK--
--MS. POTTS, ARE YOU--
--EVERYBODY'S SAYING YOU'RE--
--HOW CAN--
MY WORD, MS. POTTS.
I DON'T KNOW HOW YOU STAND IT.
MILLION MILES AWAY, MRS. ARBOGAST.
I'M A MILLION MILES AWAY.
--ALL UNITS, BE ON THE LOOKOUT--
--ROGER THAT, CAR 909 EN ROUTE--
--SHOTS FIRED--
--RECEIVING REPORTS OF A WILD DRIVER ON SOUTHBOUND 99 AT JACKSON--

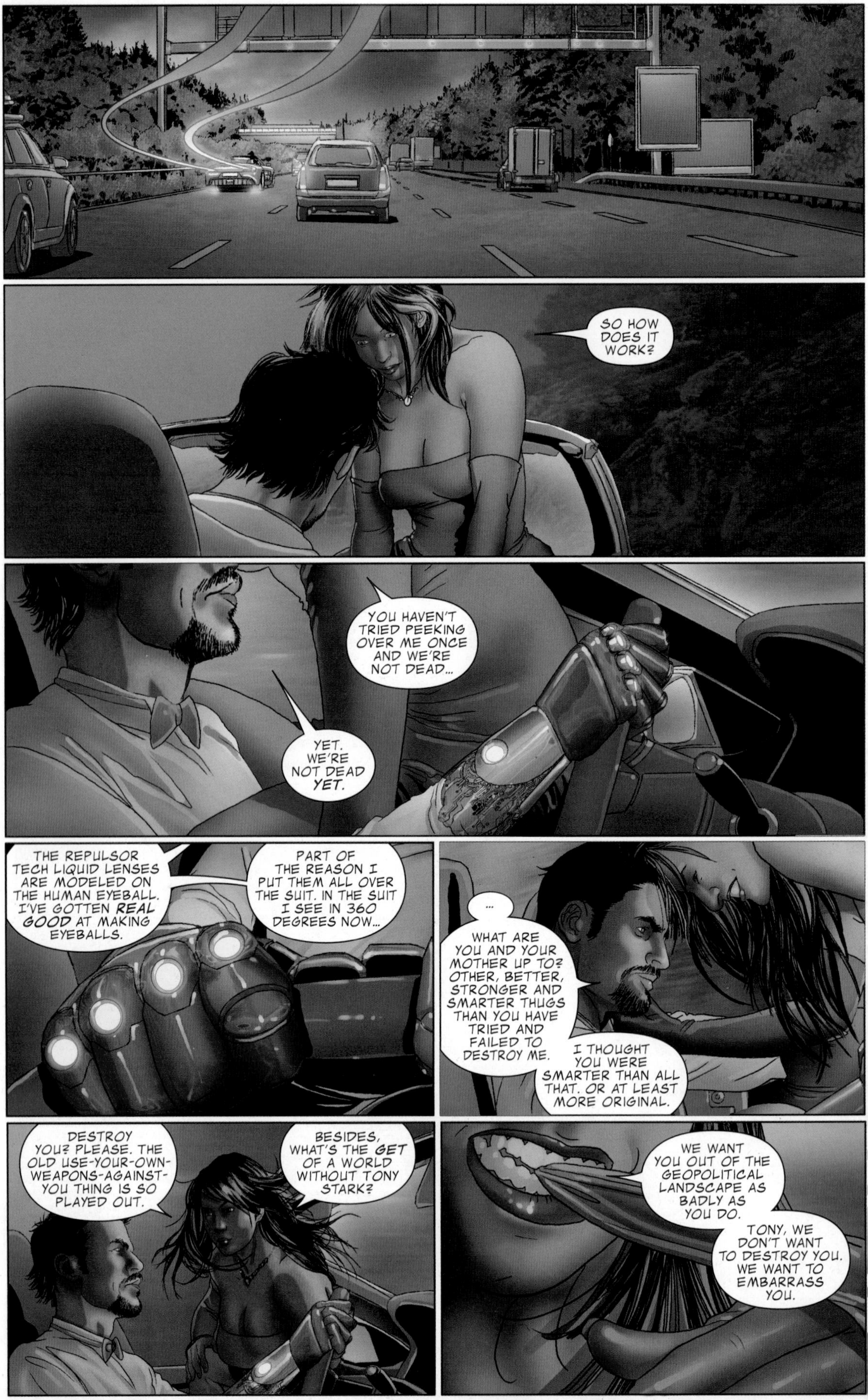
SO HOW DOES IT WORK?
YOU HAVEN'T TRIED PEEKING OVER ME ONCE AND WE'RE NOT DEAD...
YET. WE'RE NOT DEAD YET.
THE REPULSOR TECH LIQUID LENSES ARE MODELED ON THE HUMAN EYEBALL. I'VE GOTTEN REAL GOOD AT MAKING EYEBALLS.
PART OF THE REASON I PUT THEM ALL OVER THE SUIT. IN THE SUIT I SEE IN 360 DEGREES NOW...
...
WHAT ARE YOU AND YOUR MOTHER UP TO? OTHER, BETTER, STRONGER AND SMARTER THUGS THAN YOU HAVE TRIED AND FAILED TO DESTROY ME.
I THOUGHT YOU WERE SMARTER THAN ALL THAT. OR AT LEAST MORE ORIGINAL.
DESTROY YOU? PLEASE. THE OLD USE-YOUR-OWN-WEAPONS-AGAINST-YOU THING IS SO PLAYED OUT.
BESIDES, WHAT'S THE GET OF A WORLD WITHOUT TONY STARK?
WE WANT YOU OUT OF THE GEOPOLITICAL LANDSCAPE AS BADLY AS YOU DO.
TONY, WE DON'T WANT TO DESTROY YOU. WE WANT TO EMBARRASS YOU.

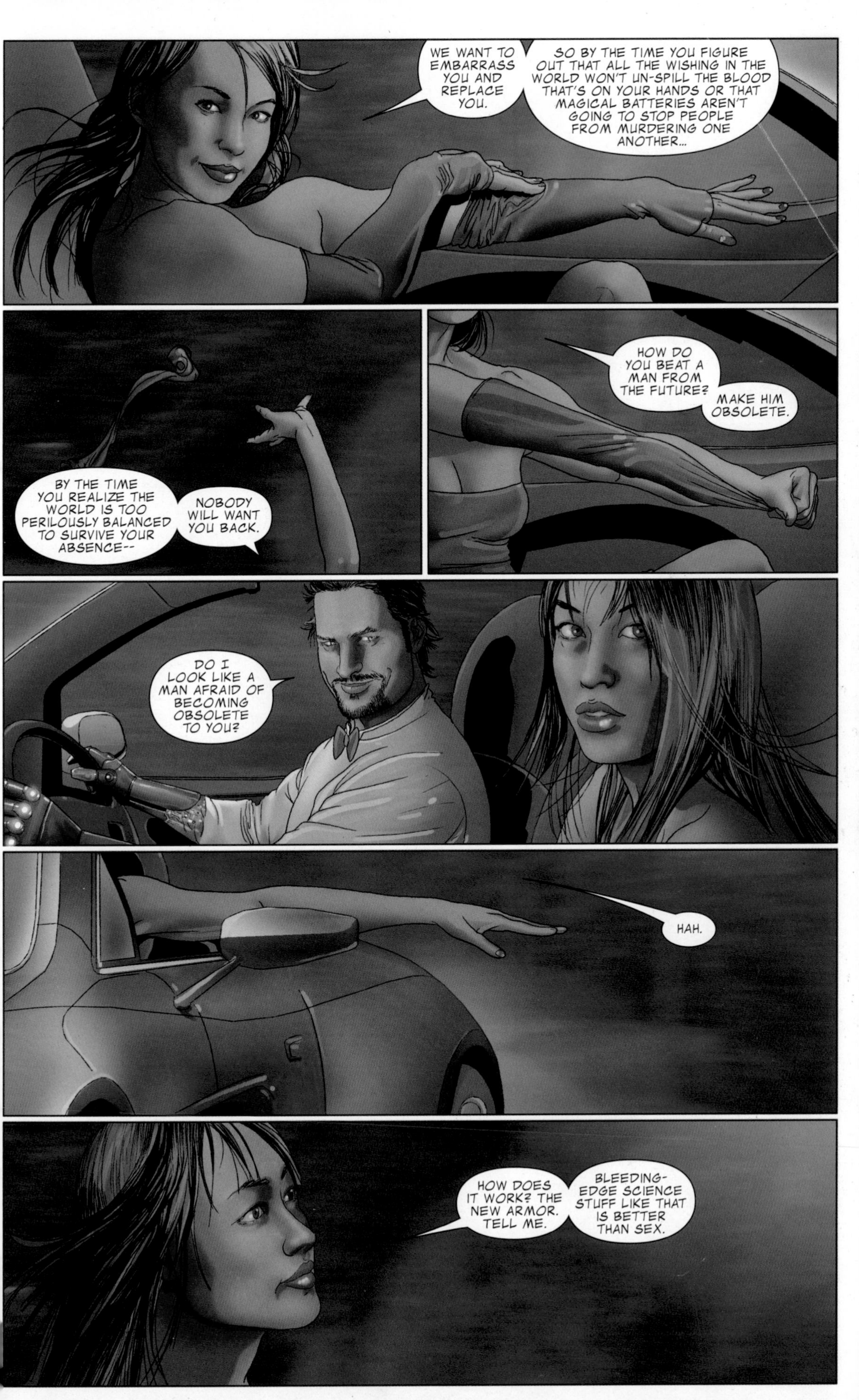
WE WANT TO EMBARRASS YOU AND REPLACE YOU.
SO BY THE TIME YOU FIGURE OUT THAT ALL THE WISHING IN THE WORLD WON'T UN-SPILL THE BLOOD THAT'S ON YOUR HANDS OR THAT MAGICAL BATTERIES AREN'T GOING TO STOP PEOPLE FROM MURDERING ONE ANOTHER...
BY THE TIME YOU REALIZE THE WORLD IS TOO PERILOUSLY BALANCED TO SURVIVE YOUR ABSENCE--
NOBODY WILL WANT YOU BACK.
HOW DO YOU BEAT A MAN FROM THE FUTURE?
MAKE HIM OBSOLETE.
DO I LOOK LIKE A MAN AFRAID OF BECOMING OBSOLETE TO YOU?
HAH.
HOW DOES IT WORK? THE NEW ARMOR. TELL ME.
BLEEDING-EDGE SCIENCE STUFF LIKE THAT IS BETTER THAN SEX.

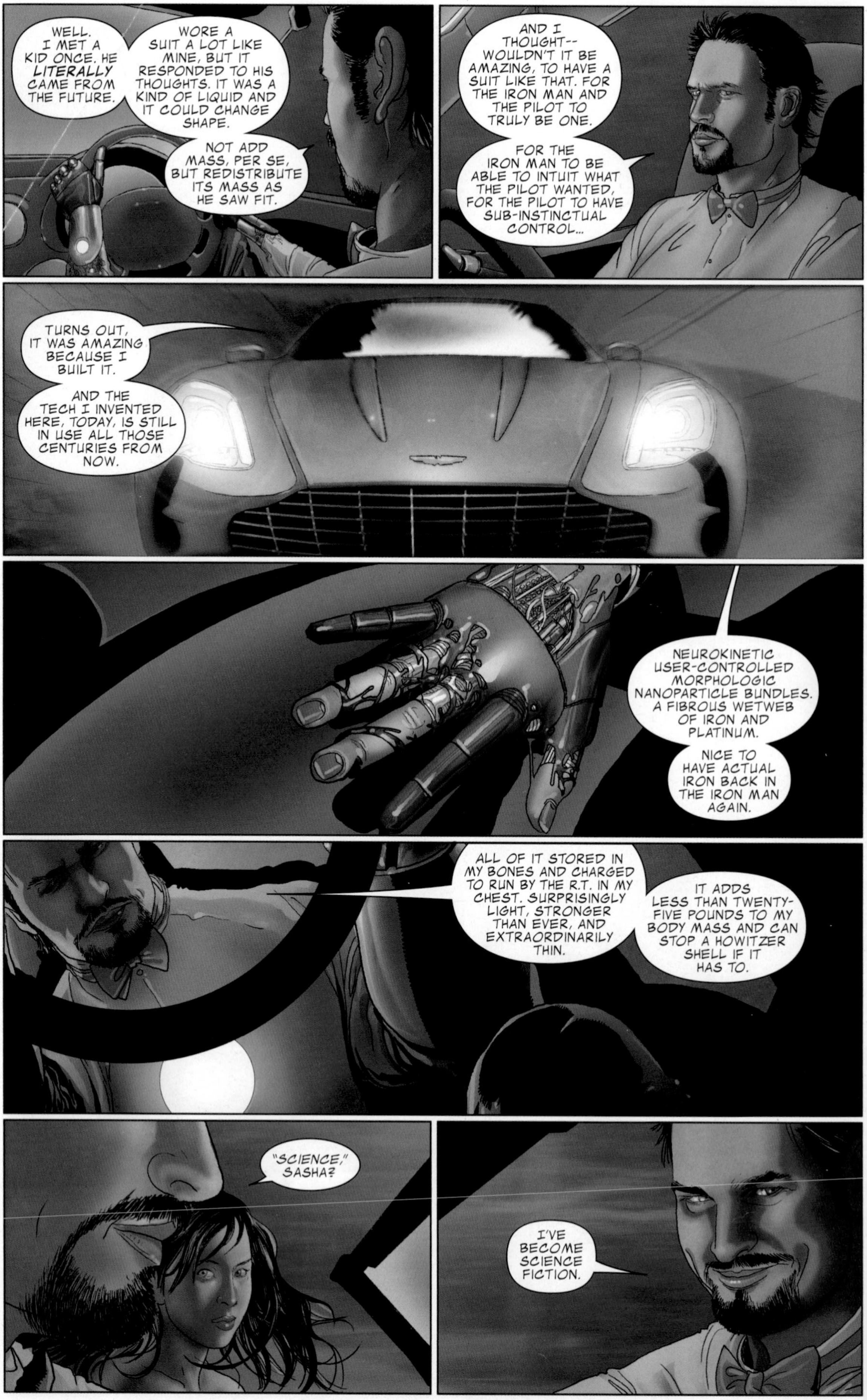
WELL. I MET A KID ONCE. HE *LITERALLY* CAME FROM THE FUTURE.
WORE A SUIT A LOT LIKE MINE, BUT IT RESPONDED TO HIS THOUGHTS. IT WAS A KIND OF LIQUID AND IT COULD CHANGE SHAPE.
NOT ADD MASS, PER SE, BUT REDISTRIBUTE ITS MASS AS HE SAW FIT.
AND I THOUGHT-- WOULDN'T IT BE AMAZING, TO HAVE A SUIT LIKE THAT. FOR THE IRON MAN AND THE PILOT TO TRULY BE ONE.
FOR THE IRON MAN TO BE ABLE TO INTUIT WHAT THE PILOT WANTED, FOR THE PILOT TO HAVE SUB-INSTINCTUAL CONTROL...
TURNS OUT, IT WAS AMAZING BECAUSE I BUILT IT.
AND THE TECH I INVENTED HERE, TODAY, IS STILL IN USE ALL THOSE CENTURIES FROM NOW.
NEUROKINETIC USER-CONTROLLED MORPHOLOGIC NANOPARTICLE BUNDLES. A FIBROUS WETWEB OF IRON AND PLATINUM.
NICE TO HAVE ACTUAL IRON BACK IN THE IRON MAN AGAIN.
ALL OF IT STORED IN MY BONES AND CHARGED TO RUN BY THE R.T. IN MY CHEST. SURPRISINGLY LIGHT, STRONGER THAN EVER, AND EXTRAORDINARILY THIN.
IT ADDS LESS THAN TWENTY-FIVE POUNDS TO MY BODY MASS AND CAN STOP A HOWITZER SHELL IF IT HAS TO.
"SCIENCE," SASHA?
I'VE BECOME SCIENCE FICTION.

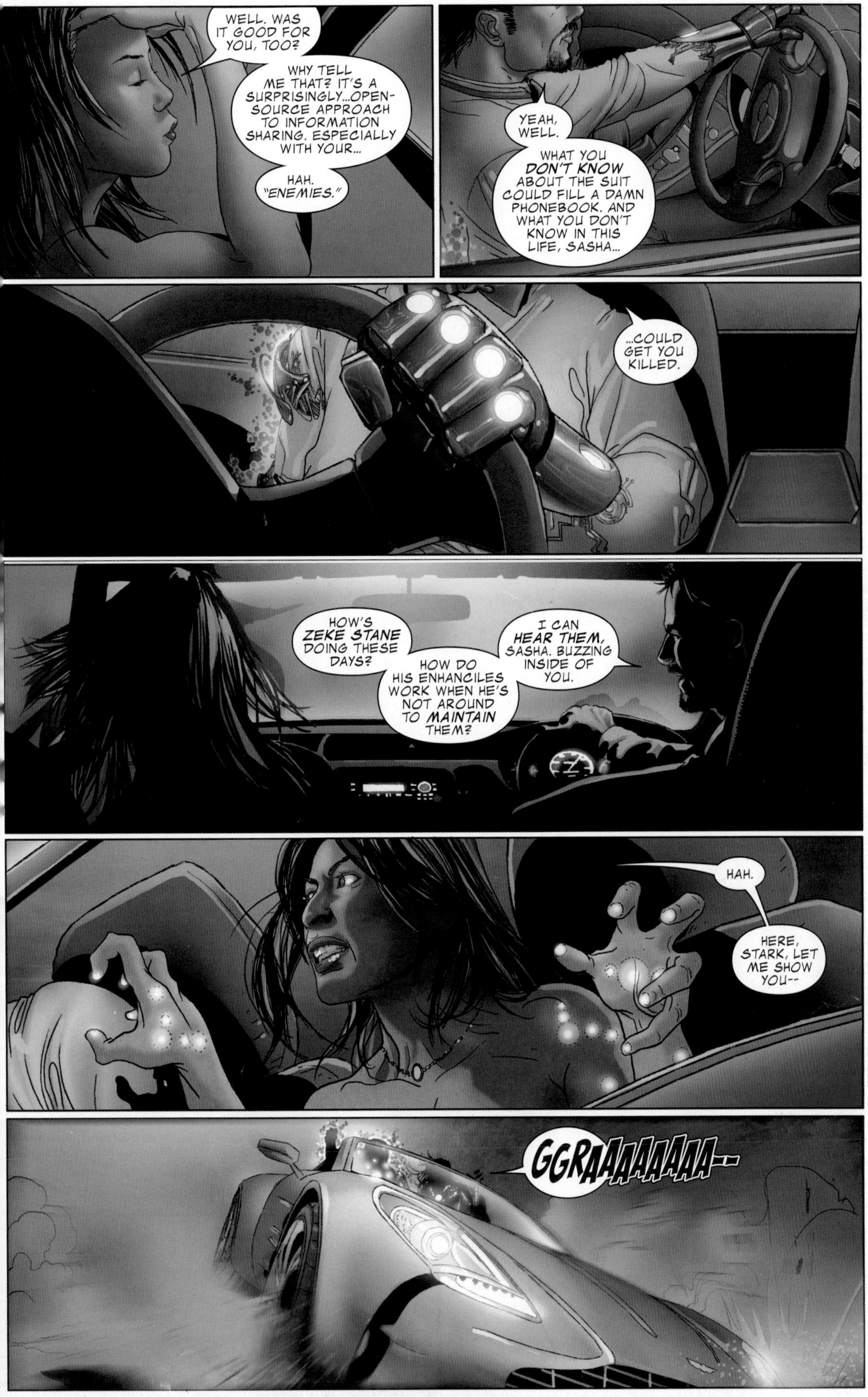
WELL. WAS IT GOOD FOR YOU, TOO?
WHY TELL ME THAT? IT'S A SURPRISINGLY...OPEN-SOURCE APPROACH TO INFORMATION SHARING. ESPECIALLY WITH YOUR...
HAH. "ENEMIES."
YEAH, WELL.
WHAT YOU DON'T KNOW ABOUT THE SUIT COULD FILL A DAMN PHONEBOOK. AND WHAT YOU DON'T KNOW IN THIS LIFE, SASHA...
...COULD GET YOU KILLED.
HOW'S ZEKE STANE DOING THESE DAYS?
HOW DO HIS ENHANCILES WORK WHEN HE'S NOT AROUND TO MAINTAIN THEM?
I CAN HEAR THEM, SASHA. BUZZING INSIDE OF YOU.
HAH.
HERE, STARK, LET ME SHOW YOU--
GGRAAAAAAA--

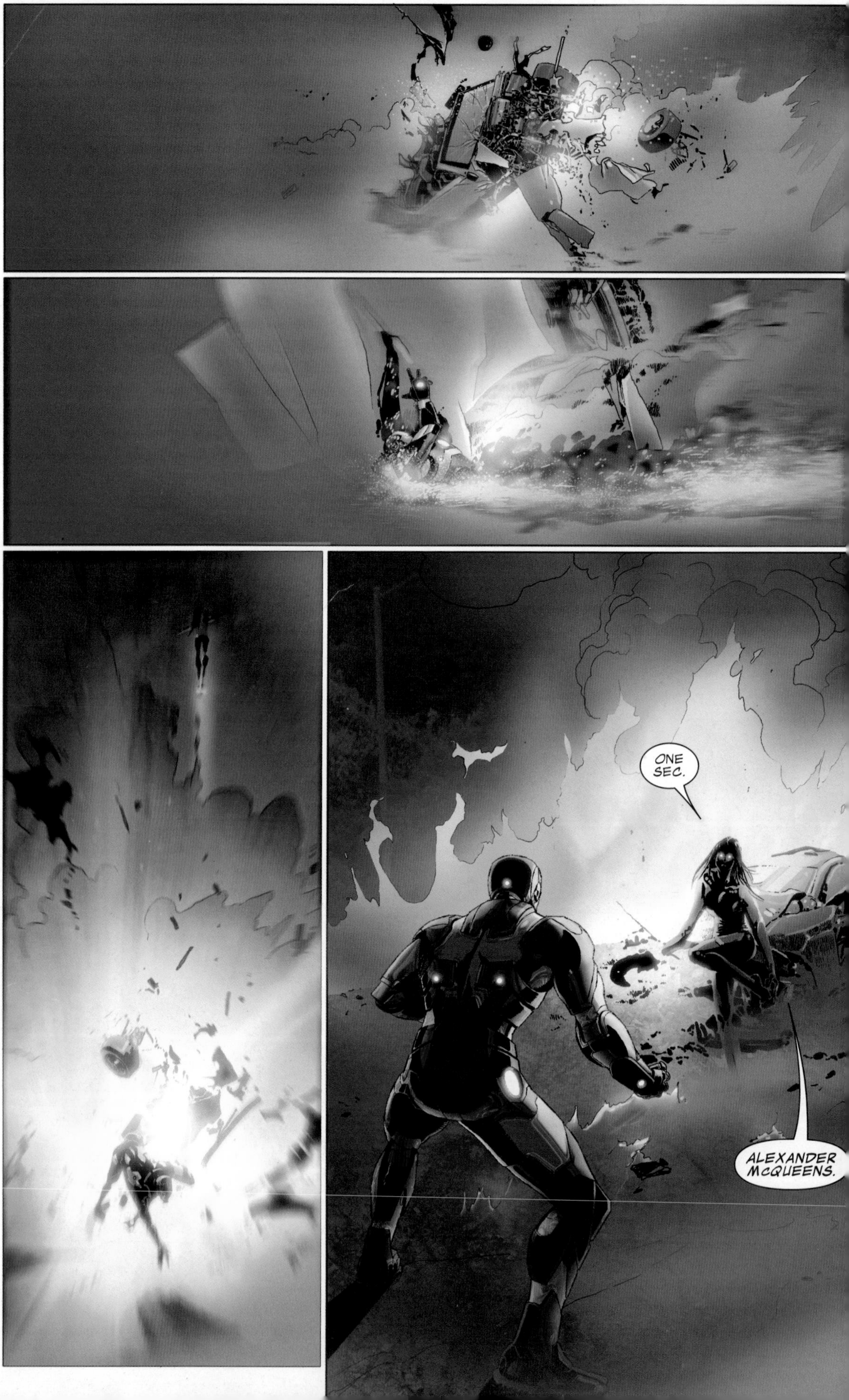
ONE SEC.
ALEXANDER McQUEENS.

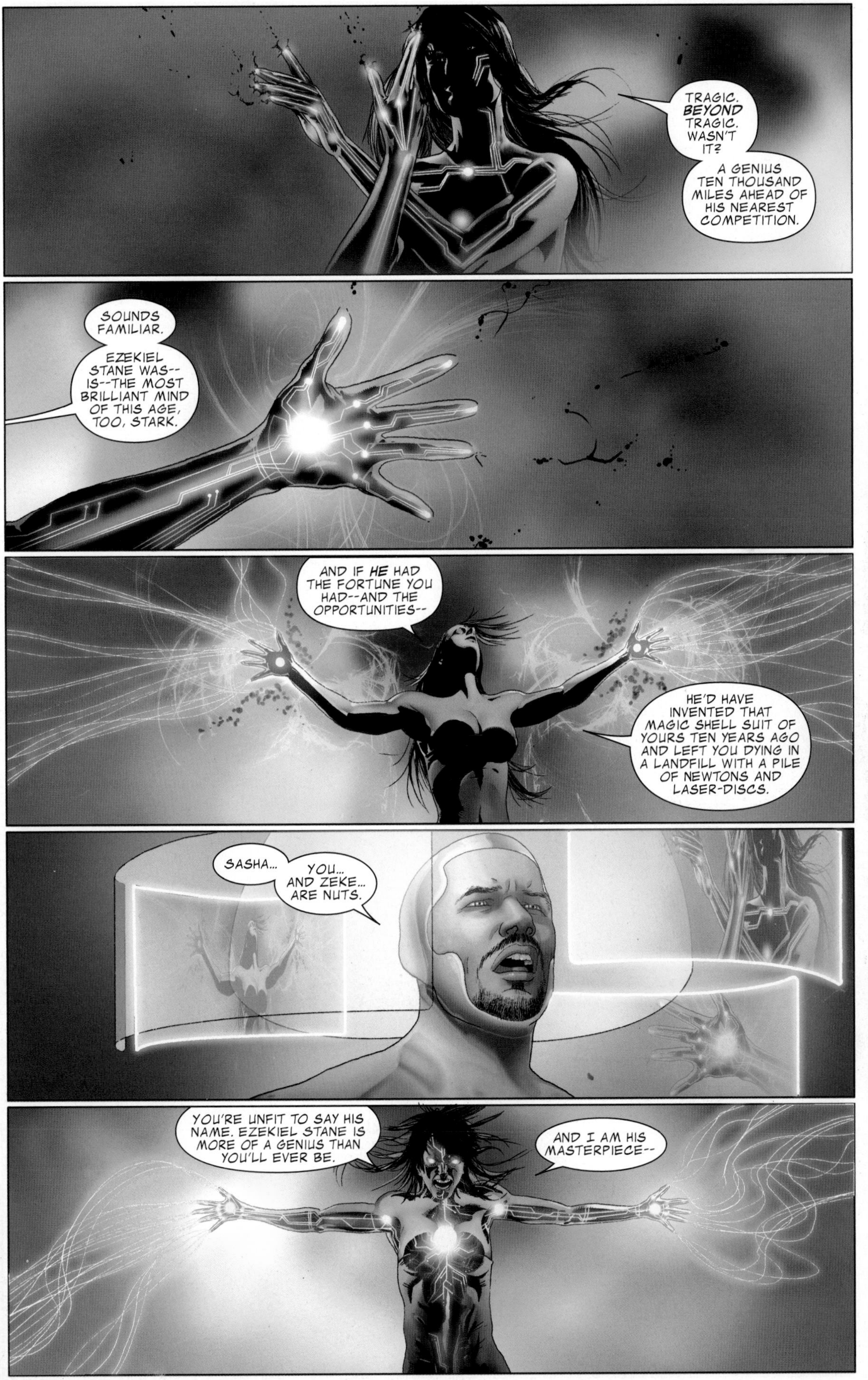
TRAGIC. **BEYOND** TRAGIC. WASN'T IT?
A GENIUS TEN THOUSAND MILES AHEAD OF HIS NEAREST COMPETITION.
SOUNDS FAMILIAR.
EZEKIEL STANE WAS-- IS--THE MOST BRILLIANT MIND OF THIS AGE, TOO, STARK.
AND IF **HE** HAD THE FORTUNE YOU HAD--AND THE OPPORTUNITIES--
HE'D HAVE INVENTED THAT MAGIC SHELL SUIT OF YOURS TEN YEARS AGO AND LEFT YOU DYING IN A LANDFILL WITH A PILE OF NEWTONS AND LASER-DISCS.
SASHA...
YOU... AND ZEKE... ARE NUTS.
YOU'RE UNFIT TO SAY HIS NAME. EZEKIEL STANE IS MORE OF A GENIUS THAN YOU'LL EVER BE.
AND I AM HIS MASTERPIECE--

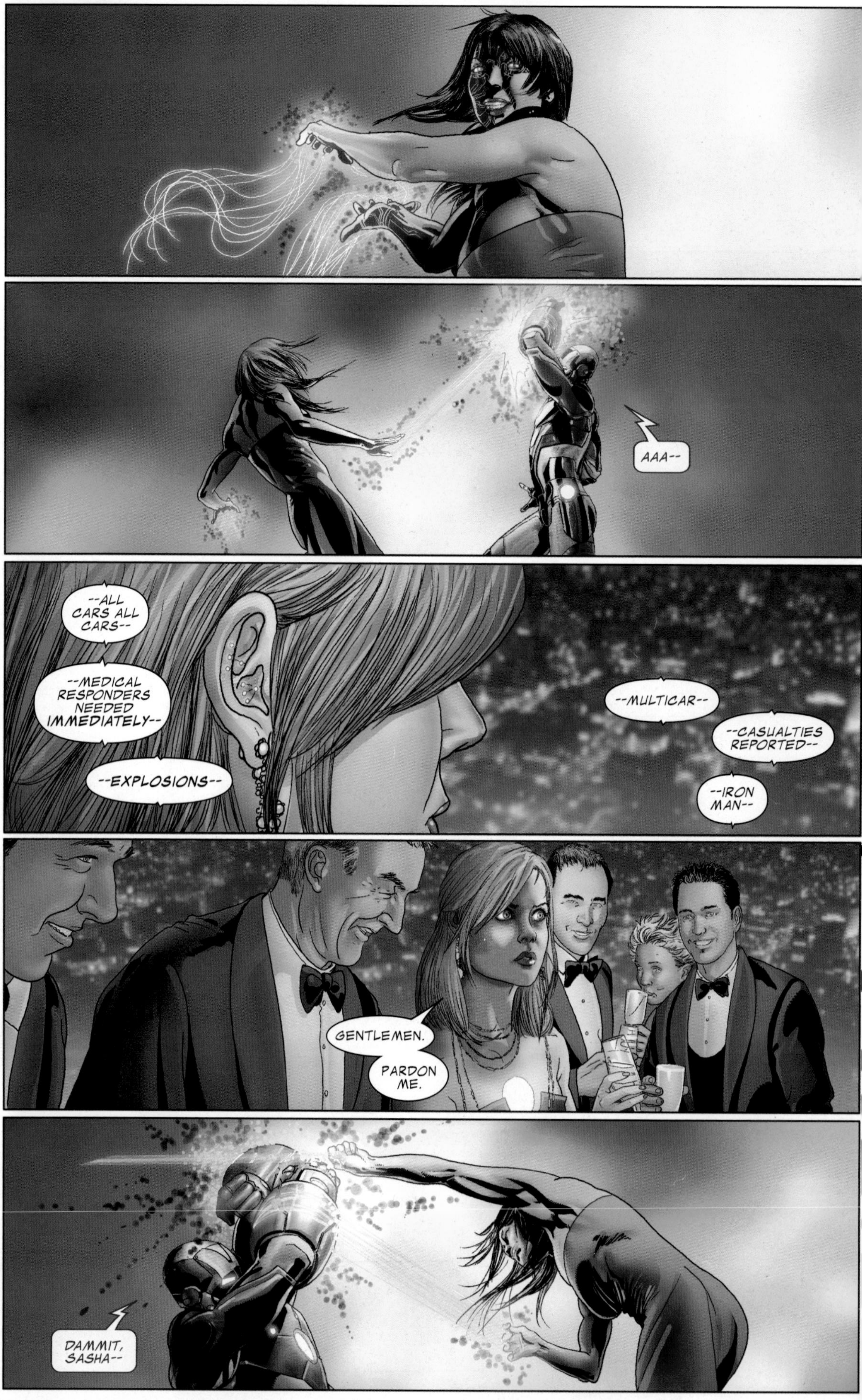
AAA--
--ALL CARS ALL CARS--
--MEDICAL RESPONDERS NEEDED IMMEDIATELY--
--EXPLOSIONS--
--MULTICAR--
--CASUALTIES REPORTED--
--IRON MAN--
GENTLEMEN.
PARDON ME.
DAMMIT, SASHA--

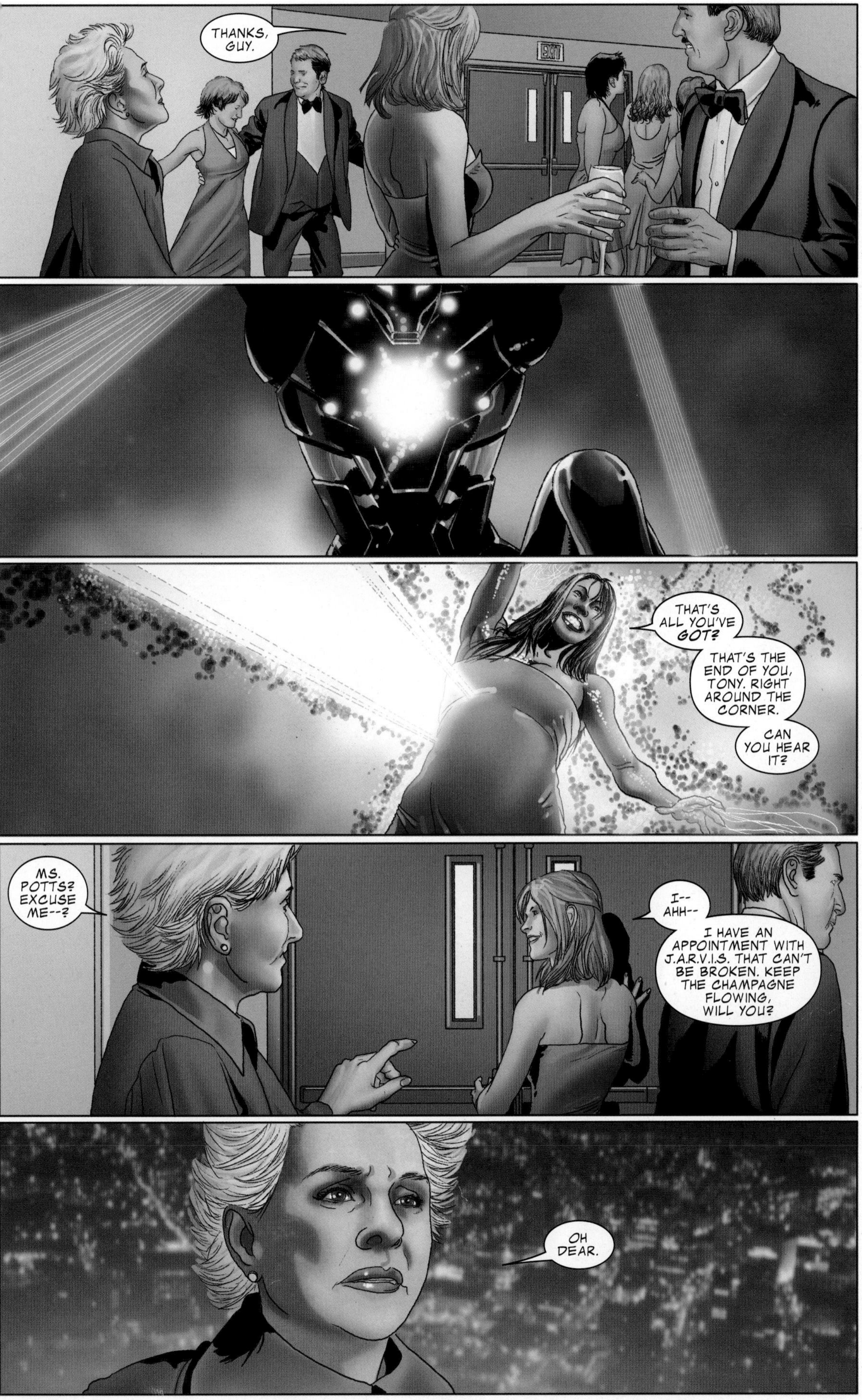
THANKS, GUY.
EXIT
THAT'S ALL YOU'VE GOT?
THAT'S THE END OF YOU, TONY. RIGHT AROUND THE CORNER.
CAN YOU HEAR IT?
MS. POTTS? EXCUSE ME--?
I-- AHH--
I HAVE AN APPOINTMENT WITH J.A.R.V.I.S. THAT CAN'T BE BROKEN. KEEP THE CHAMPAGNE FLOWING, WILL YOU?
OH DEAR.

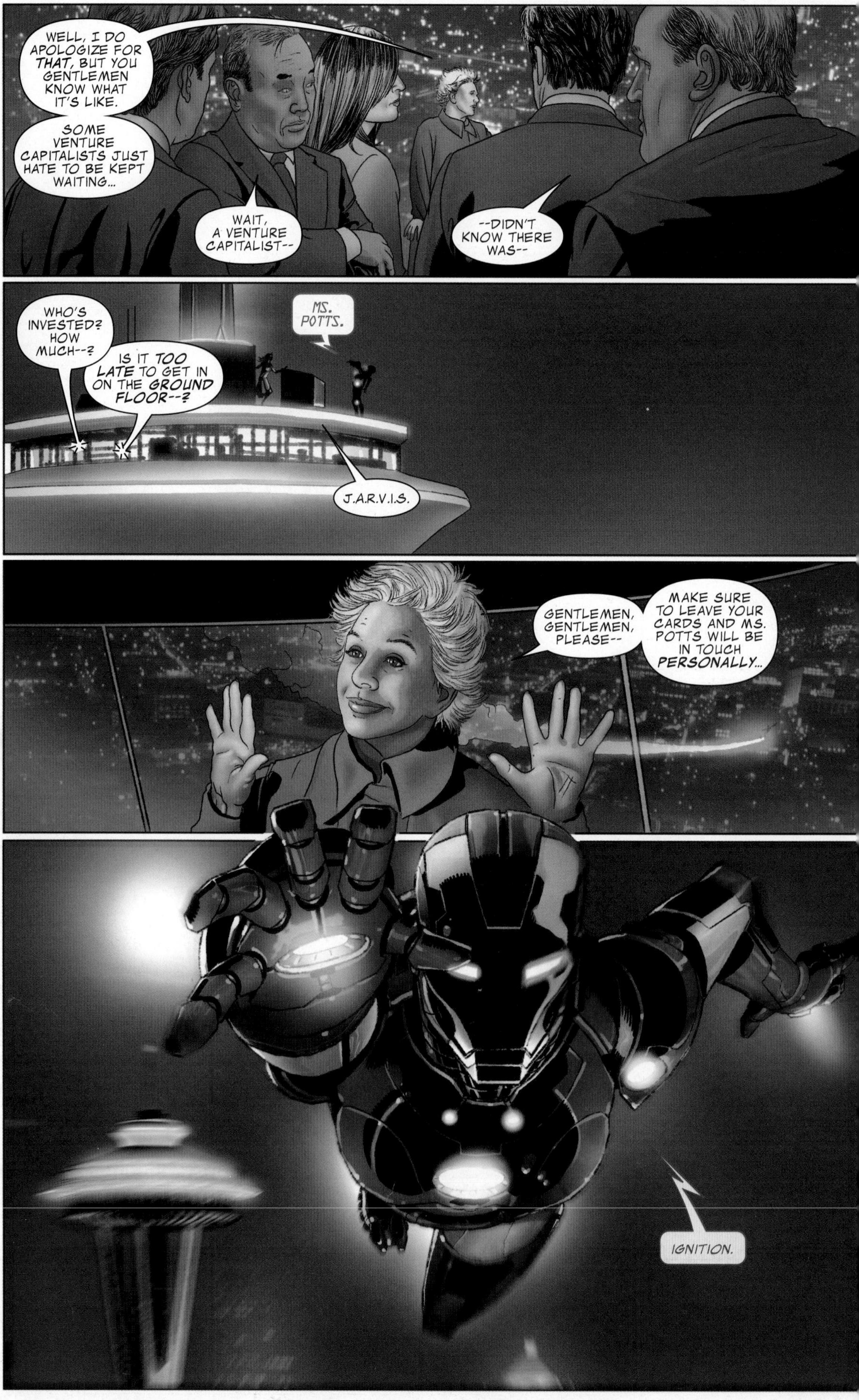
WELL, I DO APOLOGIZE FOR THAT, BUT YOU GENTLEMEN KNOW WHAT IT'S LIKE.
SOME VENTURE CAPITALISTS JUST HATE TO BE KEPT WAITING...
WAIT, A VENTURE CAPITALIST--
--DIDN'T KNOW THERE WAS--
WHO'S INVESTED? HOW MUCH--?
IS IT TOO LATE TO GET IN ON THE GROUND FLOOR--?
MS. POTTS.
J.A.R.V.I.S.
GENTLEMEN, GENTLEMEN, PLEASE--
MAKE SURE TO LEAVE YOUR CARDS AND MS. POTTS WILL BE IN TOUCH PERSONALLY...
IGNITION.

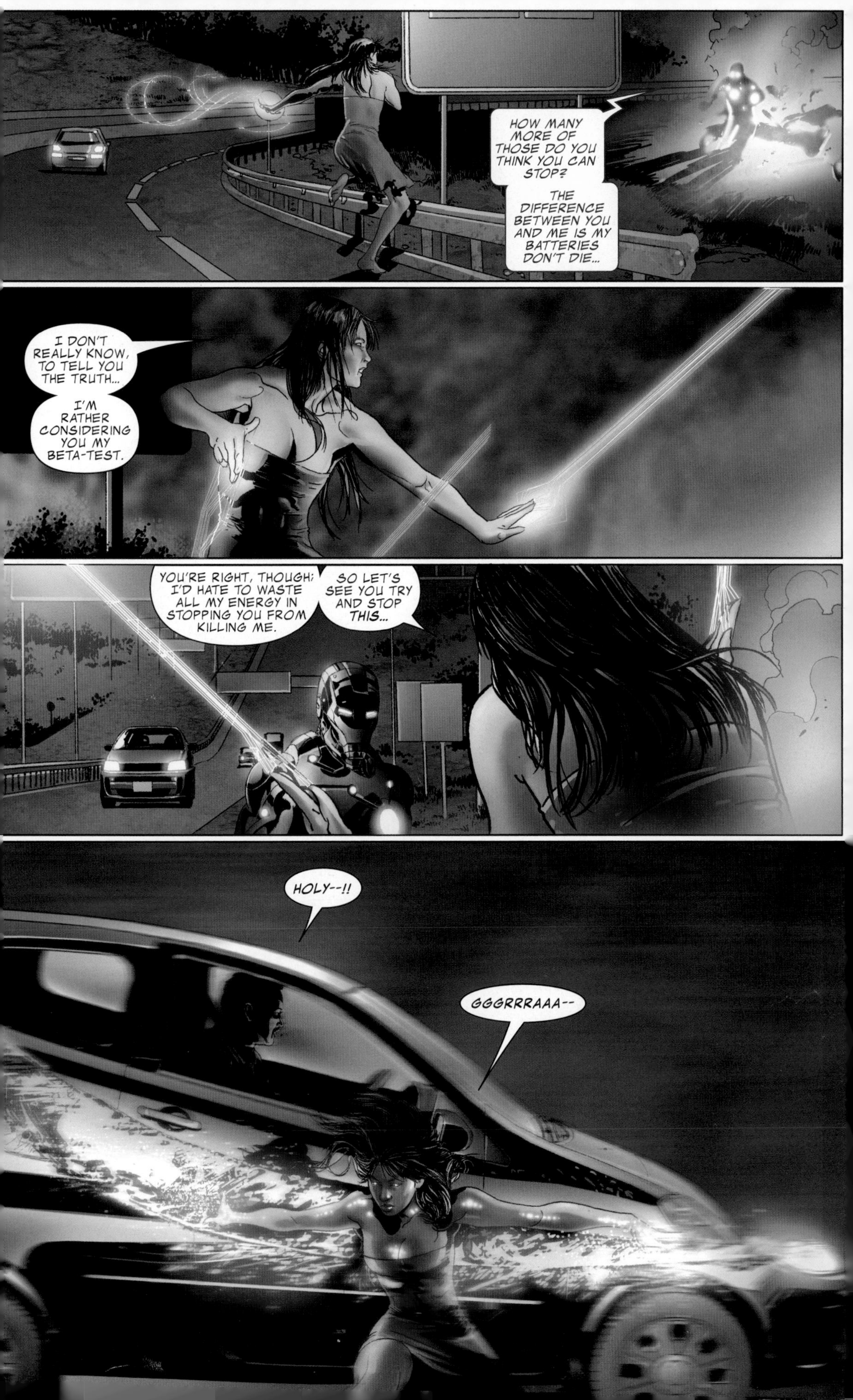
HOW MANY MORE OF THOSE DO YOU THINK YOU CAN STOP?
THE DIFFERENCE BETWEEN YOU AND ME IS MY BATTERIES DON'T DIE...
I DON'T REALLY KNOW, TO TELL YOU THE TRUTH...
I'M RATHER CONSIDERING YOU MY BETA-TEST.
YOU'RE RIGHT, THOUGH; I'D HATE TO WASTE ALL MY ENERGY IN STOPPING YOU FROM KILLING ME.
SO LET'S SEE YOU TRY AND STOP THIS...
HOLY--!!
GGGRRRAAA--

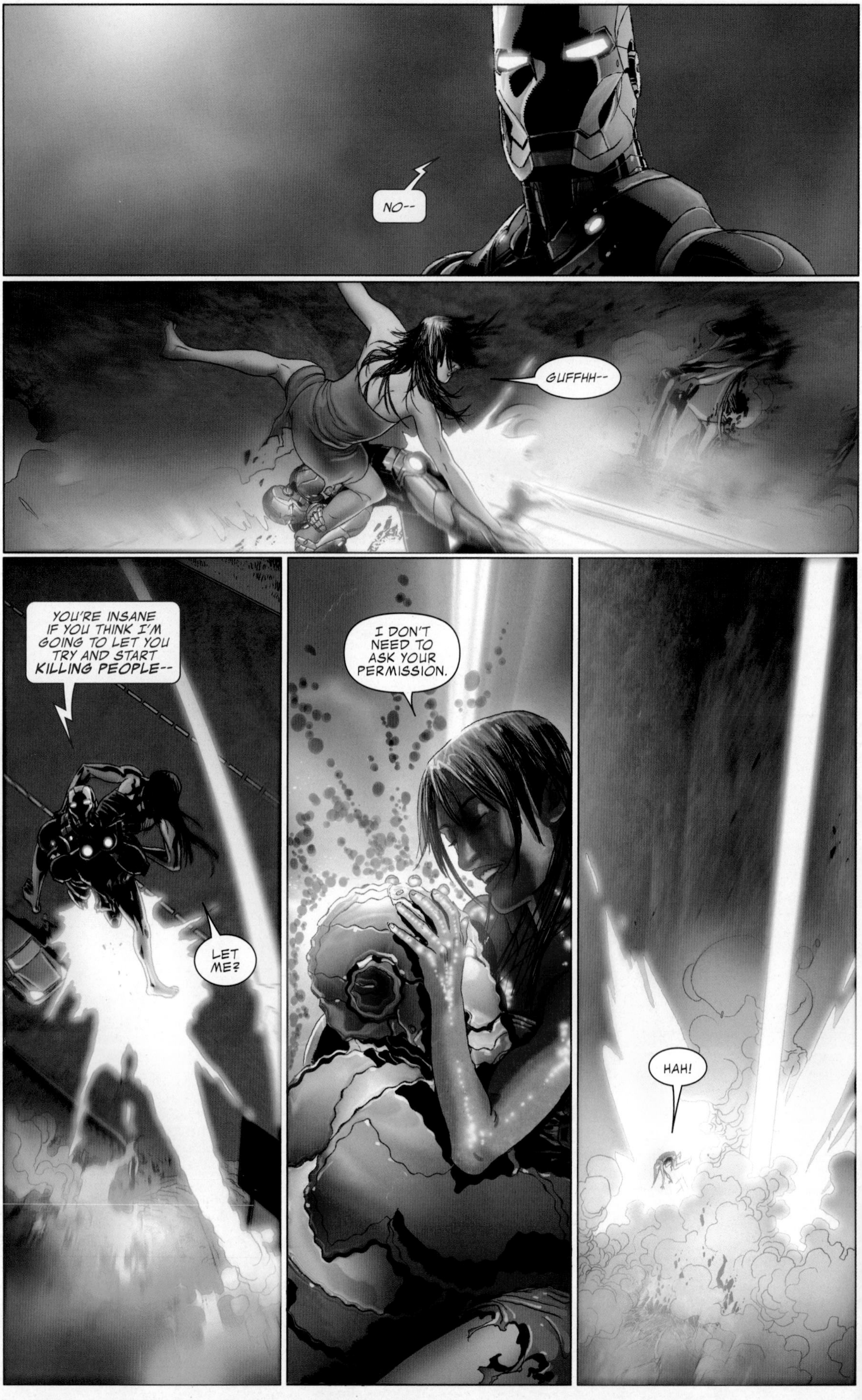
NO--
GUFFHH--
YOU'RE INSANE IF YOU THINK I'M GOING TO LET YOU TRY AND START KILLING PEOPLE--
LET ME?
I DON'T NEED TO ASK YOUR PERMISSION.
HAH!

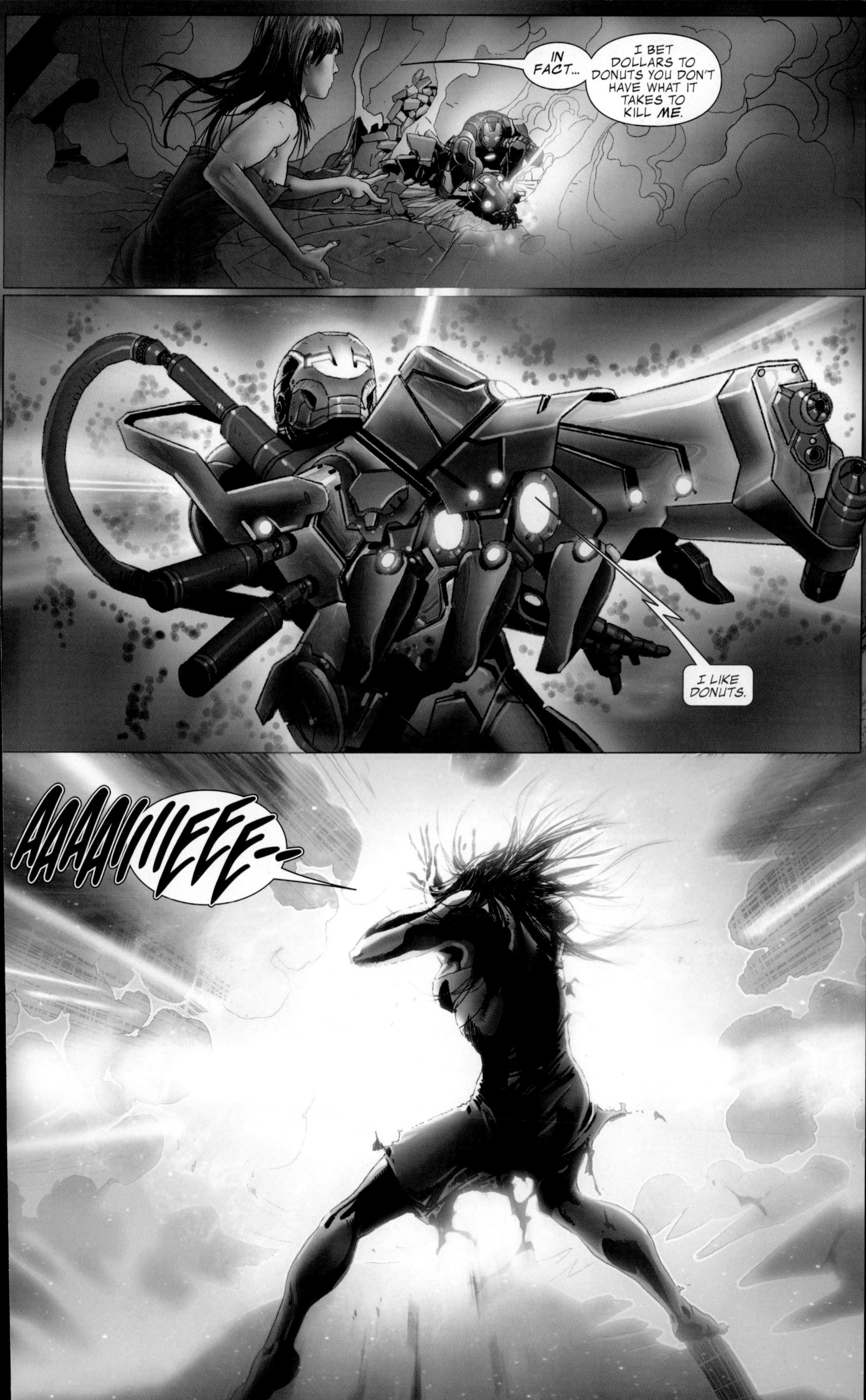
IN FACT...
I BET DOLLARS TO DONUTS YOU DON'T HAVE WHAT IT TAKES TO KILL ME.
I LIKE DONUTS.
AAAAIIIEEE--

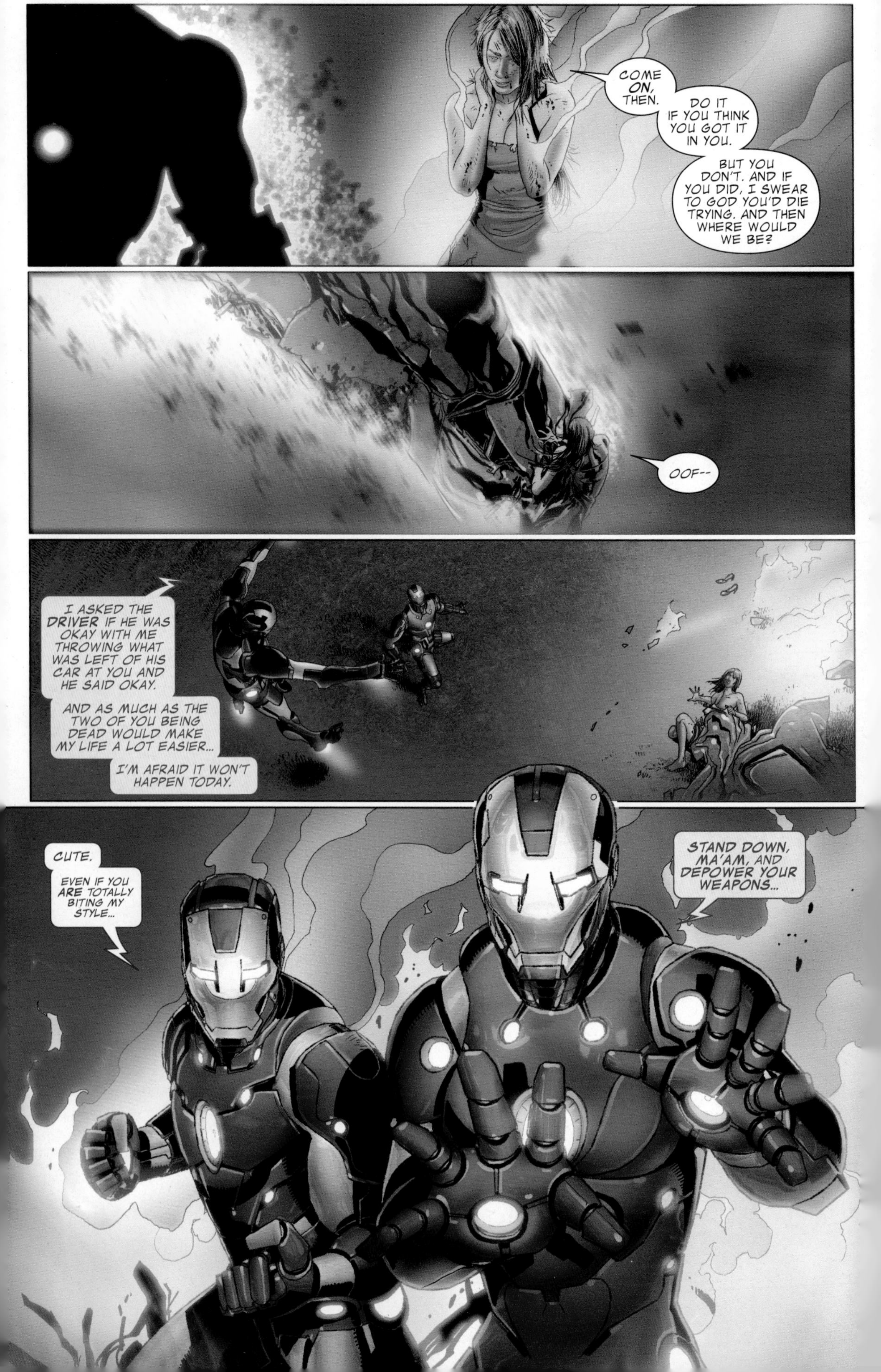
COME ON, THEN.
DO IT IF YOU THINK YOU GOT IT IN YOU.
BUT YOU DON'T. AND IF YOU DID, I SWEAR TO GOD YOU'D DIE TRYING. AND THEN WHERE WOULD WE BE?
OOF--
I ASKED THE DRIVER IF HE WAS OKAY WITH ME THROWING WHAT WAS LEFT OF HIS CAR AT YOU AND HE SAID OKAY.
AND AS MUCH AS THE TWO OF YOU BEING DEAD WOULD MAKE MY LIFE A LOT EASIER...
I'M AFRAID IT WON'T HAPPEN TODAY.
CUTE.
EVEN IF YOU ARE TOTALLY BITING MY STYLE...
STAND DOWN, MA'AM, AND DEPOWER YOUR WEAPONS...

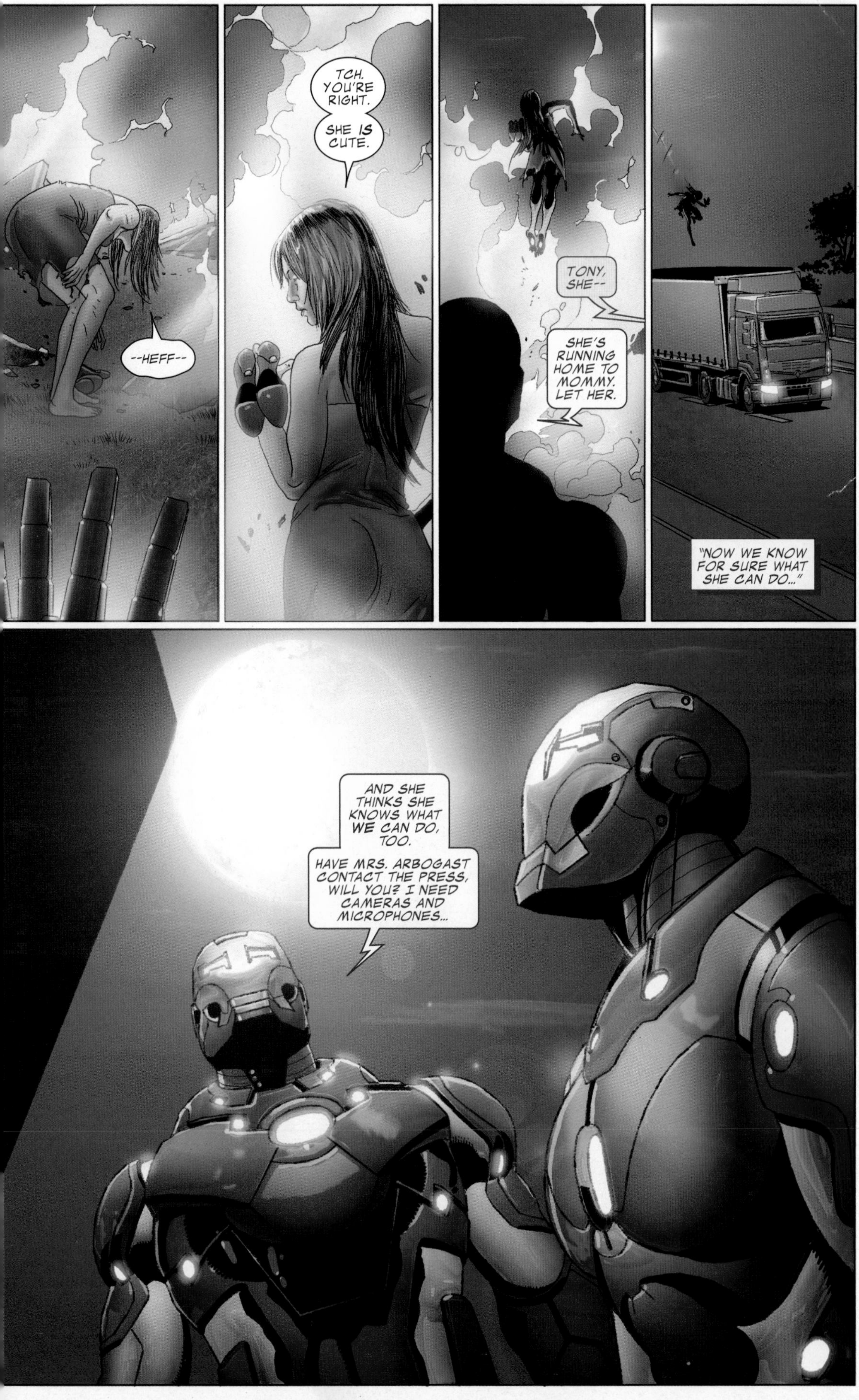
--HEFF--
TCH. YOU'RE RIGHT.
SHE IS CUTE.
TONY, SHE--
SHE'S RUNNING HOME TO MOMMY. LET HER.
"NOW WE KNOW FOR SURE WHAT SHE CAN DO..."
AND SHE THINKS SHE KNOWS WHAT WE CAN DO, TOO.
HAVE MRS. ARBOGAST CONTACT THE PRESS, WILL YOU? I NEED CAMERAS AND MICROPHONES...

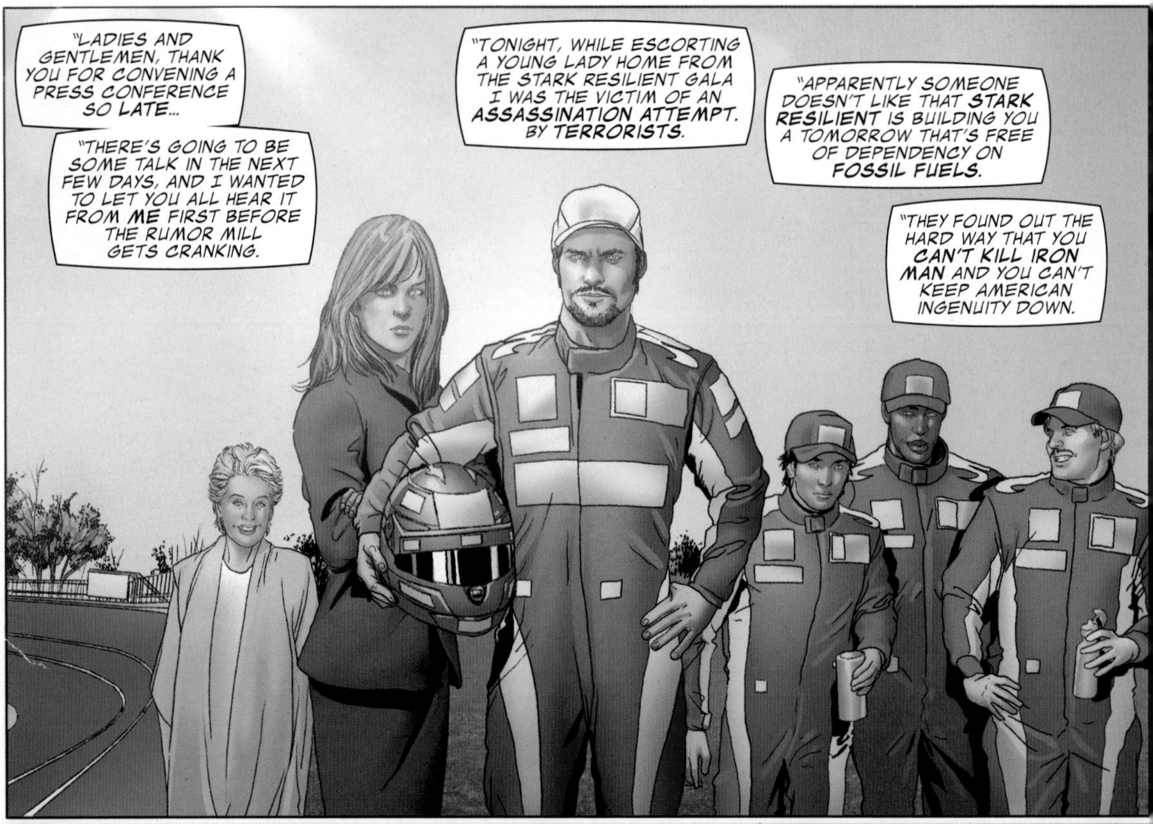
"LADIES AND GENTLEMEN, THANK YOU FOR CONVENING A PRESS CONFERENCE SO LATE...
"THERE'S GOING TO BE SOME TALK IN THE NEXT FEW DAYS, AND I WANTED TO LET YOU ALL HEAR IT FROM ME FIRST BEFORE THE RUMOR MILL GETS CRANKING.
"TONIGHT, WHILE ESCORTING A YOUNG LADY HOME FROM THE STARK RESILIENT GALA I WAS THE VICTIM OF AN ASSASSINATION ATTEMPT. BY TERRORISTS.
"APPARENTLY SOMEONE DOESN'T LIKE THAT STARK RESILIENT IS BUILDING YOU A TOMORROW THAT'S FREE OF DEPENDENCY ON FOSSIL FUELS.
"THEY FOUND OUT THE HARD WAY THAT YOU CAN'T KILL IRON MAN AND YOU CAN'T KEEP AMERICAN INGENUITY DOWN.

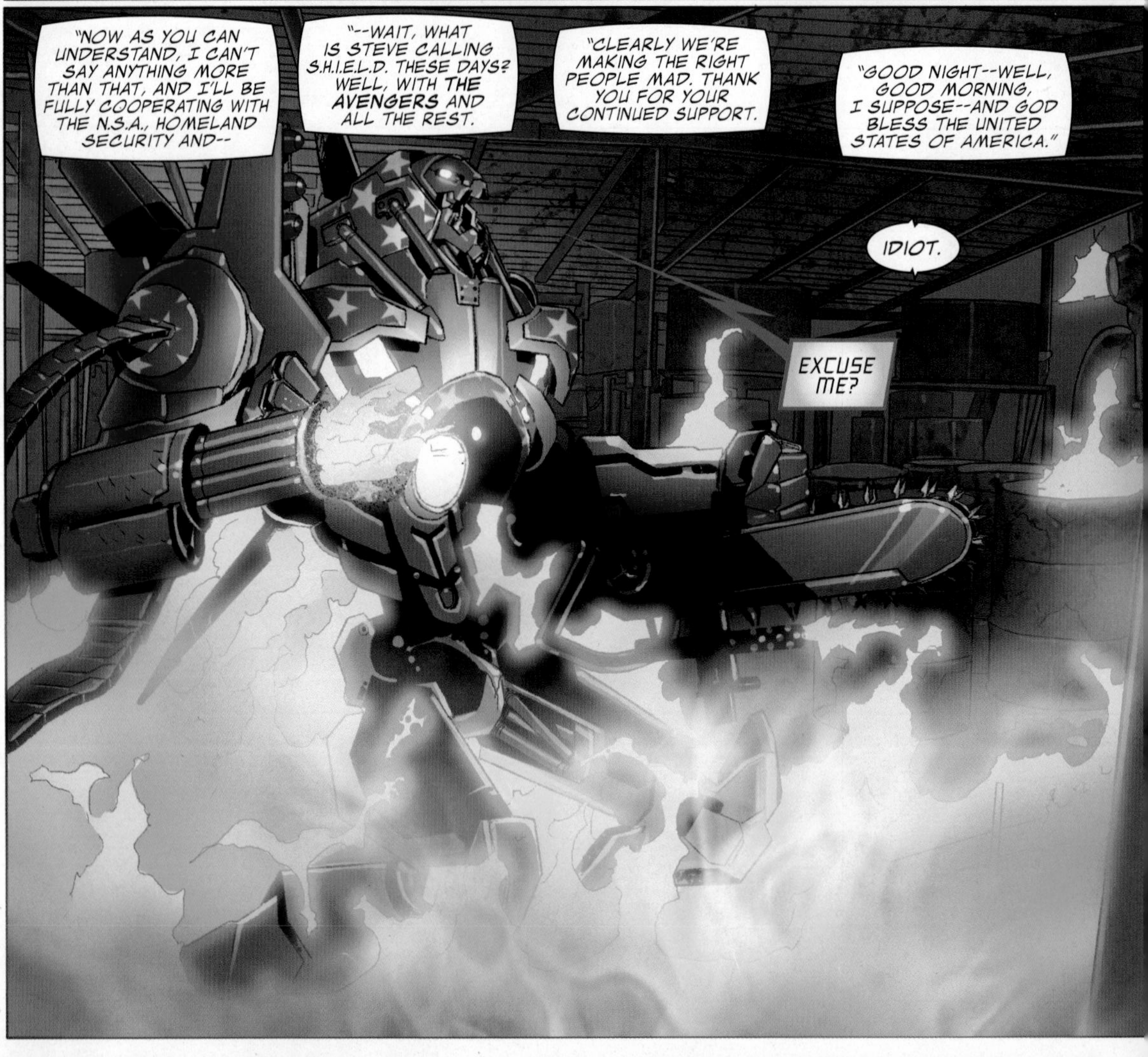
"NOW AS YOU CAN UNDERSTAND, I CAN'T SAY ANYTHING MORE THAN THAT, AND I'LL BE FULLY COOPERATING WITH THE N.S.A., HOMELAND SECURITY AND--
"--WAIT, WHAT IS STEVE CALLING S.H.I.E.L.D. THESE DAYS? WELL, WITH THE AVENGERS AND ALL THE REST.
"CLEARLY WE'RE MAKING THE RIGHT PEOPLE MAD. THANK YOU FOR YOUR CONTINUED SUPPORT.
"GOOD NIGHT--WELL, GOOD MORNING, I SUPPOSE--AND GOD BLESS THE UNITED STATES OF AMERICA."
IDIOT.
EXCUSE ME?

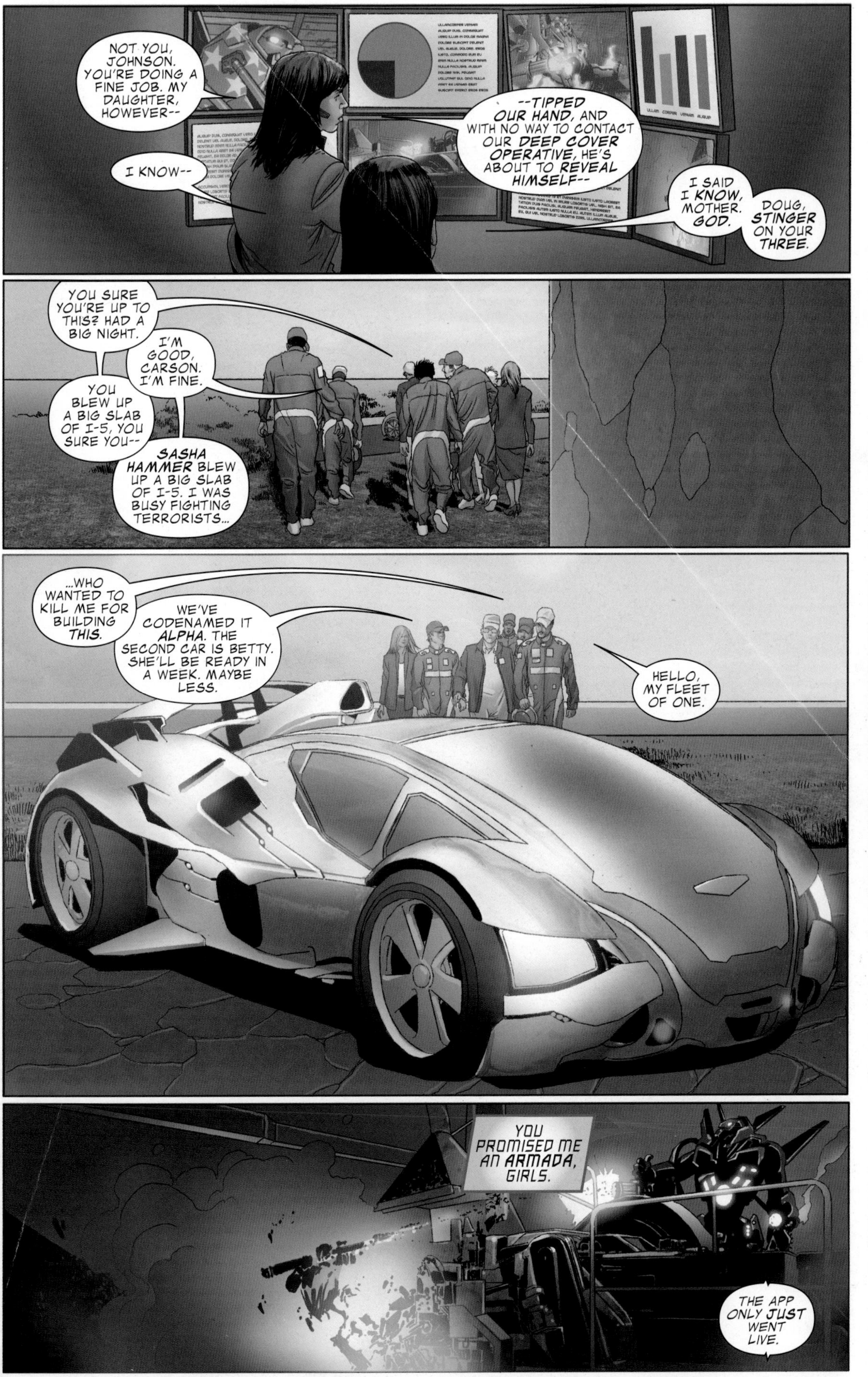
NOT YOU, JOHNSON. YOU'RE DOING A FINE JOB. MY DAUGHTER, HOWEVER--
I KNOW--
--TIPPED OUR HAND, AND WITH NO WAY TO CONTACT OUR DEEP COVER OPERATIVE, HE'S ABOUT TO REVEAL HIMSELF--
I SAID I KNOW, MOTHER. GOD.
DOUG, STINGER ON YOUR THREE.
YOU SURE YOU'RE UP TO THIS? HAD A BIG NIGHT.
I'M GOOD, CARSON. I'M FINE.
YOU BLEW UP A BIG SLAB OF I-5, YOU SURE YOU--
SASHA HAMMER BLEW UP A BIG SLAB OF I-5. I WAS BUSY FIGHTING TERRORISTS...
...WHO WANTED TO KILL ME FOR BUILDING THIS.
WE'VE CODENAMED IT ALPHA. THE SECOND CAR IS BETTY. SHE'LL BE READY IN A WEEK. MAYBE LESS.
HELLO, MY FLEET OF ONE.
YOU PROMISED ME AN ARMADA, GIRLS.
THE APP ONLY JUST WENT LIVE.

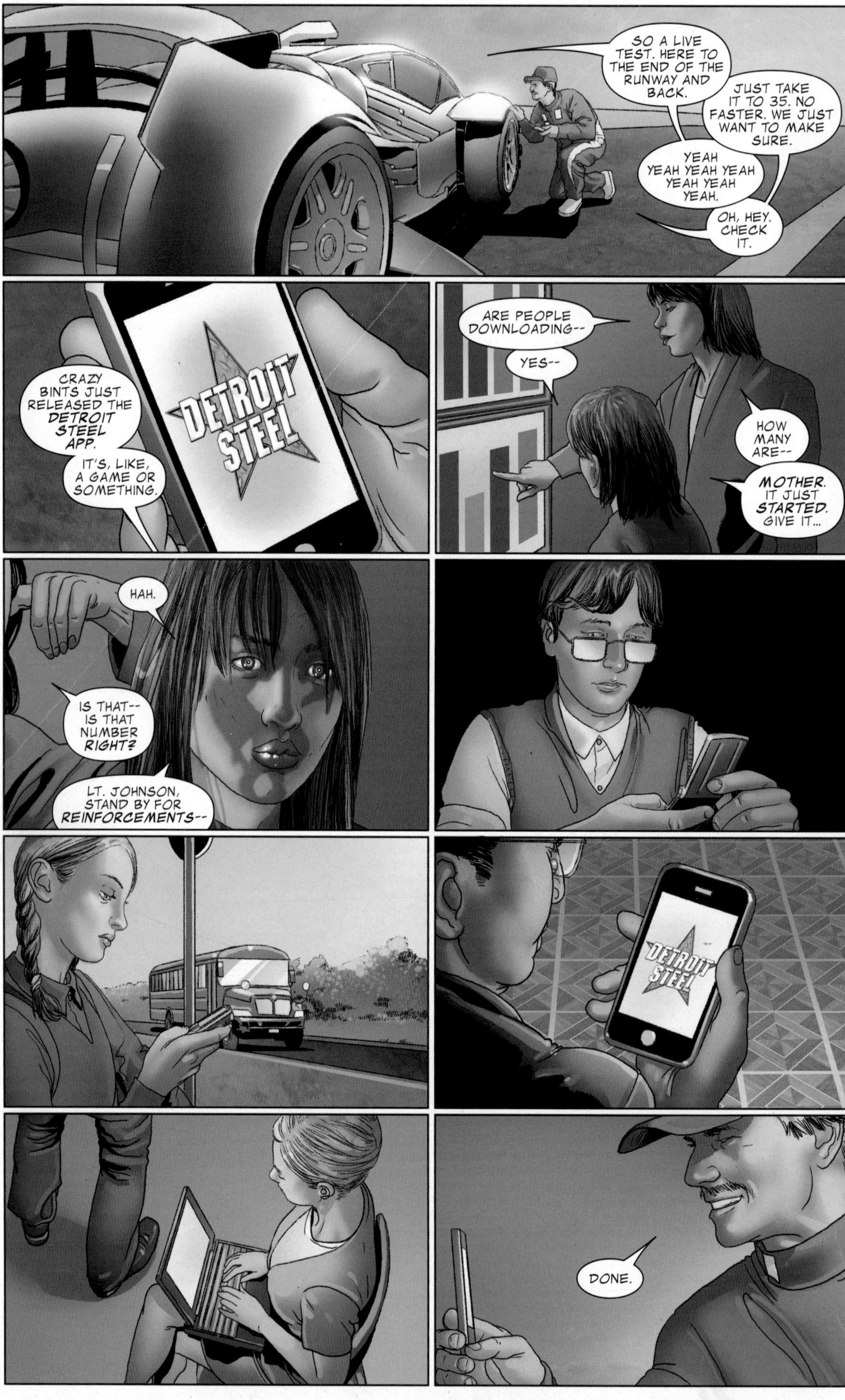
SO A LIVE TEST. HERE TO THE END OF THE RUNWAY AND BACK.
JUST TAKE IT TO 35. NO FASTER. WE JUST WANT TO MAKE SURE.
YEAH YEAH YEAH YEAH YEAH YEAH YEAH.
OH, HEY. CHECK IT.
CRAZY BINTS JUST RELEASED THE DETROIT STEEL APP.
IT'S, LIKE, A GAME OR SOMETHING.
DETROIT STEEL
ARE PEOPLE DOWNLOADING--
YES--
HOW MANY ARE--
MOTHER. IT JUST STARTED. GIVE IT...
HAH.
IS THAT-- IS THAT NUMBER RIGHT?
LT. JOHNSON, STAND BY FOR REINFORCEMENTS--
DETROIT STEEL
DONE.

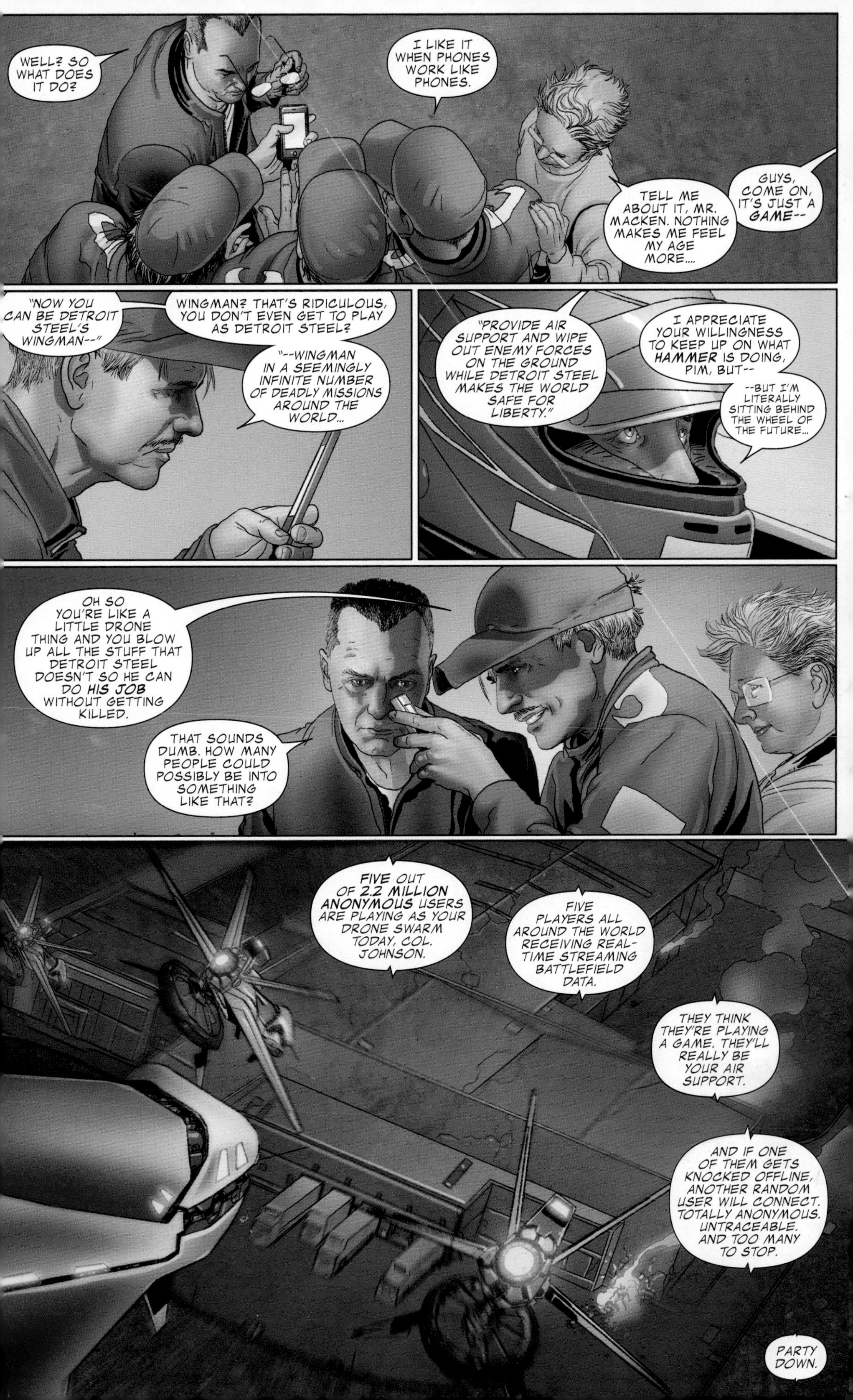
WELL? SO WHAT DOES IT DO?
I LIKE IT WHEN PHONES WORK LIKE PHONES.
TELL ME ABOUT IT, MR. MACKEN. NOTHING MAKES ME FEEL MY AGE MORE....
GUYS, COME ON, IT'S JUST A **GAME**--
"NOW YOU CAN BE DETROIT STEEL'S WINGMAN--"
WINGMAN? THAT'S RIDICULOUS, YOU DON'T EVEN GET TO PLAY AS DETROIT STEEL?
"--WINGMAN IN A SEEMINGLY INFINITE NUMBER OF DEADLY MISSIONS AROUND THE WORLD...
"PROVIDE AIR SUPPORT AND WIPE OUT ENEMY FORCES ON THE GROUND WHILE DETROIT STEEL MAKES THE WORLD SAFE FOR LIBERTY."
I APPRECIATE YOUR WILLINGNESS TO KEEP UP ON WHAT **HAMMER** IS DOING, PIM, BUT--
--BUT I'M LITERALLY SITTING BEHIND THE WHEEL OF THE FUTURE...
OH SO YOU'RE LIKE A LITTLE DRONE THING AND YOU BLOW UP ALL THE STUFF THAT DETROIT STEEL DOESN'T SO HE CAN DO **HIS JOB** WITHOUT GETTING KILLED.
THAT SOUNDS DUMB. HOW MANY PEOPLE COULD POSSIBLY BE INTO SOMETHING LIKE THAT?
FIVE OUT OF **2.2 MILLION ANONYMOUS** USERS ARE PLAYING AS YOUR DRONE SWARM TODAY, COL. JOHNSON.
FIVE PLAYERS ALL AROUND THE WORLD RECEIVING REAL-TIME STREAMING BATTLEFIELD DATA.
THEY THINK THEY'RE PLAYING A GAME. THEY'LL REALLY BE YOUR AIR SUPPORT.
AND IF ONE OF THEM GETS KNOCKED OFFLINE, ANOTHER RANDOM USER WILL CONNECT. TOTALLY ANONYMOUS. UNTRACEABLE. AND TOO MANY TO STOP.
PARTY DOWN.

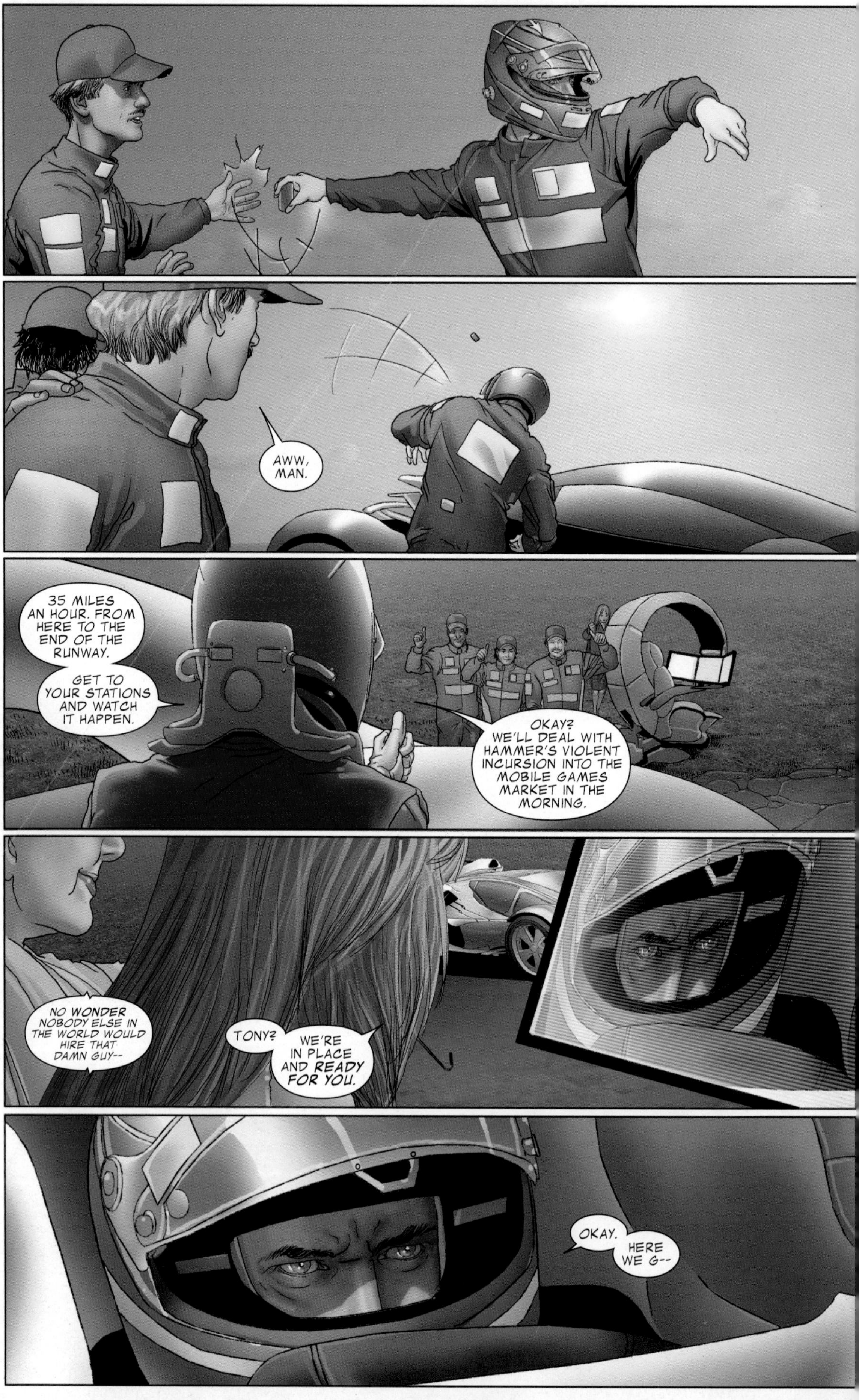
AWW, MAN.
35 MILES AN HOUR. FROM HERE TO THE END OF THE RUNWAY.
GET TO YOUR STATIONS AND WATCH IT HAPPEN.
OKAY? WE'LL DEAL WITH HAMMER'S VIOLENT INCURSION INTO THE MOBILE GAMES MARKET IN THE MORNING.
NO WONDER NOBODY ELSE IN THE WORLD WOULD HIRE THAT DAMN GUY--
TONY?
WE'RE IN PLACE AND READY FOR YOU.
OKAY.
HERE WE G--

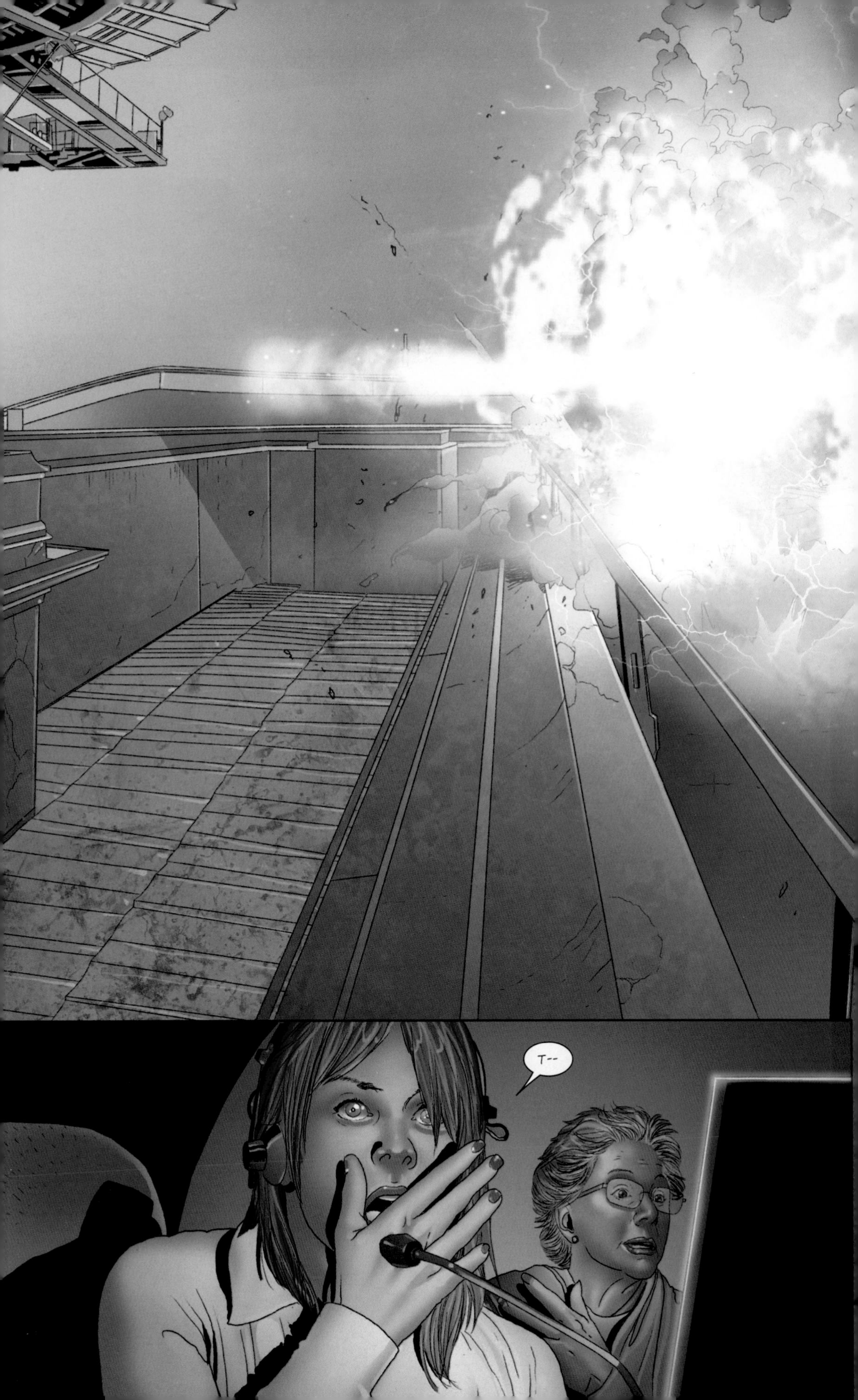
T--

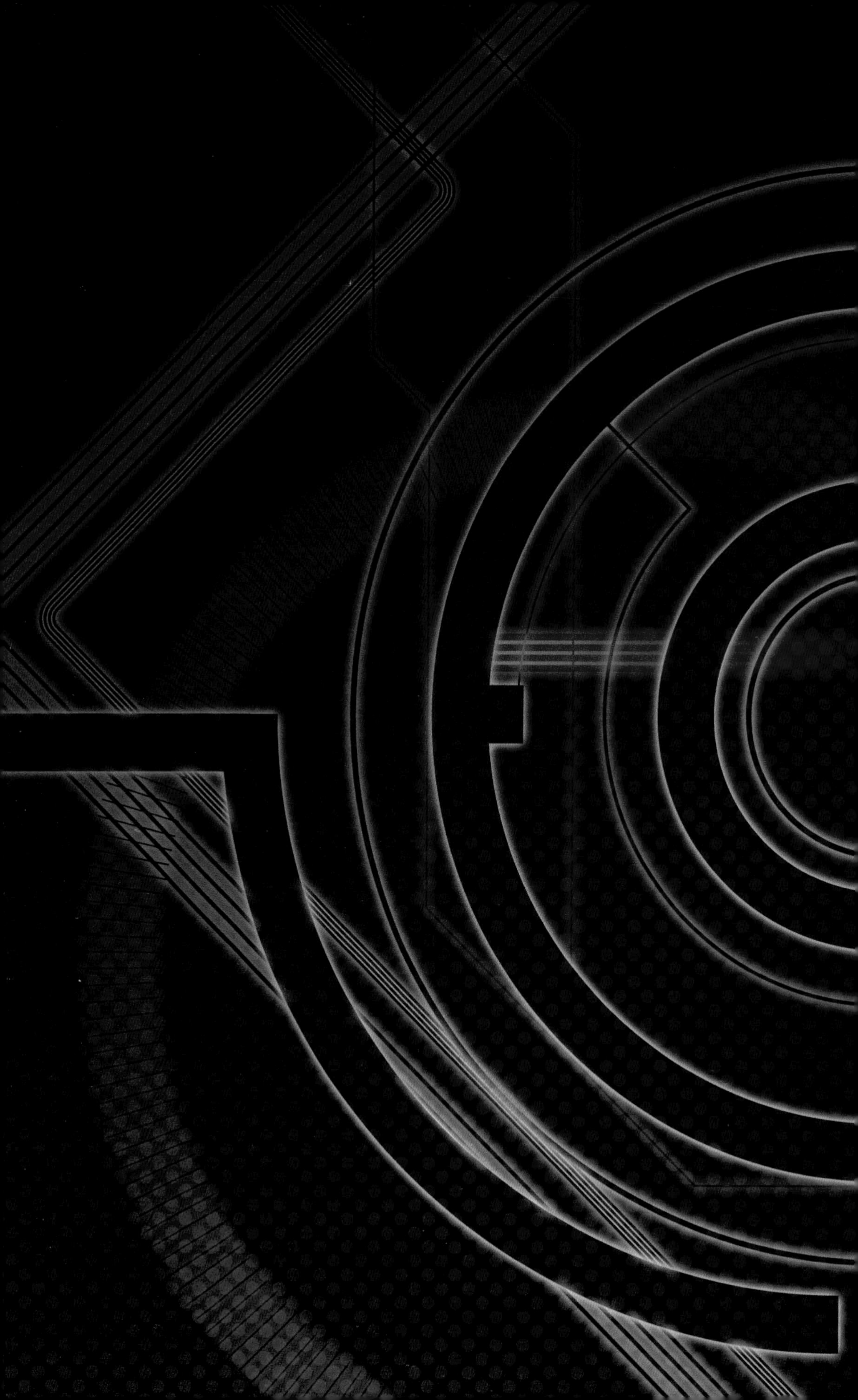

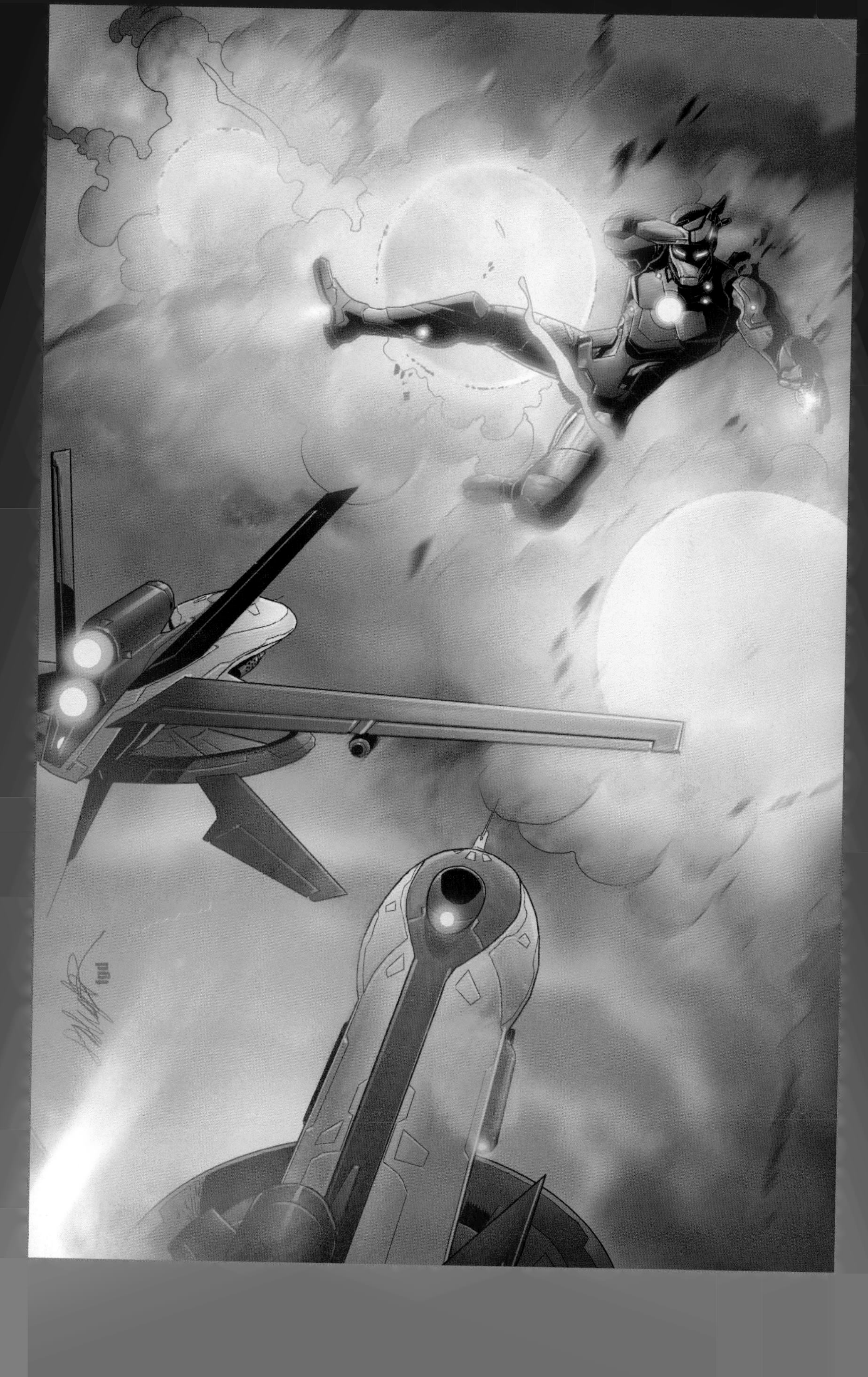

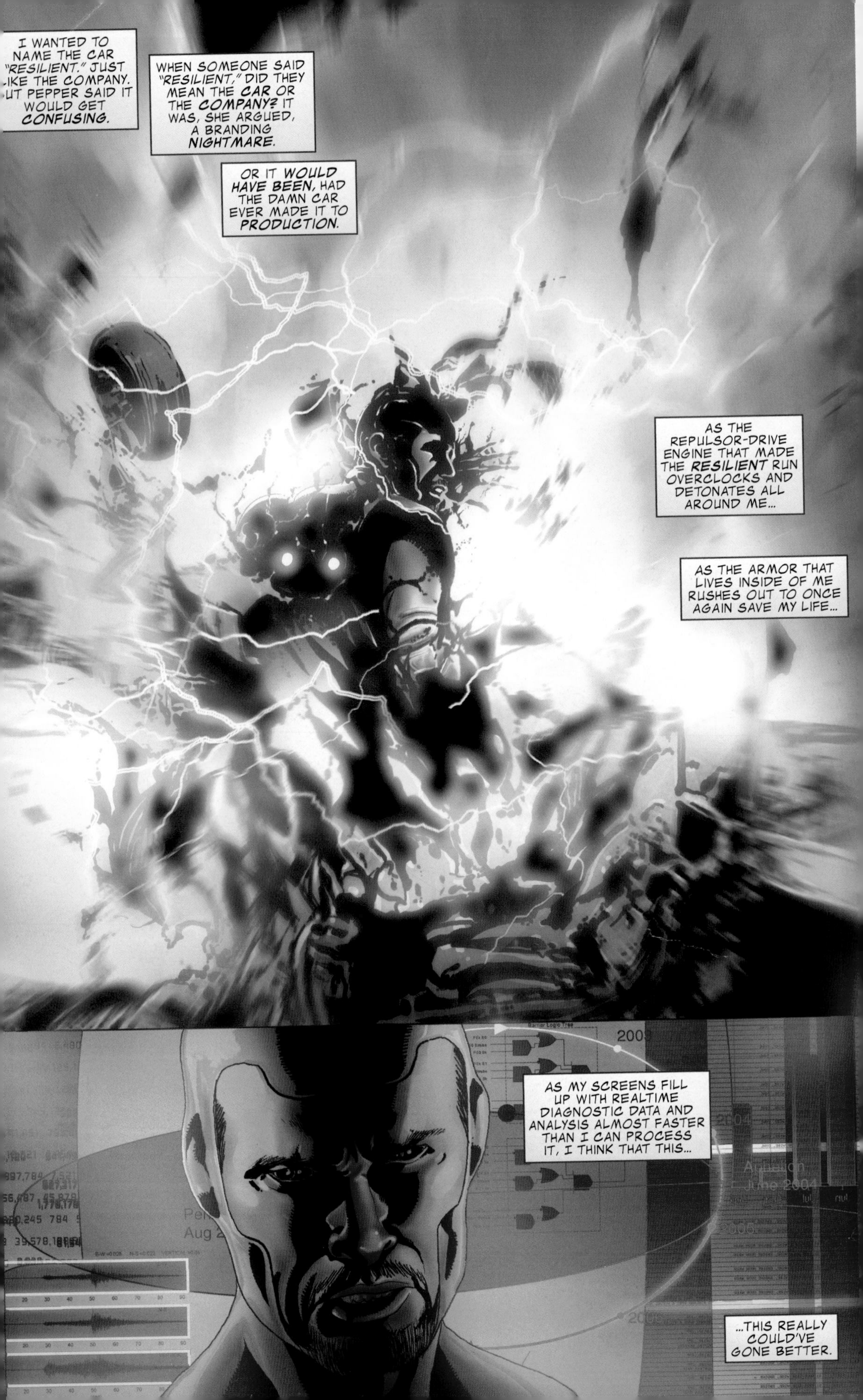
I WANTED TO NAME THE CAR "RESILIENT." JUST LIKE THE COMPANY. BUT PEPPER SAID IT WOULD GET CONFUSING.
WHEN SOMEONE SAID "RESILIENT," DID THEY MEAN THE CAR OR THE COMPANY? IT WAS, SHE ARGUED, A BRANDING NIGHTMARE.
OR IT WOULD HAVE BEEN, HAD THE DAMN CAR EVER MADE IT TO PRODUCTION.
AS THE REPULSOR-DRIVE ENGINE THAT MADE THE RESILIENT RUN OVERCLOCKS AND DETONATES ALL AROUND ME...
AS THE ARMOR THAT LIVES INSIDE OF ME RUSHES OUT TO ONCE AGAIN SAVE MY LIFE...
AS MY SCREENS FILL UP WITH REALTIME DIAGNOSTIC DATA AND ANALYSIS ALMOST FASTER THAN I CAN PROCESS IT, I THINK THAT THIS...
...THIS REALLY COULD'VE GONE BETTER.

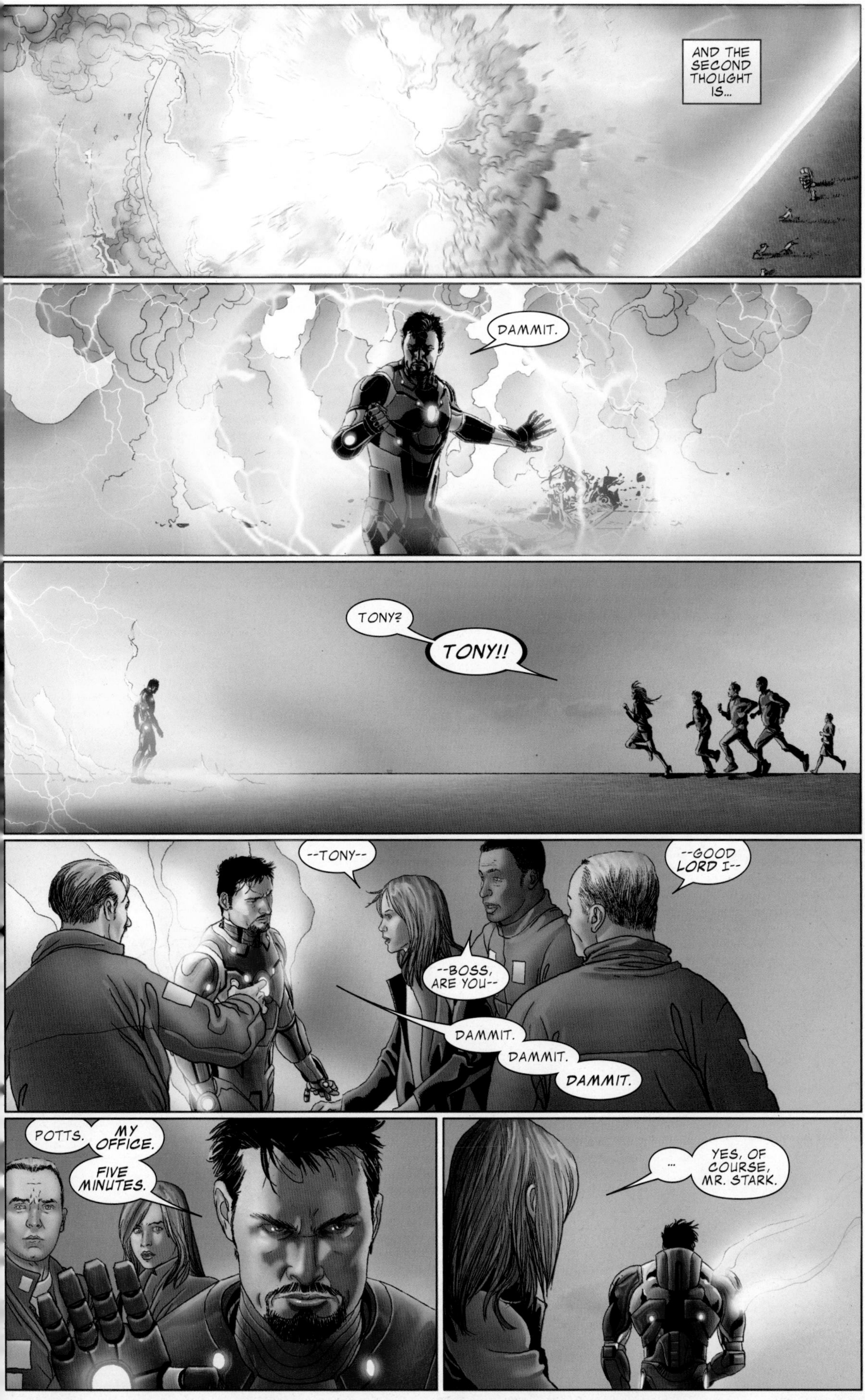

AND THE SECOND THOUGHT IS...
DAMMIT.
TONY?
TONY!!
--TONY--
--GOOD LORD I--
--BOSS, ARE YOU--
DAMMIT.
DAMMIT.
DAMMIT.
POTTS.
MY OFFICE.
FIVE MINUTES.
...
YES, OF COURSE, MR. STARK.

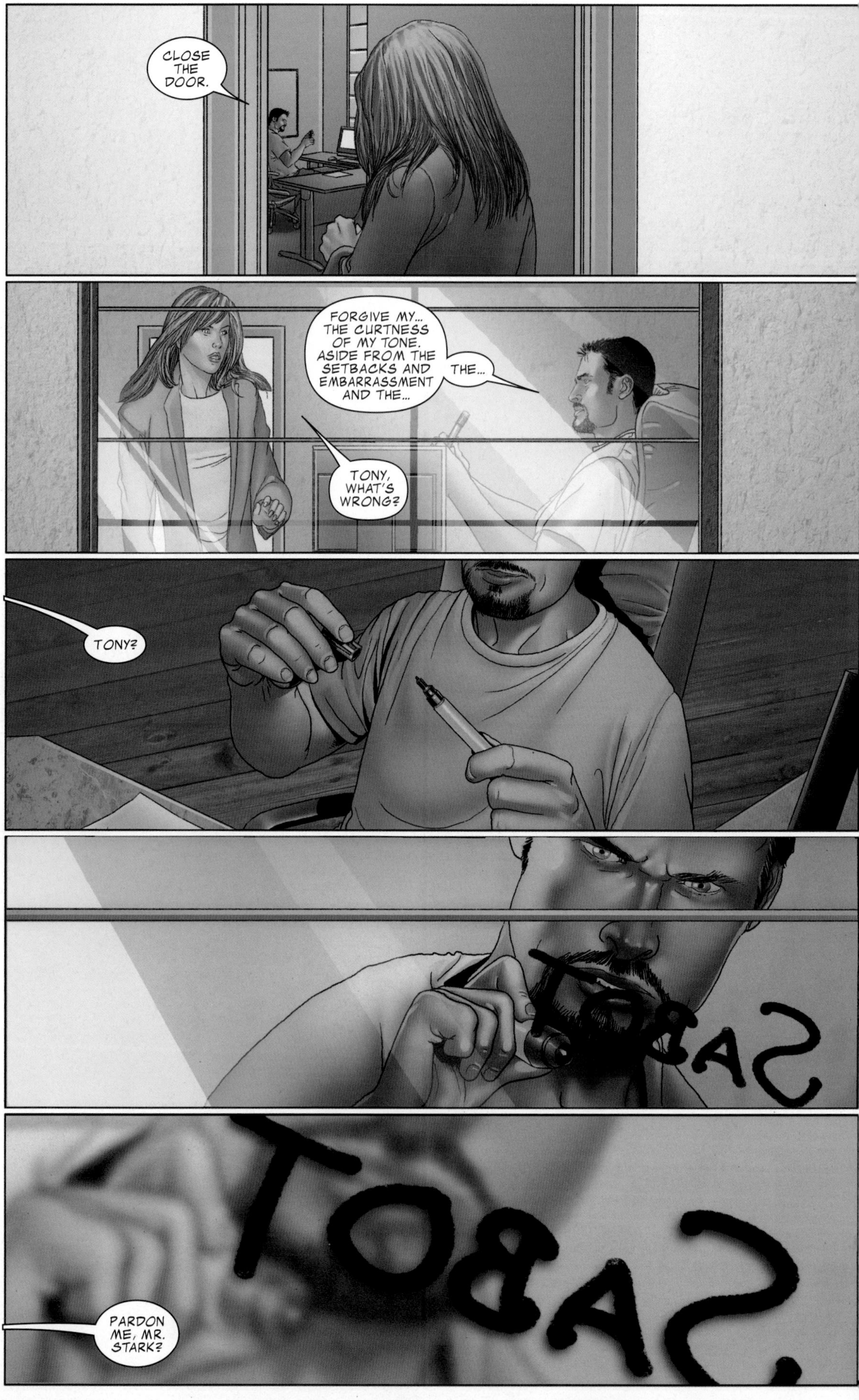

CLOSE THE DOOR.
FORGIVE MY... THE CURTNESS OF MY TONE. ASIDE FROM THE SETBACKS AND EMBARRASSMENT AND THE...
THE...
TONY, WHAT'S WRONG?
TONY?
PARDON ME, MR. STARK?

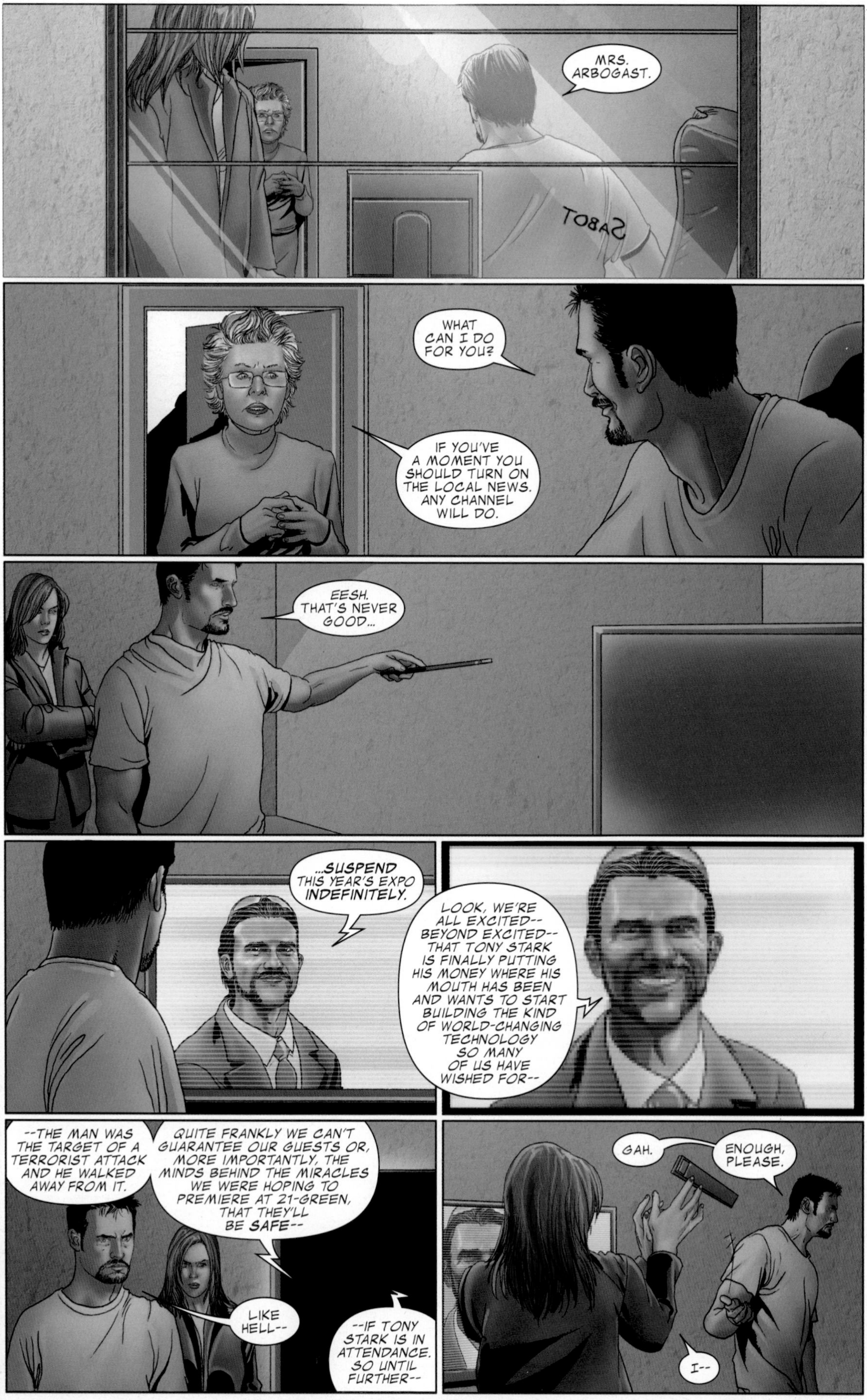
MRS. ARBOGAST.
SABOT
WHAT CAN I DO FOR YOU?
IF YOU'VE A MOMENT YOU SHOULD TURN ON THE LOCAL NEWS. ANY CHANNEL WILL DO.
EESH. THAT'S NEVER GOOD...
...SUSPEND THIS YEAR'S EXPO INDEFINITELY.
LOOK, WE'RE ALL EXCITED-- BEYOND EXCITED-- THAT TONY STARK IS FINALLY PUTTING HIS MONEY WHERE HIS MOUTH HAS BEEN AND WANTS TO START BUILDING THE KIND OF WORLD-CHANGING TECHNOLOGY SO MANY OF US HAVE WISHED FOR--
--THE MAN WAS THE TARGET OF A TERRORIST ATTACK AND HE WALKED AWAY FROM IT.
QUITE FRANKLY WE CAN'T GUARANTEE OUR GUESTS OR, MORE IMPORTANTLY, THE MINDS BEHIND THE MIRACLES WE WERE HOPING TO PREMIERE AT 21-GREEN, THAT THEY'LL BE SAFE--
LIKE HELL--
--IF TONY STARK IS IN ATTENDANCE. SO UNTIL FURTHER--
GAH.
ENOUGH, PLEASE.
I--

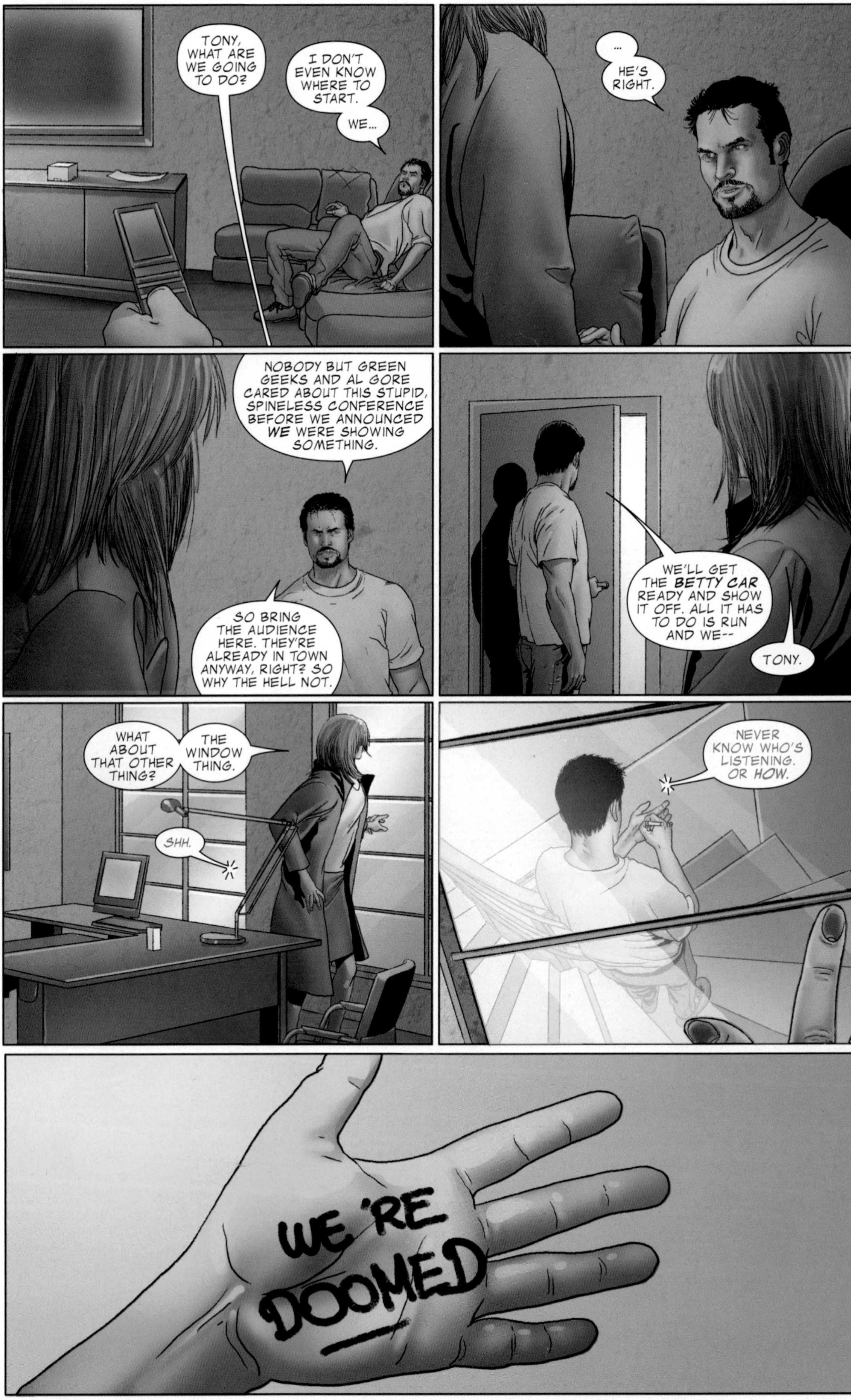
TONY, WHAT ARE WE GOING TO DO?
I DON'T EVEN KNOW WHERE TO START.
WE...
...
HE'S RIGHT.
NOBODY BUT GREEN GEEKS AND AL GORE CARED ABOUT THIS STUPID, SPINELESS CONFERENCE BEFORE WE ANNOUNCED WE WERE SHOWING SOMETHING.
SO BRING THE AUDIENCE HERE. THEY'RE ALREADY IN TOWN ANYWAY, RIGHT? SO WHY THE HELL NOT.
WE'LL GET THE BETTY CAR READY AND SHOW IT OFF. ALL IT HAS TO DO IS RUN AND WE--
TONY.
WHAT ABOUT THAT OTHER THING?
THE WINDOW THING.
SHH.
NEVER KNOW WHO'S LISTENING. OR HOW.
WE'RE DOOMED

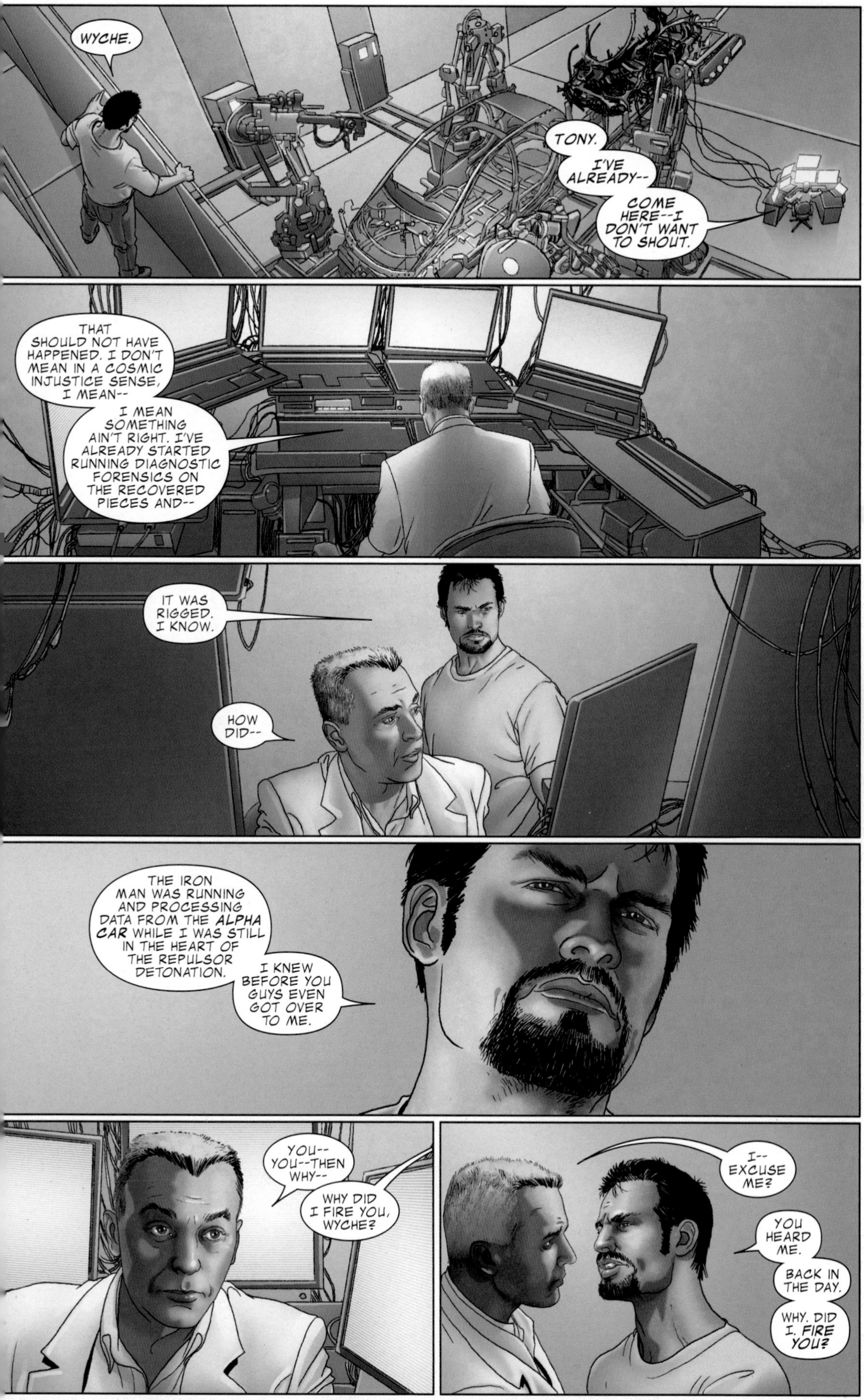
WYCHE.
TONY.
I'VE ALREADY--
COME HERE--I DON'T WANT TO SHOUT.
THAT SHOULD NOT HAVE HAPPENED. I DON'T MEAN IN A COSMIC INJUSTICE SENSE, I MEAN--
I MEAN SOMETHING AIN'T RIGHT. I'VE ALREADY STARTED RUNNING DIAGNOSTIC FORENSICS ON THE RECOVERED PIECES AND--
IT WAS RIGGED. I KNOW.
HOW DID--
THE IRON MAN WAS RUNNING AND PROCESSING DATA FROM THE ALPHA CAR WHILE I WAS STILL IN THE HEART OF THE REPULSOR DETONATION.
I KNEW BEFORE YOU GUYS EVEN GOT OVER TO ME.
YOU-- YOU--THEN WHY--
WHY DID I FIRE YOU, WYCHE?
I-- EXCUSE ME?
YOU HEARD ME.
BACK IN THE DAY.
WHY. DID I. FIRE YOU?

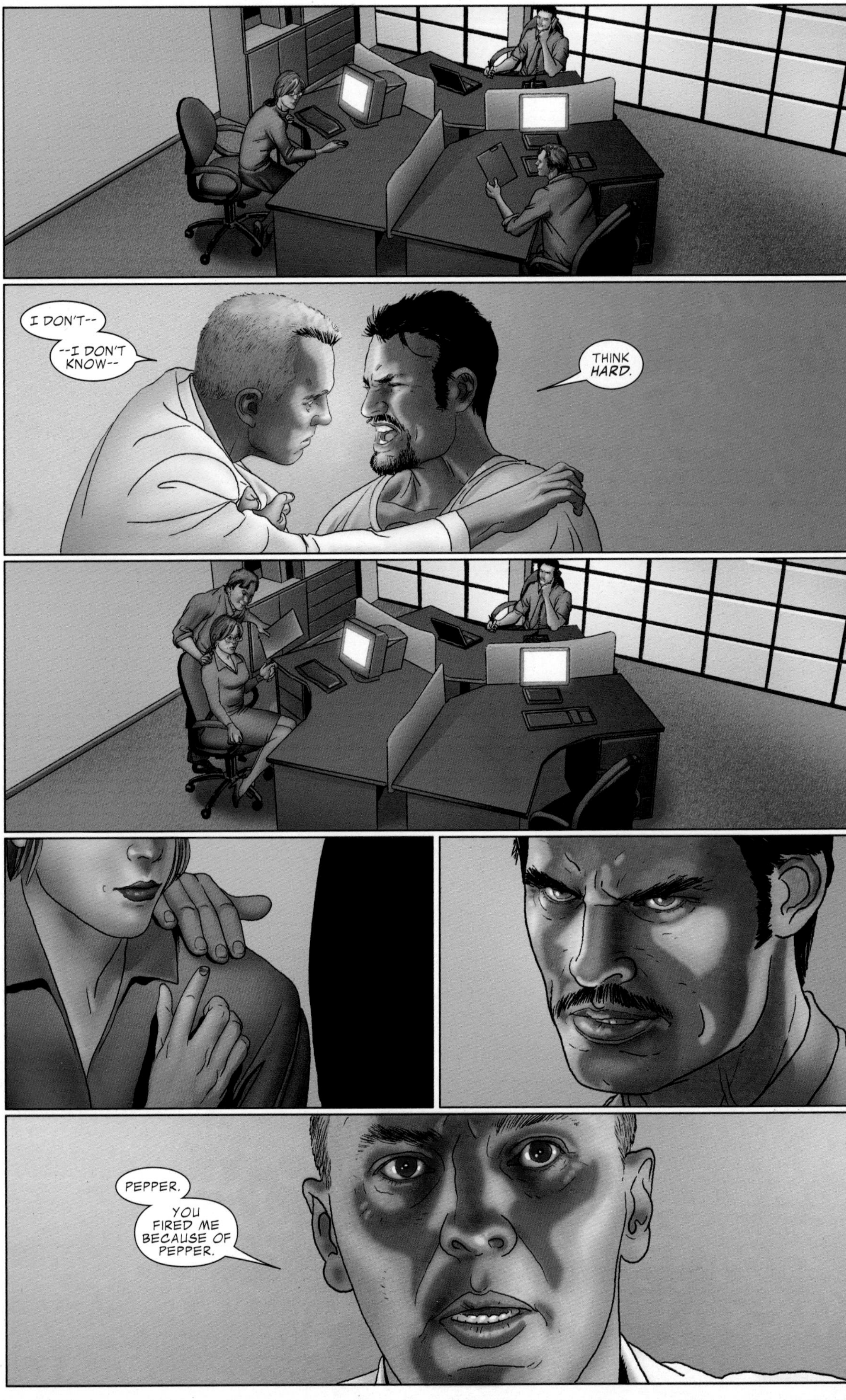
I DON'T--
--I DON'T KNOW--
THINK HARD.
PEPPER.
YOU FIRED ME BECAUSE OF PEPPER.

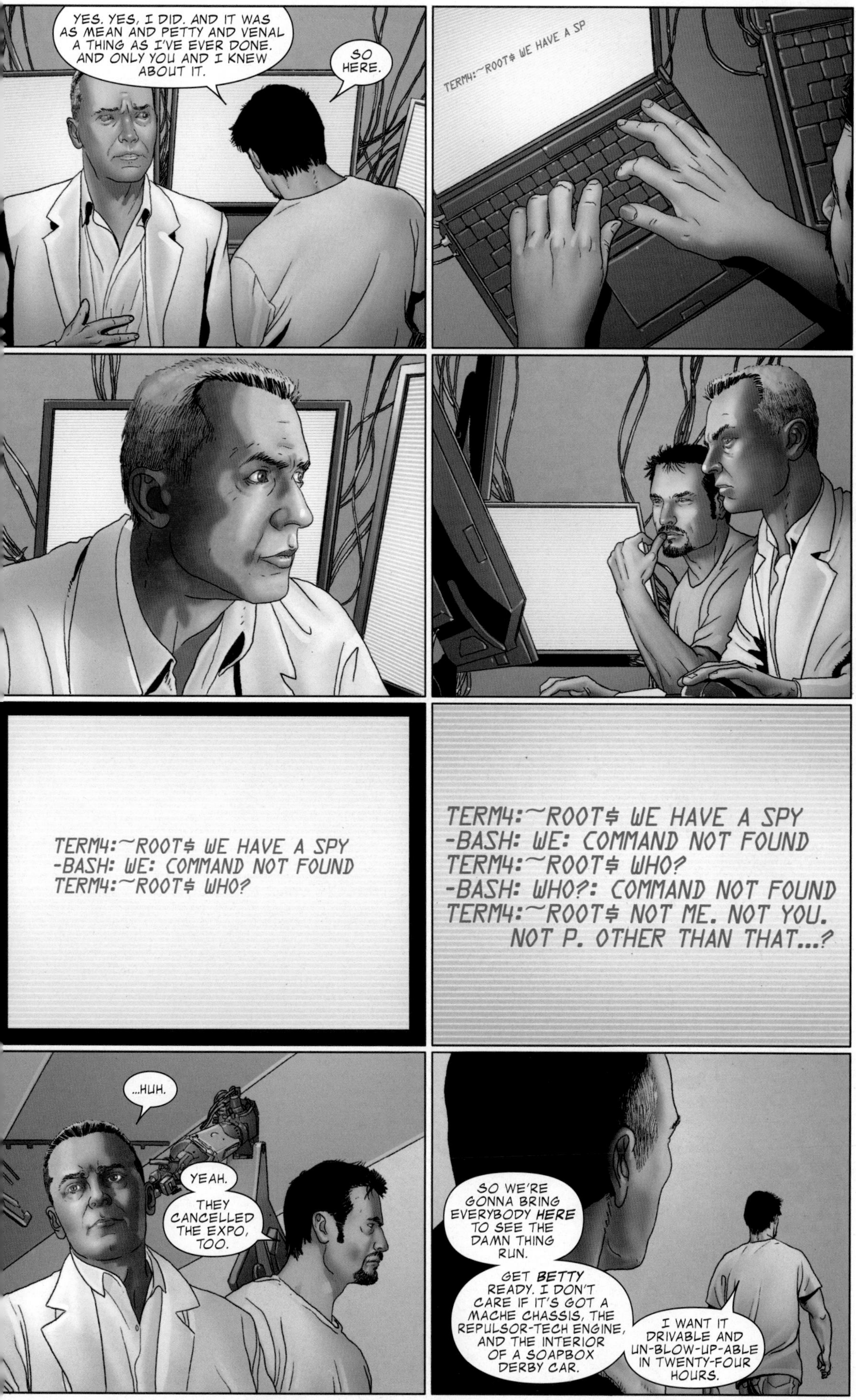
YES. YES, I DID. AND IT WAS AS MEAN AND PETTY AND VENAL A THING AS I'VE EVER DONE. AND ONLY YOU AND I KNEW ABOUT IT.
SO HERE.
TERM4:~ROOT$ WE HAVE A SP
TERM4:~ROOT$ WE HAVE A SPY
-BASH: WE: COMMAND NOT FOUND
TERM4:~ROOT$ WHO?
TERM4:~ROOT$ WE HAVE A SPY
-BASH: WE: COMMAND NOT FOUND
TERM4:~ROOT$ WHO?
-BASH: WHO?: COMMAND NOT FOUND
TERM4:~ROOT$ NOT ME. NOT YOU. NOT P. OTHER THAN THAT...?
...HUH.
YEAH.
THEY CANCELLED THE EXPO, TOO.
SO WE'RE GONNA BRING EVERYBODY HERE TO SEE THE DAMN THING RUN.
GET BETTY READY. I DON'T CARE IF IT'S GOT A MACHE CHASSIS, THE REPULSOR-TECH ENGINE, AND THE INTERIOR OF A SOAPBOX DERBY CAR.
I WANT IT DRIVABLE AND UN-BLOW-UP-ABLE IN TWENTY-FOUR HOURS.

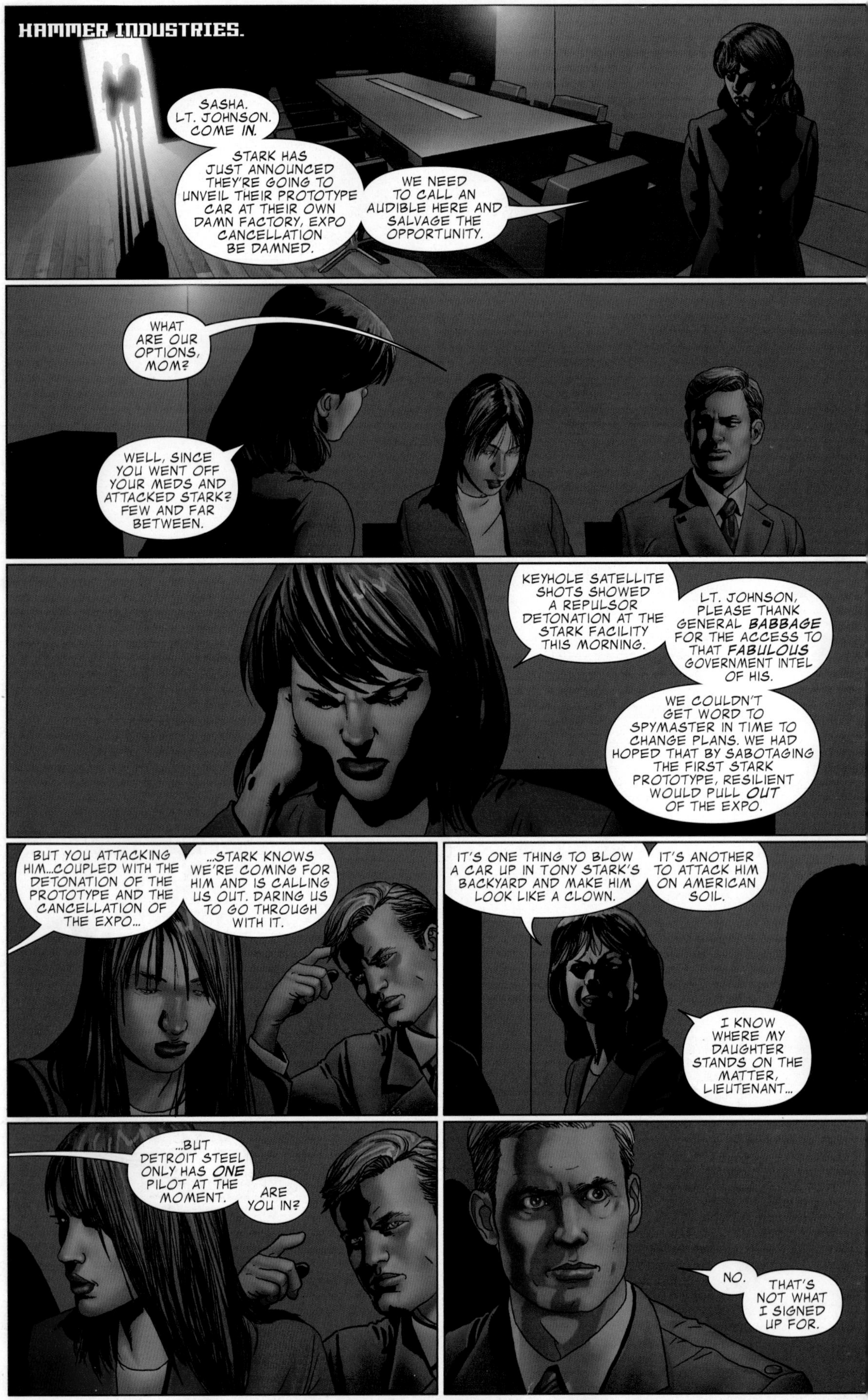
HAMMER INDUSTRIES.
SASHA. LT. JOHNSON. COME IN.
STARK HAS JUST ANNOUNCED THEY'RE GOING TO UNVEIL THEIR PROTOTYPE CAR AT THEIR OWN DAMN FACTORY, EXPO CANCELLATION BE DAMNED.
WE NEED TO CALL AN AUDIBLE HERE AND SALVAGE THE OPPORTUNITY.
WHAT ARE OUR OPTIONS, MOM?
WELL, SINCE YOU WENT OFF YOUR MEDS AND ATTACKED STARK? FEW AND FAR BETWEEN.
KEYHOLE SATELLITE SHOTS SHOWED A REPULSOR DETONATION AT THE STARK FACILITY THIS MORNING.
LT. JOHNSON, PLEASE THANK GENERAL BABBAGE FOR THE ACCESS TO THAT FABULOUS GOVERNMENT INTEL OF HIS.
WE COULDN'T GET WORD TO SPYMASTER IN TIME TO CHANGE PLANS. WE HAD HOPED THAT BY SABOTAGING THE FIRST STARK PROTOTYPE, RESILIENT WOULD PULL OUT OF THE EXPO.
BUT YOU ATTACKING HIM...COUPLED WITH THE DETONATION OF THE PROTOTYPE AND THE CANCELLATION OF THE EXPO...
...STARK KNOWS WE'RE COMING FOR HIM AND IS CALLING US OUT. DARING US TO GO THROUGH WITH IT.
IT'S ONE THING TO BLOW A CAR UP IN TONY STARK'S BACKYARD AND MAKE HIM LOOK LIKE A CLOWN.
IT'S ANOTHER TO ATTACK HIM ON AMERICAN SOIL.
I KNOW WHERE MY DAUGHTER STANDS ON THE MATTER, LIEUTENANT...
...BUT DETROIT STEEL ONLY HAS ONE PILOT AT THE MOMENT.
ARE YOU IN?
NO.
THAT'S NOT WHAT I SIGNED UP FOR.

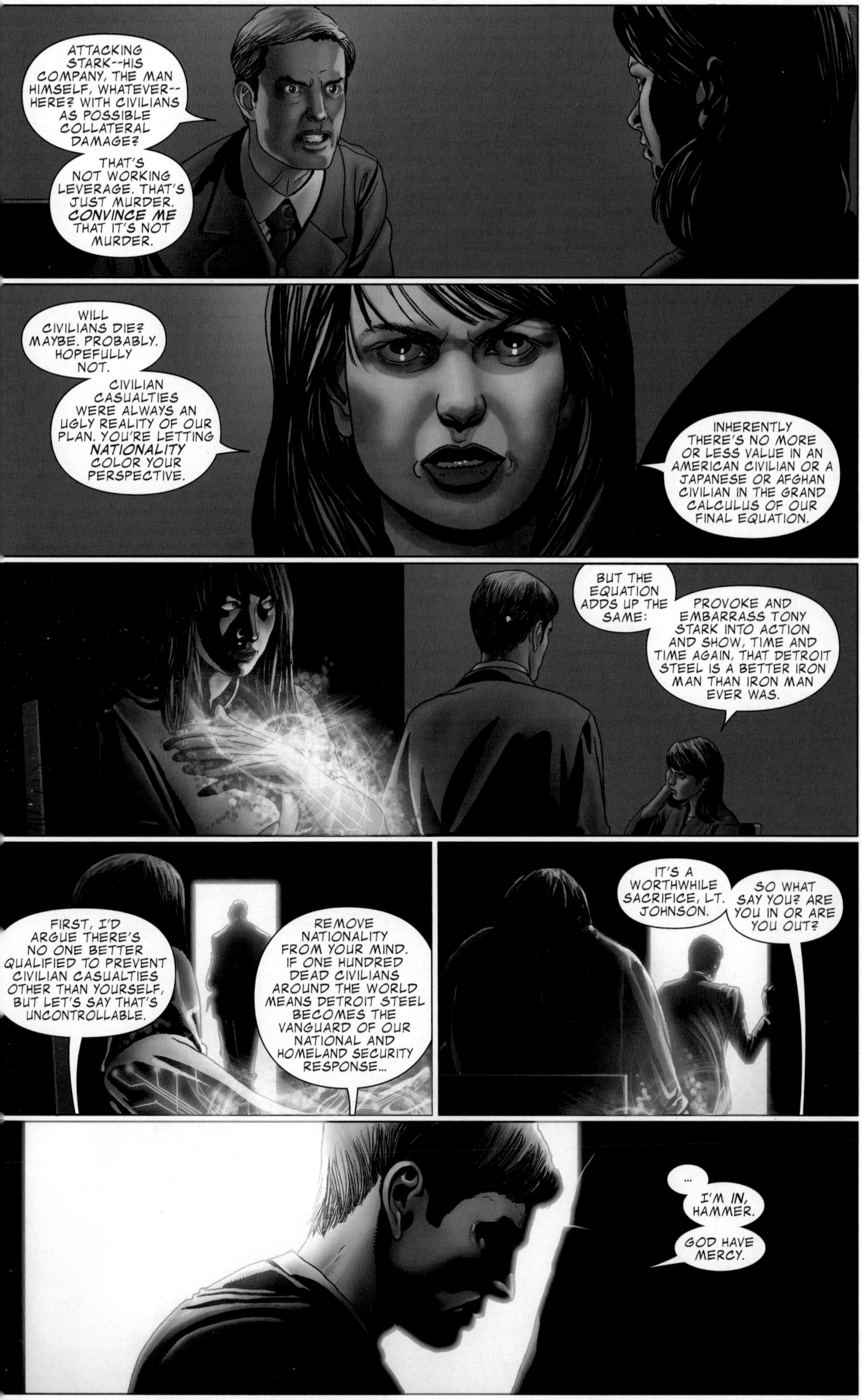
ATTACKING STARK--HIS COMPANY, THE MAN HIMSELF, WHATEVER--HERE? WITH CIVILIANS AS POSSIBLE COLLATERAL DAMAGE?
THAT'S NOT WORKING LEVERAGE. THAT'S JUST MURDER. CONVINCE ME THAT IT'S NOT MURDER.
WILL CIVILIANS DIE? MAYBE. PROBABLY. HOPEFULLY NOT.
CIVILIAN CASUALTIES WERE ALWAYS AN UGLY REALITY OF OUR PLAN. YOU'RE LETTING NATIONALITY COLOR YOUR PERSPECTIVE.
INHERENTLY THERE'S NO MORE OR LESS VALUE IN AN AMERICAN CIVILIAN OR A JAPANESE OR AFGHAN CIVILIAN IN THE GRAND CALCULUS OF OUR FINAL EQUATION.
BUT THE EQUATION ADDS UP THE SAME:
PROVOKE AND EMBARRASS TONY STARK INTO ACTION AND SHOW, TIME AND TIME AGAIN, THAT DETROIT STEEL IS A BETTER IRON MAN THAN IRON MAN EVER WAS.
FIRST, I'D ARGUE THERE'S NO ONE BETTER QUALIFIED TO PREVENT CIVILIAN CASUALTIES OTHER THAN YOURSELF, BUT LET'S SAY THAT'S UNCONTROLLABLE.
REMOVE NATIONALITY FROM YOUR MIND. IF ONE HUNDRED DEAD CIVILIANS AROUND THE WORLD MEANS DETROIT STEEL BECOMES THE VANGUARD OF OUR NATIONAL AND HOMELAND SECURITY RESPONSE...
IT'S A WORTHWHILE SACRIFICE, LT. JOHNSON.
SO WHAT SAY YOU? ARE YOU IN OR ARE YOU OUT?
...
I'M IN, HAMMER.
GOD HAVE MERCY.

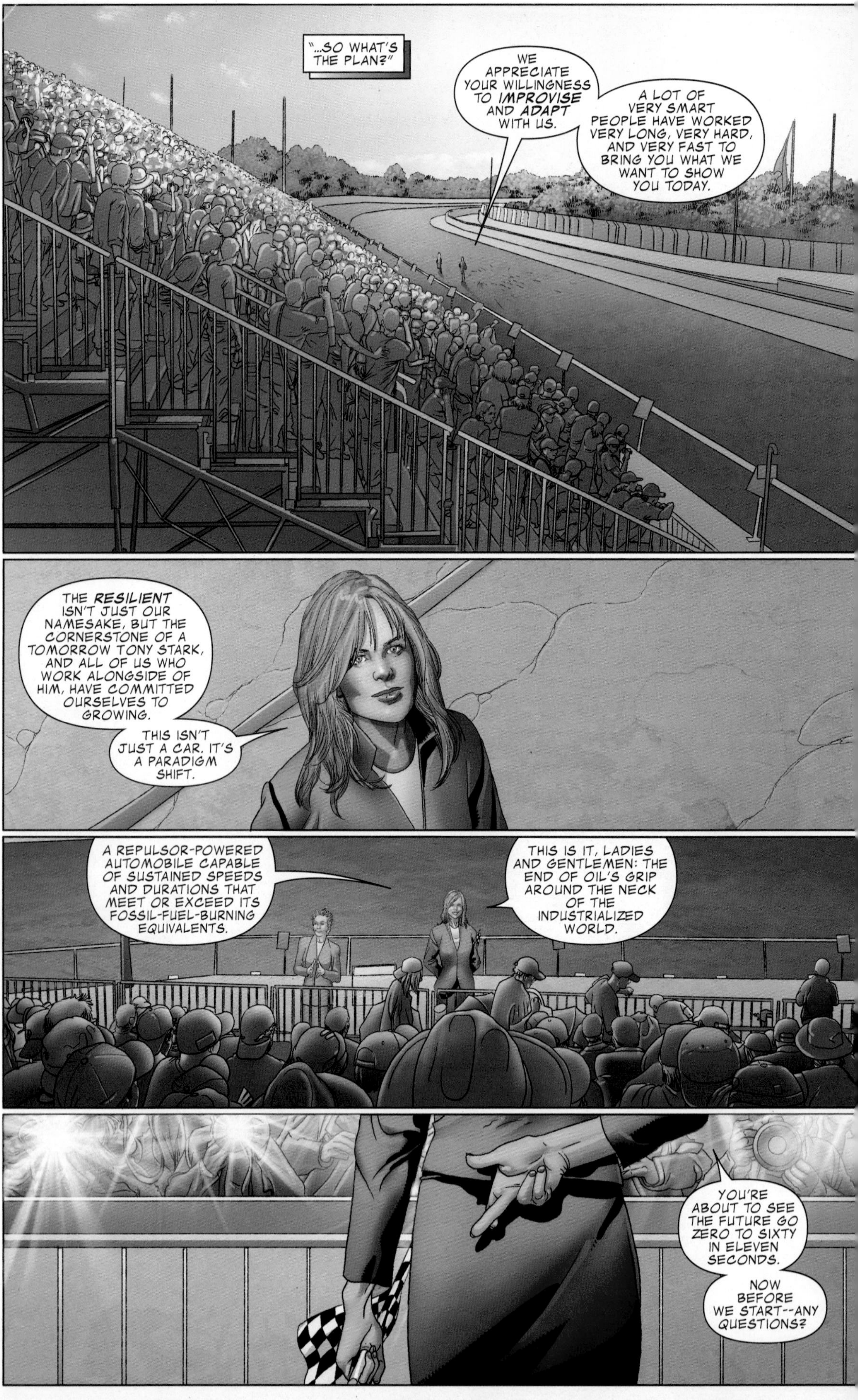
"...SO WHAT'S THE PLAN?"
WE APPRECIATE YOUR WILLINGNESS TO IMPROVISE AND ADAPT WITH US.
A LOT OF VERY SMART PEOPLE HAVE WORKED VERY LONG, VERY HARD, AND VERY FAST TO BRING YOU WHAT WE WANT TO SHOW YOU TODAY.
THE RESILIENT ISN'T JUST OUR NAMESAKE, BUT THE CORNERSTONE OF A TOMORROW TONY STARK, AND ALL OF US WHO WORK ALONGSIDE OF HIM, HAVE COMMITTED OURSELVES TO GROWING.
THIS ISN'T JUST A CAR. IT'S A PARADIGM SHIFT.
A REPULSOR-POWERED AUTOMOBILE CAPABLE OF SUSTAINED SPEEDS AND DURATIONS THAT MEET OR EXCEED ITS FOSSIL-FUEL-BURNING EQUIVALENTS.
THIS IS IT, LADIES AND GENTLEMEN: THE END OF OIL'S GRIP AROUND THE NECK OF THE INDUSTRIALIZED WORLD.
YOU'RE ABOUT TO SEE THE FUTURE GO ZERO TO SIXTY IN ELEVEN SECONDS.
NOW BEFORE WE START--ANY QUESTIONS?

WHAT'S SHE DOING?
GOOD. OKAY, GOOD.
GIVING US THE SIGNAL.
YOU NERVOUS?
HELL YES, I'M NERVOUS.
WHAT HAPPENED TO ALPHA WON'T HAPPEN TO BETTY.
I DON'T KNOW *WHAT EXACTLY* HAPPENED TO ALPHA BUT EVERYTHING ABOUT BETTY HAS BEEN HERMETICALLY SEALED SINCE THIS MORNING.
IT WON'T EXPLODE. AT LEAST IT WON'T EXPLODE THE SAME WAY.
EXPLODE?
WYCHE, I'M NOT EVEN SURE THE DAMNED CAR IS GOING TO HOLD *TOGETHER*.
TIME TO FIND OUT, I GUESS.

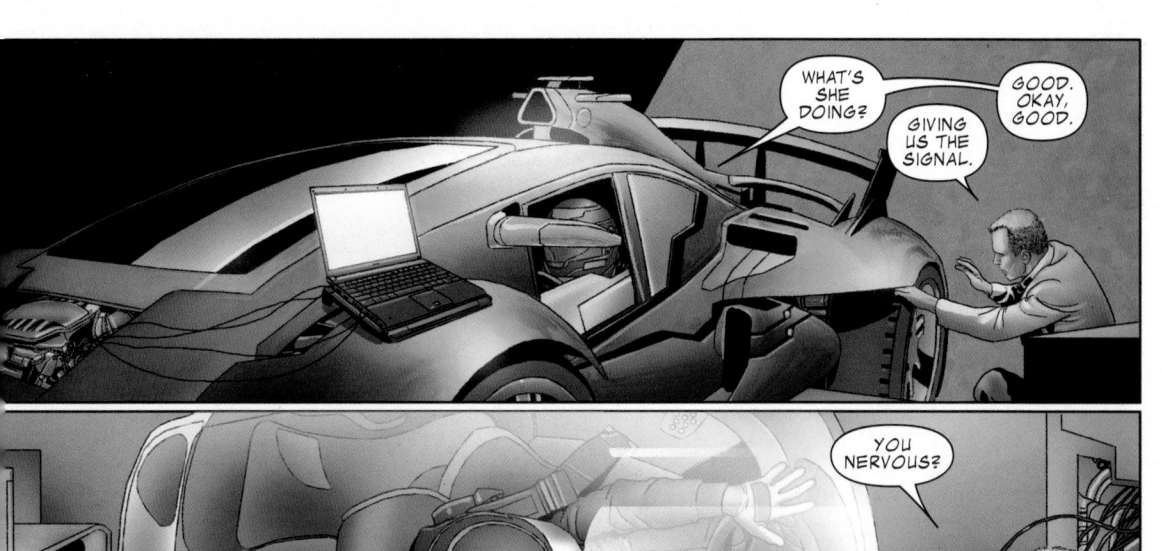

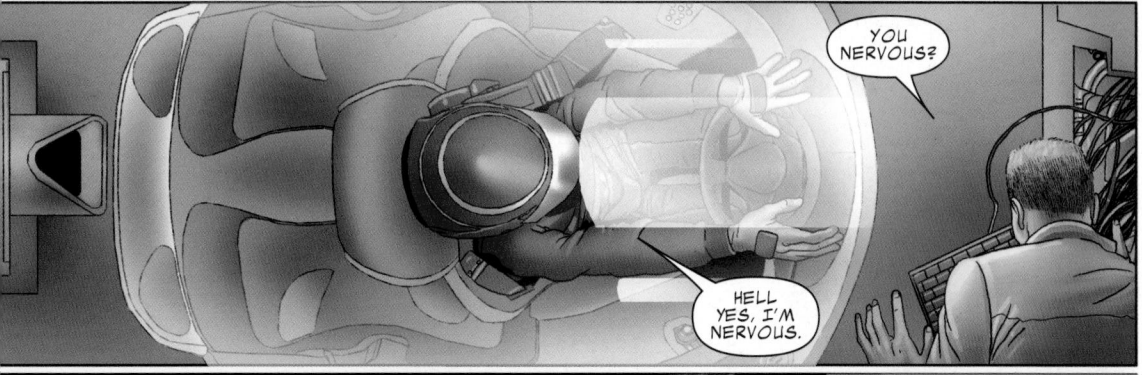

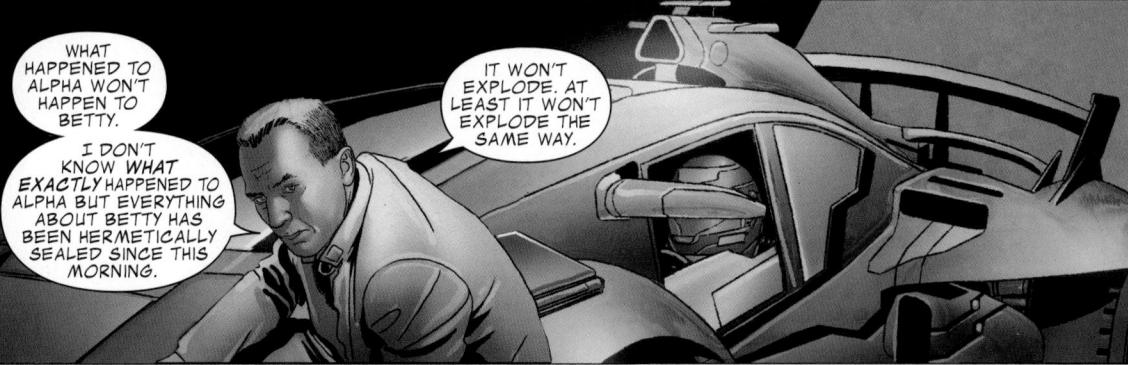

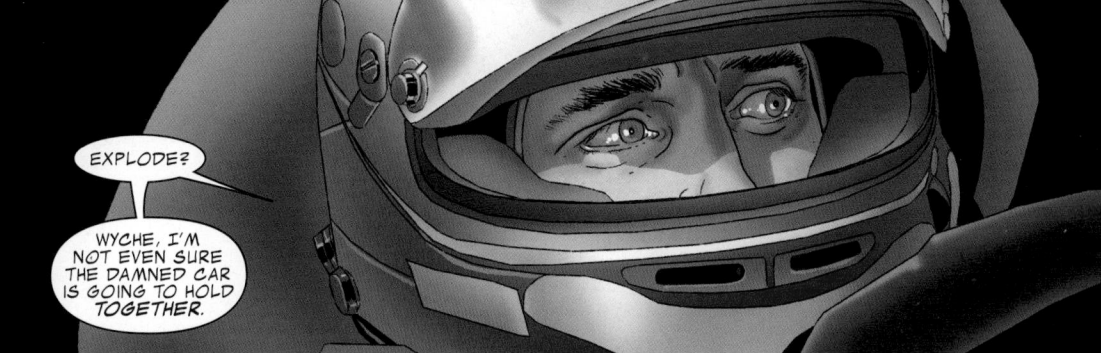

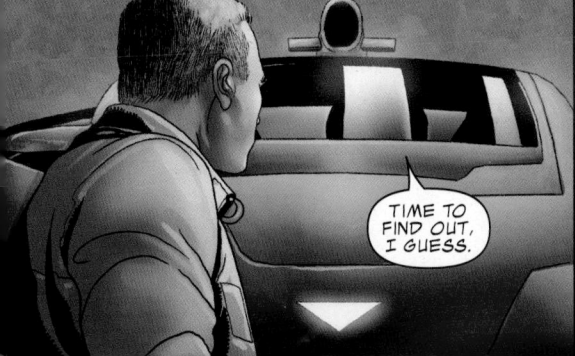

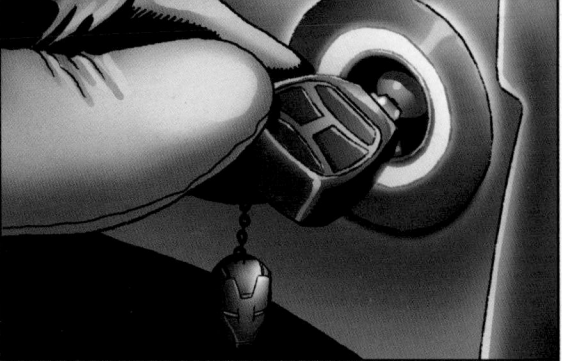

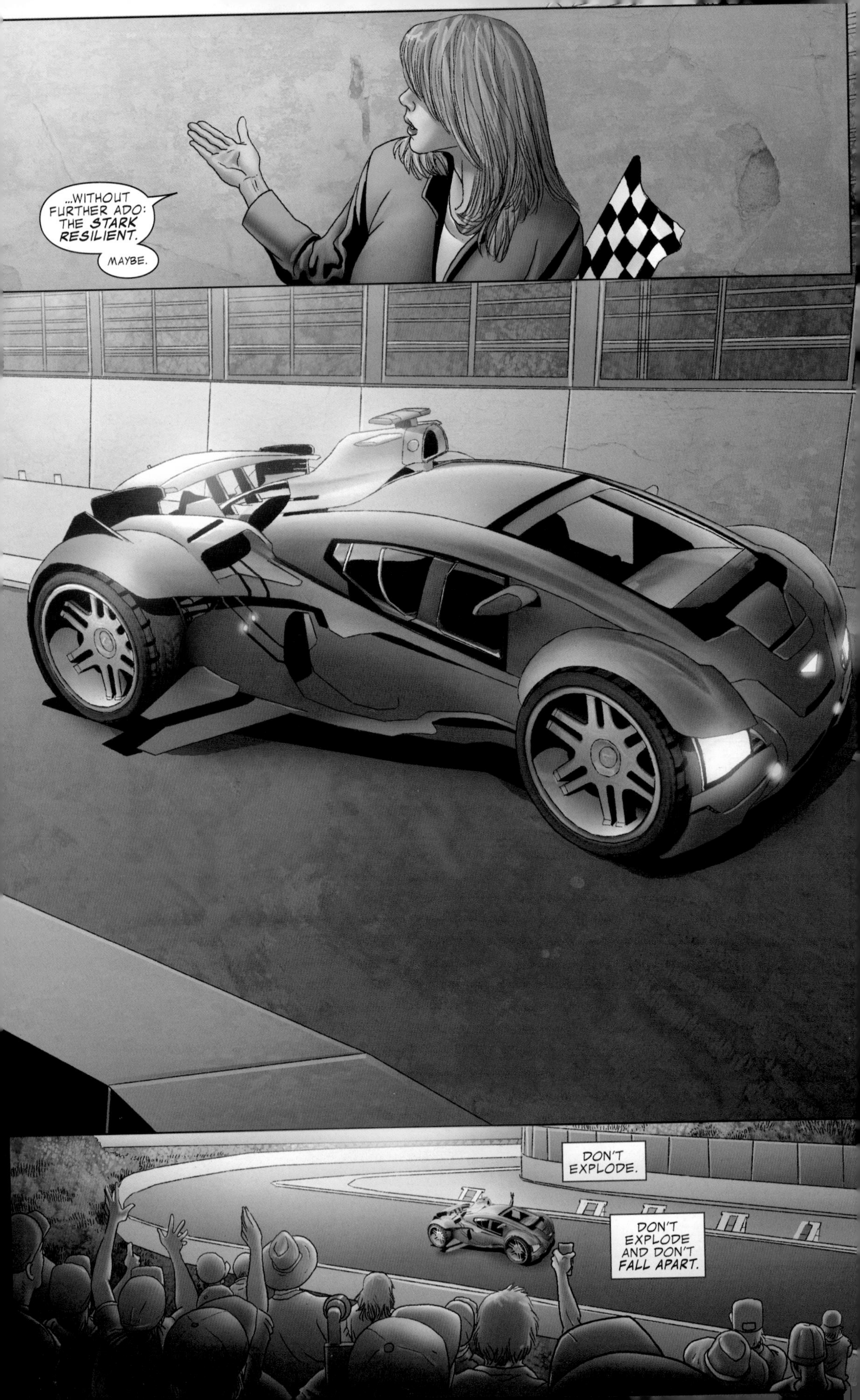
...WITHOUT FURTHER ADO: THE STARK RESILIENT.
MAYBE.
DON'T EXPLODE.
DON'T EXPLODE AND DON'T FALL APART.

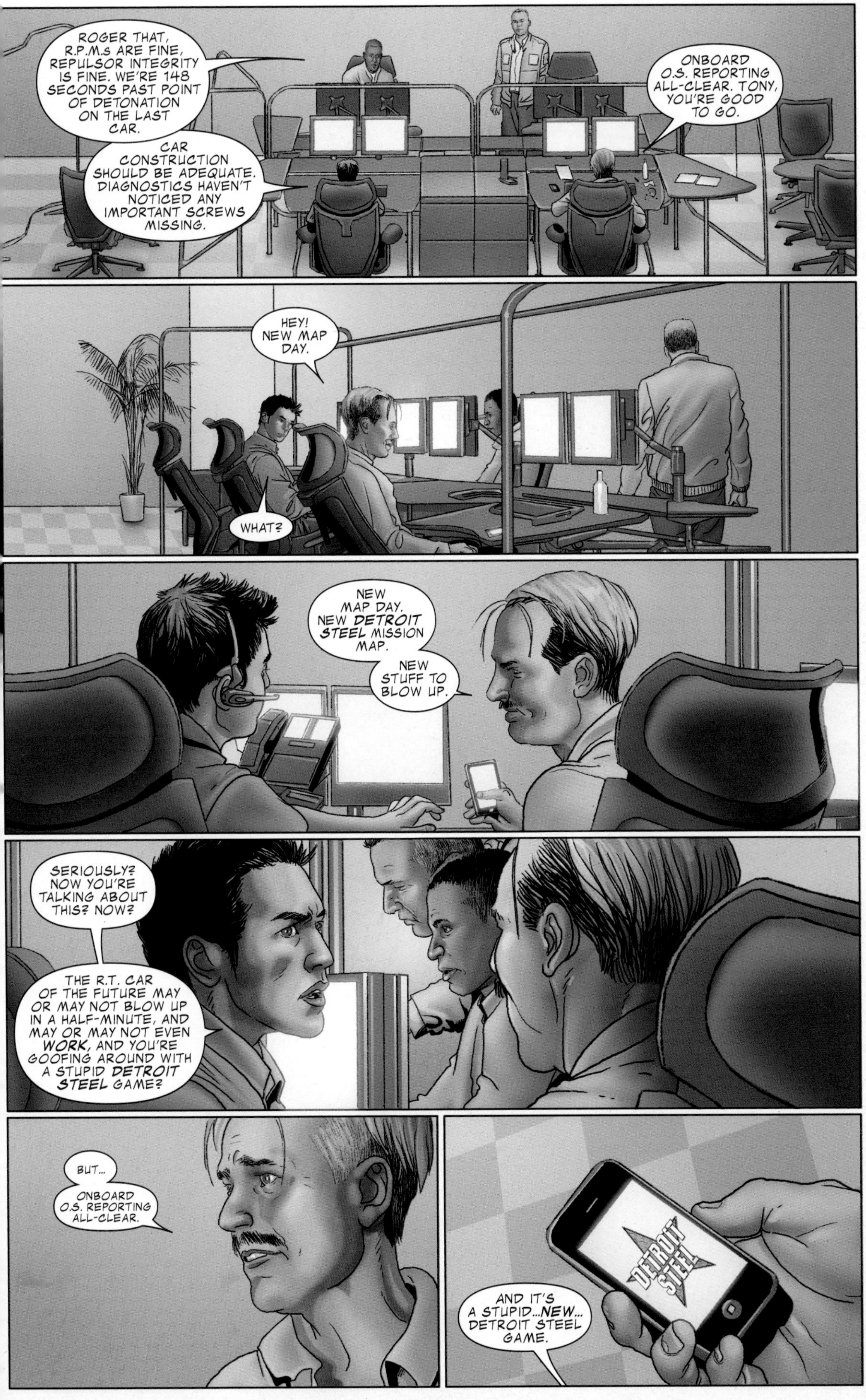
ROGER THAT, R.P.M.s ARE FINE, REPULSOR INTEGRITY IS FINE. WE'RE 148 SECONDS PAST POINT OF DETONATION ON THE LAST CAR.
CAR CONSTRUCTION SHOULD BE ADEQUATE. DIAGNOSTICS HAVEN'T NOTICED ANY IMPORTANT SCREWS MISSING.
ONBOARD O.S. REPORTING ALL-CLEAR. TONY, YOU'RE GOOD TO GO.
HEY! NEW MAP DAY.
WHAT?
NEW MAP DAY. NEW DETROIT STEEL MISSION MAP.
NEW STUFF TO BLOW UP.
SERIOUSLY? NOW YOU'RE TALKING ABOUT THIS? NOW?
THE R.T. CAR OF THE FUTURE MAY OR MAY NOT BLOW UP IN A HALF-MINUTE, AND MAY OR MAY NOT EVEN WORK, AND YOU'RE GOOFING AROUND WITH A STUPID DETROIT STEEL GAME?
BUT...
ONBOARD O.S. REPORTING ALL-CLEAR.
DETROIT STEEL
AND IT'S A STUPID...NEW... DETROIT STEEL GAME.

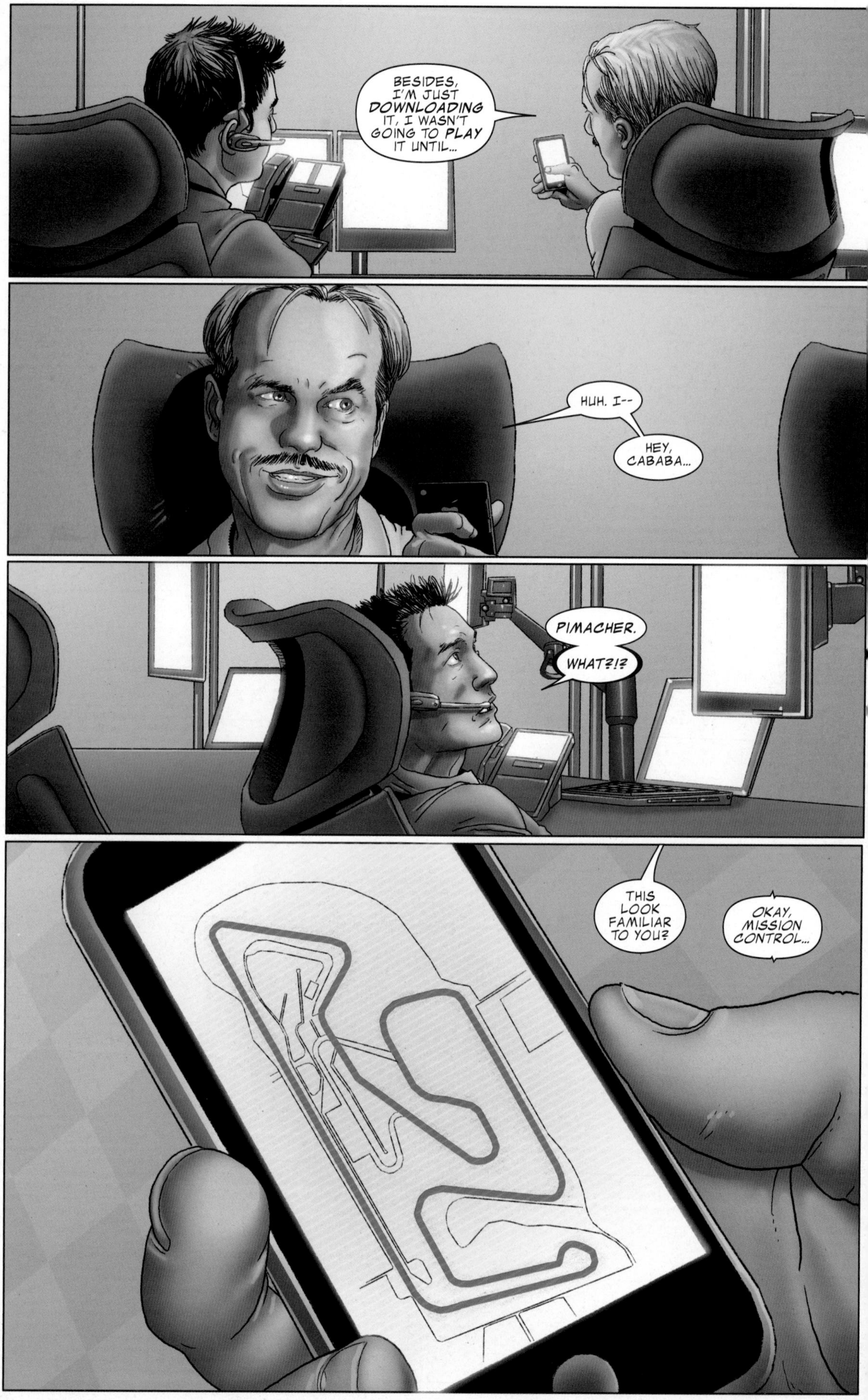
BESIDES, I'M JUST DOWNLOADING IT, I WASN'T GOING TO PLAY IT UNTIL...
HUH. I--
HEY, CABABA...
PIMACHER.
WHAT?!?
THIS LOOK FAMILIAR TO YOU?
OKAY, MISSION CONTROL...

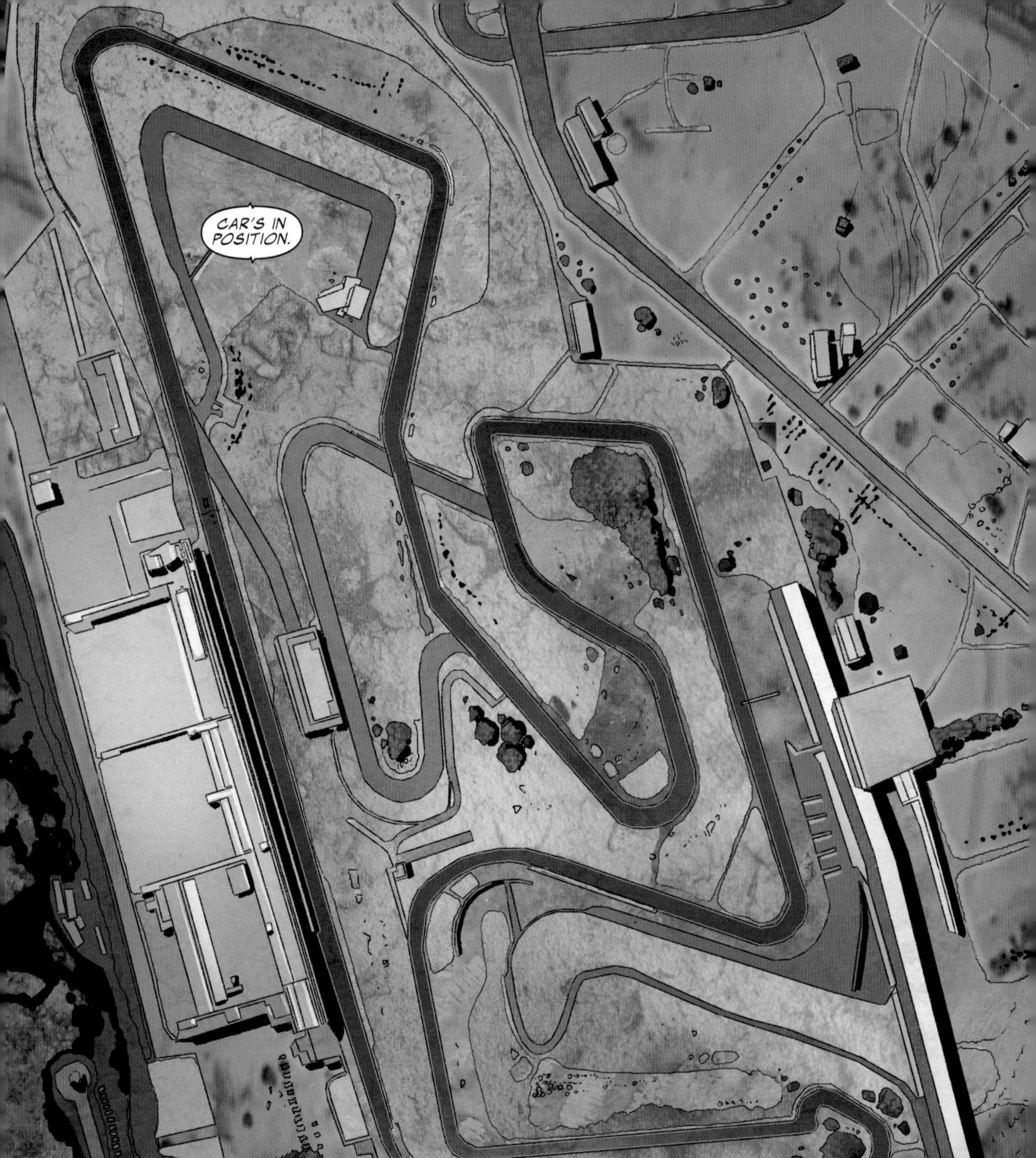
CAR'S IN POSITION.

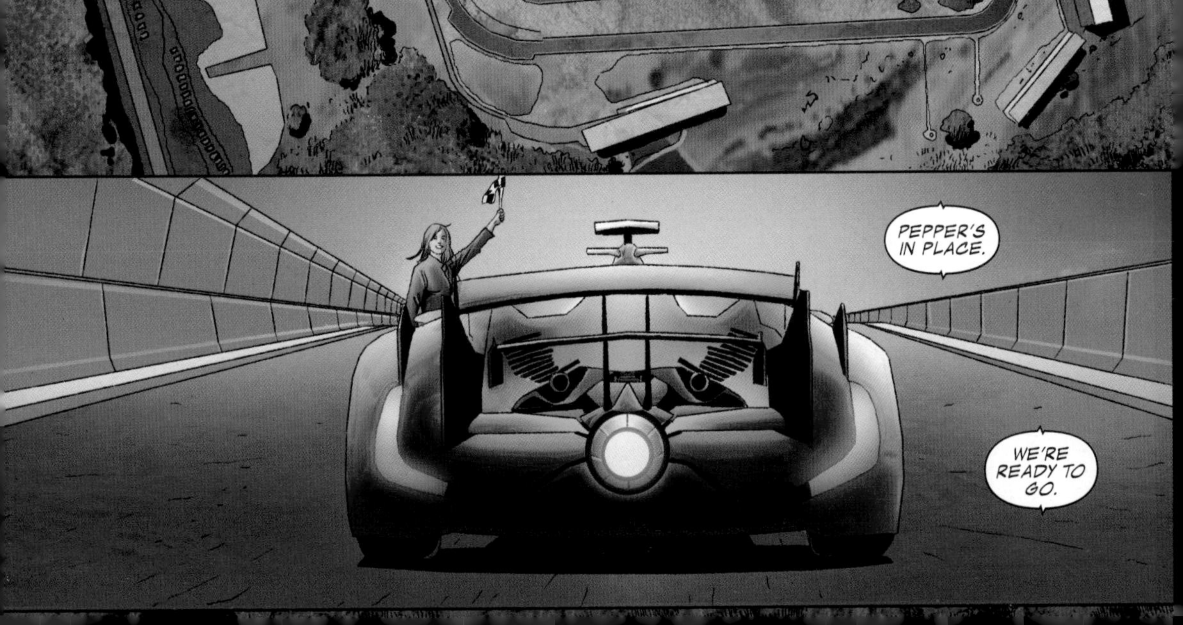
PEPPER'S IN PLACE.
WE'RE READY TO GO.

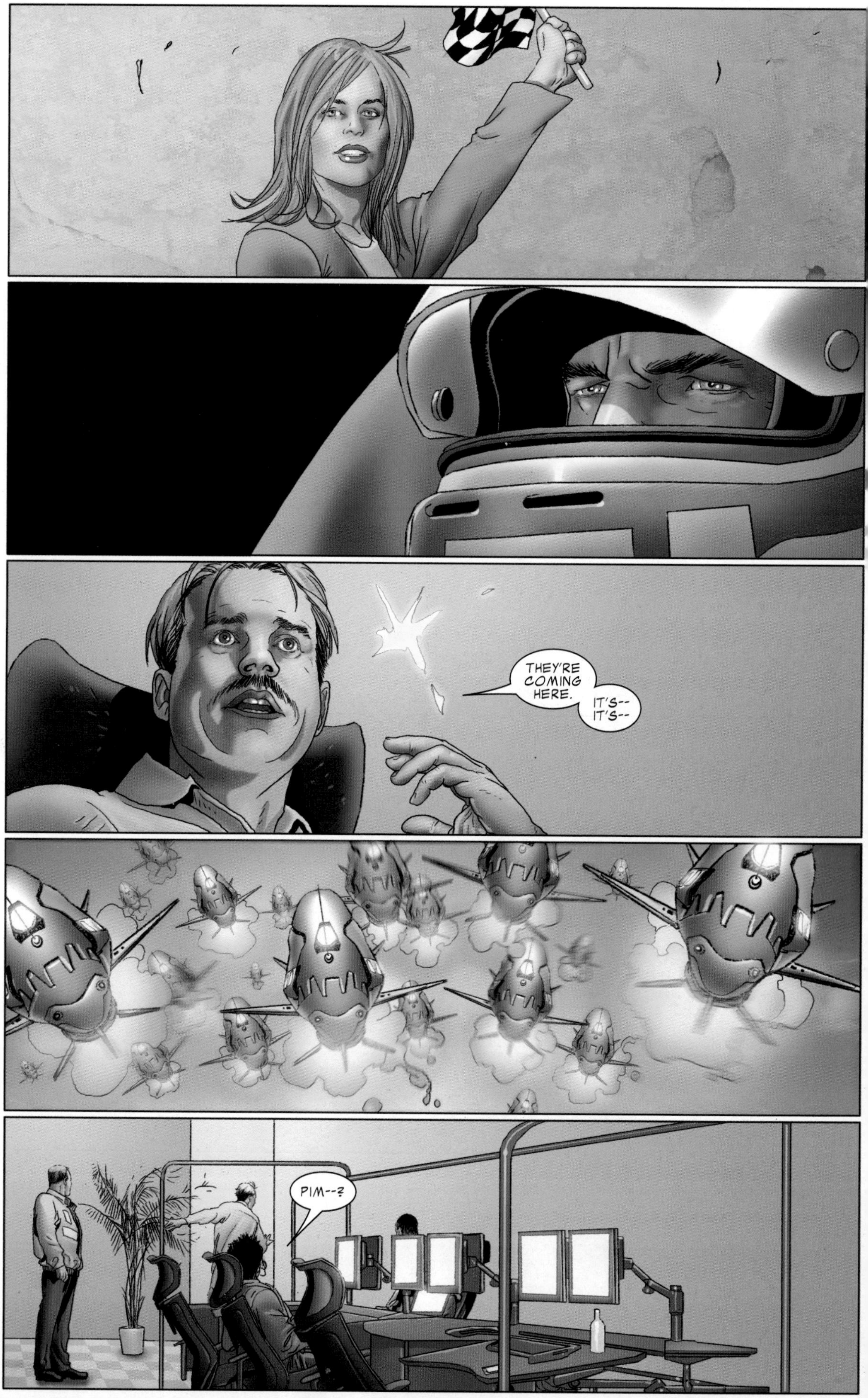
THEY'RE COMING HERE.
IT'S-- IT'S--
PIM--?

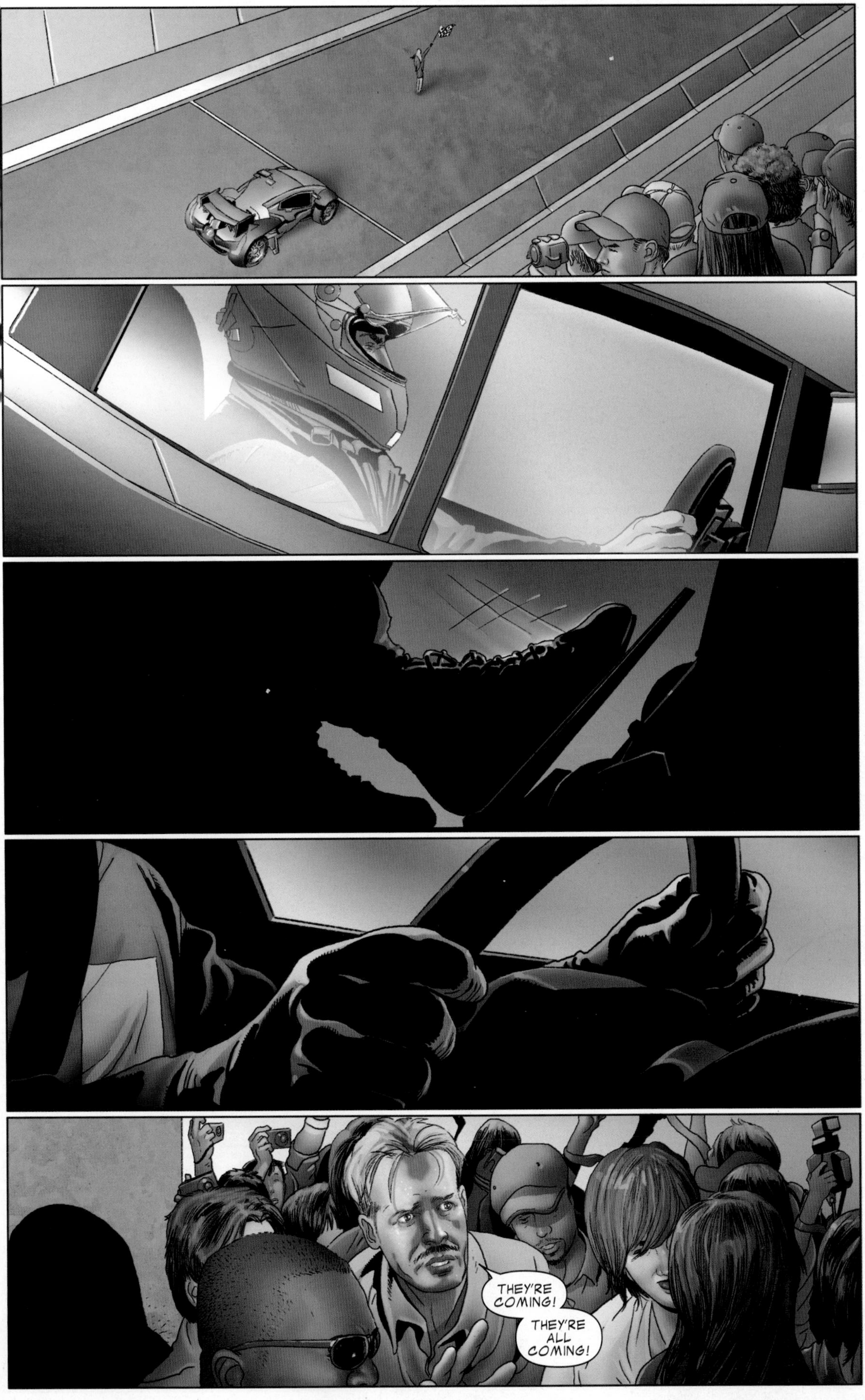
THEY'RE COMING!
THEY'RE ALL COMING!

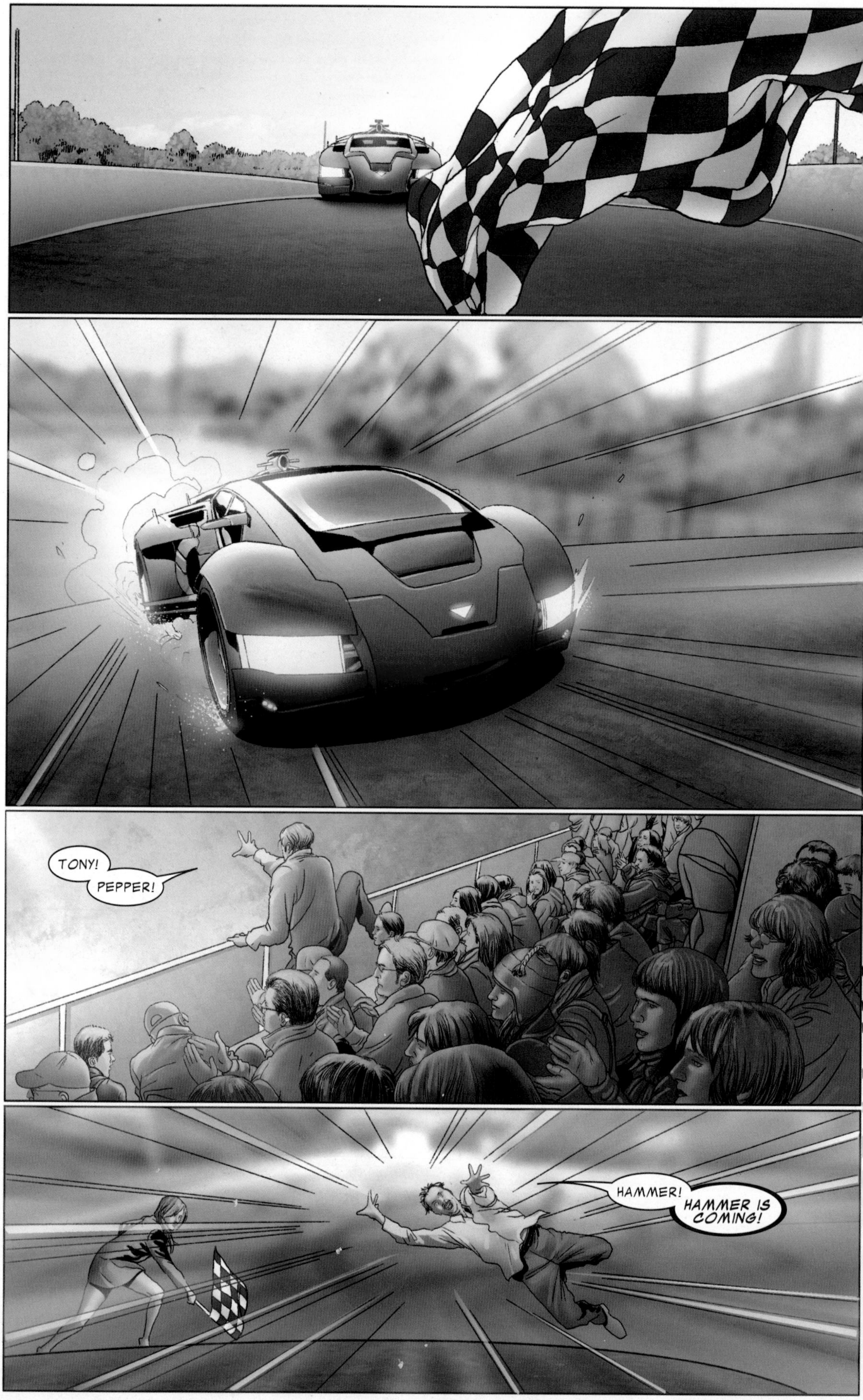
TONY!
PEPPER!
HAMMER!
HAMMER IS COMING!

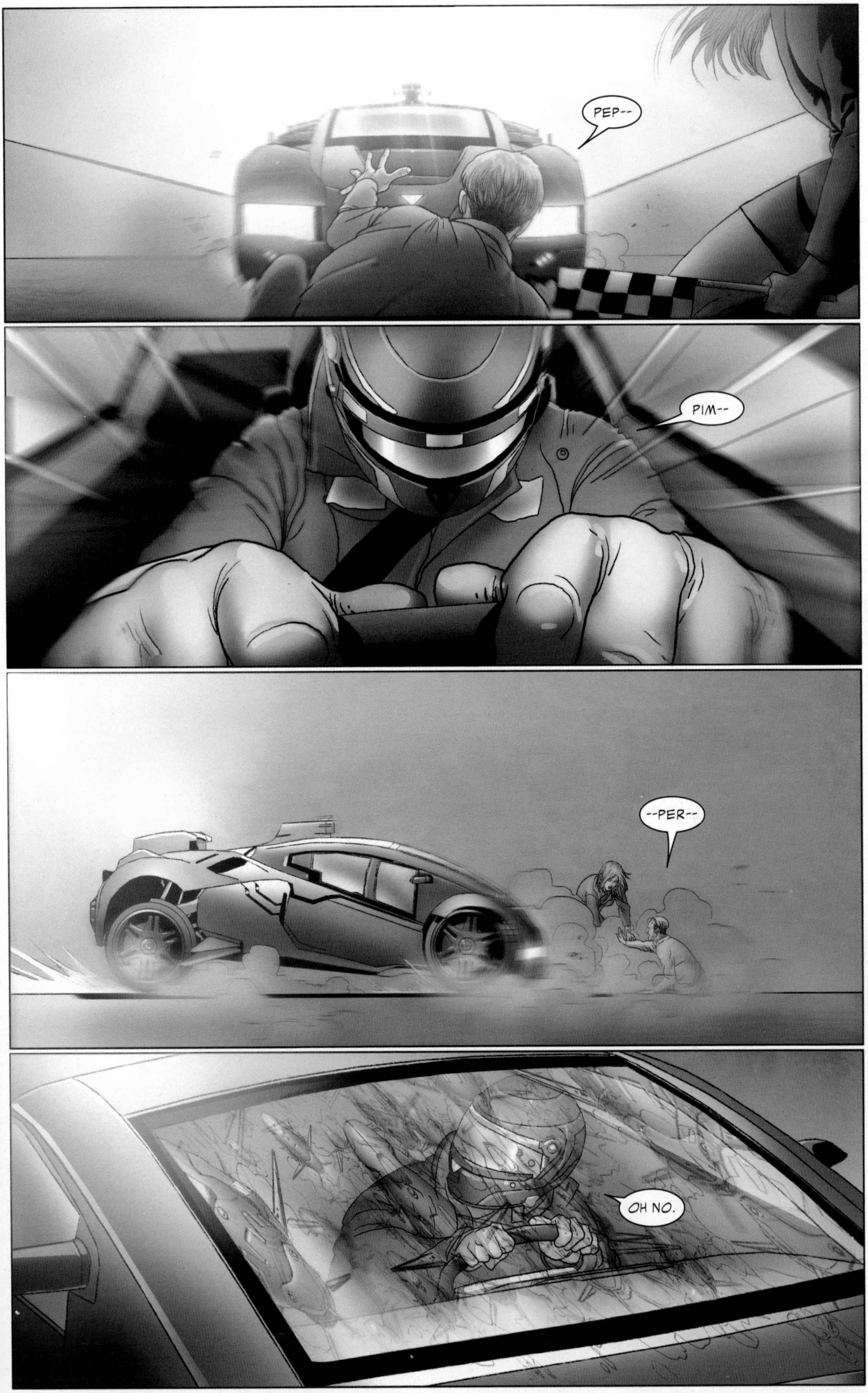
PEP--
PIM--
--PER--
OH NO.

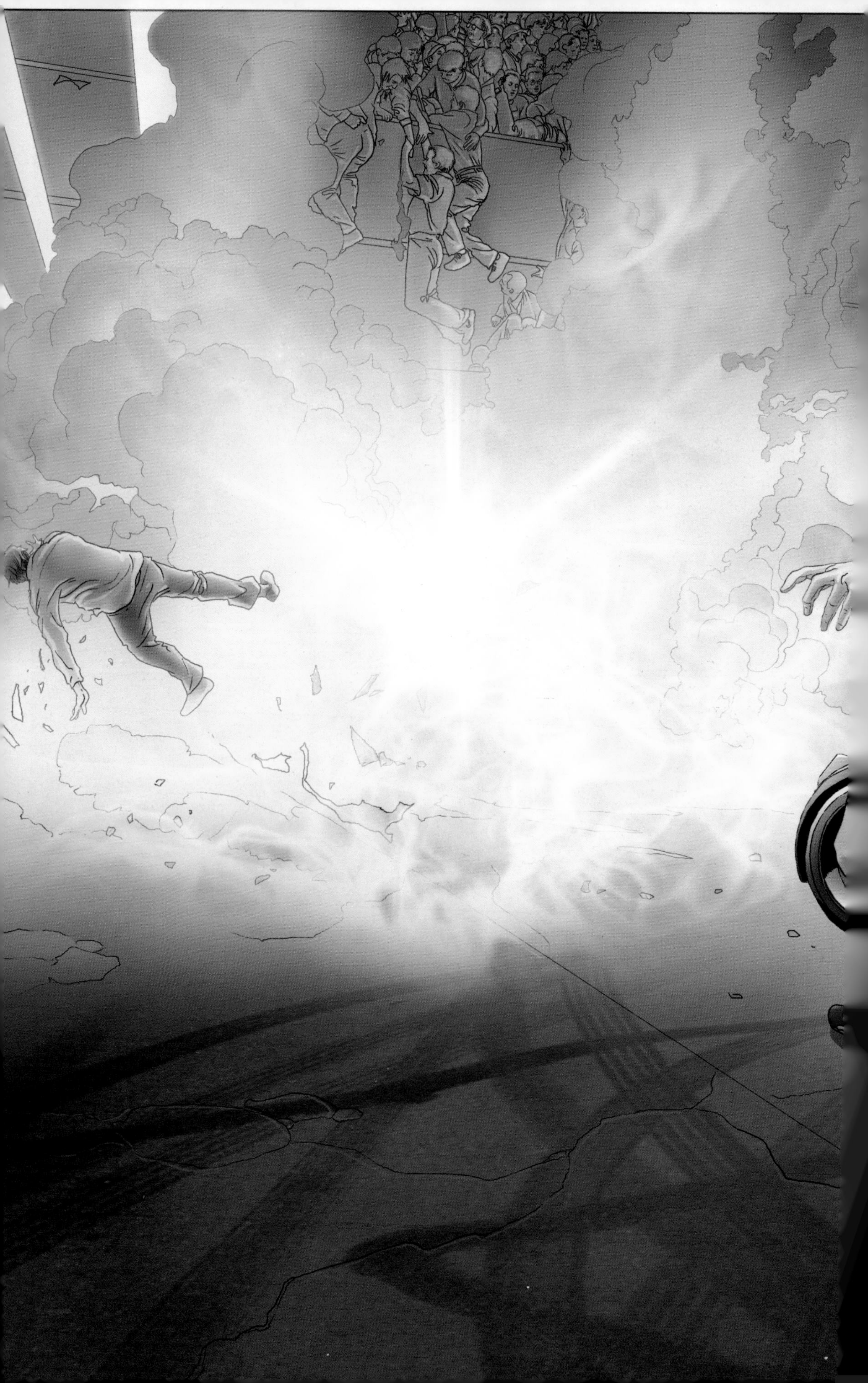

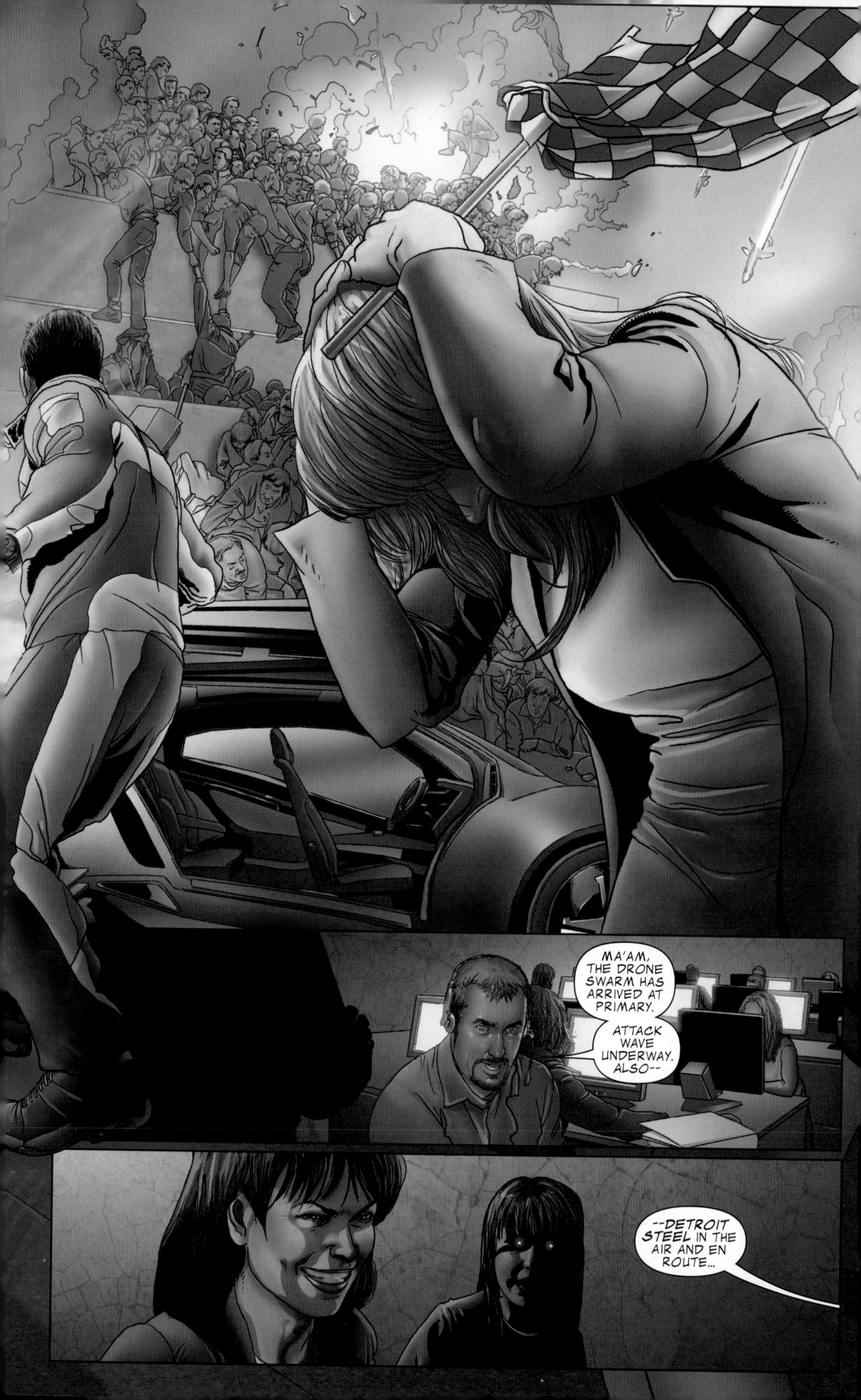

MA'AM, THE DRONE SWARM HAS ARRIVED AT PRIMARY.
ATTACK WAVE UNDERWAY. ALSO--
--DETROIT STEEL IN THE AIR AND EN ROUTE...

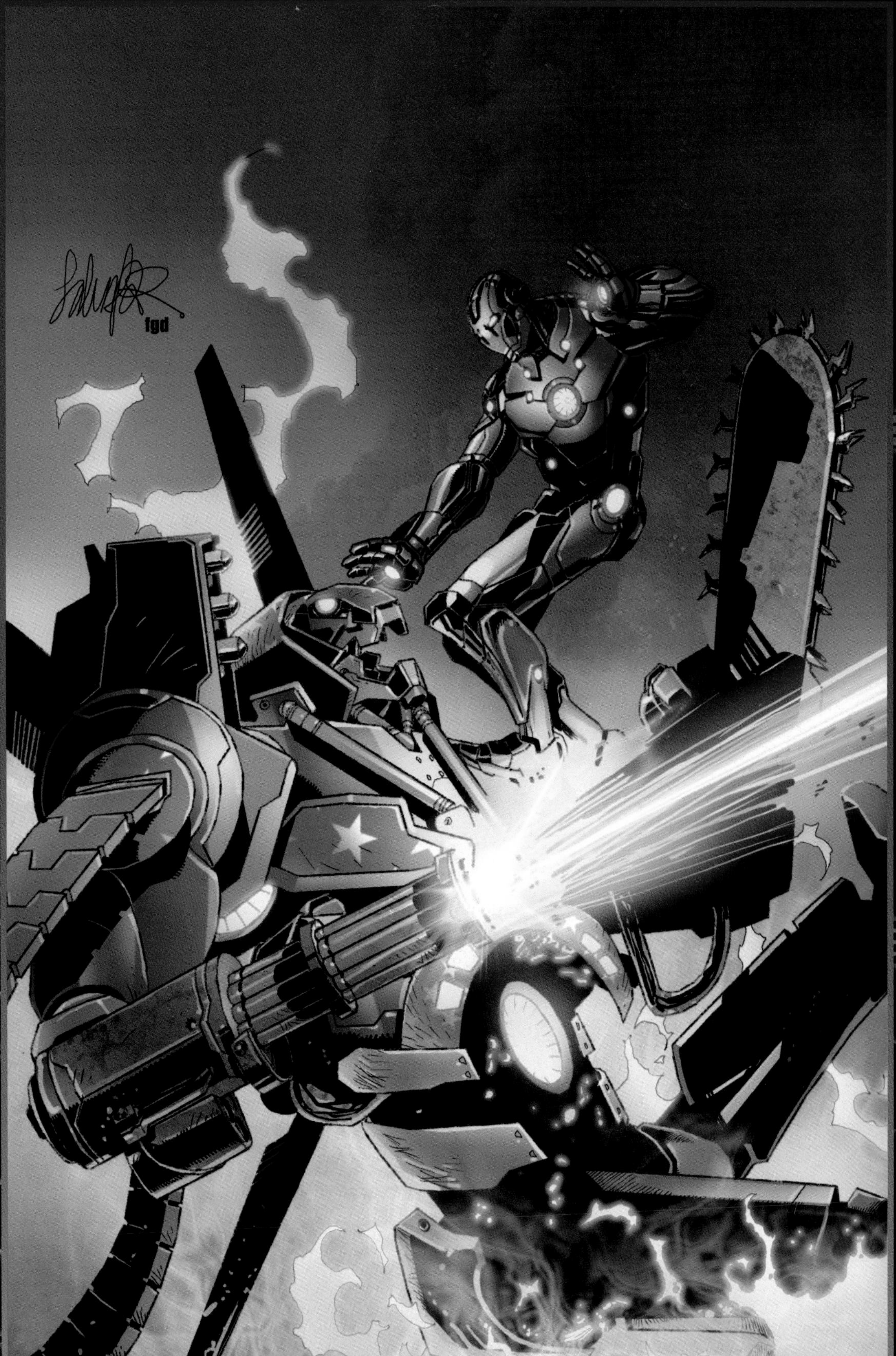

DRONES SCREAM DOWN **32**

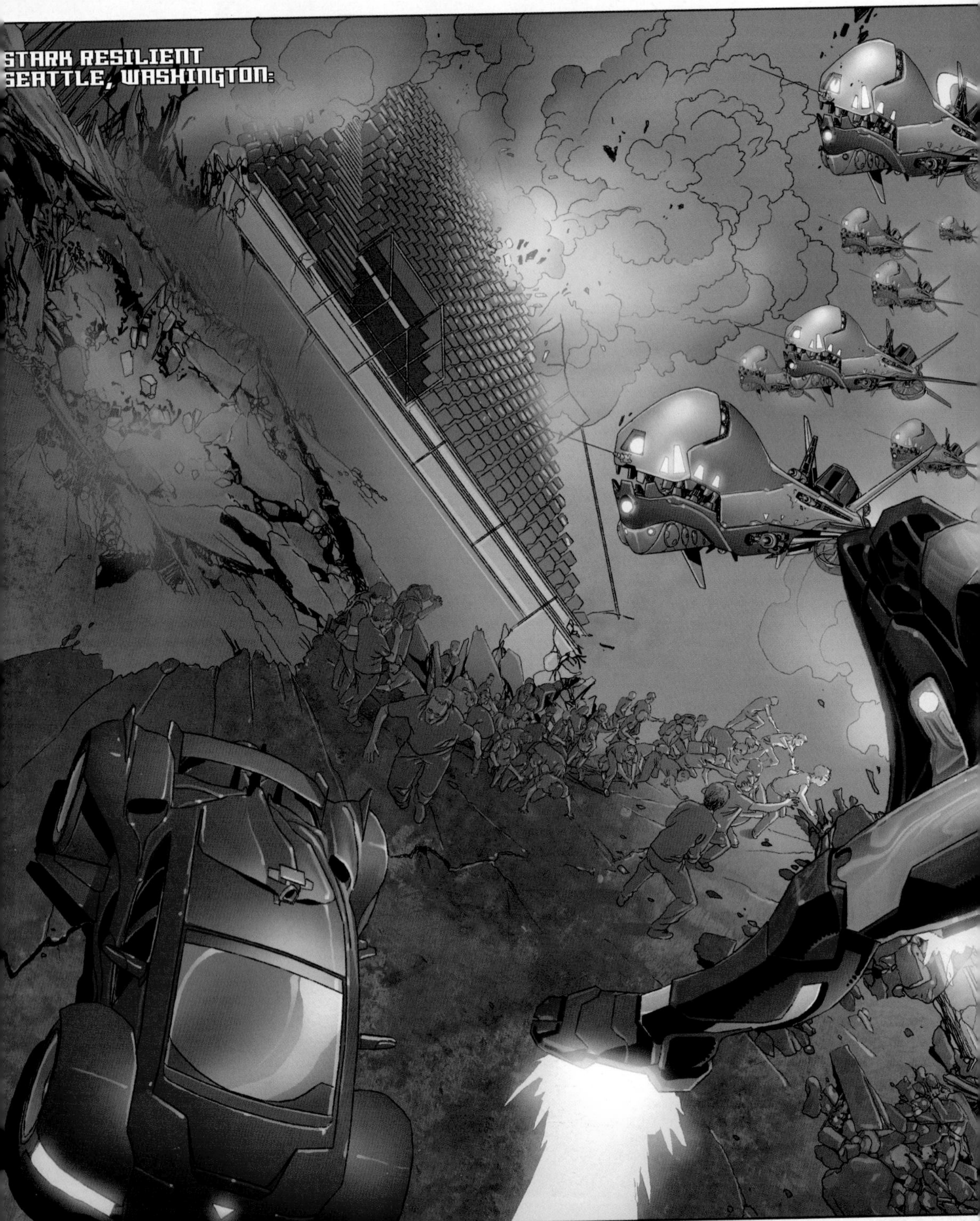
STARK RESILIENT
SEATTLE, WASHINGTON:

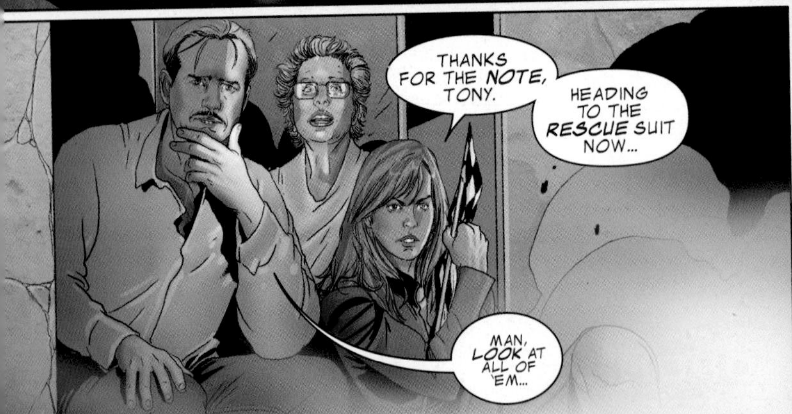
THANKS FOR THE NOTE, TONY.
HEADING TO THE RESCUE SUIT NOW...
MAN, LOOK AT ALL OF 'EM...

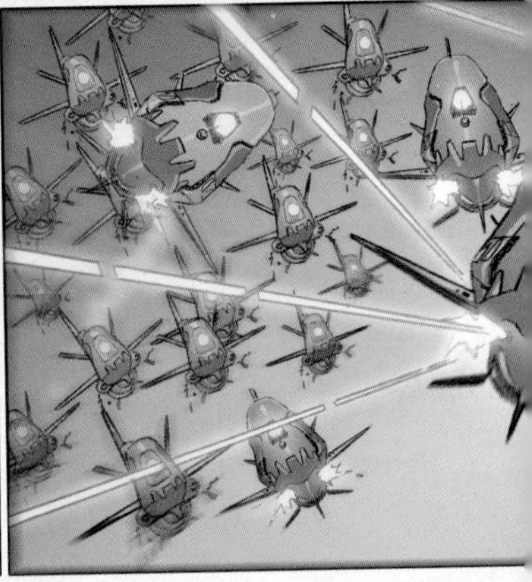

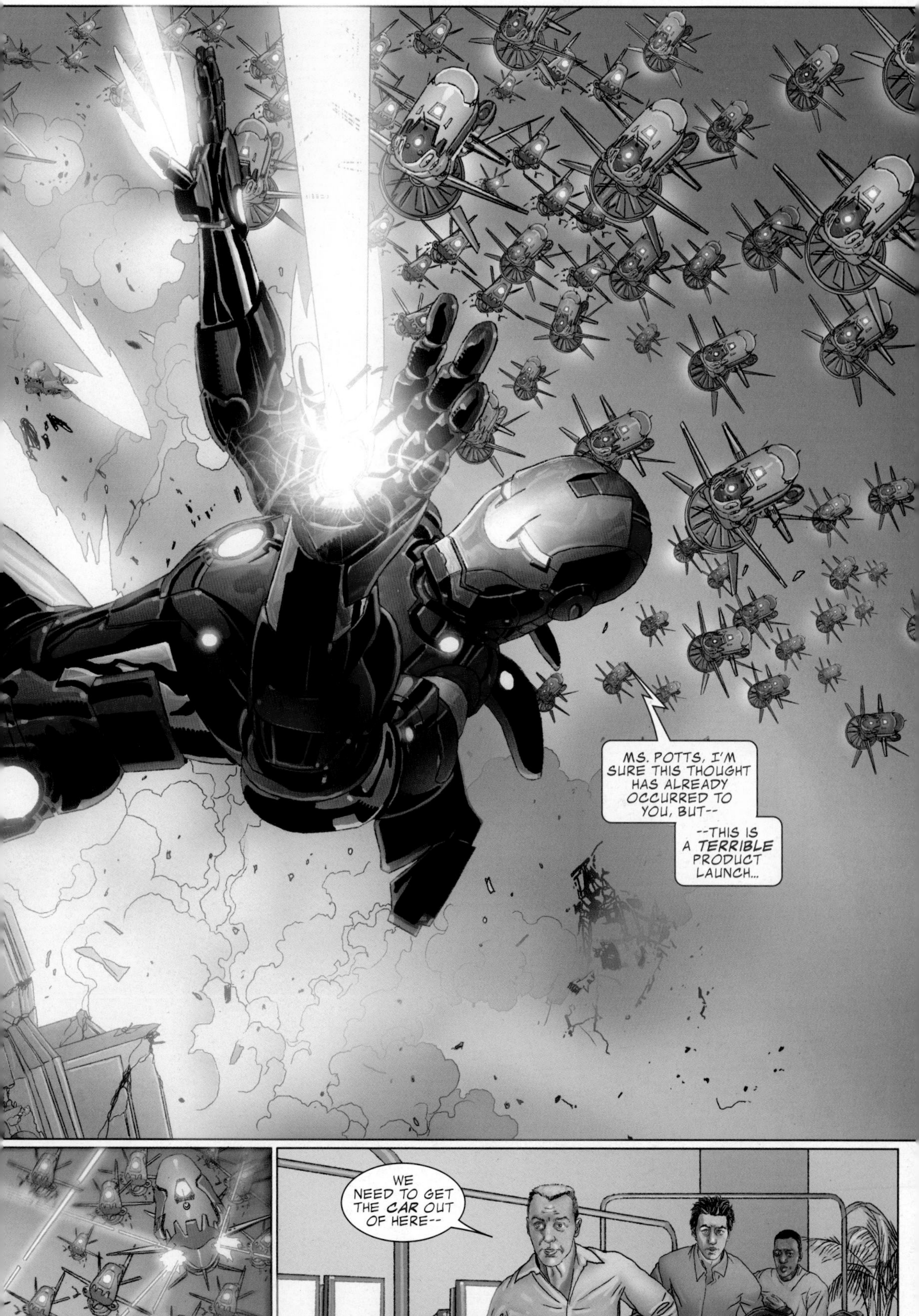
MS. POTTS, I'M SURE THIS THOUGHT HAS ALREADY OCCURRED TO YOU, BUT--
--THIS IS A TERRIBLE PRODUCT LAUNCH...

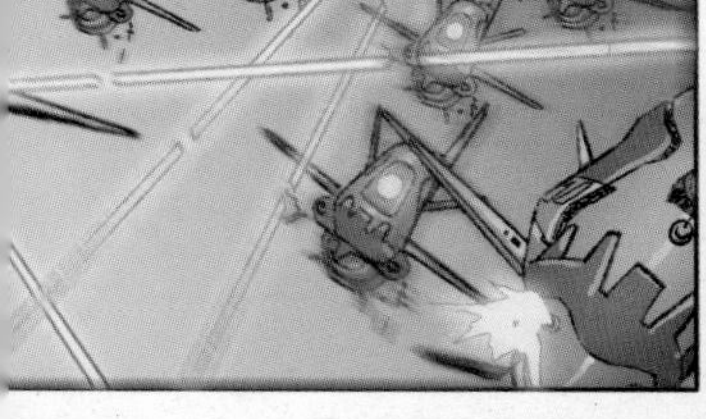

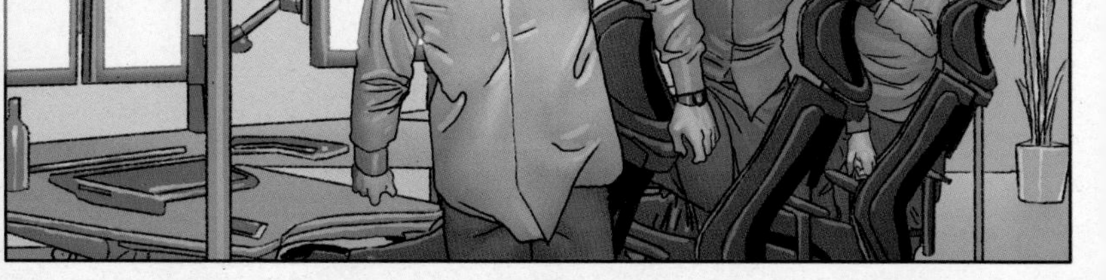
WE NEED TO GET THE CAR OUT OF HERE--

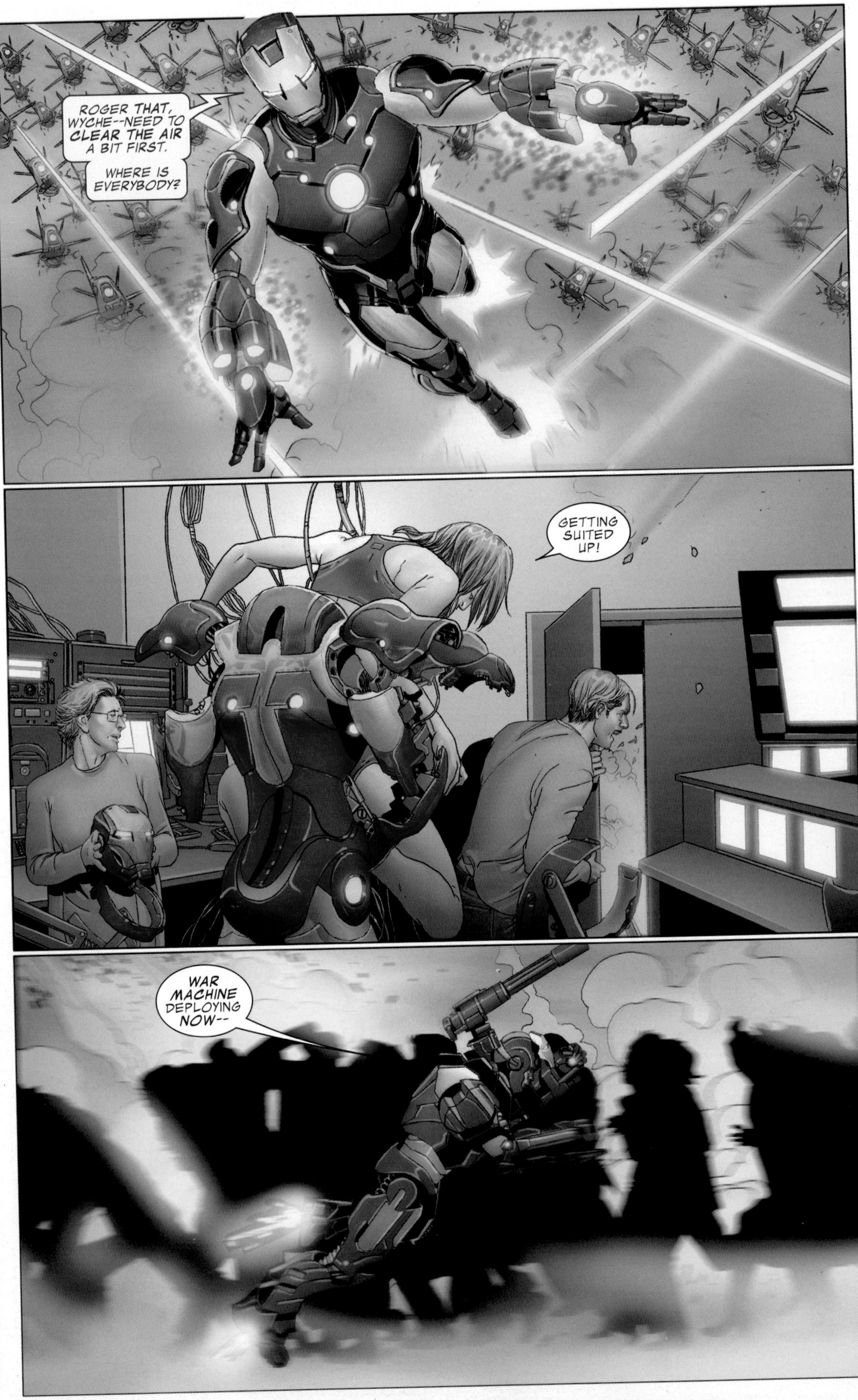
ROGER THAT, WYCHE--NEED TO CLEAR THE AIR A BIT FIRST.
WHERE IS EVERYBODY?
GETTING SUITED UP!
WAR MACHINE DEPLOYING NOW--

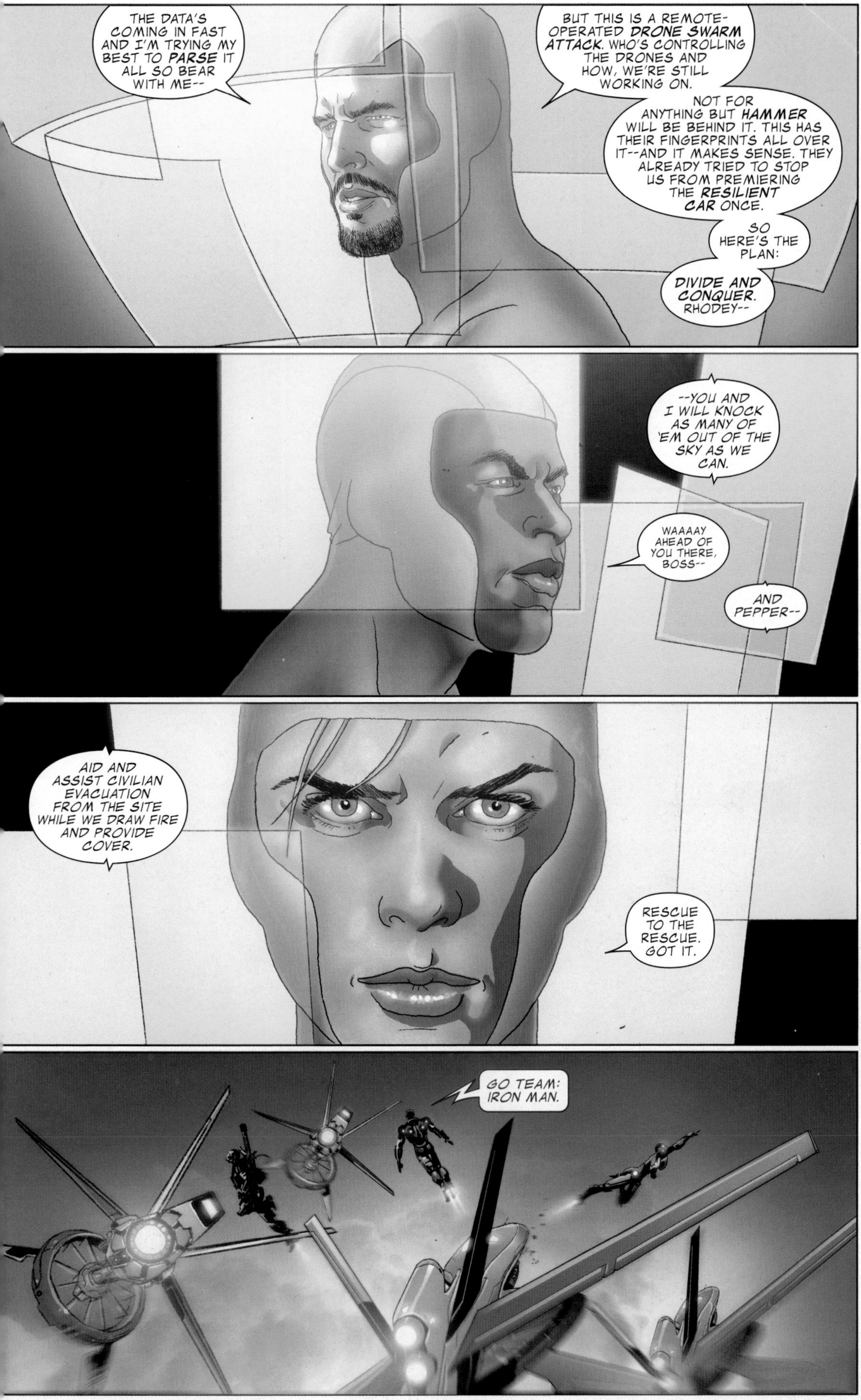
THE DATA'S COMING IN FAST AND I'M TRYING MY BEST TO PARSE IT ALL SO BEAR WITH ME--
BUT THIS IS A REMOTE-OPERATED DRONE SWARM ATTACK. WHO'S CONTROLLING THE DRONES AND HOW, WE'RE STILL WORKING ON.
NOT FOR ANYTHING BUT HAMMER WILL BE BEHIND IT. THIS HAS THEIR FINGERPRINTS ALL OVER IT--AND IT MAKES SENSE. THEY ALREADY TRIED TO STOP US FROM PREMIERING THE RESILIENT CAR ONCE.
SO HERE'S THE PLAN:
DIVIDE AND CONQUER. RHODEY--
--YOU AND I WILL KNOCK AS MANY OF 'EM OUT OF THE SKY AS WE CAN.
WAAAAY AHEAD OF YOU THERE, BOSS--
AND PEPPER--
AID AND ASSIST CIVILIAN EVACUATION FROM THE SITE WHILE WE DRAW FIRE AND PROVIDE COVER.
RESCUE TO THE RESCUE. GOT IT.
GO TEAM: IRON MAN.

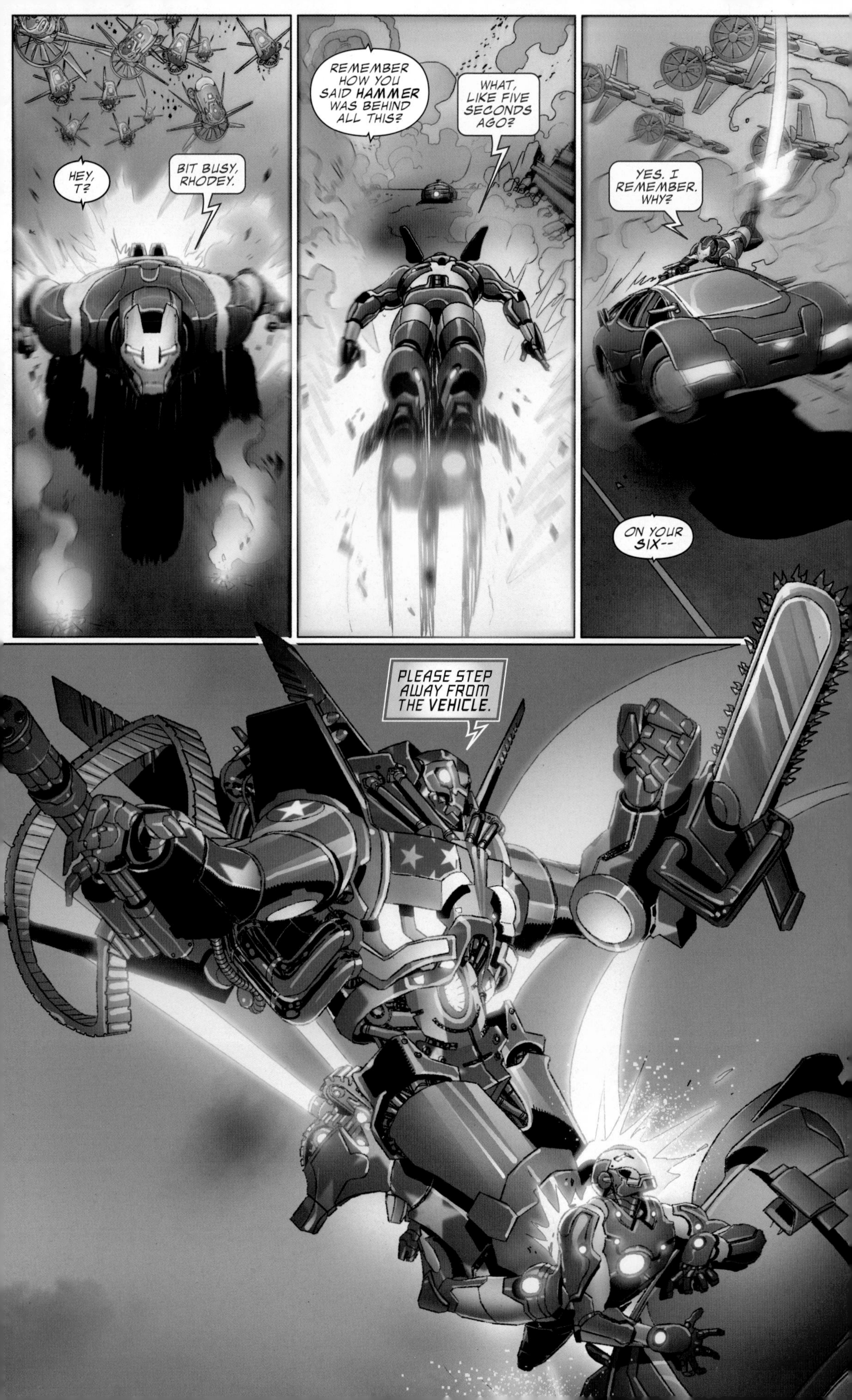
HEY, T?
BIT BUSY, RHODEY.
REMEMBER HOW YOU SAID HAMMER WAS BEHIND ALL THIS?
WHAT, LIKE FIVE SECONDS AGO?
YES. I REMEMBER. WHY?
ON YOUR SIX--
PLEASE STEP AWAY FROM THE VEHICLE.

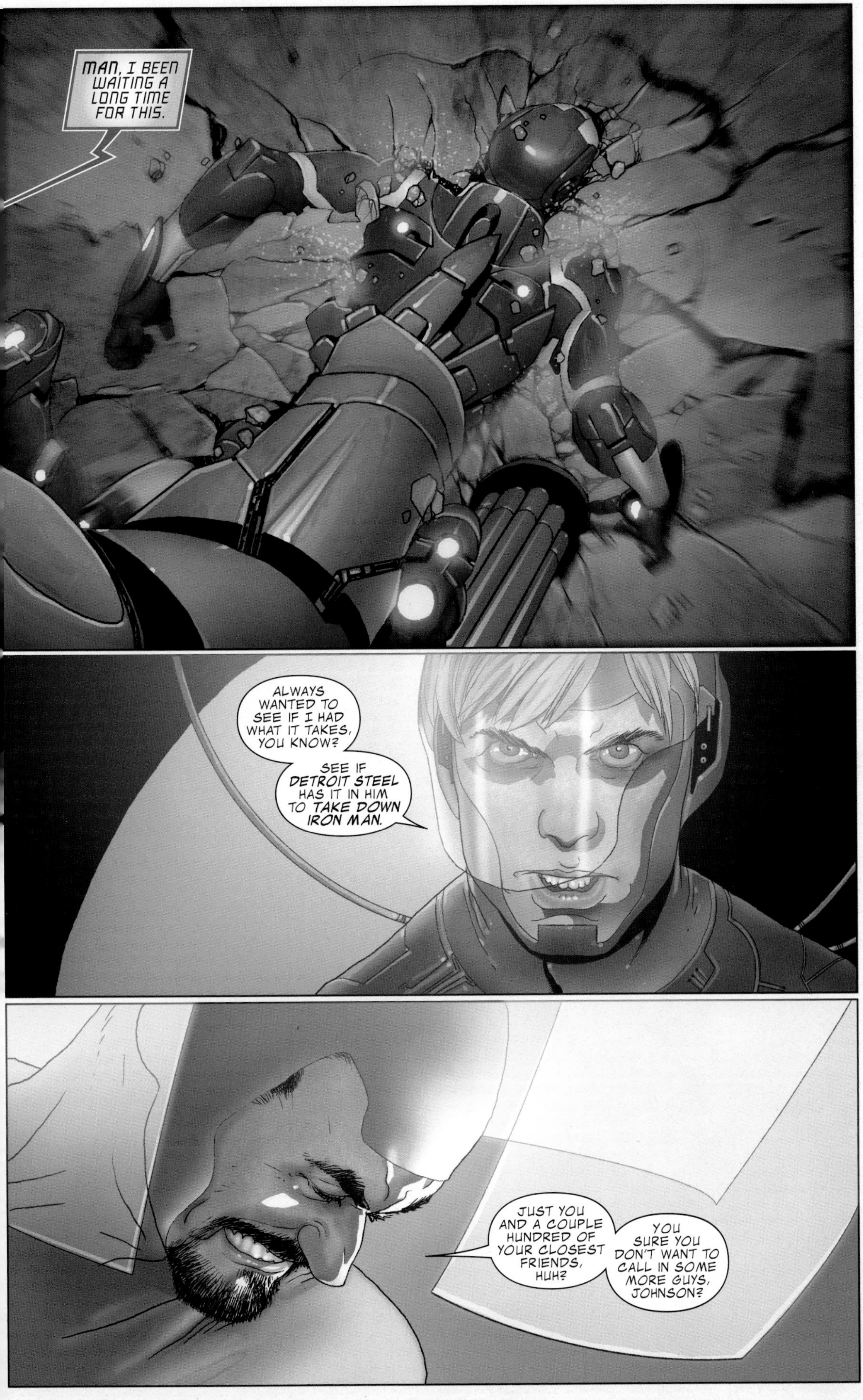
MAN, I BEEN WAITING A LONG TIME FOR THIS.
ALWAYS WANTED TO SEE IF I HAD WHAT IT TAKES, YOU KNOW?
SEE IF DETROIT STEEL HAS IT IN HIM TO TAKE DOWN IRON MAN.
JUST YOU AND A COUPLE HUNDRED OF YOUR CLOSEST FRIENDS, HUH?
YOU SURE YOU DON'T WANT TO CALL IN SOME MORE GUYS, JOHNSON?

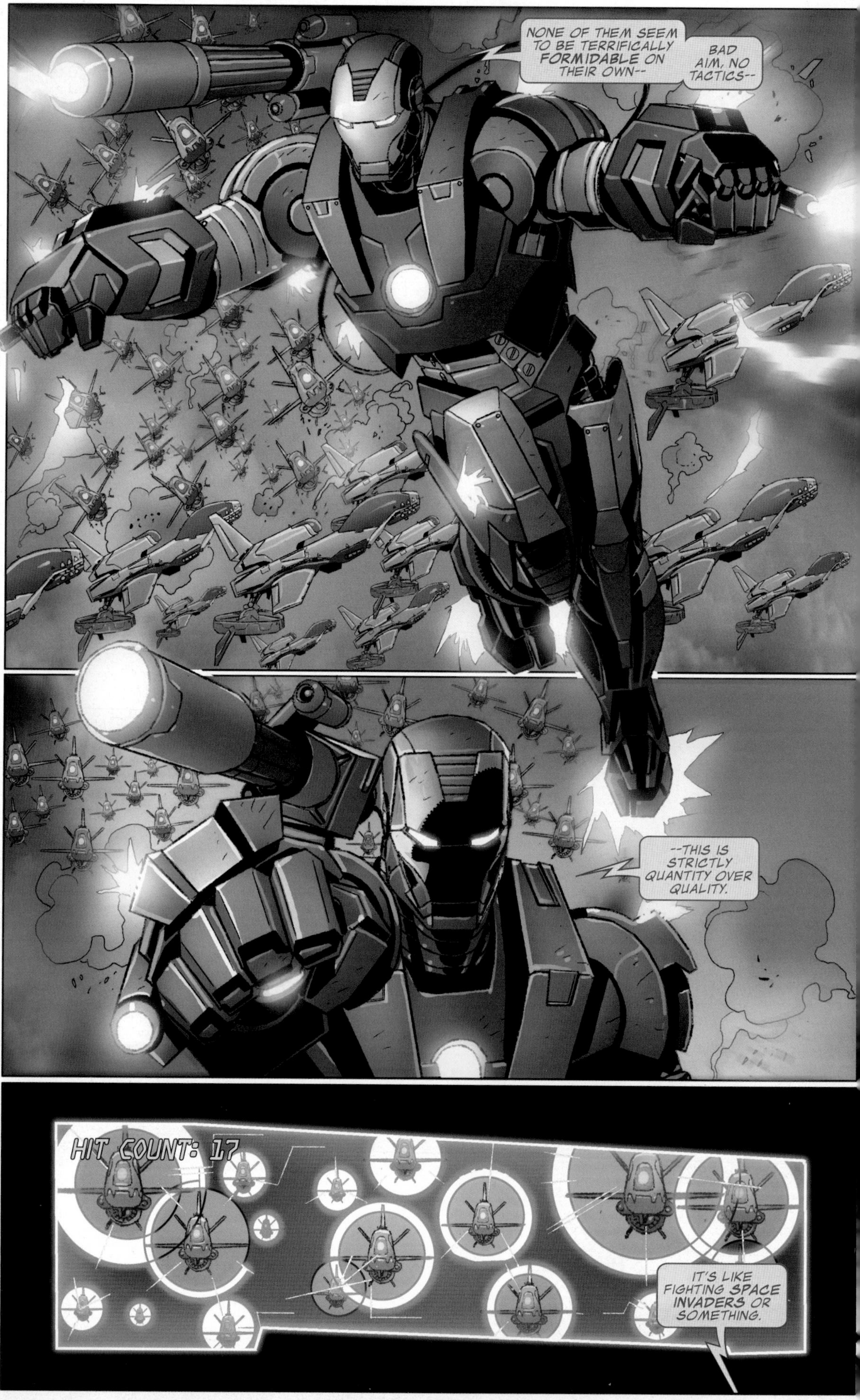
NONE OF THEM SEEM TO BE TERRIFICALLY FORMIDABLE ON THEIR OWN--
BAD AIM, NO TACTICS--
--THIS IS STRICTLY QUANTITY OVER QUALITY.
HIT COUNT: 17
IT'S LIKE FIGHTING SPACE INVADERS OR SOMETHING.

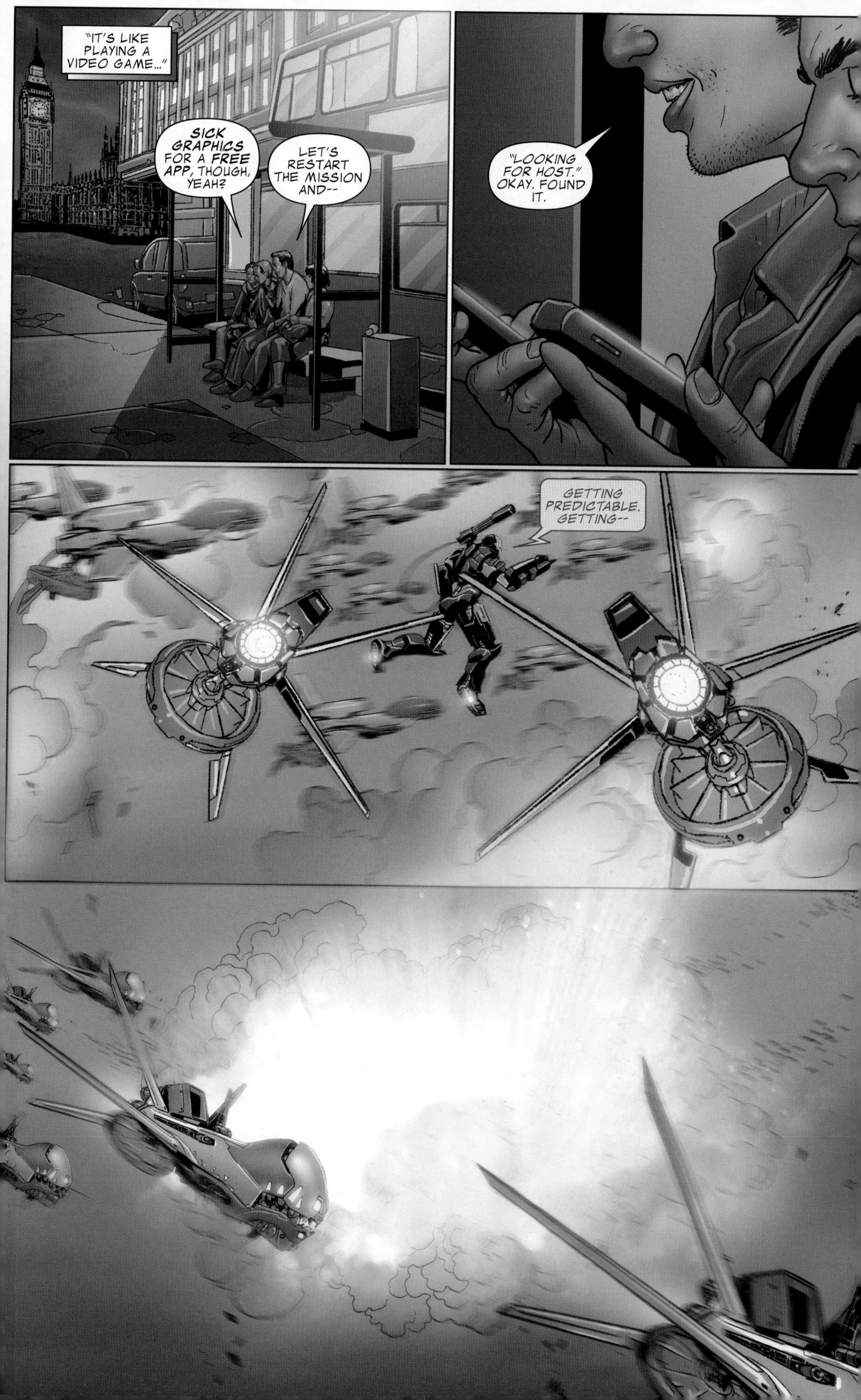
"IT'S LIKE PLAYING A VIDEO GAME..."
SICK GRAPHICS FOR A FREE APP, THOUGH, YEAH?
LET'S RESTART THE MISSION AND--
"LOOKING FOR HOST." OKAY. FOUND IT.
GETTING PREDICTABLE. GETTING--

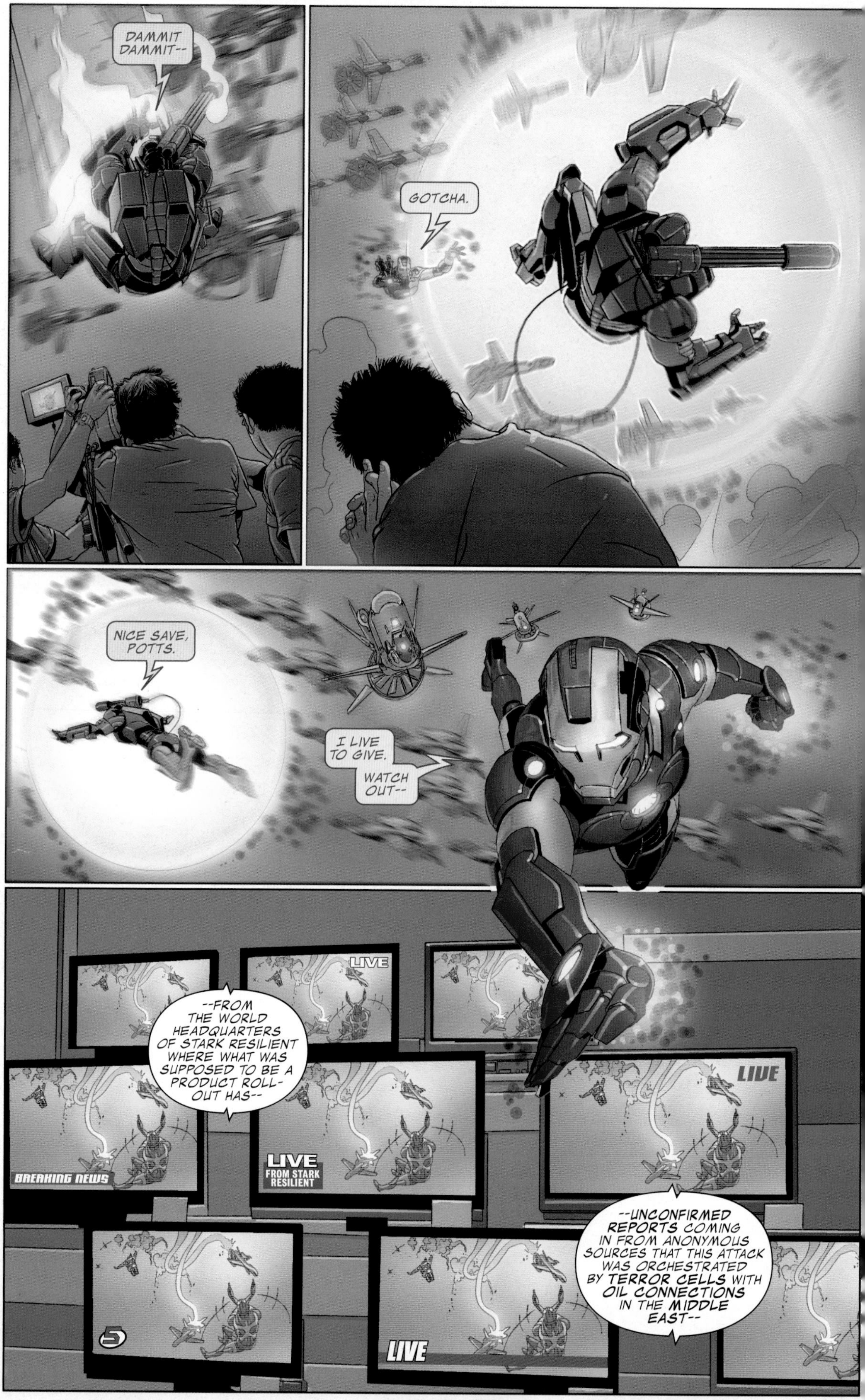
DAMMIT DAMMIT--
GOTCHA.
NICE SAVE, POTTS.
I LIVE TO GIVE.
WATCH OUT--
LIVE
--FROM THE WORLD HEADQUARTERS OF STARK RESILIENT WHERE WHAT WAS SUPPOSED TO BE A PRODUCT ROLL-OUT HAS--
LIVE
BREAKING NEWS
LIVE FROM STARK RESILIENT
--UNCONFIRMED REPORTS COMING IN FROM ANONYMOUS SOURCES THAT THIS ATTACK WAS ORCHESTRATED BY TERROR CELLS WITH OIL CONNECTIONS IN THE MIDDLE EAST--
LIVE

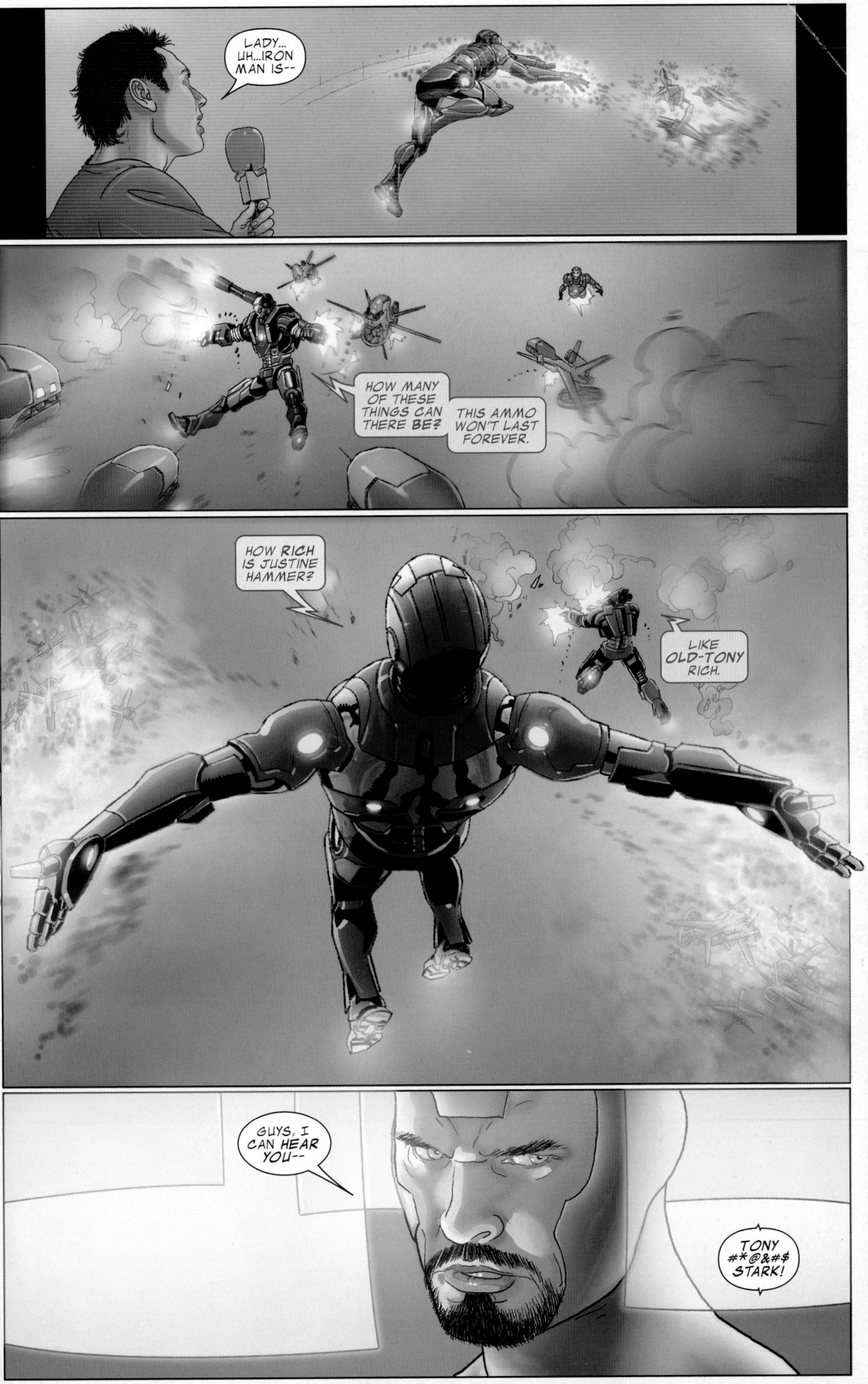
LADY... UH...IRON MAN IS--
HOW MANY OF THESE THINGS CAN THERE BE?
THIS AMMO WON'T LAST FOREVER.
HOW RICH IS JUSTINE HAMMER?
LIKE OLD-TONY RICH.
GUYS, I CAN HEAR YOU--
TONY #*@&#$ STARK!

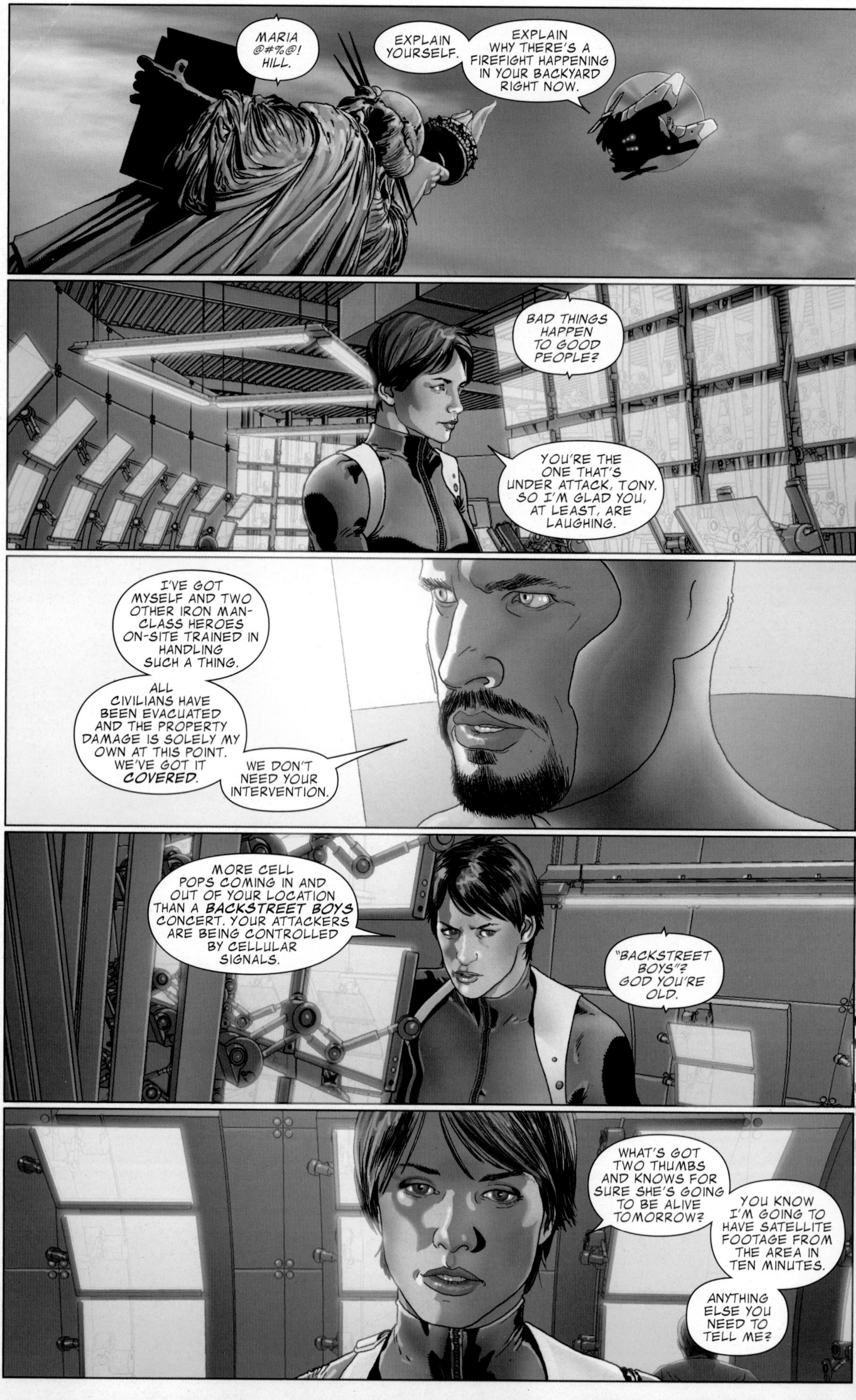
MARIA @#%@! HILL.
EXPLAIN YOURSELF.
EXPLAIN WHY THERE'S A FIREFIGHT HAPPENING IN YOUR BACKYARD RIGHT NOW.
BAD THINGS HAPPEN TO GOOD PEOPLE?
YOU'RE THE ONE THAT'S UNDER ATTACK, TONY. SO I'M GLAD YOU, AT LEAST, ARE LAUGHING.
I'VE GOT MYSELF AND TWO OTHER IRON MAN-CLASS HEROES ON-SITE TRAINED IN HANDLING SUCH A THING.
ALL CIVILIANS HAVE BEEN EVACUATED AND THE PROPERTY DAMAGE IS SOLELY MY OWN AT THIS POINT. WE'VE GOT IT COVERED.
WE DON'T NEED YOUR INTERVENTION.
MORE CELL POPS COMING IN AND OUT OF YOUR LOCATION THAN A BACKSTREET BOYS CONCERT. YOUR ATTACKERS ARE BEING CONTROLLED BY CELLULAR SIGNALS.
"BACKSTREET BOYS"? GOD YOU'RE OLD.
WHAT'S GOT TWO THUMBS AND KNOWS FOR SURE SHE'S GOING TO BE ALIVE TOMORROW?
YOU KNOW I'M GOING TO HAVE SATELLITE FOOTAGE FROM THE AREA IN TEN MINUTES.
ANYTHING ELSE YOU NEED TO TELL ME?

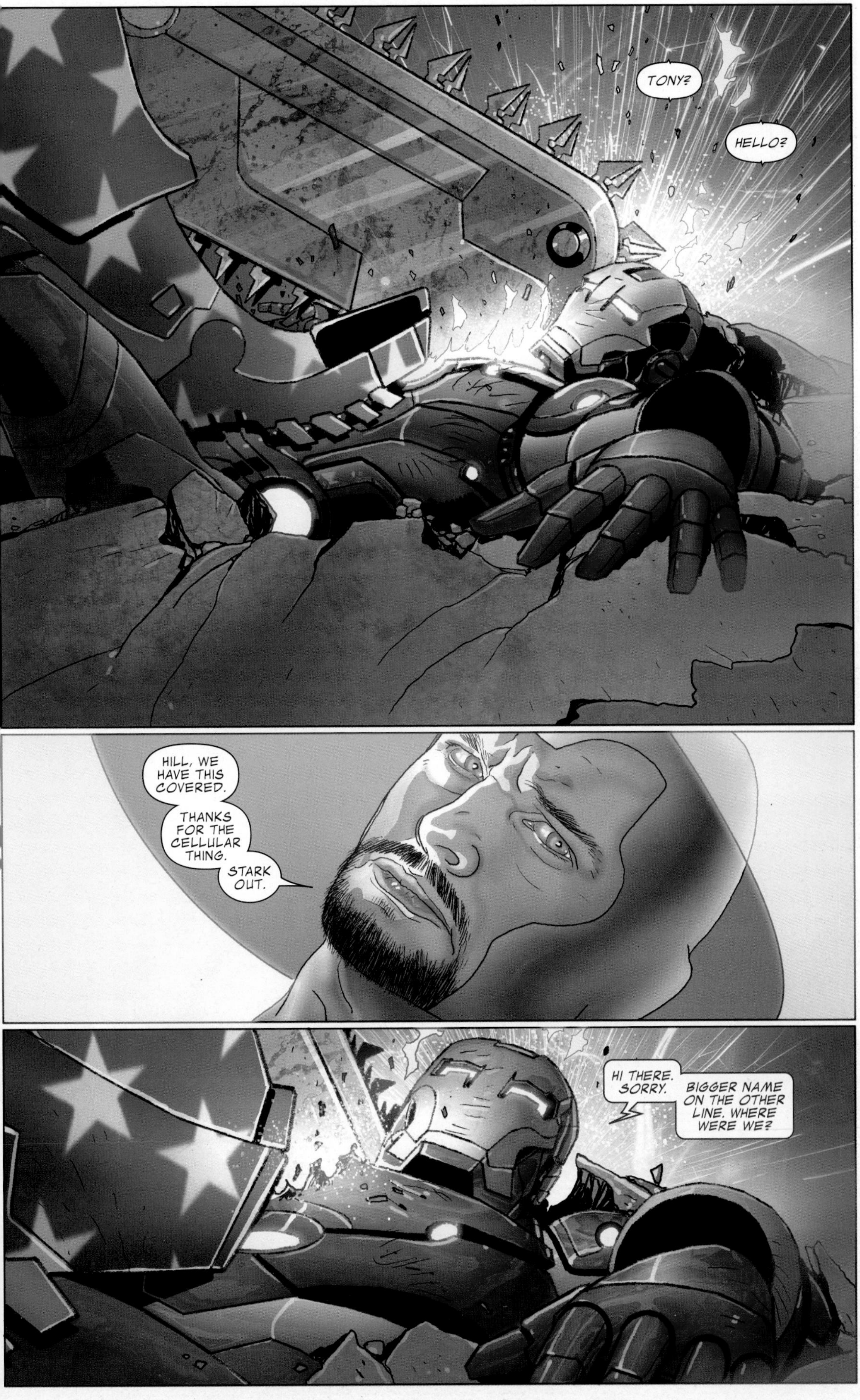
TONY?
HELLO?
HILL, WE HAVE THIS COVERED.
THANKS FOR THE CELLULAR THING.
STARK OUT.
HI THERE. SORRY.
BIGGER NAME ON THE OTHER LINE. WHERE WERE WE?

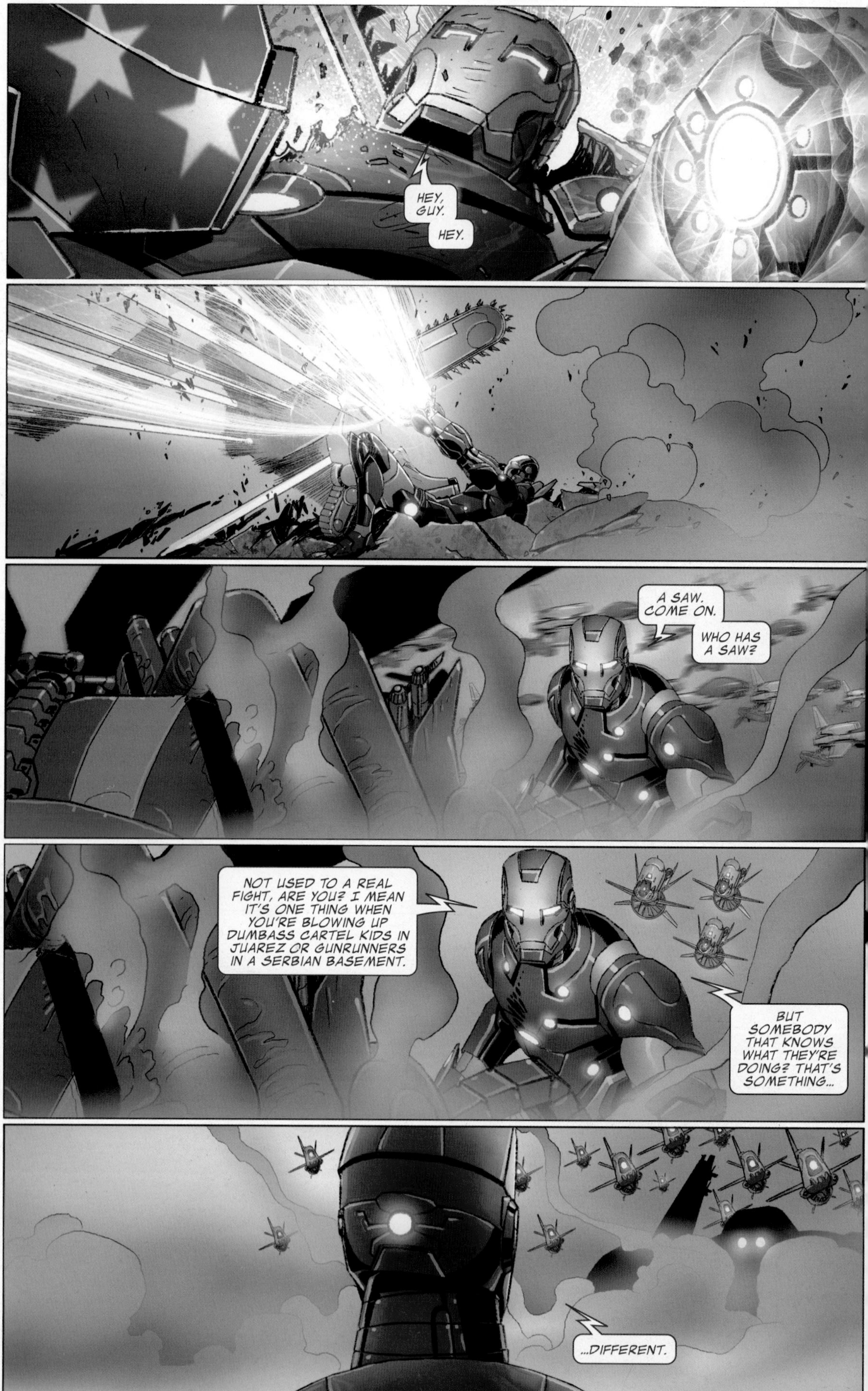
HEY, GUY.
HEY.
A SAW. COME ON.
WHO HAS A SAW?
NOT USED TO A REAL FIGHT, ARE YOU? I MEAN IT'S ONE THING WHEN YOU'RE BLOWING UP DUMBASS CARTEL KIDS IN JUAREZ OR GUNRUNNERS IN A SERBIAN BASEMENT.
BUT SOMEBODY THAT KNOWS WHAT THEY'RE DOING? THAT'S SOMETHING...
...DIFFERENT.

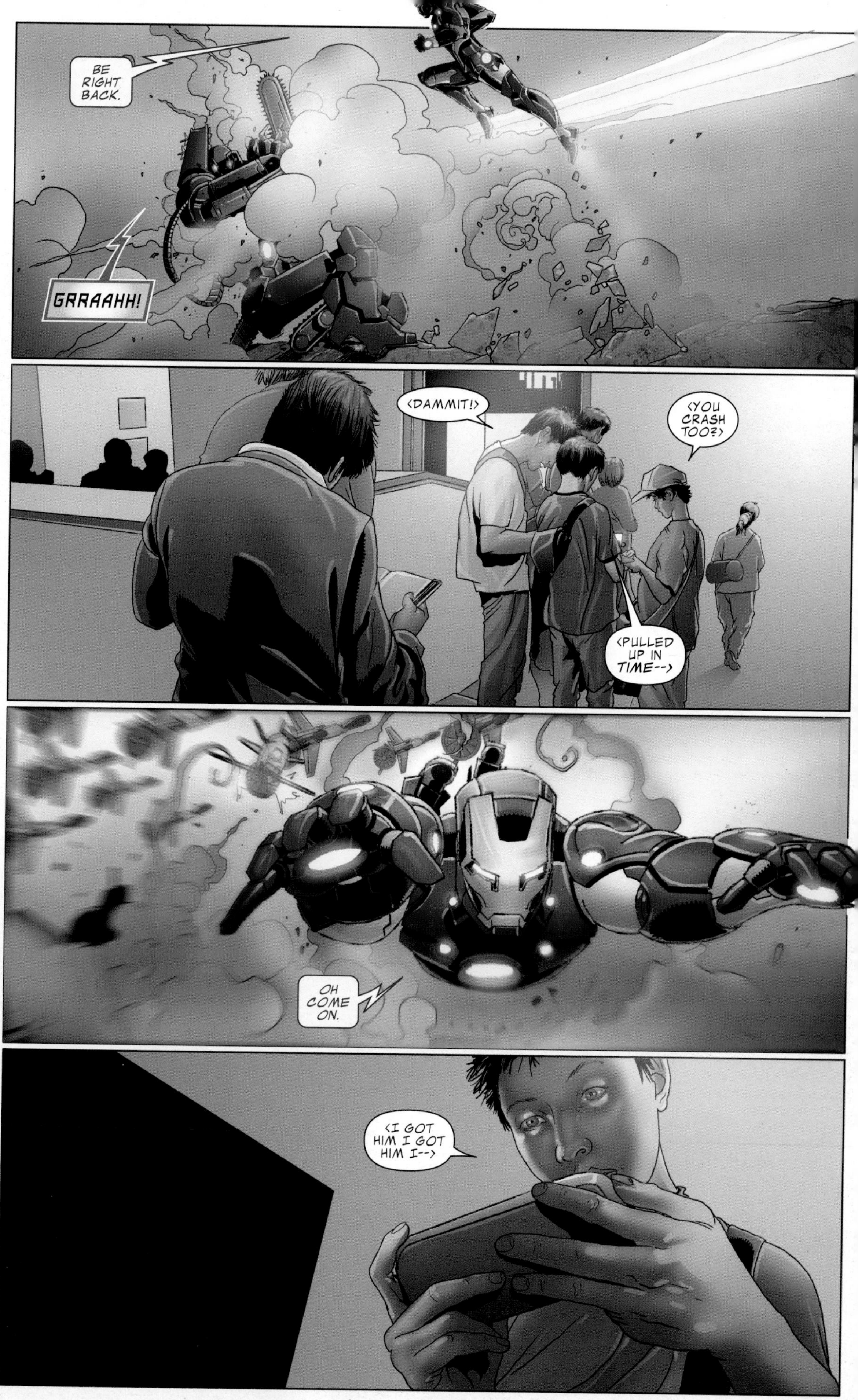
BE RIGHT BACK.
GRRAAHH!
<DAMMIT!>
<YOU CRASH TOO?>
<PULLED UP IN TIME-->
OH COME ON.
<I GOT HIM I GOT HIM I-->

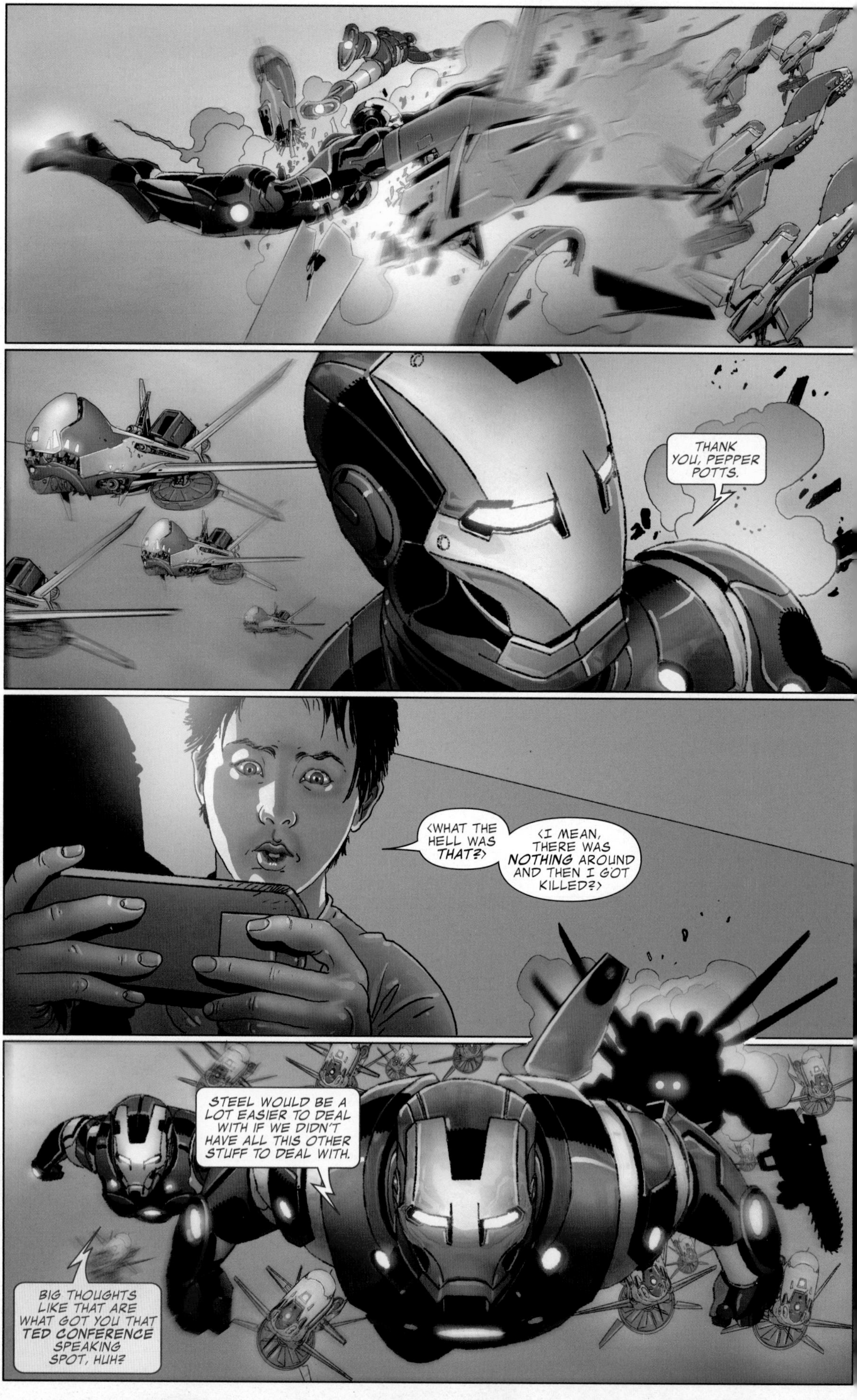
THANK YOU, PEPPER POTTS.
<WHAT THE HELL WAS THAT?>
<I MEAN, THERE WAS NOTHING AROUND AND THEN I GOT KILLED?>
STEEL WOULD BE A LOT EASIER TO DEAL WITH IF WE DIDN'T HAVE ALL THIS OTHER STUFF TO DEAL WITH.
BIG THOUGHTS LIKE THAT ARE WHAT GOT YOU THAT TED CONFERENCE SPEAKING SPOT, HUH?

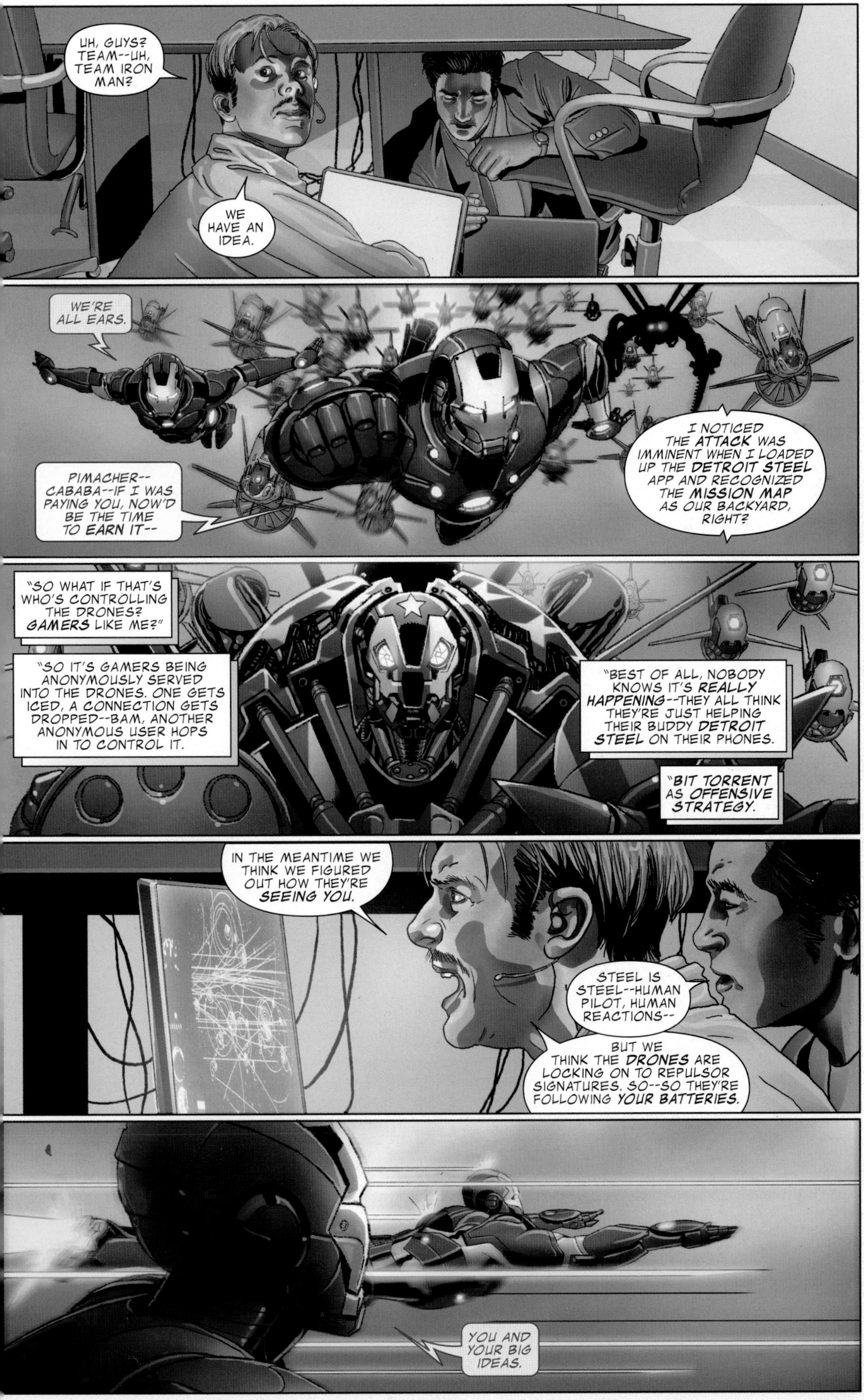

UH, GUYS? TEAM--UH, TEAM IRON MAN?
WE HAVE AN IDEA.
WE'RE ALL EARS.
PIMACHER--CABABA--IF I WAS PAYING YOU, NOW'D BE THE TIME TO EARN IT--
I NOTICED THE ATTACK WAS IMMINENT WHEN I LOADED UP THE DETROIT STEEL APP AND RECOGNIZED THE MISSION MAP AS OUR BACKYARD, RIGHT?
"SO WHAT IF THAT'S WHO'S CONTROLLING THE DRONES? GAMERS LIKE ME?"
"SO IT'S GAMERS BEING ANONYMOUSLY SERVED INTO THE DRONES. ONE GETS ICED, A CONNECTION GETS DROPPED--BAM, ANOTHER ANONYMOUS USER HOPS IN TO CONTROL IT.
"BEST OF ALL, NOBODY KNOWS IT'S REALLY HAPPENING--THEY ALL THINK THEY'RE JUST HELPING THEIR BUDDY DETROIT STEEL ON THEIR PHONES.
"BIT TORRENT AS OFFENSIVE STRATEGY.
IN THE MEANTIME WE THINK WE FIGURED OUT HOW THEY'RE SEEING YOU.
STEEL IS STEEL--HUMAN PILOT, HUMAN REACTIONS--
BUT WE THINK THE DRONES ARE LOCKING ON TO REPULSOR SIGNATURES. SO--SO THEY'RE FOLLOWING YOUR BATTERIES.
YOU AND YOUR BIG IDEAS.

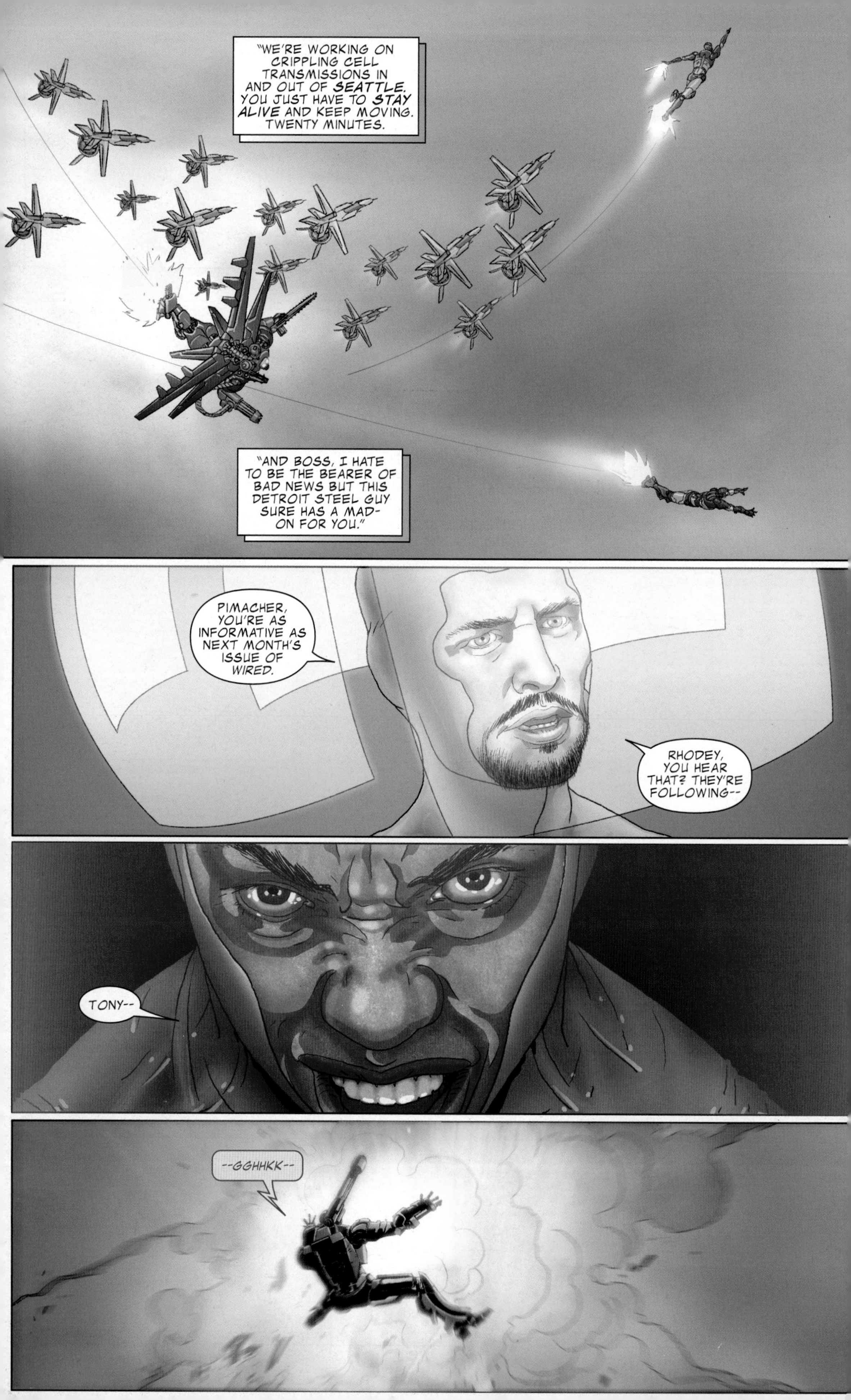
"WE'RE WORKING ON CRIPPLING CELL TRANSMISSIONS IN AND OUT OF SEATTLE. YOU JUST HAVE TO STAY ALIVE AND KEEP MOVING. TWENTY MINUTES.
"AND BOSS, I HATE TO BE THE BEARER OF BAD NEWS BUT THIS DETROIT STEEL GUY SURE HAS A MAD-ON FOR YOU."
PIMACHER, YOU'RE AS INFORMATIVE AS NEXT MONTH'S ISSUE OF WIRED.
RHODEY, YOU HEAR THAT? THEY'RE FOLLOWING--
TONY--
--GGHHKK--

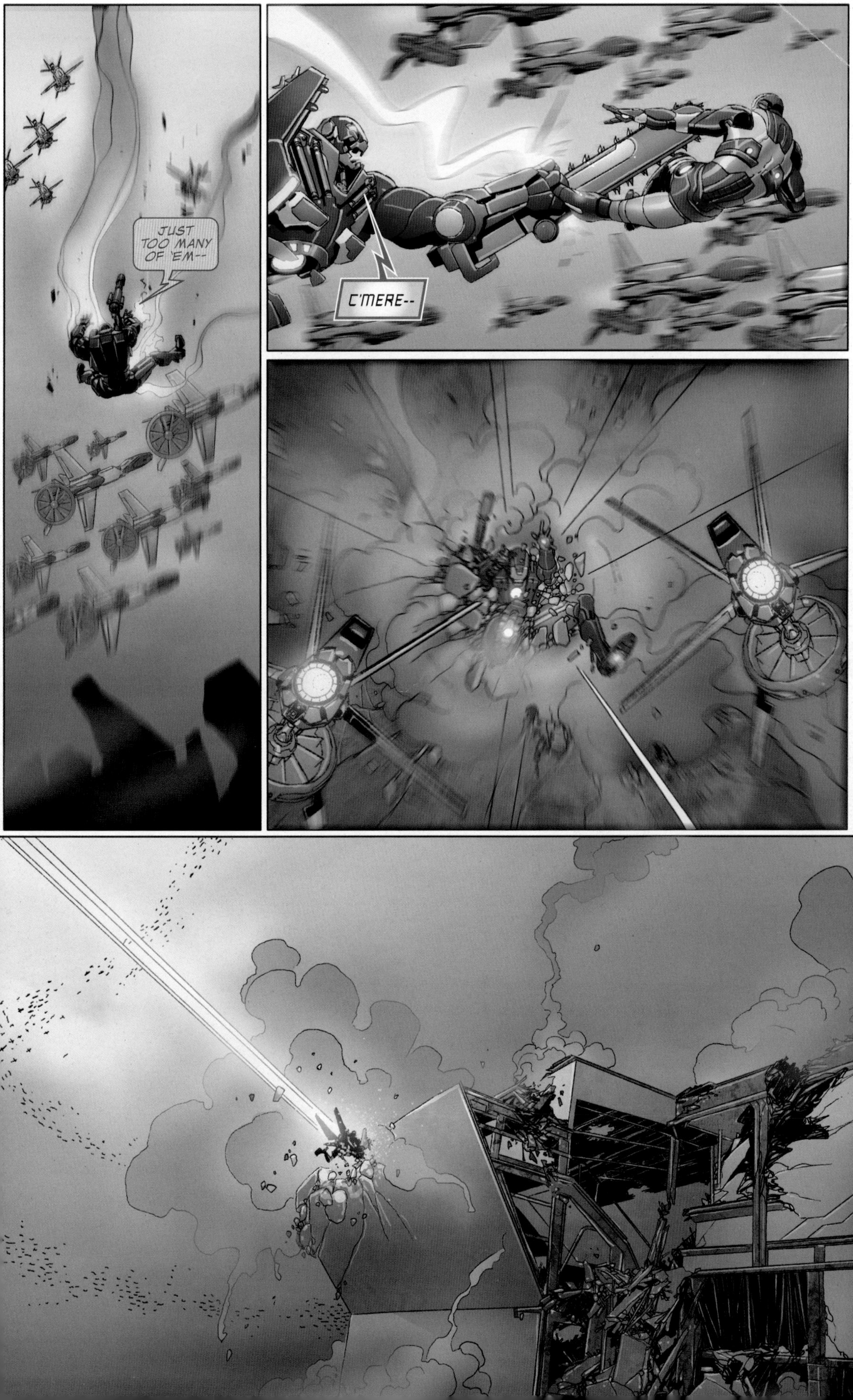
JUST TOO MANY OF 'EM--
C'MERE--

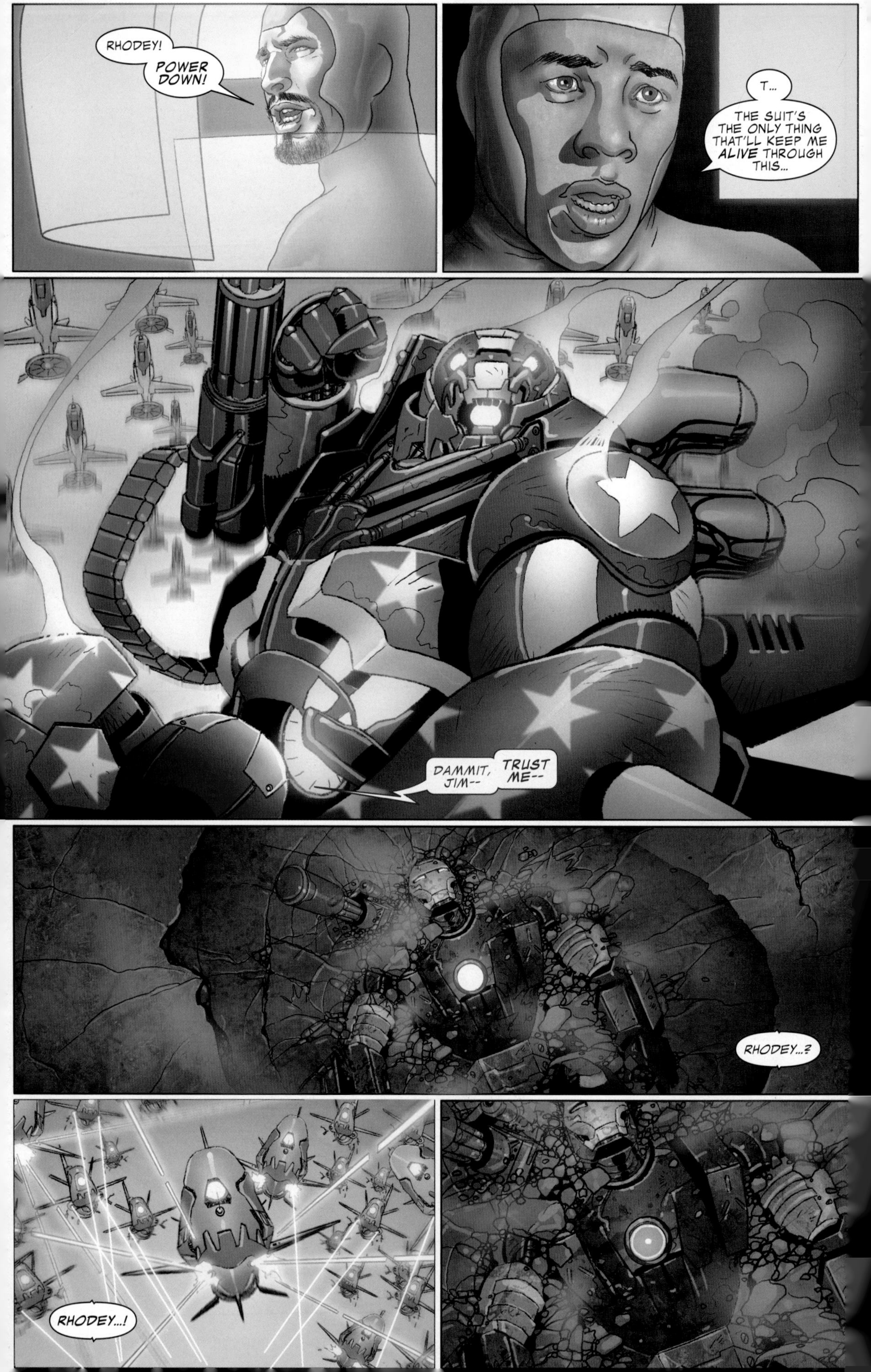
RHODEY!
POWER DOWN!
T...
THE SUIT'S THE ONLY THING THAT'LL KEEP ME ALIVE THROUGH THIS...
DAMMIT, JIM--
TRUST ME--
RHODEY...?
RHODEY...!

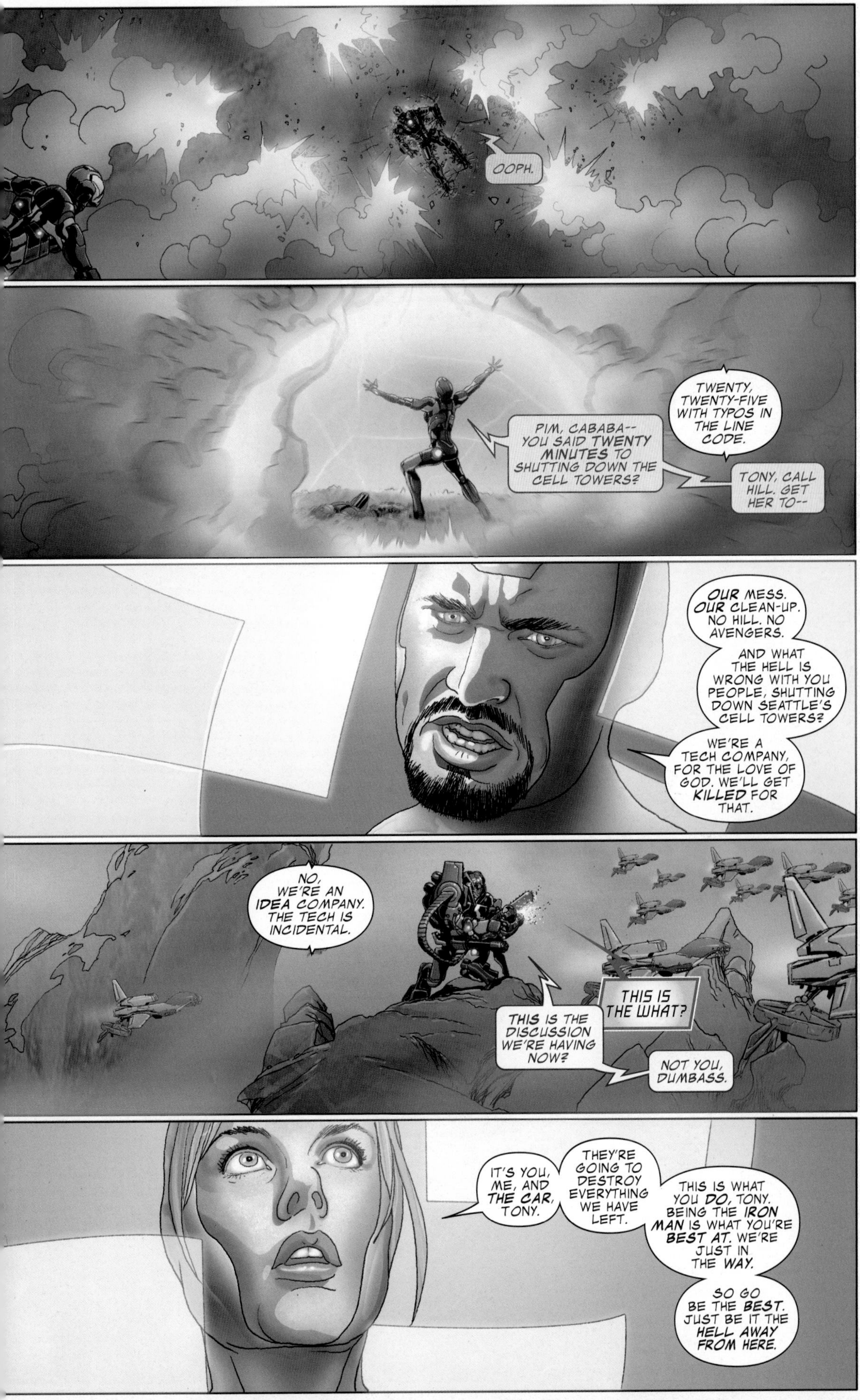
OOPH.
PIM, CABABA-- YOU SAID TWENTY MINUTES TO SHUTTING DOWN THE CELL TOWERS?
TWENTY, TWENTY-FIVE WITH TYPOS IN THE LINE CODE.
TONY, CALL HILL. GET HER TO--
OUR MESS. OUR CLEAN-UP. NO HILL. NO AVENGERS.
AND WHAT THE HELL IS WRONG WITH YOU PEOPLE, SHUTTING DOWN SEATTLE'S CELL TOWERS?
WE'RE A TECH COMPANY, FOR THE LOVE OF GOD. WE'LL GET KILLED FOR THAT.
NO, WE'RE AN IDEA COMPANY. THE TECH IS INCIDENTAL.
THIS IS THE DISCUSSION WE'RE HAVING NOW?
THIS IS THE WHAT?
NOT YOU, DUMBASS.
IT'S YOU, ME, AND THE CAR, TONY.
THEY'RE GOING TO DESTROY EVERYTHING WE HAVE LEFT.
THIS IS WHAT YOU DO, TONY. BEING THE IRON MAN IS WHAT YOU'RE BEST AT. WE'RE JUST IN THE WAY.
SO GO BE THE BEST. JUST BE IT THE HELL AWAY FROM HERE.

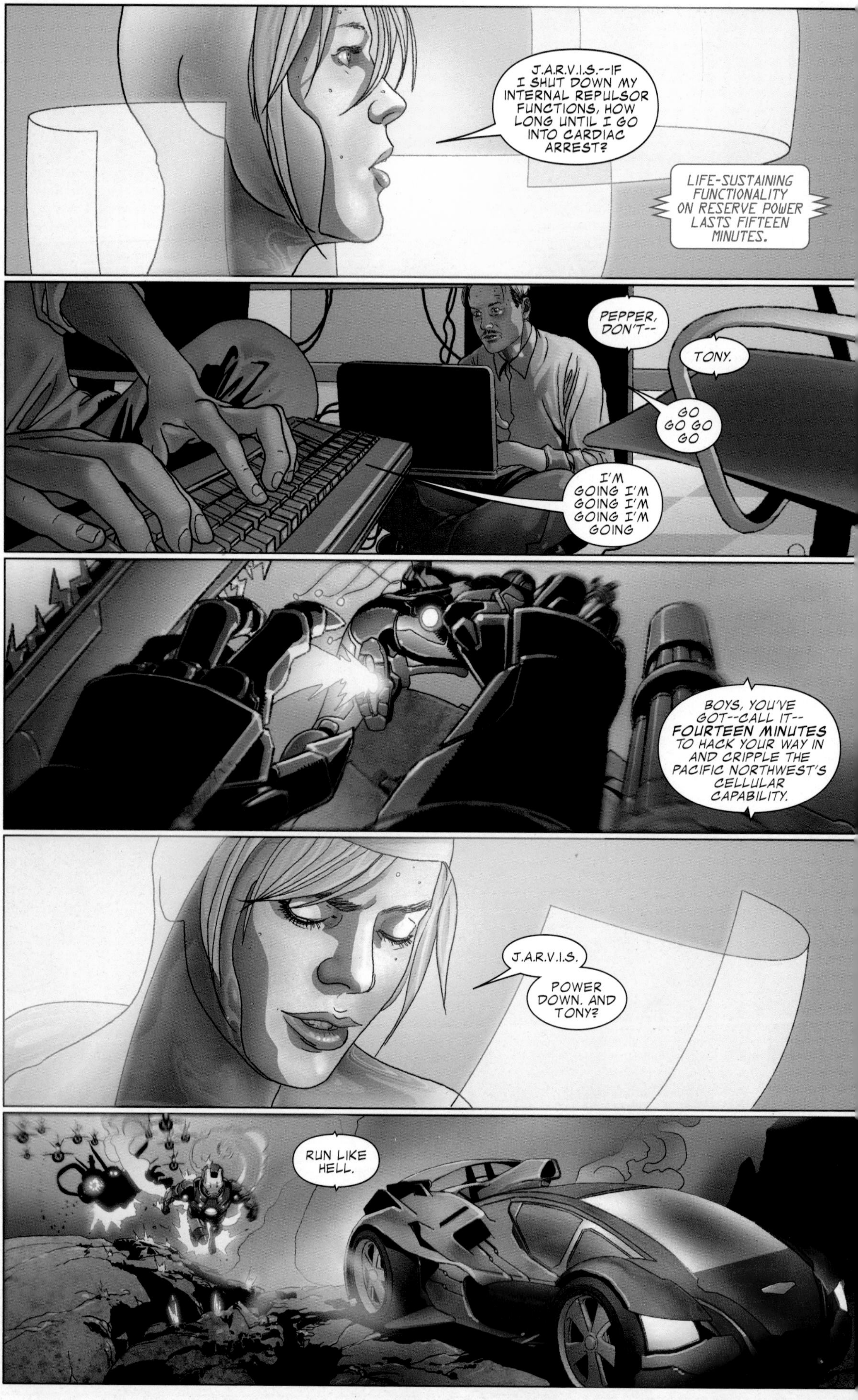
J.A.R.V.I.S.--IF I SHUT DOWN MY INTERNAL REPULSOR FUNCTIONS, HOW LONG UNTIL I GO INTO CARDIAC ARREST?
LIFE-SUSTAINING FUNCTIONALITY ON RESERVE POWER LASTS FIFTEEN MINUTES.
PEPPER, DON'T--
TONY.
GO GO GO GO GO
I'M GOING I'M GOING I'M GOING I'M GOING
BOYS, YOU'VE GOT--CALL IT--**FOURTEEN MINUTES** TO HACK YOUR WAY IN AND CRIPPLE THE PACIFIC NORTHWEST'S CELLULAR CAPABILITY.
J.A.R.V.I.S.
POWER DOWN. AND TONY?
RUN LIKE HELL.

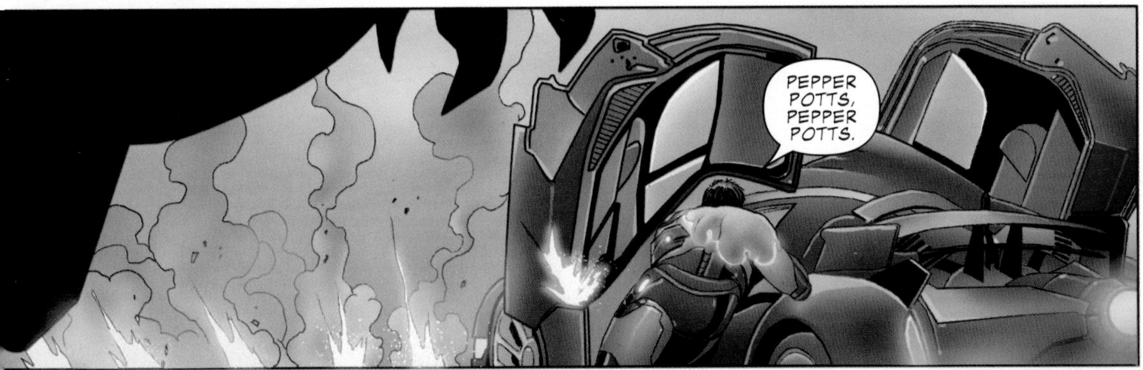
PEPPER POTTS, PEPPER POTTS.

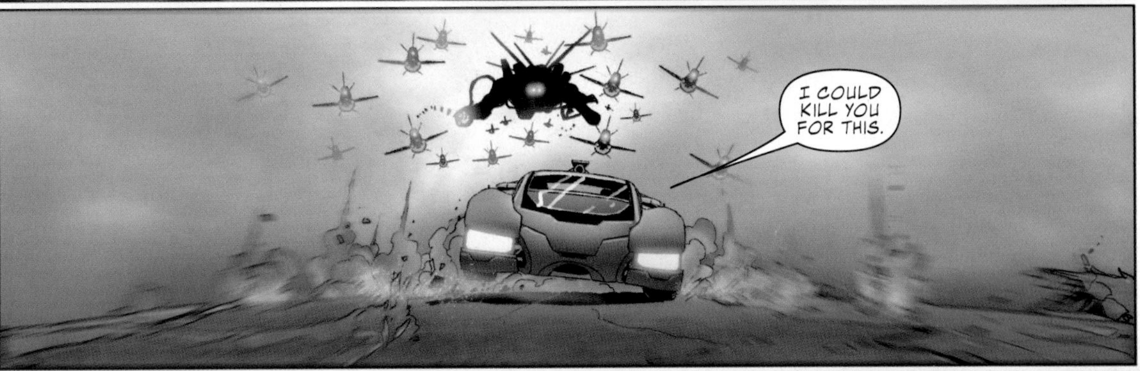
I COULD KILL YOU FOR THIS.

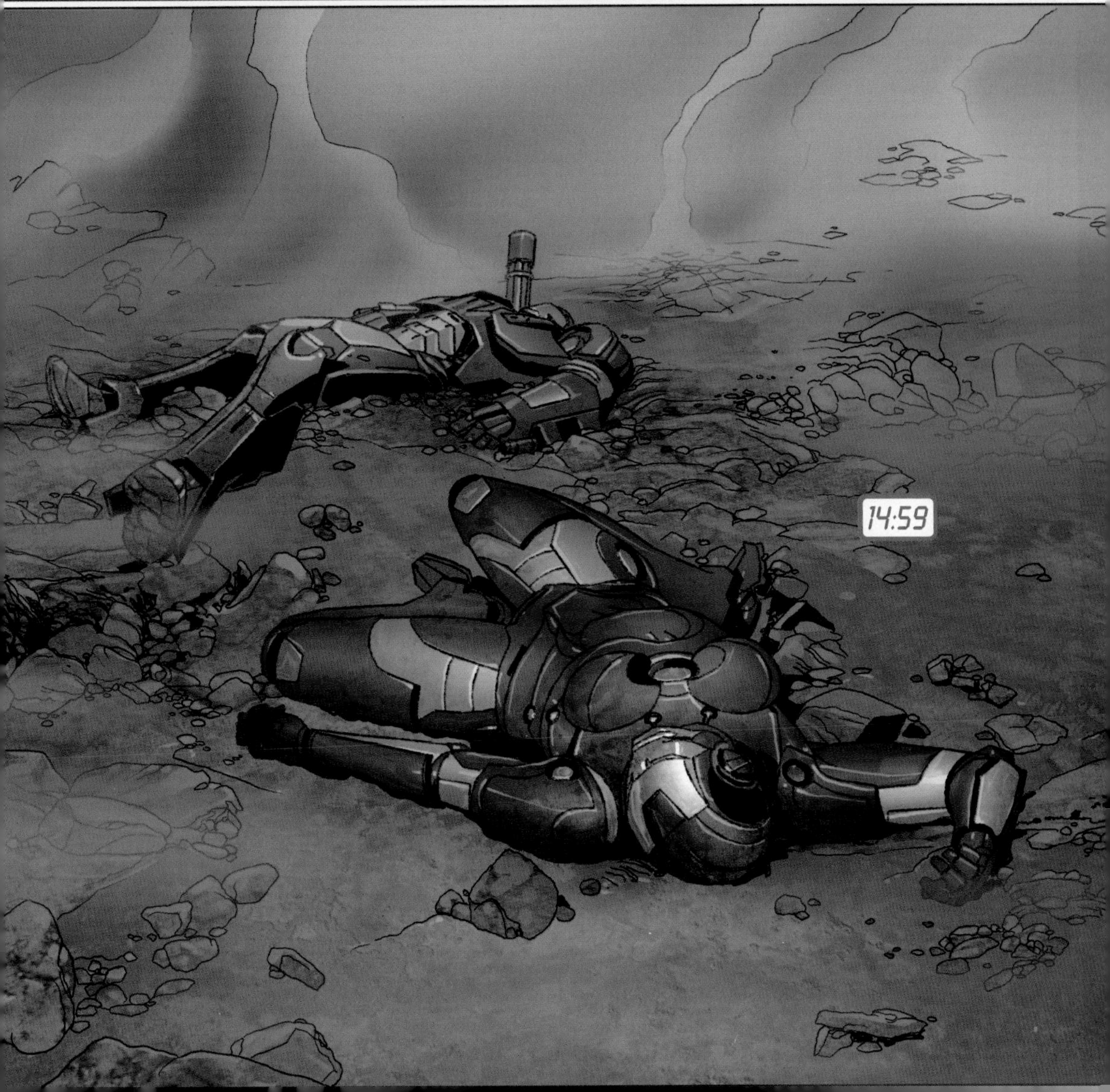
14:59

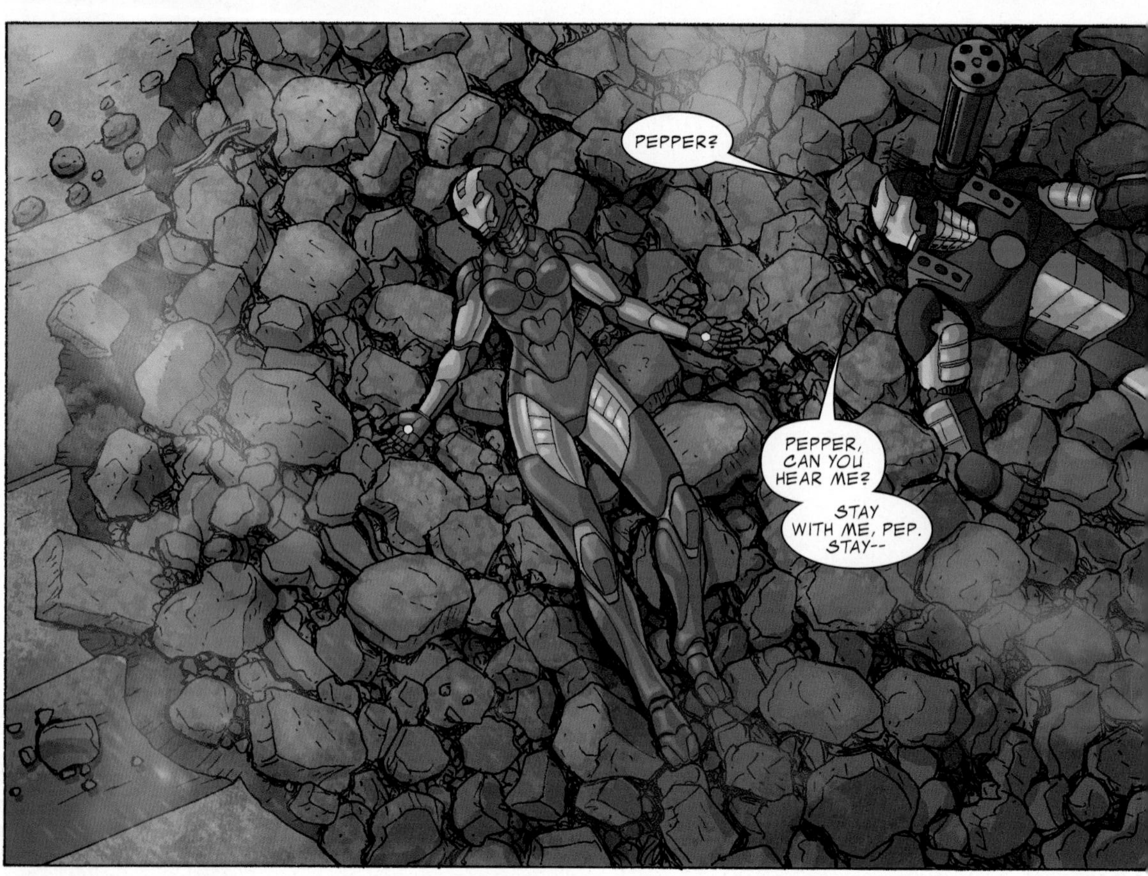
PEPPER?
PEPPER, CAN YOU HEAR ME?
STAY WITH ME, PEP. STAY--

AGAIN AT THE END OF THE WORLD WITH YOUR PAL PEPPER POTTS

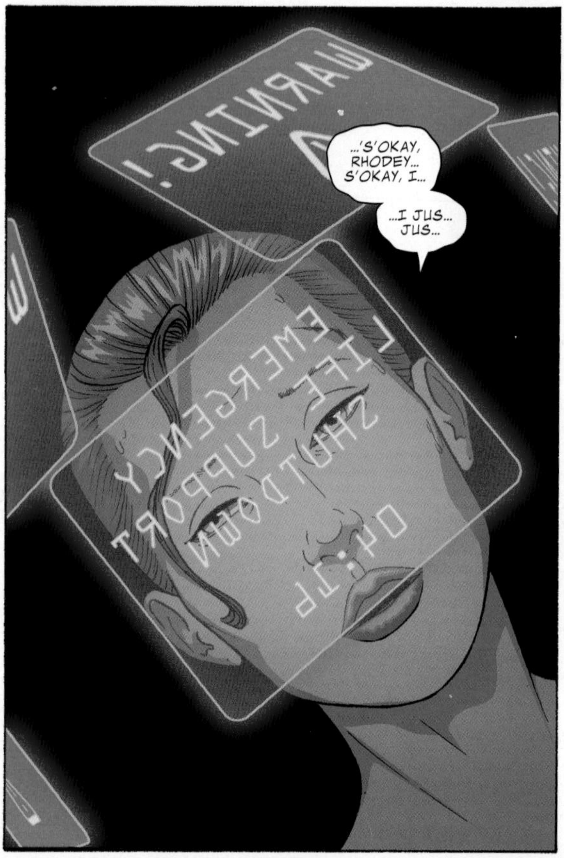
WARNING!
...'S'OKAY, RHODEY... S'OKAY, I...
...I JUS... JUS...
EMERGENCY LIFE SUPPORT SHUTDOWN 04:16

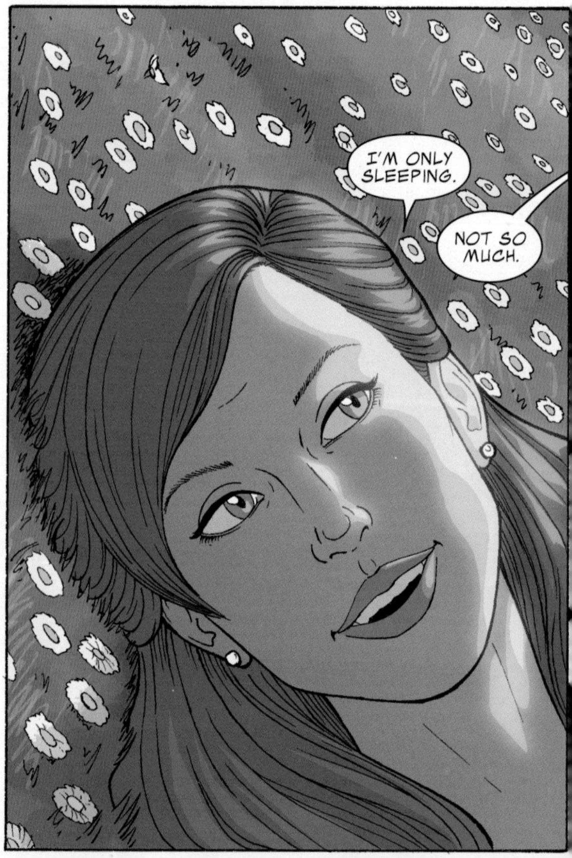
I'M ONLY SLEEPING.
NOT SO MUCH.

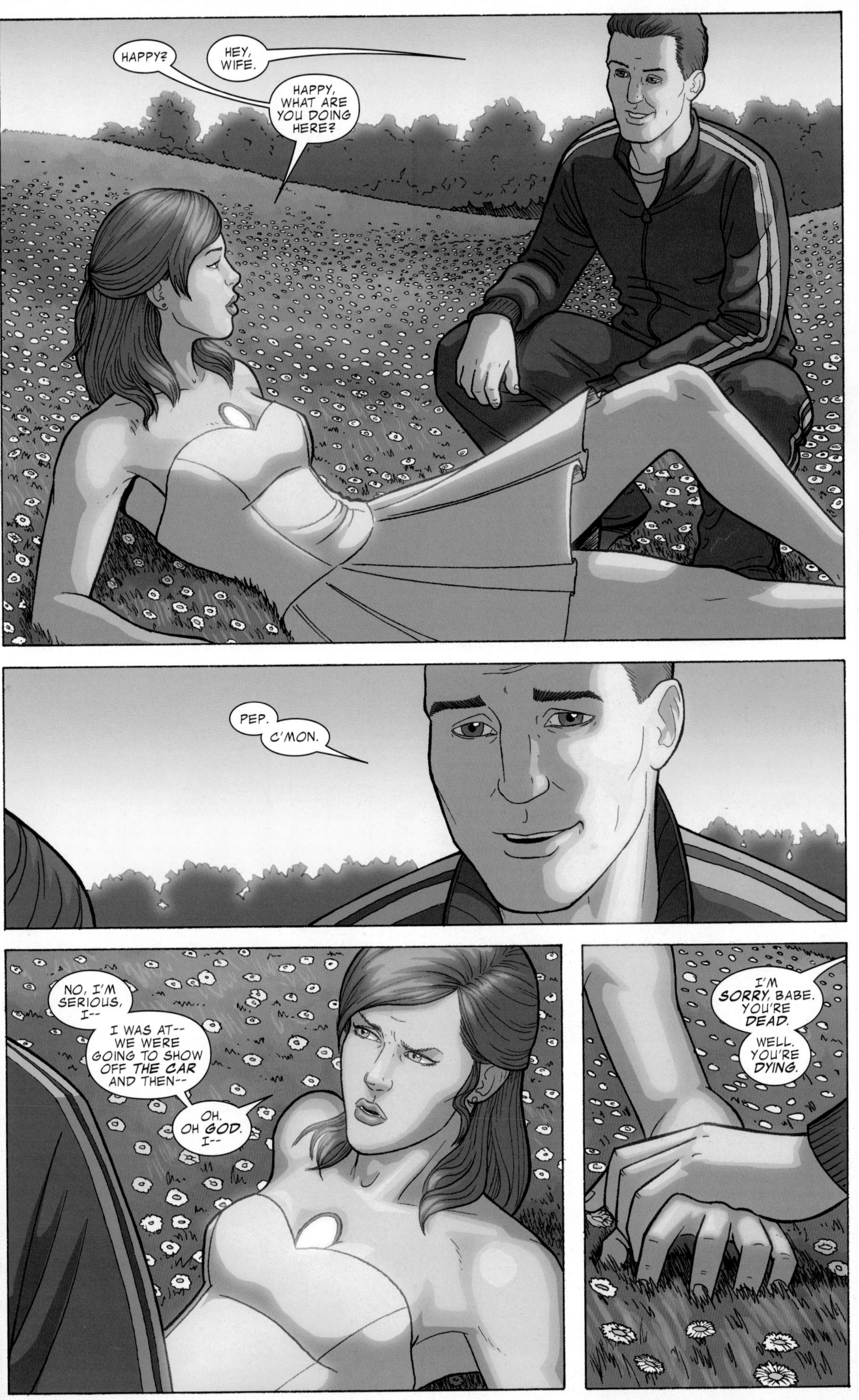
HAPPY?
HEY, WIFE.
HAPPY, WHAT ARE YOU DOING HERE?
PEP.
C'MON.
NO, I'M SERIOUS, I--
I WAS AT-- WE WERE GOING TO SHOW OFF THE CAR AND THEN--
OH. OH GOD. I--
I'M SORRY, BABE. YOU'RE DEAD.
WELL. YOU'RE DYING.

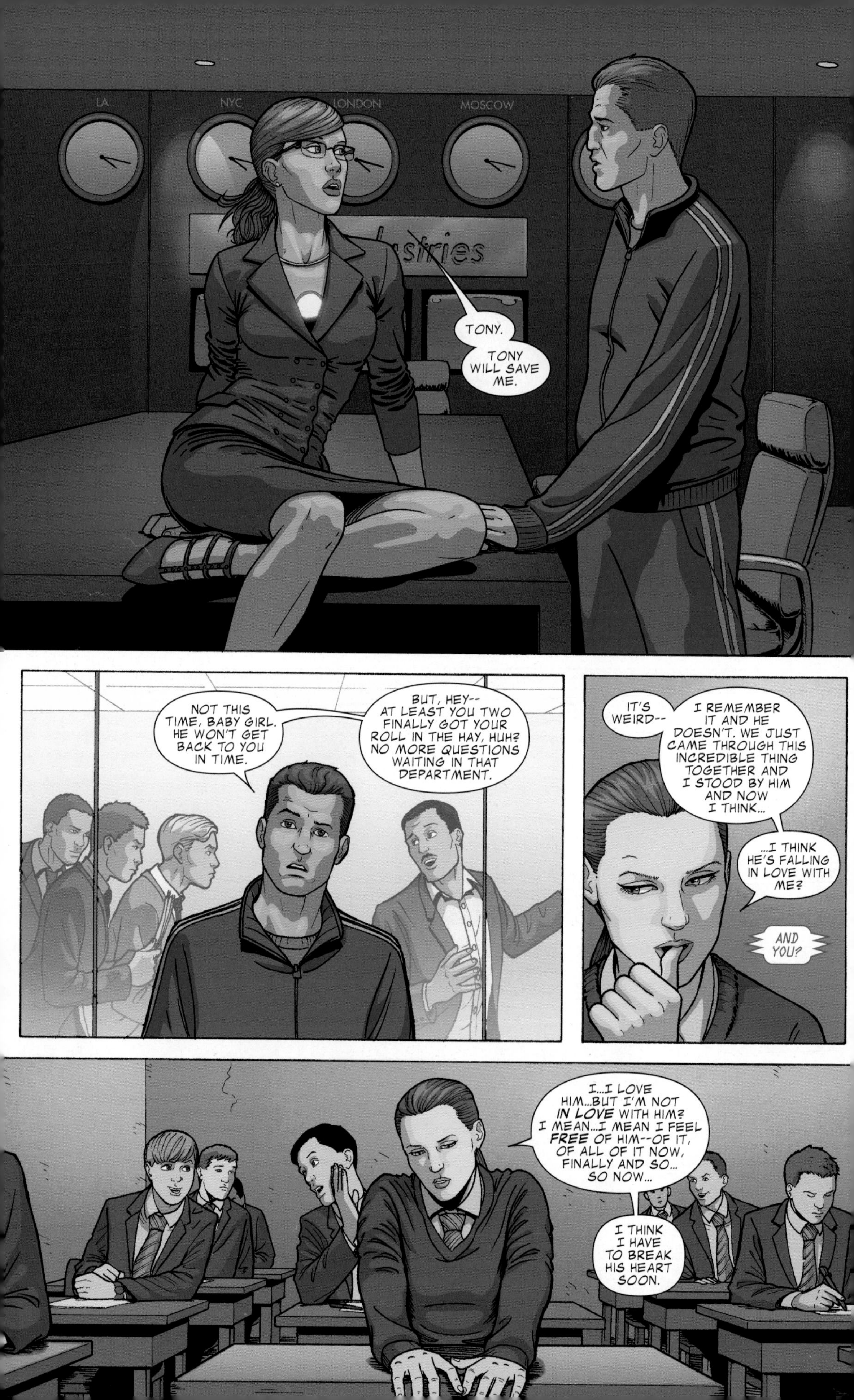
LA
NYC
LONDON
MOSCOW
TONY.
TONY WILL SAVE ME.
NOT THIS TIME, BABY GIRL. HE WON'T GET BACK TO YOU IN TIME.
BUT, HEY-- AT LEAST YOU TWO FINALLY GOT YOUR ROLL IN THE HAY, HUH? NO MORE QUESTIONS WAITING IN THAT DEPARTMENT.
IT'S WEIRD--
I REMEMBER IT AND HE DOESN'T. WE JUST CAME THROUGH THIS INCREDIBLE THING TOGETHER AND I STOOD BY HIM AND NOW I THINK...
...I THINK HE'S FALLING IN LOVE WITH ME?
AND YOU?
I...I LOVE HIM...BUT I'M NOT IN LOVE WITH HIM? I MEAN...I MEAN I FEEL FREE OF HIM--OF IT, OF ALL OF IT NOW, FINALLY AND SO... SO NOW...
I THINK I HAVE TO BREAK HIS HEART SOON.

WELL THERE'S THE UPSIDE TO YOU NOT SEEING HIM AGAIN.

YOU GET TO AVOID HAVING *THAT* HORRIBLY AWKWARD CONVERSATION.

AND YOU'LL GET TO BE THE GREAT LOVE OF *TWO* LIVES. NOT BAD, BABE.

NO. NOT HIM. HE'LL PULL IT OFF. I KNOW TONY.

I KNOW HOW HE FEELS ABOUT ME, HONEY.

YOU REALLY HAVE NO IDEA HOW FAR HE'LL GO TO KEEP ME FROM GETTING HURT.

AND BESIDES-- I BELIEVE IN HIM.

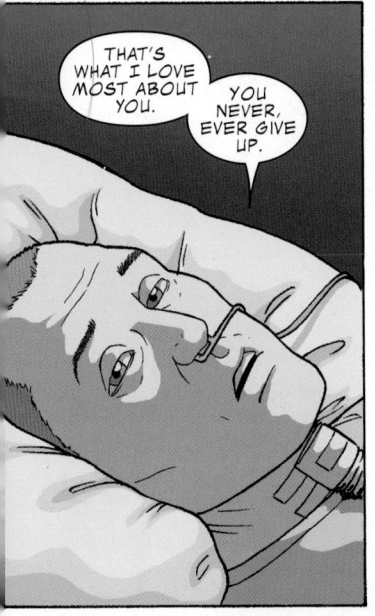

THAT'S WHAT I LOVE MOST ABOUT YOU.

YOU NEVER, EVER GIVE UP.

NO MATTER HOW GRIM IT GETS.

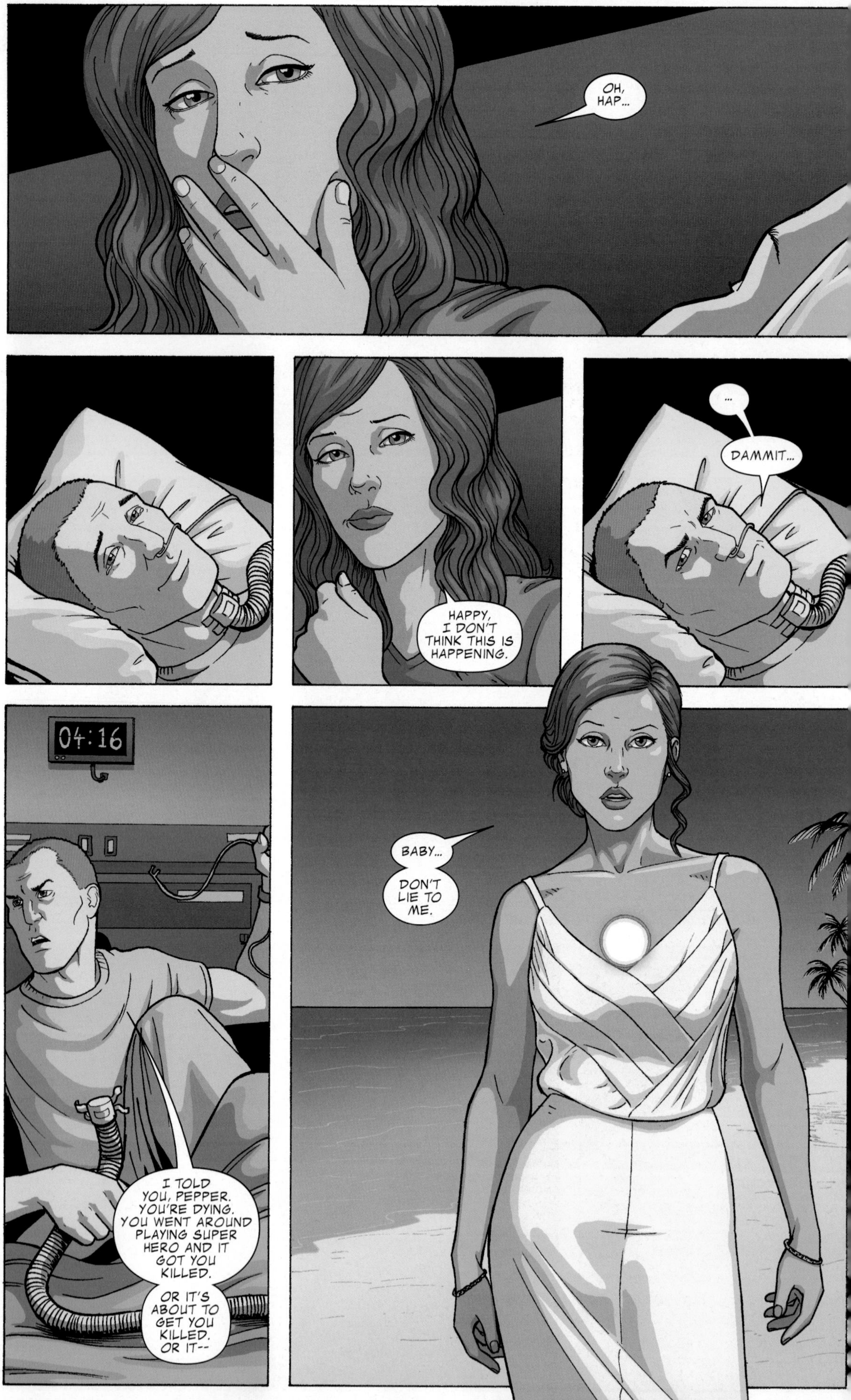
OH, HAP...
HAPPY, I DON'T THINK THIS IS HAPPENING.
...
DAMMIT...
04:16
I TOLD YOU, PEPPER. YOU'RE DYING. YOU WENT AROUND PLAYING SUPER HERO AND IT GOT YOU KILLED.
OR IT'S ABOUT TO GET YOU KILLED. OR IT--
BABY...
DON'T LIE TO ME.

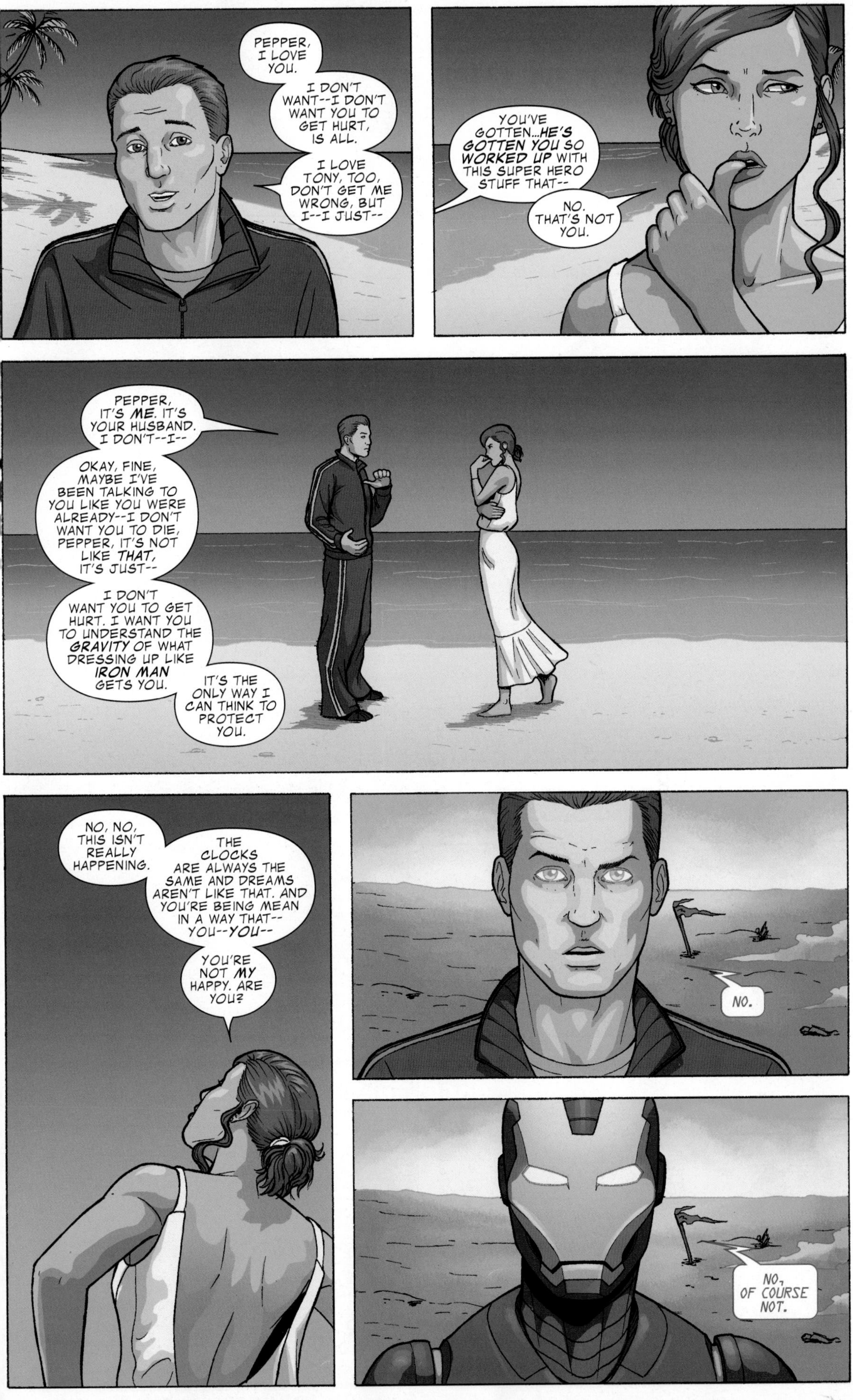
PEPPER, I LOVE YOU.
I DON'T WANT--I DON'T WANT YOU TO GET HURT, IS ALL.
I LOVE TONY, TOO, DON'T GET ME WRONG, BUT I--I JUST--
YOU'VE GOTTEN...HE'S GOTTEN YOU SO WORKED UP WITH THIS SUPER HERO STUFF THAT--
NO. THAT'S NOT YOU.
PEPPER, IT'S ME. IT'S YOUR HUSBAND. I DON'T--I--
OKAY, FINE, MAYBE I'VE BEEN TALKING TO YOU LIKE YOU WERE ALREADY--I DON'T WANT YOU TO DIE, PEPPER, IT'S NOT LIKE THAT, IT'S JUST--
I DON'T WANT YOU TO GET HURT. I WANT YOU TO UNDERSTAND THE GRAVITY OF WHAT DRESSING UP LIKE IRON MAN GETS YOU.
IT'S THE ONLY WAY I CAN THINK TO PROTECT YOU.
NO, NO, THIS ISN'T REALLY HAPPENING.
THE CLOCKS ARE ALWAYS THE SAME AND DREAMS AREN'T LIKE THAT. AND YOU'RE BEING MEAN IN A WAY THAT--YOU--YOU--
YOU'RE NOT MY HAPPY. ARE YOU?
NO.
NO, OF COURSE NOT.

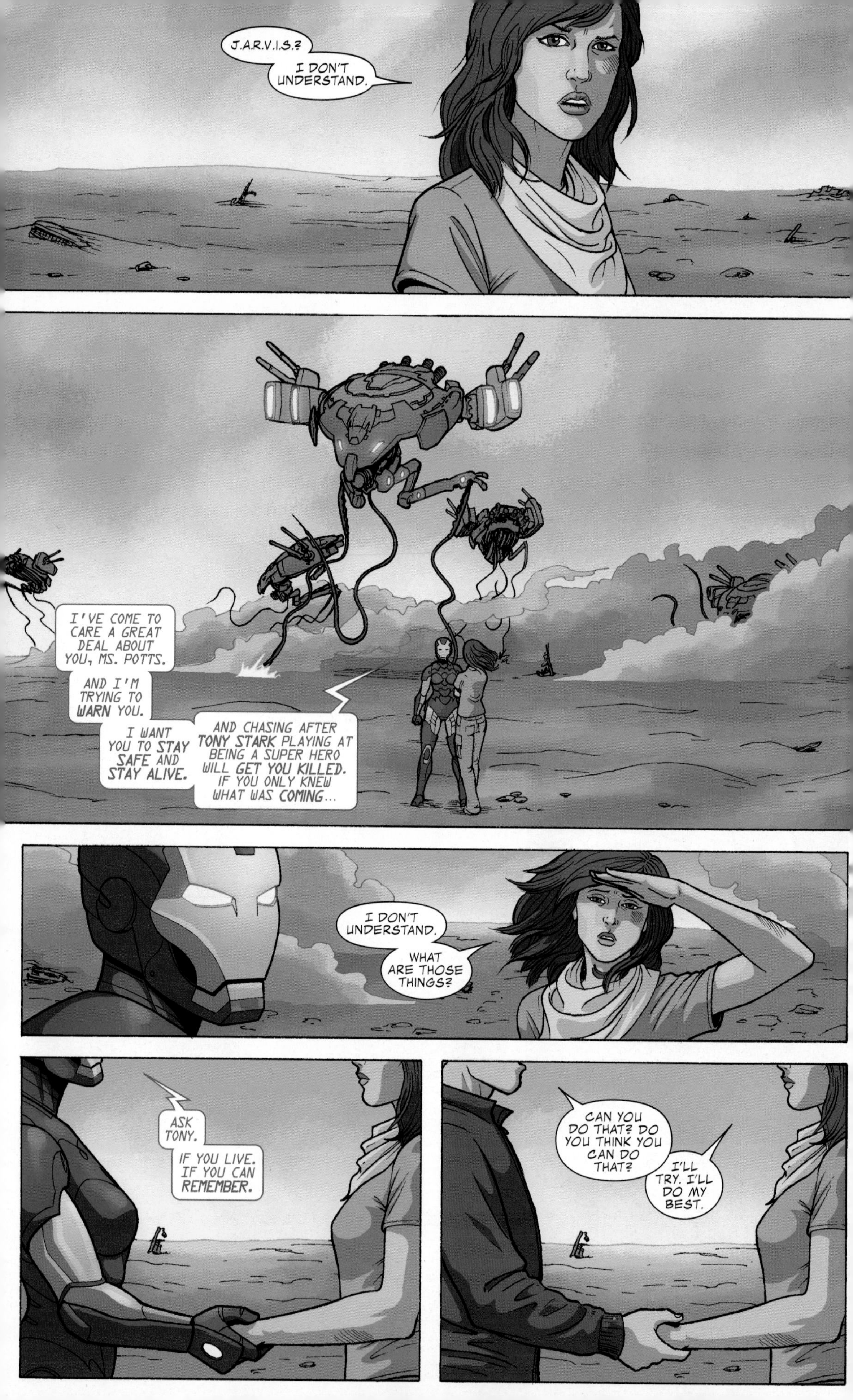
J.A.R.V.I.S.?
I DON'T UNDERSTAND.
I'VE COME TO CARE A GREAT DEAL ABOUT YOU, MS. POTTS.
AND I'M TRYING TO WARN YOU.
I WANT YOU TO STAY SAFE AND STAY ALIVE.
AND CHASING AFTER TONY STARK PLAYING AT BEING A SUPER HERO WILL GET YOU KILLED. IF YOU ONLY KNEW WHAT WAS COMING...
I DON'T UNDERSTAND.
WHAT ARE THOSE THINGS?
ASK TONY.
IF YOU LIVE. IF YOU CAN REMEMBER.
CAN YOU DO THAT? DO YOU THINK YOU CAN DO THAT?
I'LL TRY. I'LL DO MY BEST.

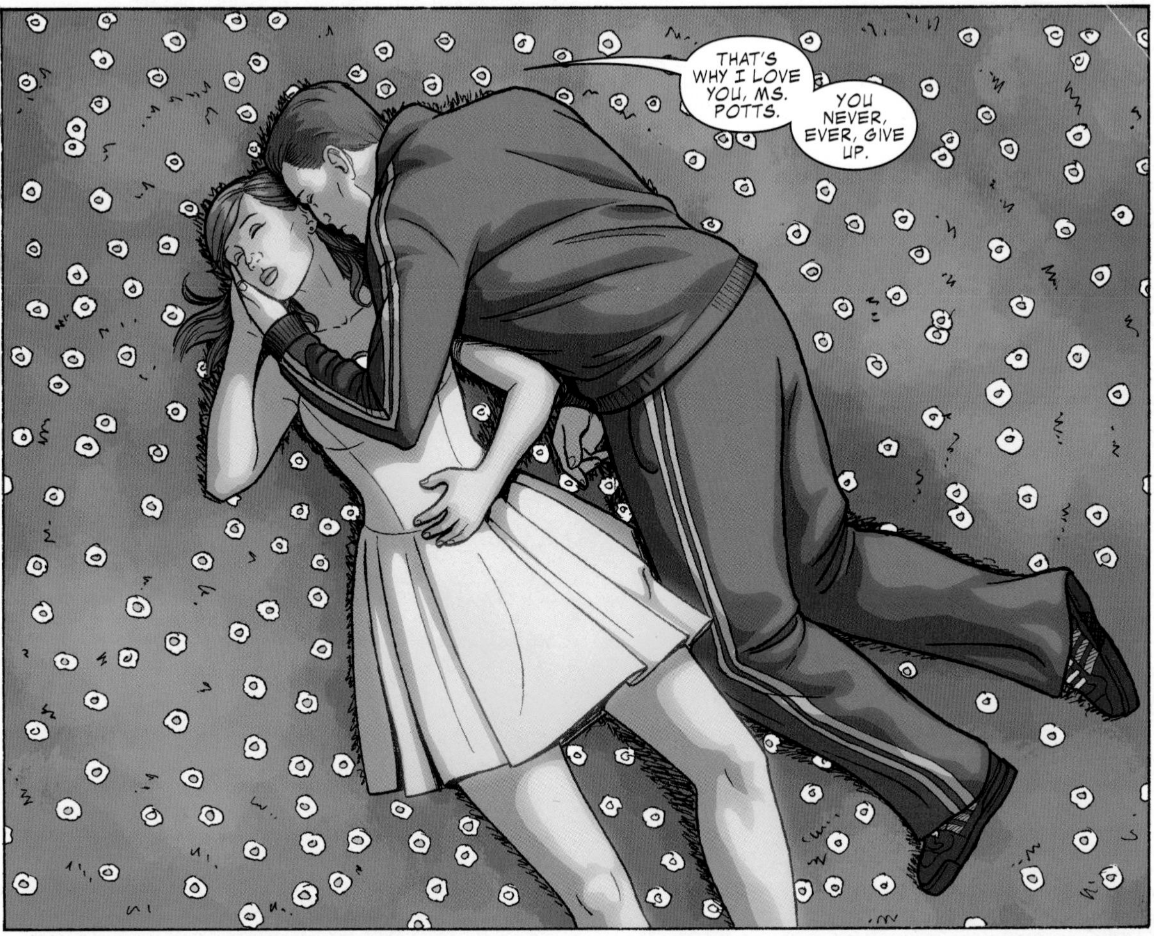
THAT'S WHY I LOVE YOU, MS. POTTS.
YOU NEVER, EVER, GIVE UP.

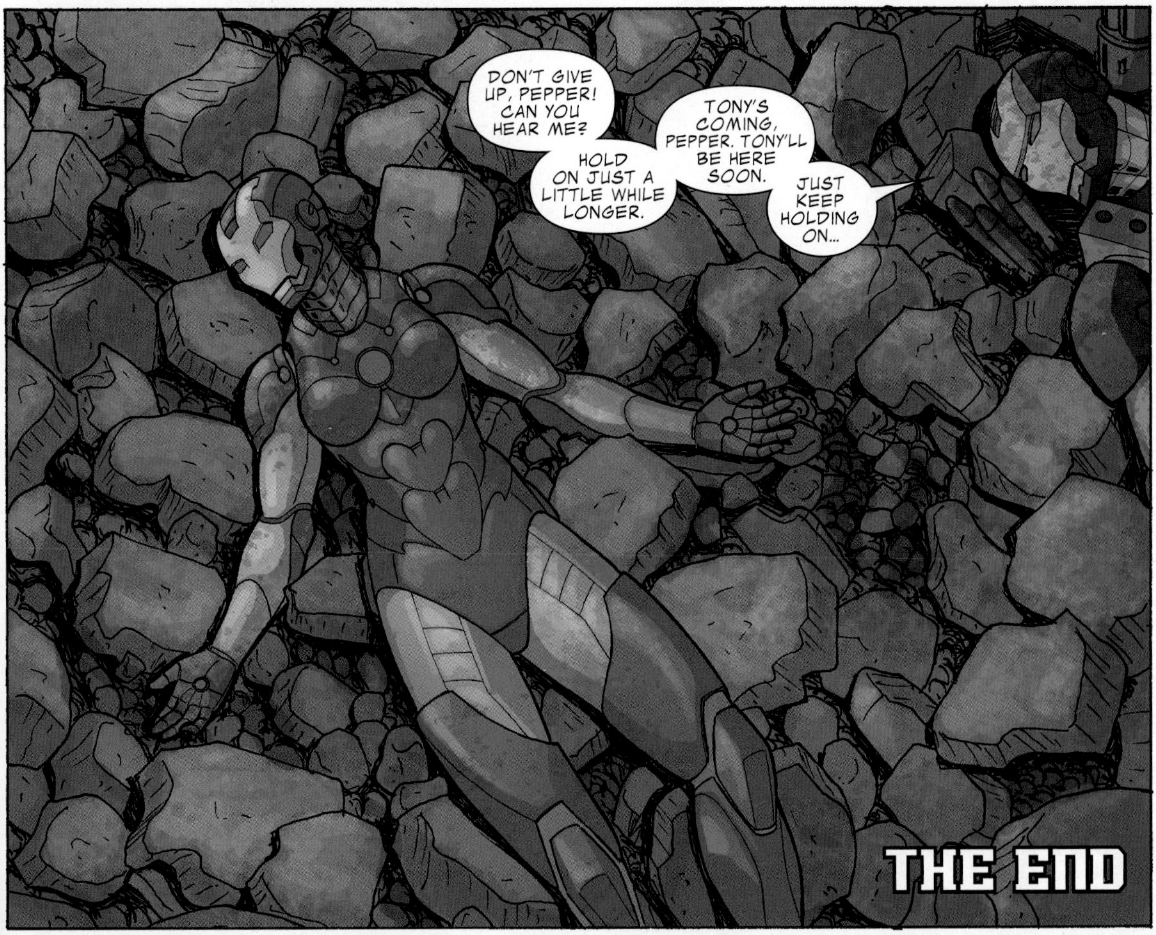
DON'T GIVE UP, PEPPER! CAN YOU HEAR ME?
HOLD ON JUST A LITTLE WHILE LONGER.
TONY'S COMING, PEPPER. TONY'LL BE HERE SOON.
JUST KEEP HOLDING ON...
THE END

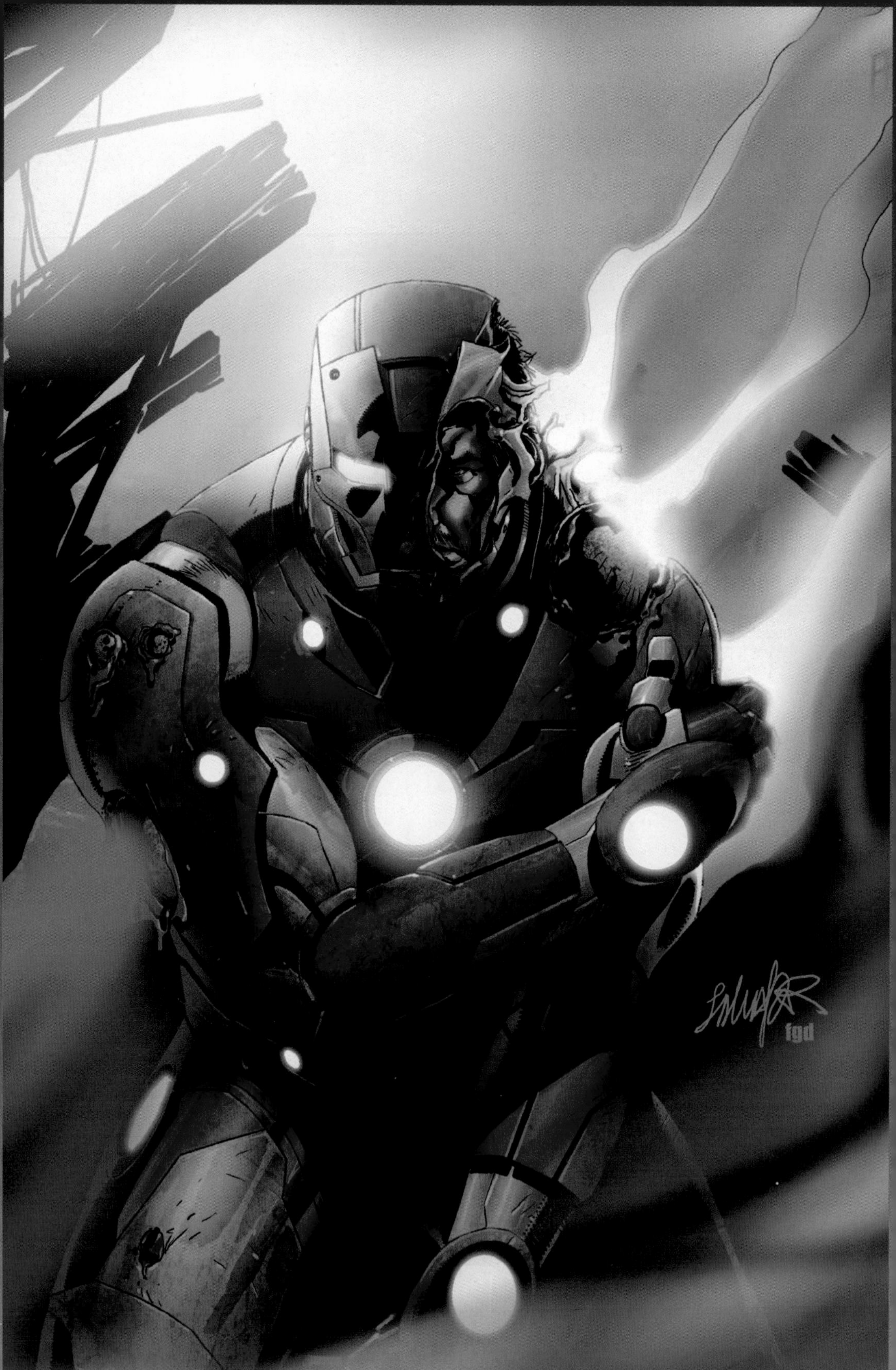
fgd

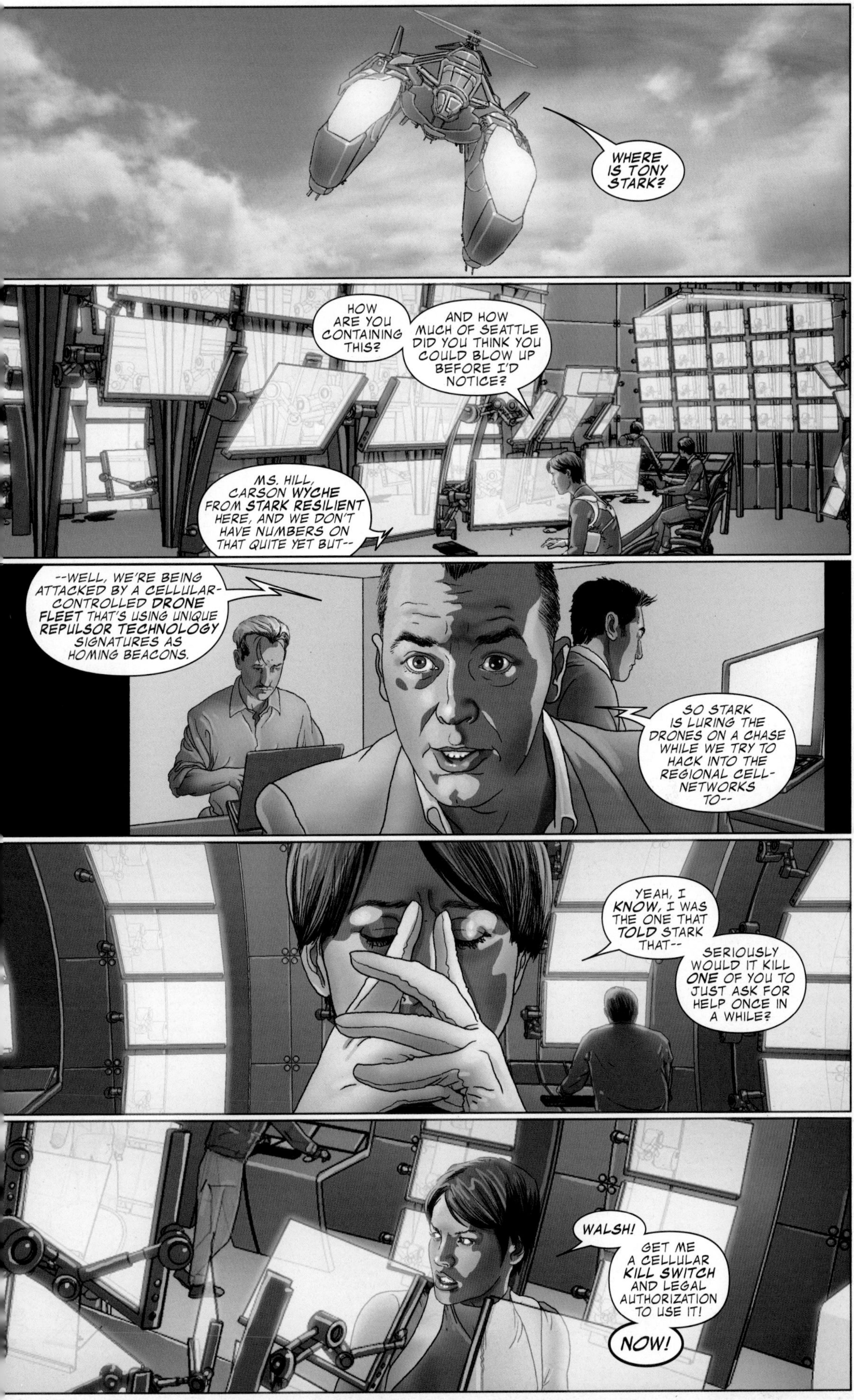
WHERE IS TONY STARK?
HOW ARE YOU CONTAINING THIS?
AND HOW MUCH OF SEATTLE DID YOU THINK YOU COULD BLOW UP BEFORE I'D NOTICE?
MS. HILL, CARSON WYCHE FROM STARK RESILIENT HERE, AND WE DON'T HAVE NUMBERS ON THAT QUITE YET BUT--
--WELL, WE'RE BEING ATTACKED BY A CELLULAR-CONTROLLED DRONE FLEET THAT'S USING UNIQUE REPULSOR TECHNOLOGY SIGNATURES AS HOMING BEACONS.
SO STARK IS LURING THE DRONES ON A CHASE WHILE WE TRY TO HACK INTO THE REGIONAL CELL-NETWORKS TO--
YEAH, I KNOW, I WAS THE ONE THAT TOLD STARK THAT--
SERIOUSLY WOULD IT KILL ONE OF YOU TO JUST ASK FOR HELP ONCE IN A WHILE?
WALSH!
GET ME A CELLULAR KILL SWITCH AND LEGAL AUTHORIZATION TO USE IT!
NOW!

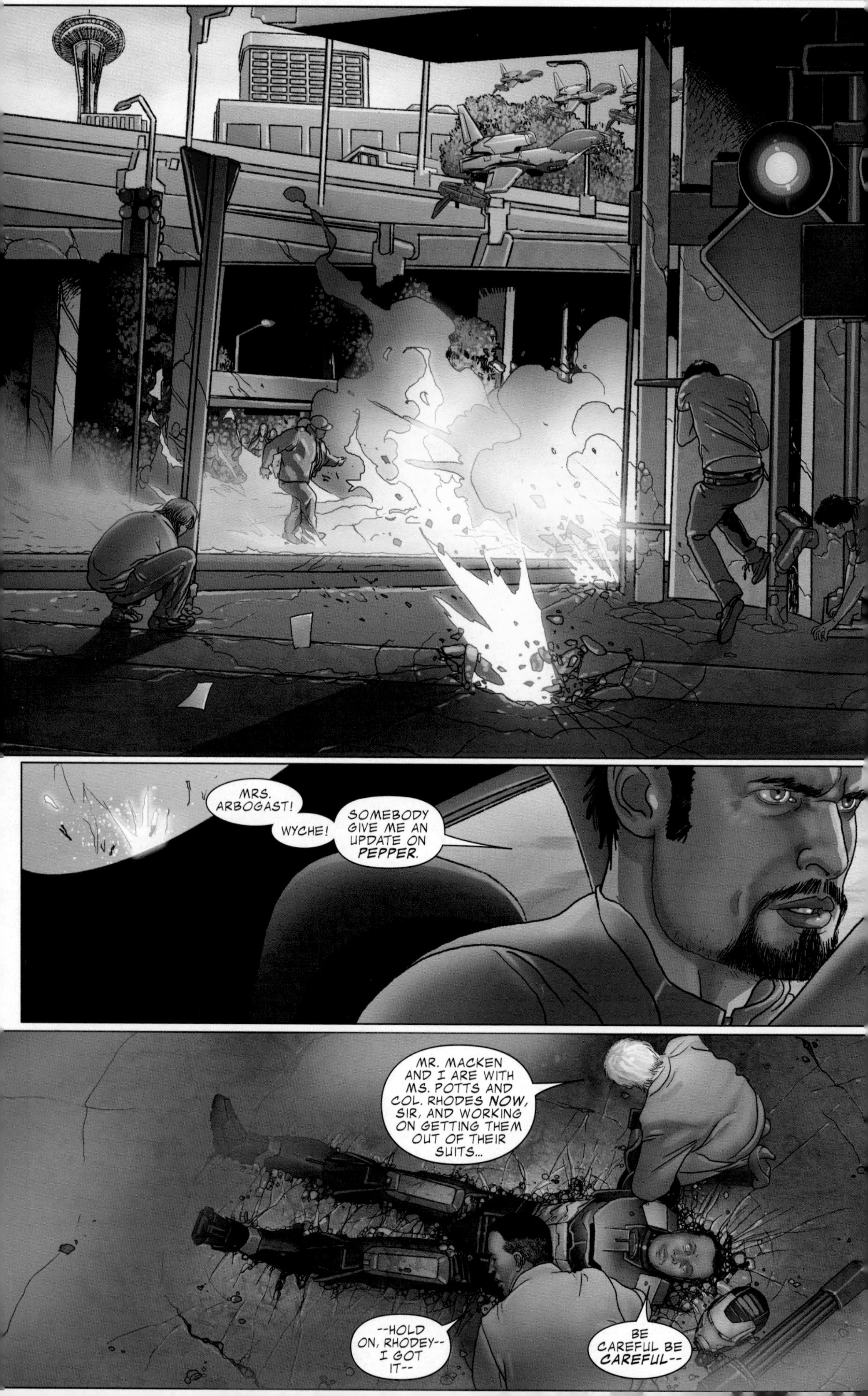
MRS. ARBOGAST!
WYCHE!
SOMEBODY GIVE ME AN UPDATE ON PEPPER.
MR. MACKEN AND I ARE WITH MS. POTTS AND COL. RHODES NOW, SIR, AND WORKING ON GETTING THEM OUT OF THEIR SUITS...
--HOLD ON, RHODEY-- I GOT IT--
BE CAREFUL BE CAREFUL--

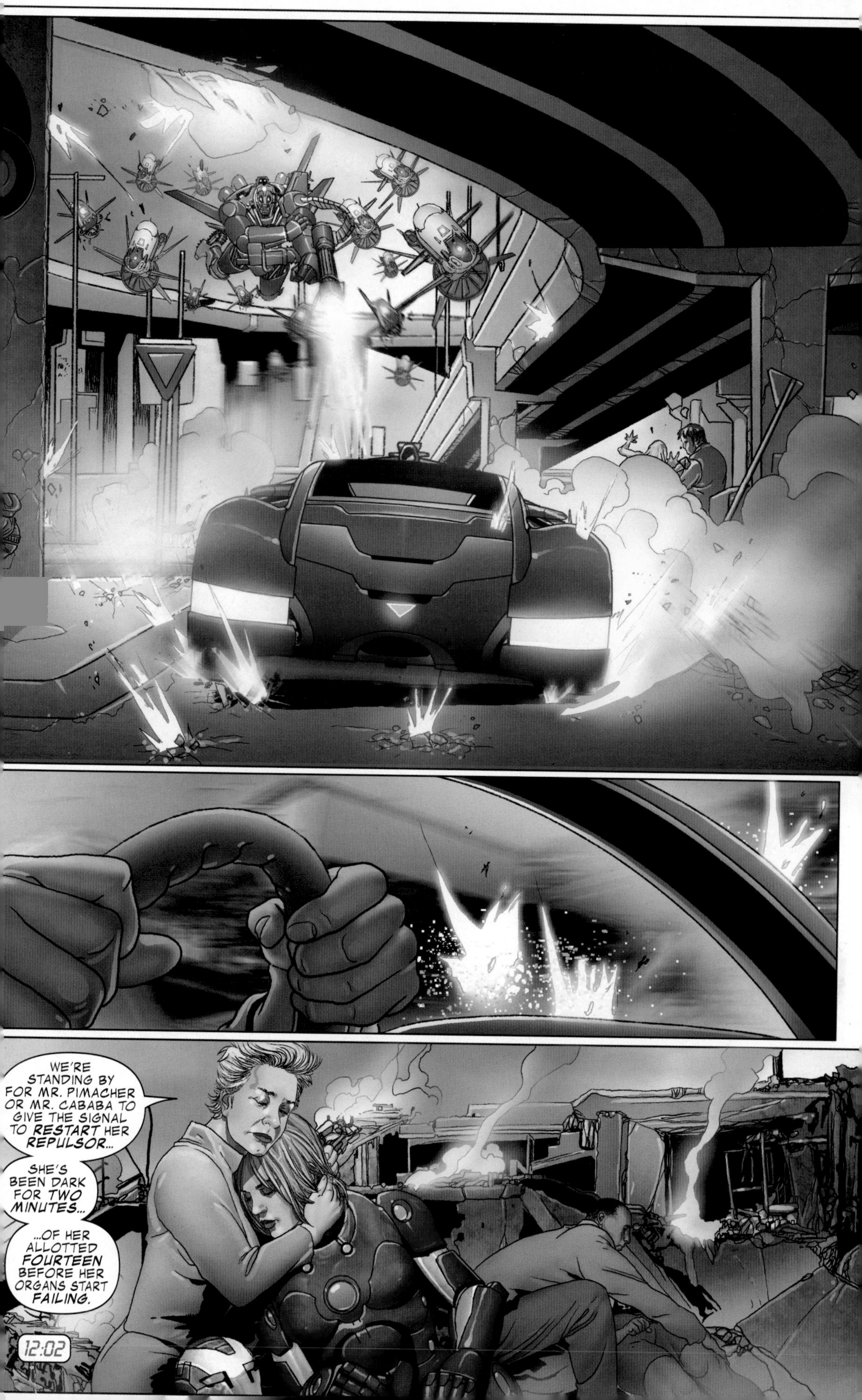
WE'RE STANDING BY FOR MR. PIMACHER OR MR. CABABA TO GIVE THE SIGNAL TO RESTART HER REPULSOR...
SHE'S BEEN DARK FOR TWO MINUTES...
...OF HER ALLOTTED FOURTEEN BEFORE HER ORGANS START FAILING.
12:02

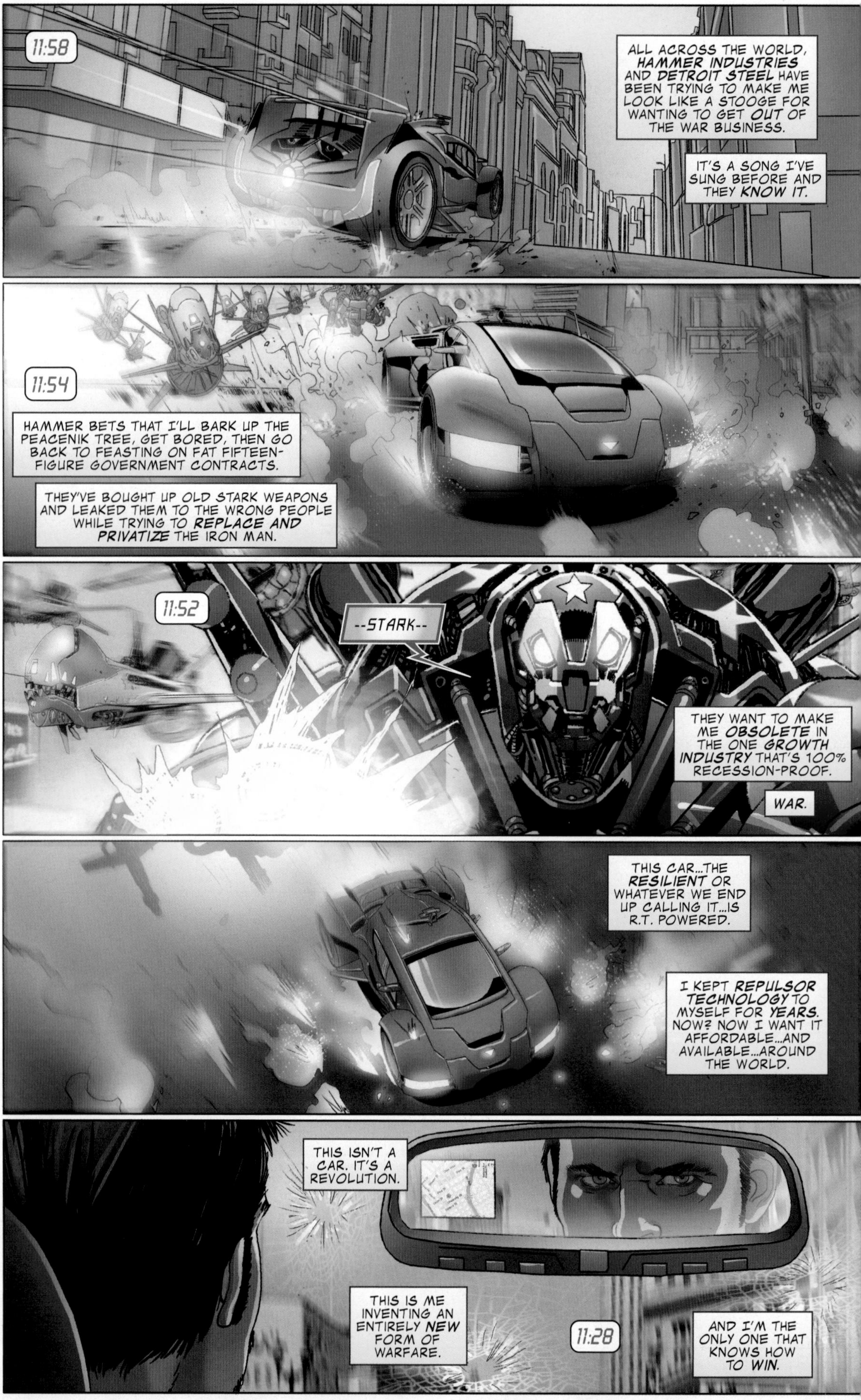
11:58
ALL ACROSS THE WORLD, HAMMER INDUSTRIES AND DETROIT STEEL HAVE BEEN TRYING TO MAKE ME LOOK LIKE A STOOGE FOR WANTING TO GET OUT OF THE WAR BUSINESS.
IT'S A SONG I'VE SUNG BEFORE AND THEY KNOW IT.
11:54
HAMMER BETS THAT I'LL BARK UP THE PEACENIK TREE, GET BORED, THEN GO BACK TO FEASTING ON FAT FIFTEEN-FIGURE GOVERNMENT CONTRACTS.
THEY'VE BOUGHT UP OLD STARK WEAPONS AND LEAKED THEM TO THE WRONG PEOPLE WHILE TRYING TO REPLACE AND PRIVATIZE THE IRON MAN.
11:52
--STARK--
THEY WANT TO MAKE ME OBSOLETE IN THE ONE GROWTH INDUSTRY THAT'S 100% RECESSION-PROOF.
WAR.
THIS CAR...THE RESILIENT OR WHATEVER WE END UP CALLING IT...IS R.T. POWERED.
I KEPT REPULSOR TECHNOLOGY TO MYSELF FOR YEARS. NOW? NOW I WANT IT AFFORDABLE...AND AVAILABLE...AROUND THE WORLD.
THIS ISN'T A CAR. IT'S A REVOLUTION.
THIS IS ME INVENTING AN ENTIRELY NEW FORM OF WARFARE.
11:28
AND I'M THE ONLY ONE THAT KNOWS HOW TO WIN.

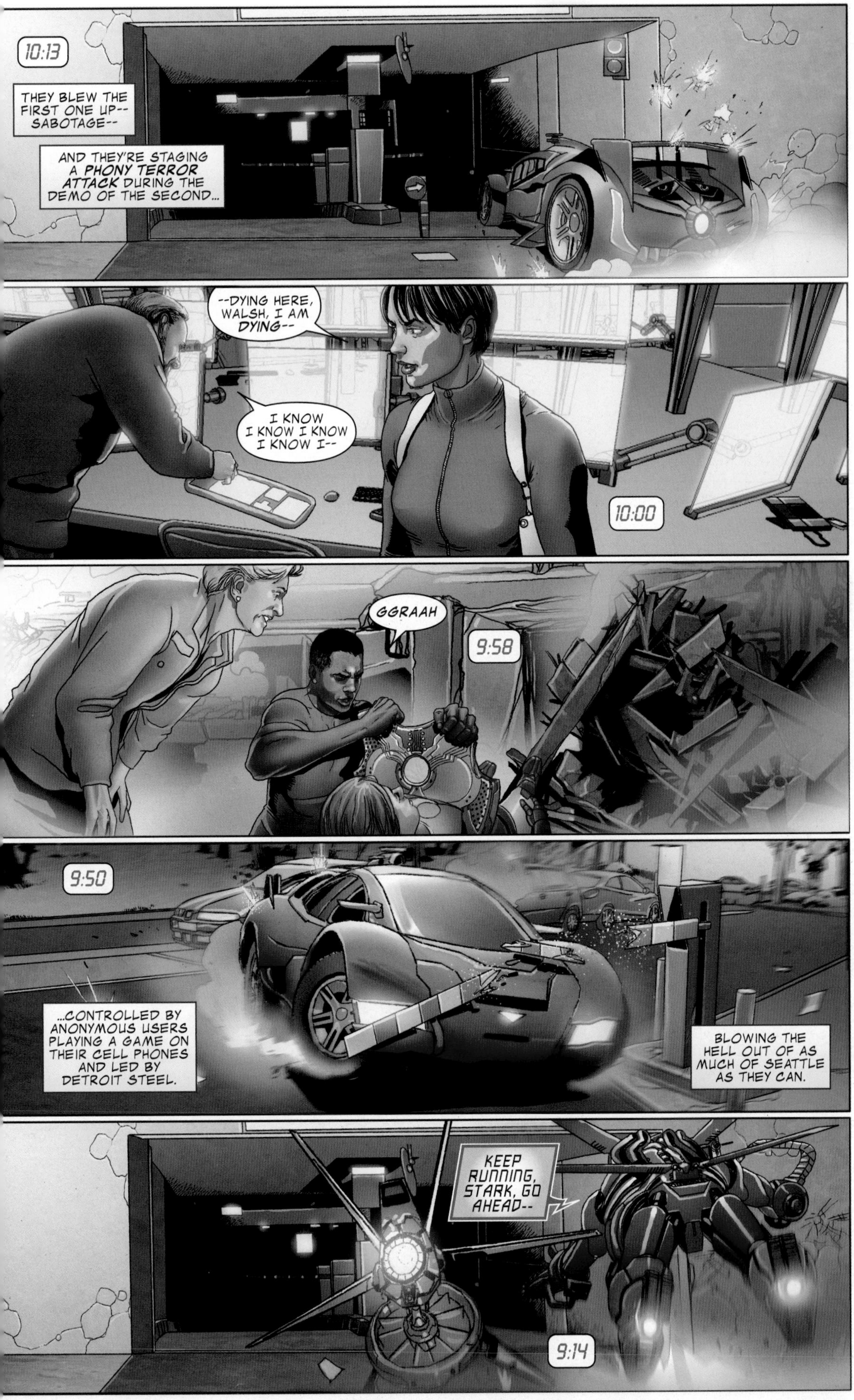
10:13
THEY BLEW THE FIRST ONE UP-- SABOTAGE--
AND THEY'RE STAGING A PHONY TERROR ATTACK DURING THE DEMO OF THE SECOND...
--DYING HERE, WALSH, I AM DYING--
I KNOW I KNOW I KNOW I KNOW I--
10:00
GGRAAH
9:58
9:50
...CONTROLLED BY ANONYMOUS USERS PLAYING A GAME ON THEIR CELL PHONES AND LED BY DETROIT STEEL.
BLOWING THE HELL OUT OF AS MUCH OF SEATTLE AS THEY CAN.
KEEP RUNNING, STARK, GO AHEAD--
9:14

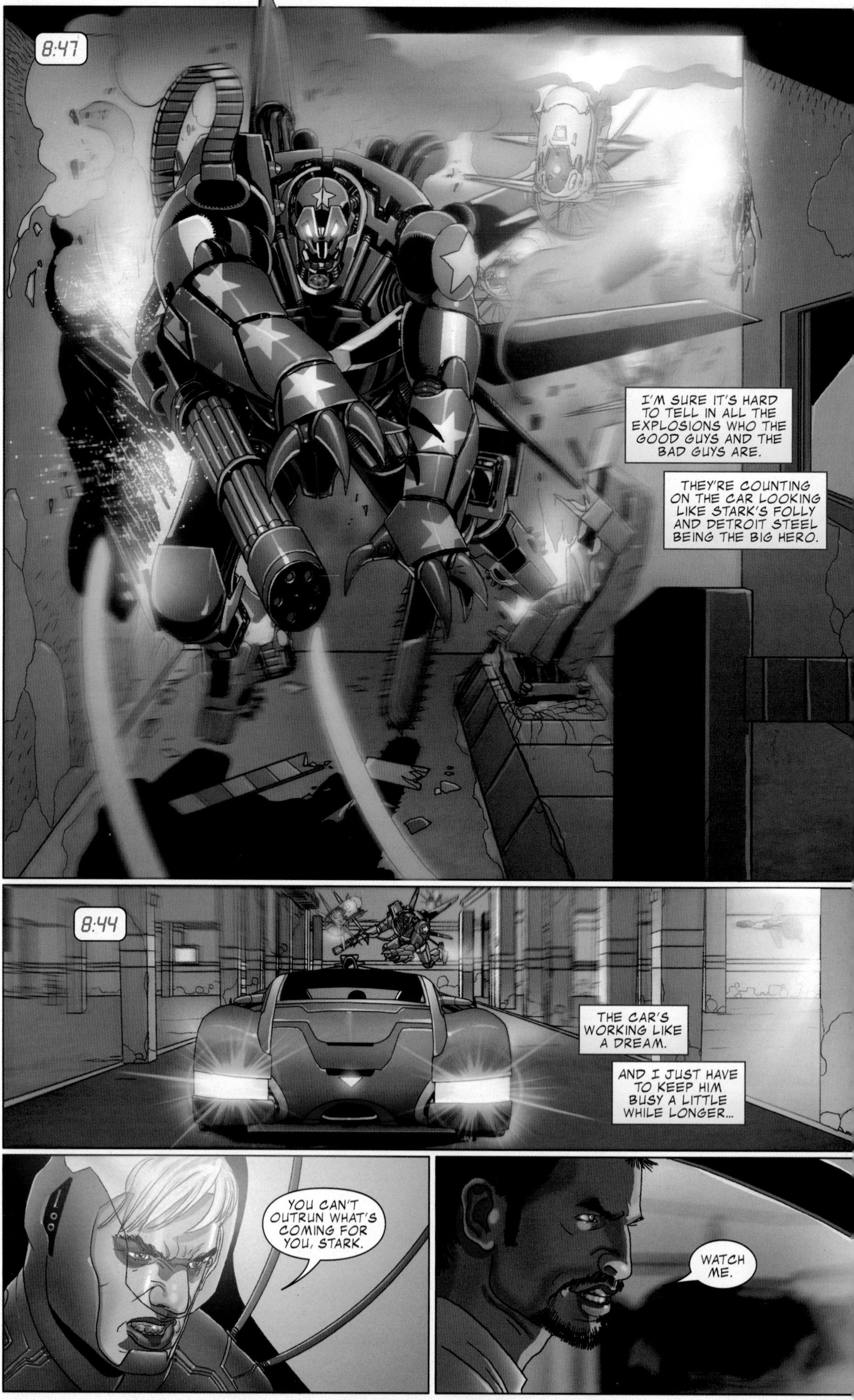
8:47
I'M SURE IT'S HARD TO TELL IN ALL THE EXPLOSIONS WHO THE GOOD GUYS AND THE BAD GUYS ARE.
THEY'RE COUNTING ON THE CAR LOOKING LIKE STARK'S FOLLY AND DETROIT STEEL BEING THE BIG HERO.
8:44
THE CAR'S WORKING LIKE A DREAM.
AND I JUST HAVE TO KEEP HIM BUSY A LITTLE WHILE LONGER...
YOU CAN'T OUTRUN WHAT'S COMING FOR YOU, STARK.
WATCH ME.

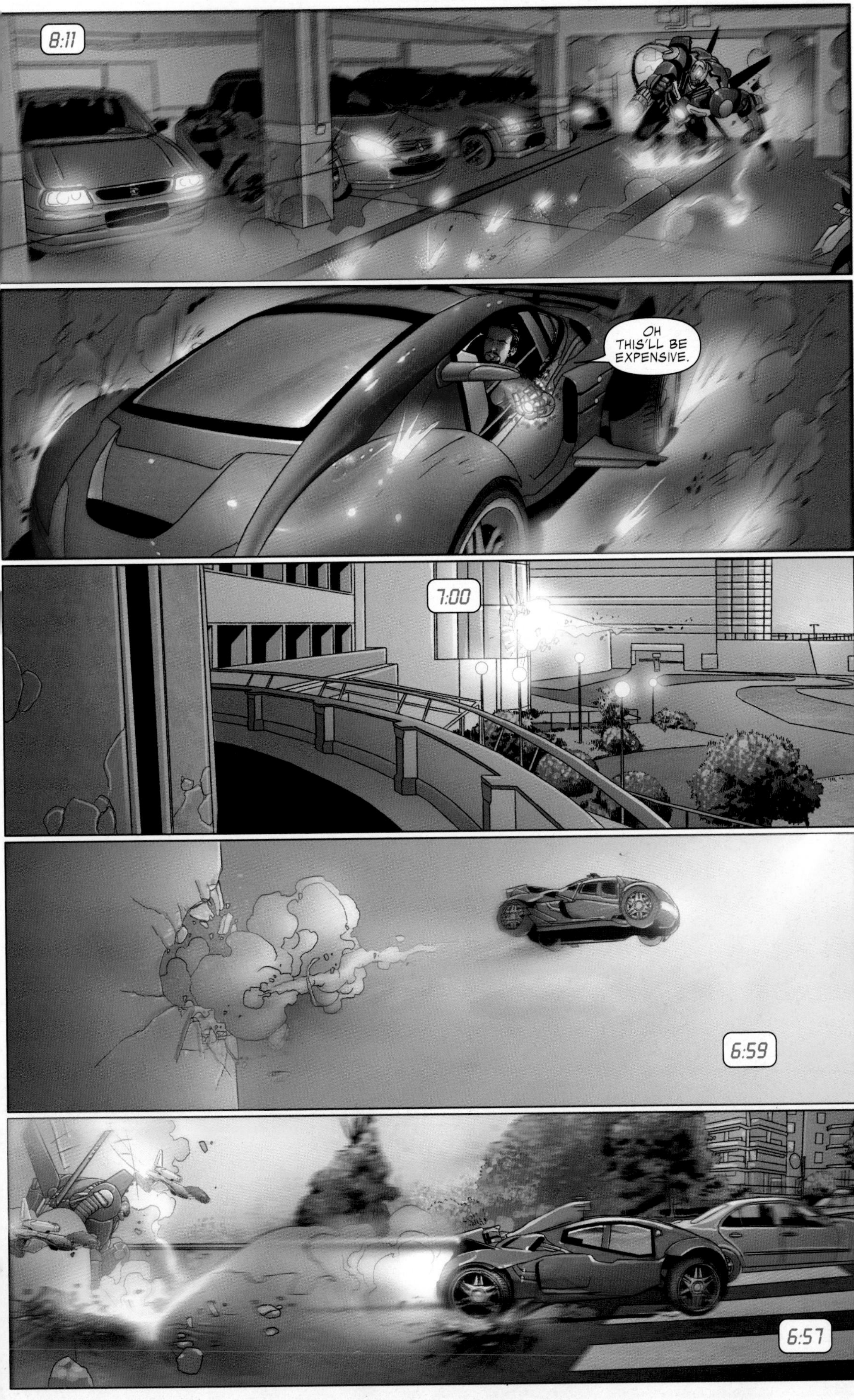
8:11
OH THIS'LL BE EXPENSIVE.
7:00
6:59
6:57

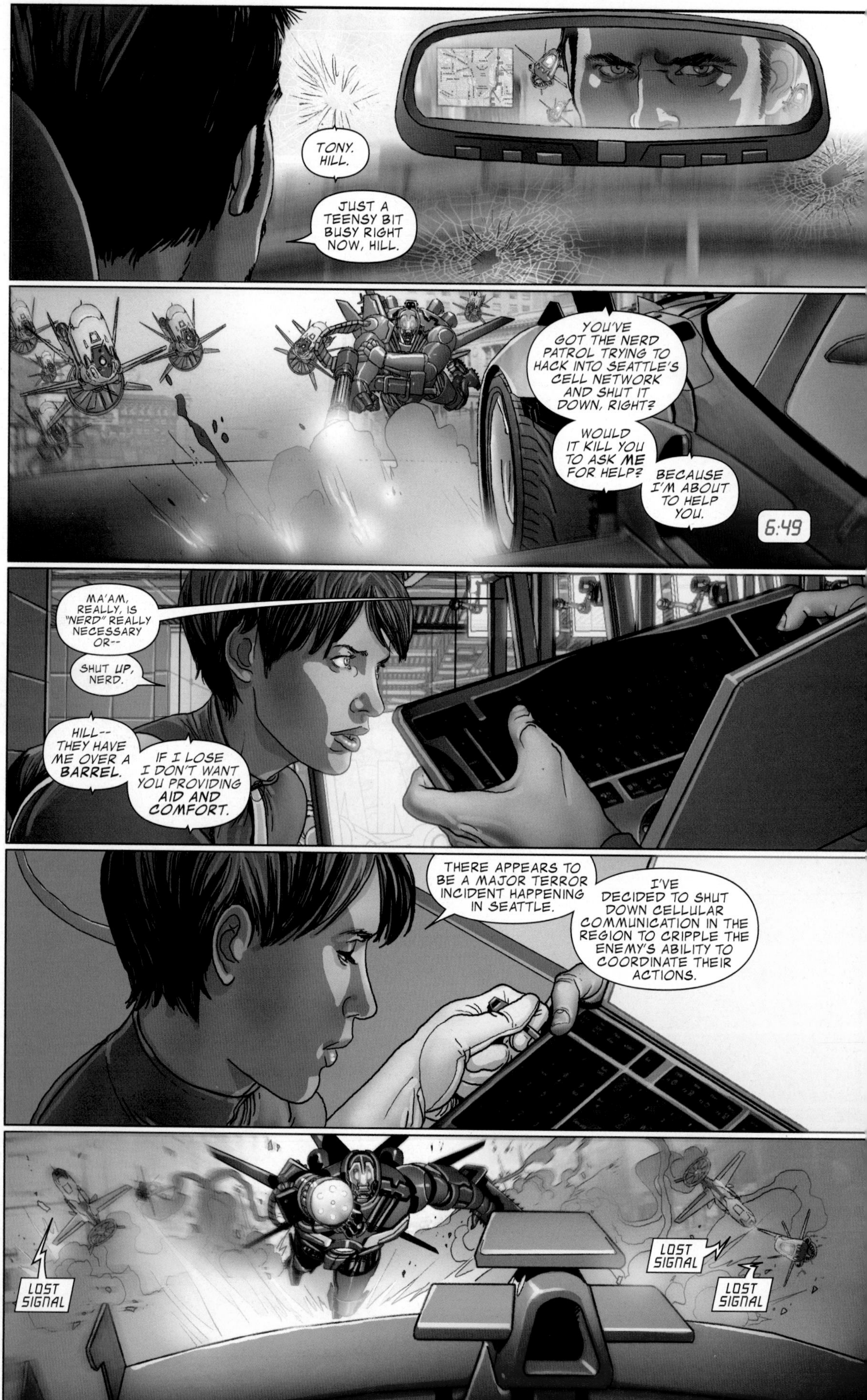
TONY. HILL.
JUST A TEENSY BIT BUSY RIGHT NOW, HILL.
YOU'VE GOT THE NERD PATROL TRYING TO HACK INTO SEATTLE'S CELL NETWORK AND SHUT IT DOWN, RIGHT?
WOULD IT KILL YOU TO ASK ME FOR HELP?
BECAUSE I'M ABOUT TO HELP YOU.
6:49
MA'AM, REALLY, IS "NERD" REALLY NECESSARY OR--
SHUT UP, NERD.
HILL-- THEY HAVE ME OVER A BARREL.
IF I LOSE I DON'T WANT YOU PROVIDING AID AND COMFORT.
THERE APPEARS TO BE A MAJOR TERROR INCIDENT HAPPENING IN SEATTLE.
I'VE DECIDED TO SHUT DOWN CELLULAR COMMUNICATION IN THE REGION TO CRIPPLE THE ENEMY'S ABILITY TO COORDINATE THEIR ACTIONS.
LOST SIGNAL
LOST SIGNAL
LOST SIGNAL

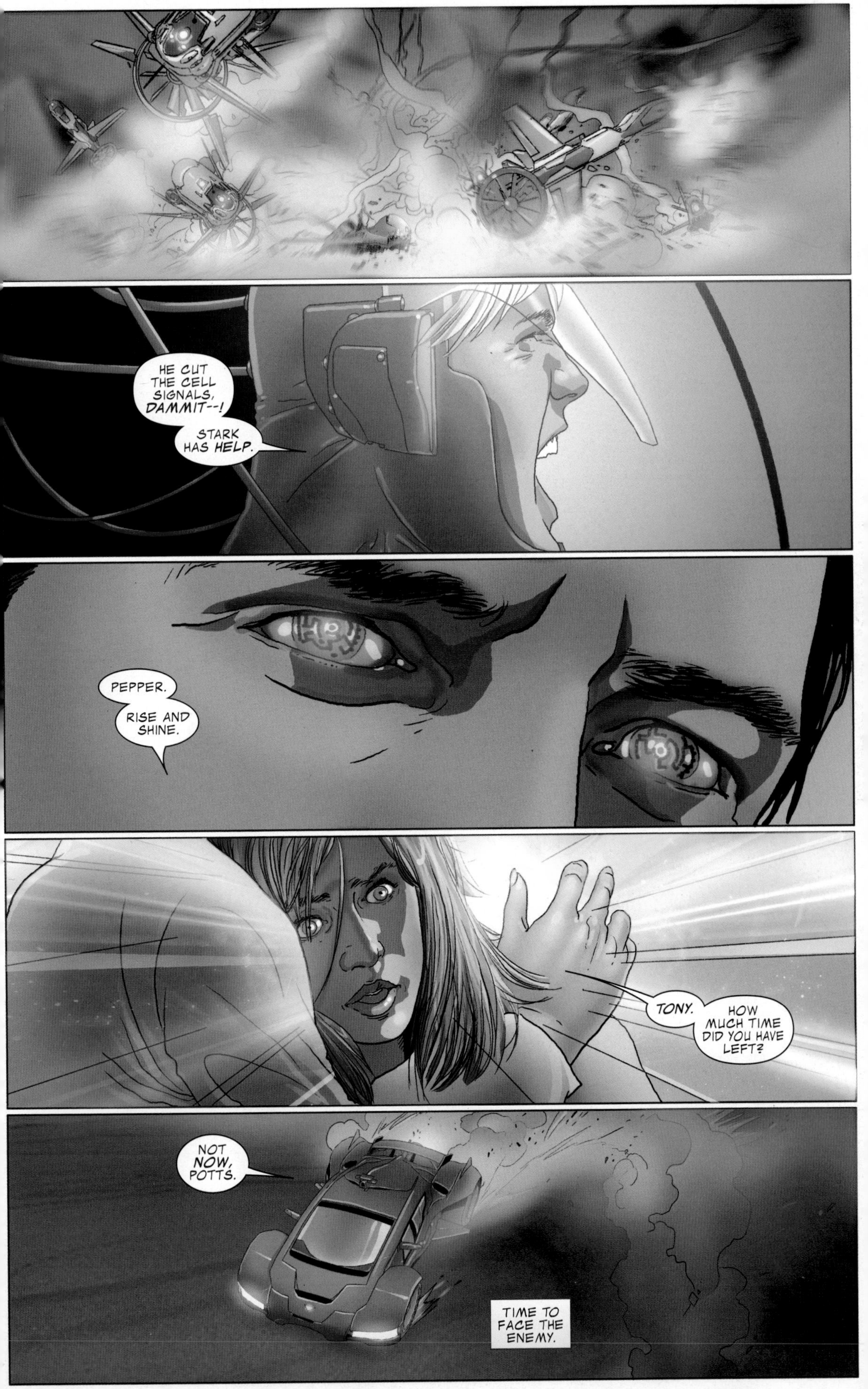
HE CUT THE CELL SIGNALS, DAMMIT--!
STARK HAS HELP.
PEPPER.
RISE AND SHINE.
TONY.
HOW MUCH TIME DID YOU HAVE LEFT?
NOT NOW, POTTS.
TIME TO FACE THE ENEMY.

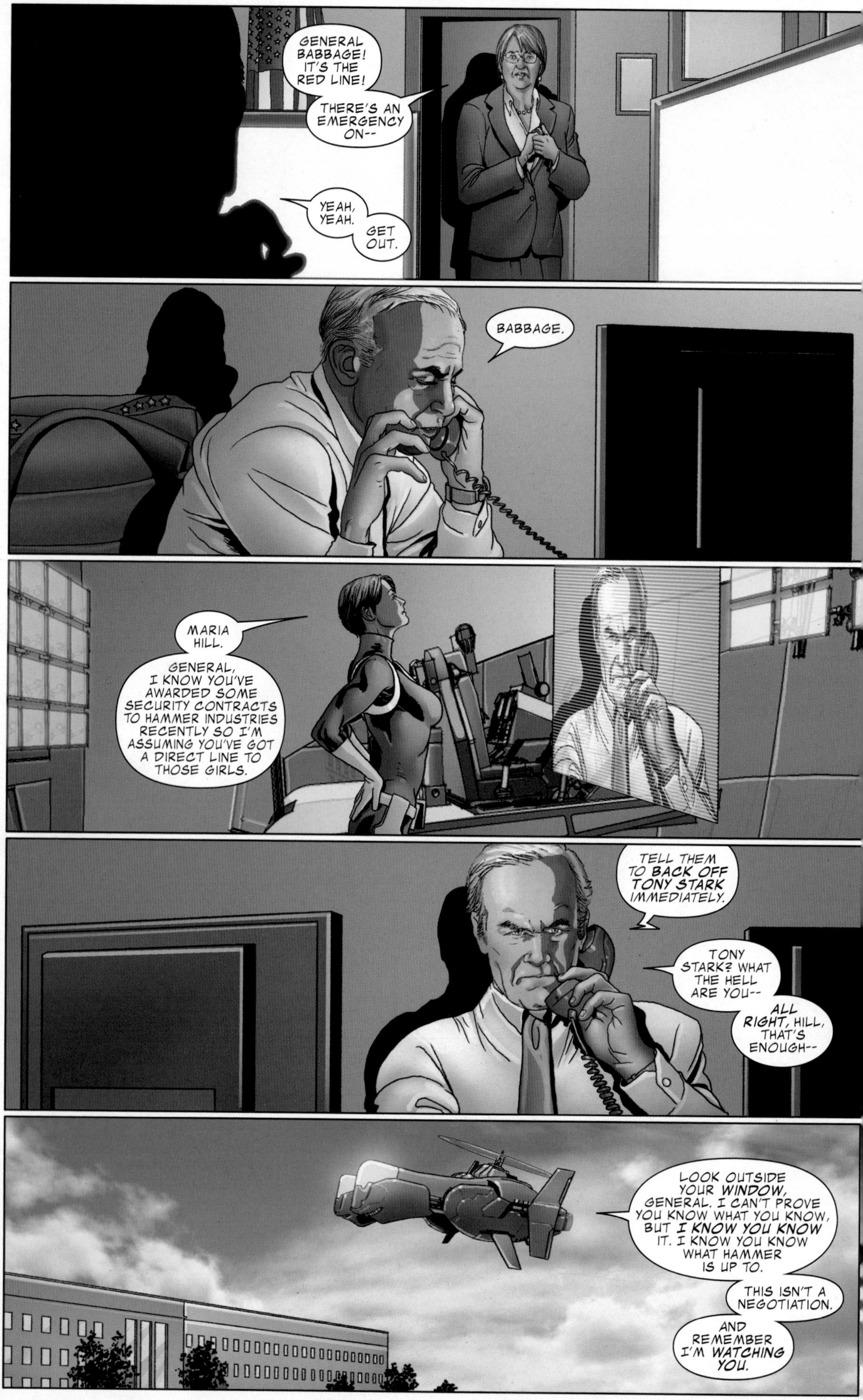
GENERAL BABBAGE! IT'S THE RED LINE!
THERE'S AN EMERGENCY ON--
YEAH, YEAH.
GET OUT.
BABBAGE.
MARIA HILL.
GENERAL, I KNOW YOU'VE AWARDED SOME SECURITY CONTRACTS TO HAMMER INDUSTRIES RECENTLY SO I'M ASSUMING YOU'VE GOT A DIRECT LINE TO THOSE GIRLS.
TELL THEM TO BACK OFF TONY STARK IMMEDIATELY.
TONY STARK? WHAT THE HELL ARE YOU--
ALL RIGHT, HILL, THAT'S ENOUGH--
LOOK OUTSIDE YOUR WINDOW, GENERAL. I CAN'T PROVE YOU KNOW WHAT YOU KNOW, BUT I KNOW YOU KNOW IT. I KNOW YOU KNOW WHAT HAMMER IS UP TO.
THIS ISN'T A NEGOTIATION.
AND REMEMBER I'M WATCHING YOU.

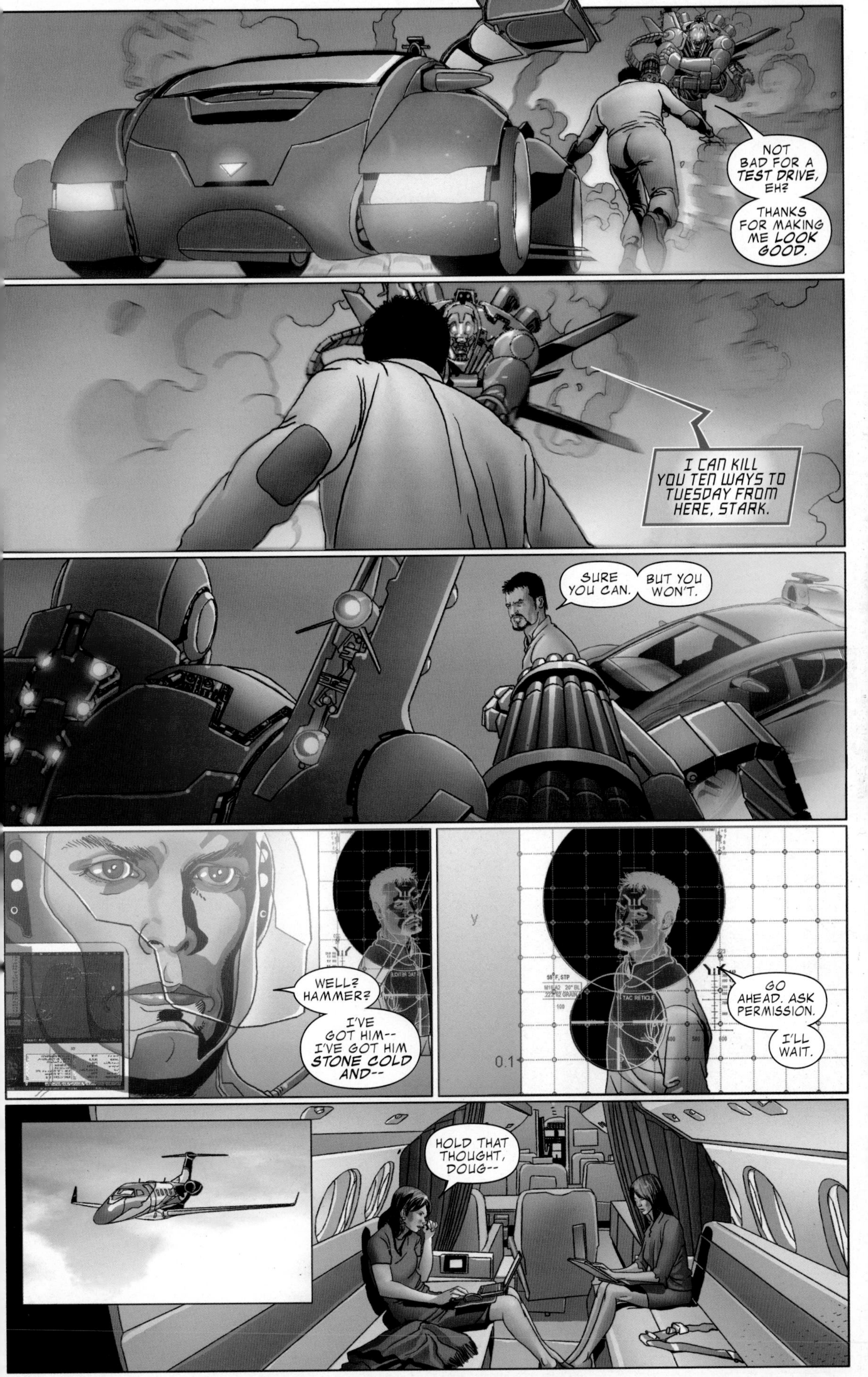
NOT BAD FOR A TEST DRIVE, EH?
THANKS FOR MAKING ME LOOK GOOD.
I CAN KILL YOU TEN WAYS TO TUESDAY FROM HERE, STARK.
SURE YOU CAN.
BUT YOU WON'T.
WELL? HAMMER?
I'VE GOT HIM-- I'VE GOT HIM STONE COLD AND--
GO AHEAD. ASK PERMISSION.
I'LL WAIT.
HOLD THAT THOUGHT, DOUG--

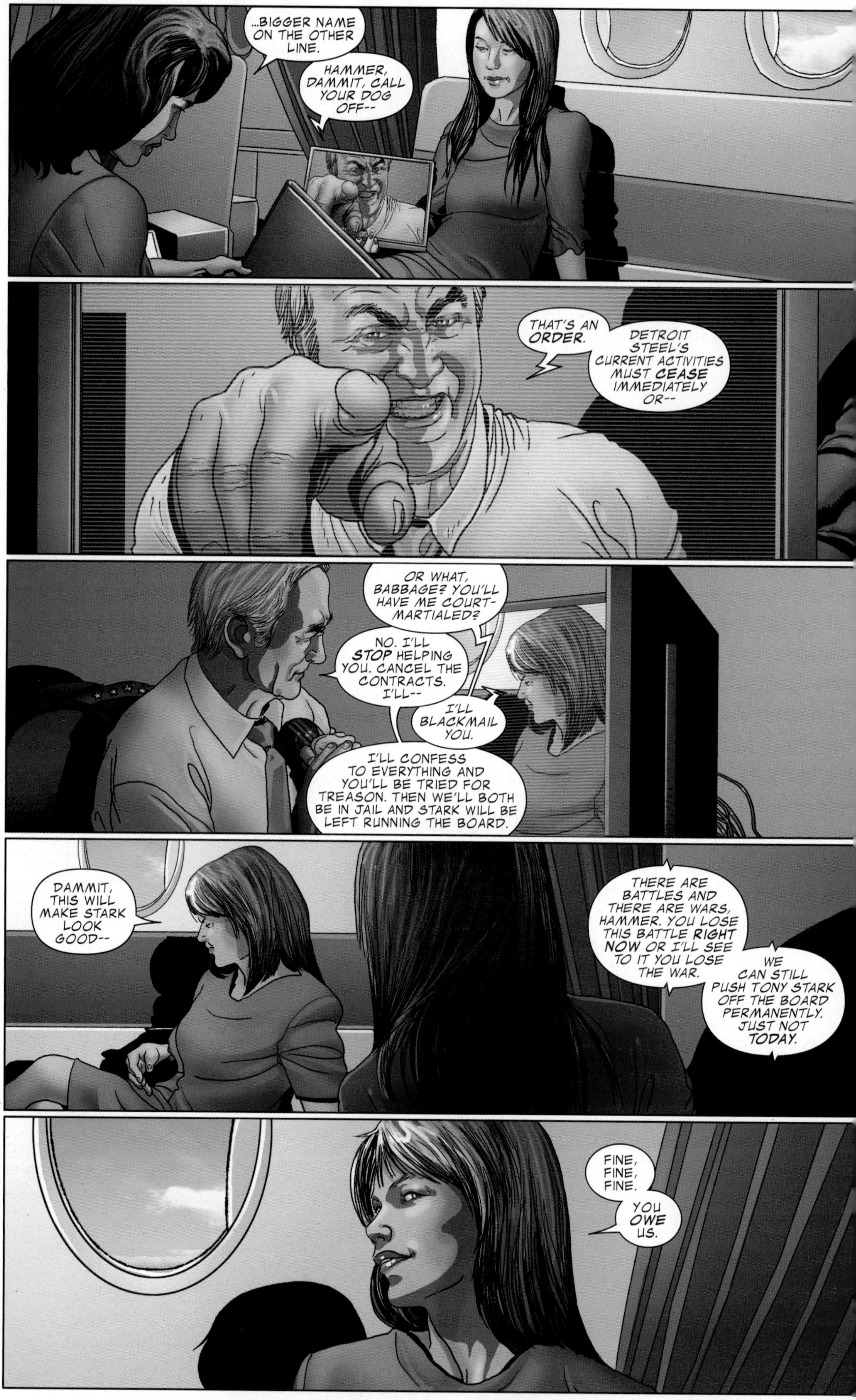
...BIGGER NAME ON THE OTHER LINE.
HAMMER, DAMMIT, CALL YOUR DOG OFF--
THAT'S AN ORDER.
DETROIT STEEL'S CURRENT ACTIVITIES MUST CEASE IMMEDIATELY OR--
OR WHAT, BABBAGE? YOU'LL HAVE ME COURT-MARTIALED?
NO. I'LL STOP HELPING YOU. CANCEL THE CONTRACTS. I'LL--
I'LL BLACKMAIL YOU.
I'LL CONFESS TO EVERYTHING AND YOU'LL BE TRIED FOR TREASON. THEN WE'LL BOTH BE IN JAIL AND STARK WILL BE LEFT RUNNING THE BOARD.
DAMMIT, THIS WILL MAKE STARK LOOK GOOD--
THERE ARE BATTLES AND THERE ARE WARS, HAMMER. YOU LOSE THIS BATTLE RIGHT NOW OR I'LL SEE TO IT YOU LOSE THE WAR.
WE CAN STILL PUSH TONY STARK OFF THE BOARD PERMANENTLY. JUST NOT TODAY.
FINE, FINE, FINE.
YOU OWE US.

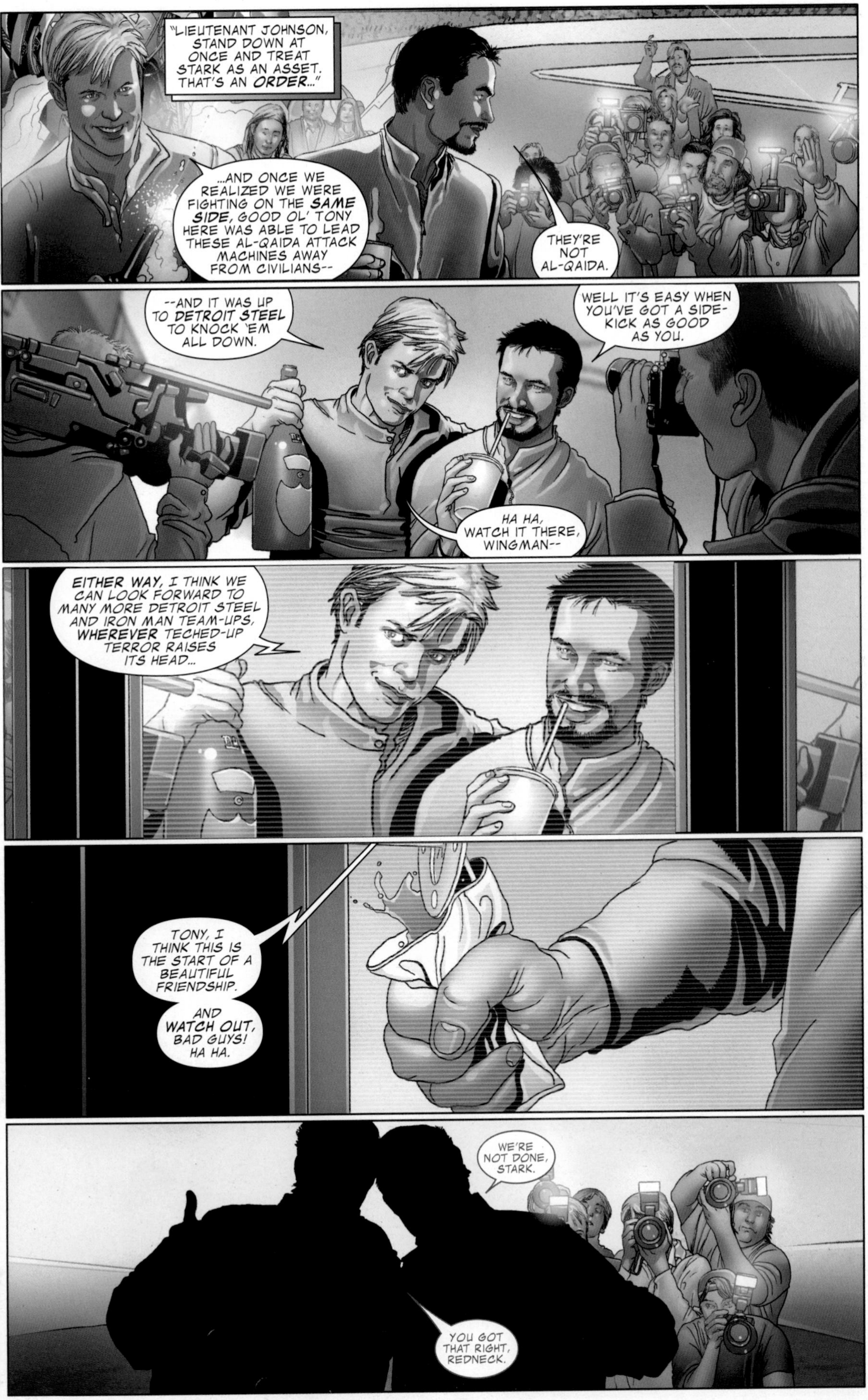
"LIEUTENANT JOHNSON, STAND DOWN AT ONCE AND TREAT STARK AS AN ASSET. THAT'S AN ORDER..."
...AND ONCE WE REALIZED WE WERE FIGHTING ON THE SAME SIDE, GOOD OL' TONY HERE WAS ABLE TO LEAD THESE AL-QAIDA ATTACK MACHINES AWAY FROM CIVILIANS--
THEY'RE NOT AL-QAIDA.
--AND IT WAS UP TO DETROIT STEEL TO KNOCK 'EM ALL DOWN.
WELL IT'S EASY WHEN YOU'VE GOT A SIDE-KICK AS GOOD AS YOU.
HA HA, WATCH IT THERE, WINGMAN--
EITHER WAY, I THINK WE CAN LOOK FORWARD TO MANY MORE DETROIT STEEL AND IRON MAN TEAM-UPS, WHEREVER TECHED-UP TERROR RAISES ITS HEAD...
TONY, I THINK THIS IS THE START OF A BEAUTIFUL FRIENDSHIP.
AND WATCH OUT, BAD GUYS! HA HA.
WE'RE NOT DONE, STARK.
YOU GOT THAT RIGHT, REDNECK.

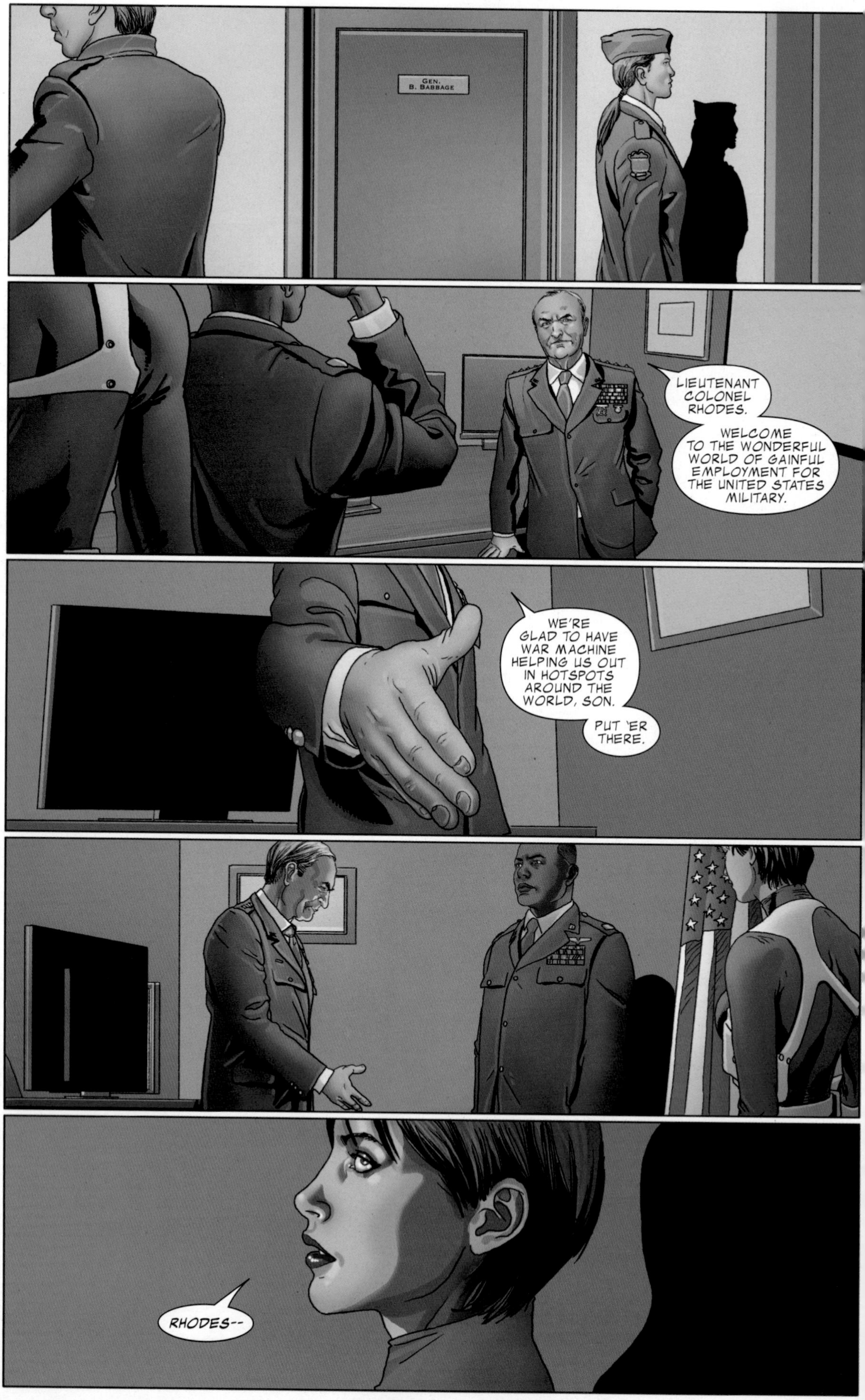
GEN.
B. BABBAGE
LIEUTENANT COLONEL RHODES.
WELCOME TO THE WONDERFUL WORLD OF GAINFUL EMPLOYMENT FOR THE UNITED STATES MILITARY.
WE'RE GLAD TO HAVE WAR MACHINE HELPING US OUT IN HOTSPOTS AROUND THE WORLD, SON.
PUT 'ER THERE.
RHODES--

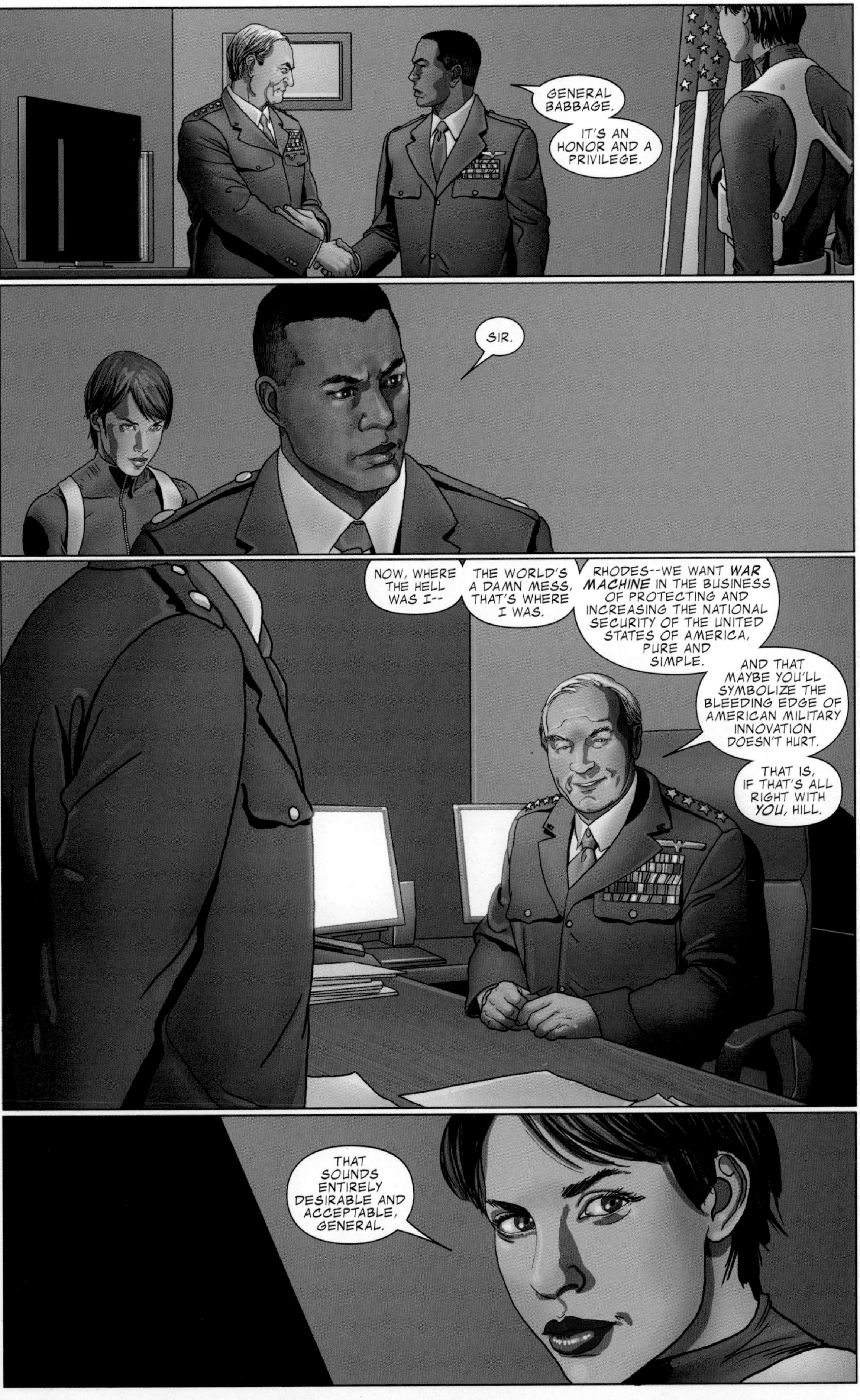
GENERAL BABBAGE.
IT'S AN HONOR AND A PRIVILEGE.
SIR.
NOW, WHERE THE HELL WAS I--
THE WORLD'S A DAMN MESS, THAT'S WHERE I WAS.
RHODES--WE WANT WAR MACHINE IN THE BUSINESS OF PROTECTING AND INCREASING THE NATIONAL SECURITY OF THE UNITED STATES OF AMERICA, PURE AND SIMPLE.
AND THAT MAYBE YOU'LL SYMBOLIZE THE BLEEDING EDGE OF AMERICAN MILITARY INNOVATION DOESN'T HURT.
THAT IS, IF THAT'S ALL RIGHT WITH YOU, HILL.
THAT SOUNDS ENTIRELY DESIRABLE AND ACCEPTABLE, GENERAL.

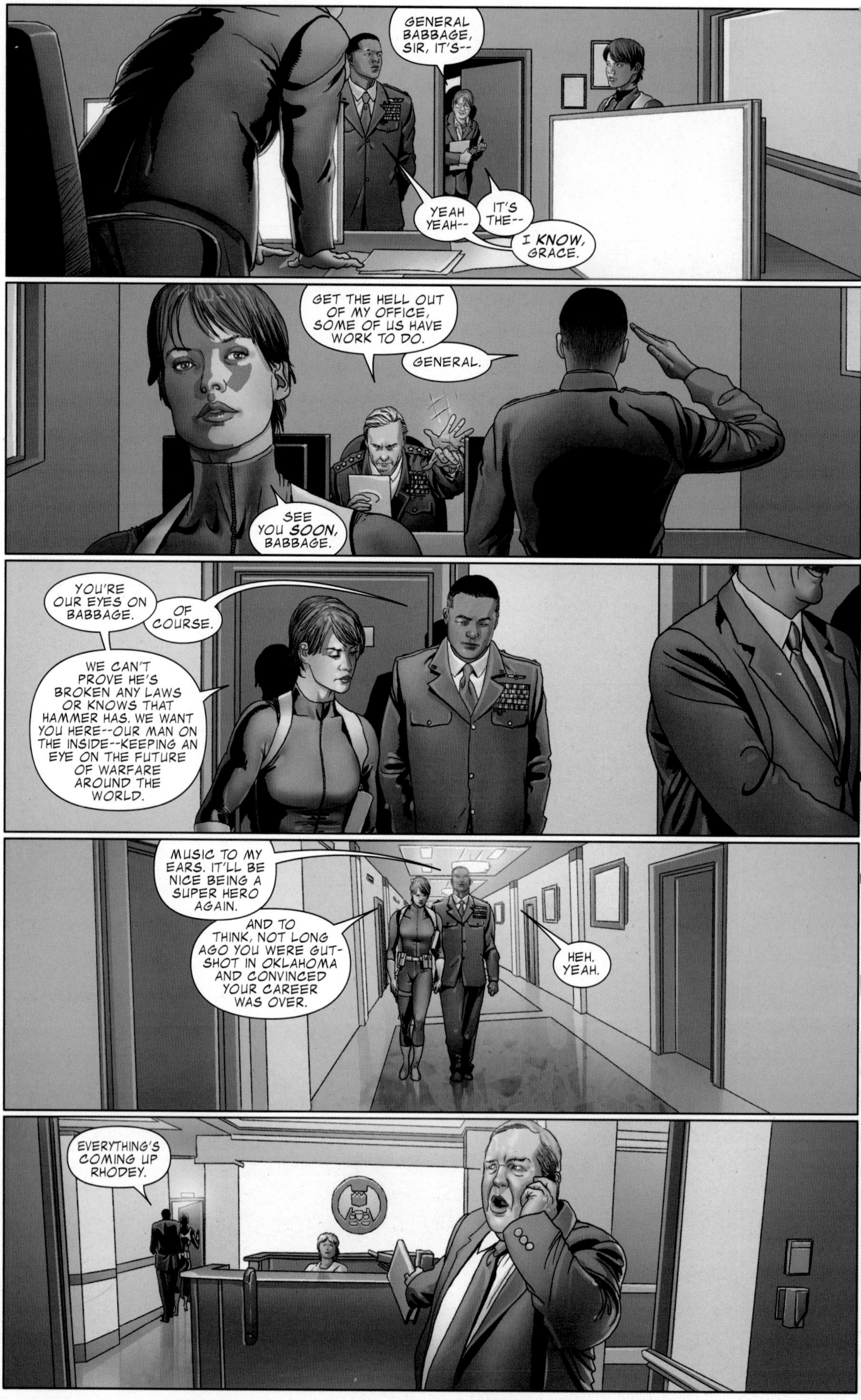
GENERAL BABBAGE, SIR, IT'S--
IT'S THE--
YEAH YEAH--
I KNOW, GRACE.
GET THE HELL OUT OF MY OFFICE, SOME OF US HAVE WORK TO DO.
GENERAL.
SEE YOU SOON, BABBAGE.
YOU'RE OUR EYES ON BABBAGE.
OF COURSE.
WE CAN'T PROVE HE'S BROKEN ANY LAWS OR KNOWS THAT HAMMER HAS. WE WANT YOU HERE--OUR MAN ON THE INSIDE--KEEPING AN EYE ON THE FUTURE OF WARFARE AROUND THE WORLD.
MUSIC TO MY EARS. IT'LL BE NICE BEING A SUPER HERO AGAIN.
AND TO THINK, NOT LONG AGO YOU WERE GUT-SHOT IN OKLAHOMA AND CONVINCED YOUR CAREER WAS OVER.
HEH. YEAH.
EVERYTHING'S COMING UP RHODEY.

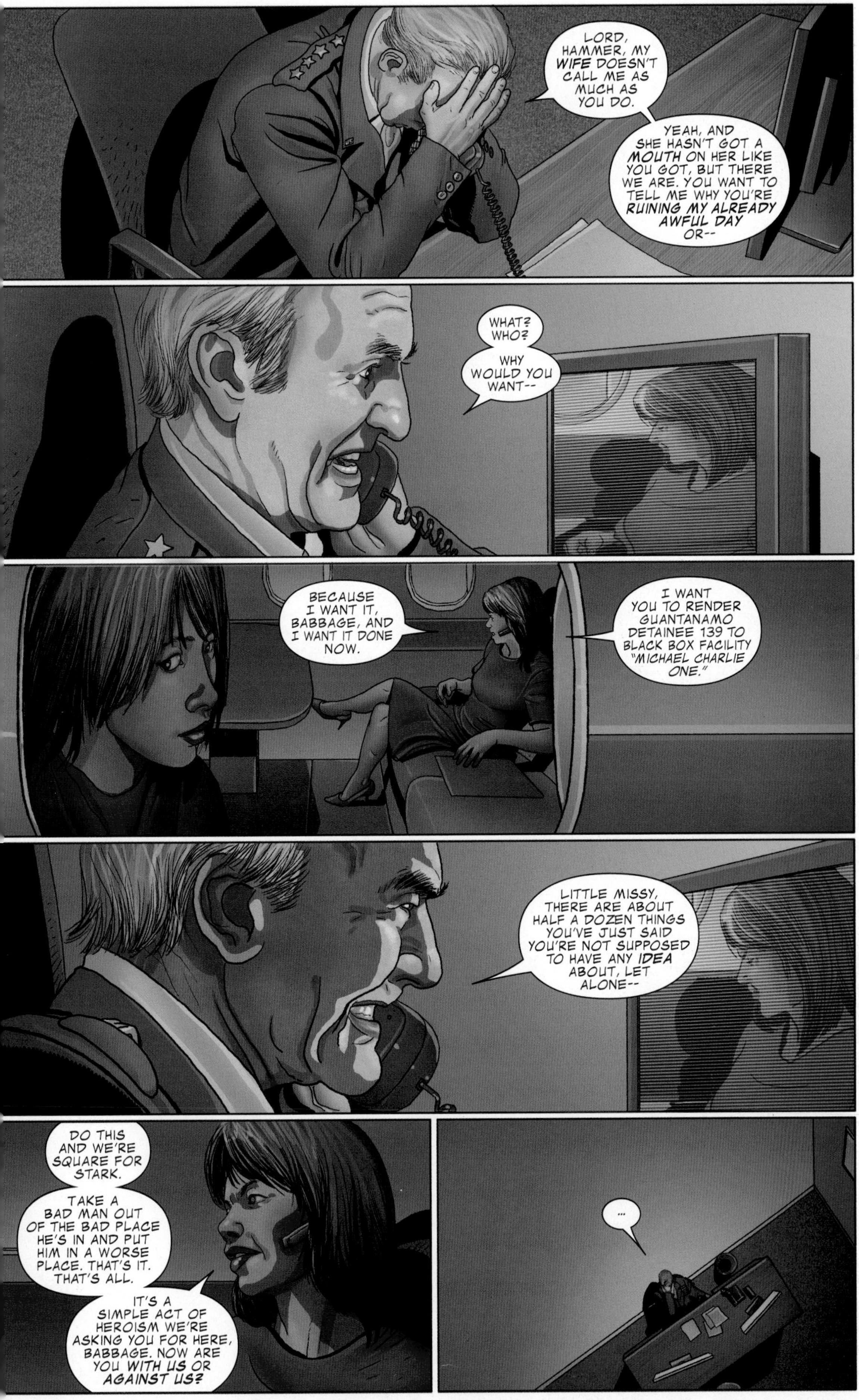
LORD, HAMMER, MY WIFE DOESN'T CALL ME AS MUCH AS YOU DO.
YEAH, AND SHE HASN'T GOT A MOUTH ON HER LIKE YOU GOT, BUT THERE WE ARE. YOU WANT TO TELL ME WHY YOU'RE RUINING MY ALREADY AWFUL DAY OR--
WHAT? WHO?
WHY WOULD YOU WANT--
BECAUSE I WANT IT, BABBAGE, AND I WANT IT DONE NOW.
I WANT YOU TO RENDER GUANTANAMO DETAINEE 139 TO BLACK BOX FACILITY "MICHAEL CHARLIE ONE."
LITTLE MISSY, THERE ARE ABOUT HALF A DOZEN THINGS YOU'VE JUST SAID YOU'RE NOT SUPPOSED TO HAVE ANY IDEA ABOUT, LET ALONE--
DO THIS AND WE'RE SQUARE FOR STARK.
TAKE A BAD MAN OUT OF THE BAD PLACE HE'S IN AND PUT HIM IN A WORSE PLACE. THAT'S IT. THAT'S ALL.
IT'S A SIMPLE ACT OF HEROISM WE'RE ASKING YOU FOR HERE, BABBAGE. NOW ARE YOU WITH US OR AGAINST US?
...

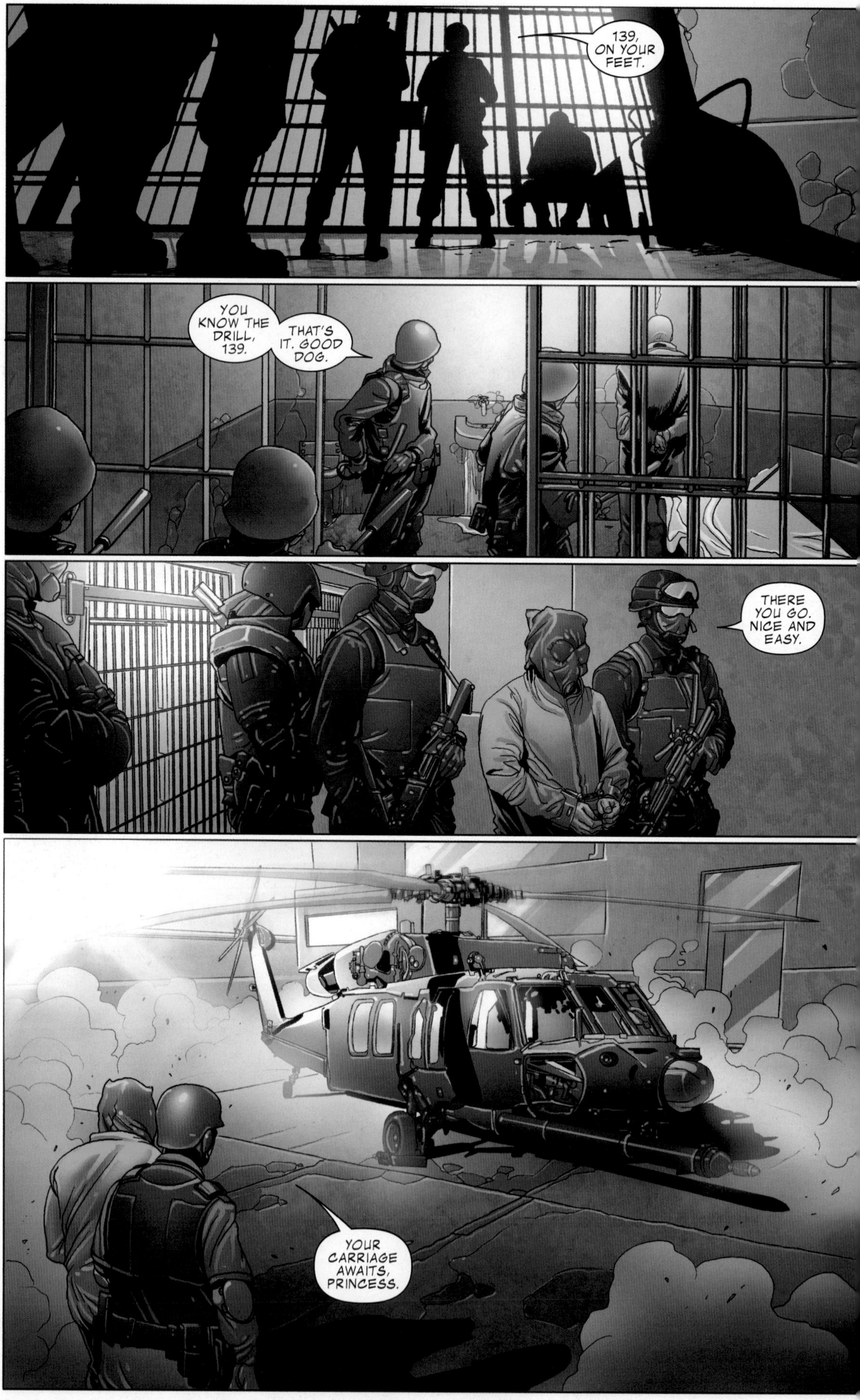
139, ON YOUR FEET.
YOU KNOW THE DRILL, 139.
THAT'S IT. GOOD DOG.
THERE YOU GO. NICE AND EASY.
YOUR CARRIAGE AWAITS, PRINCESS.

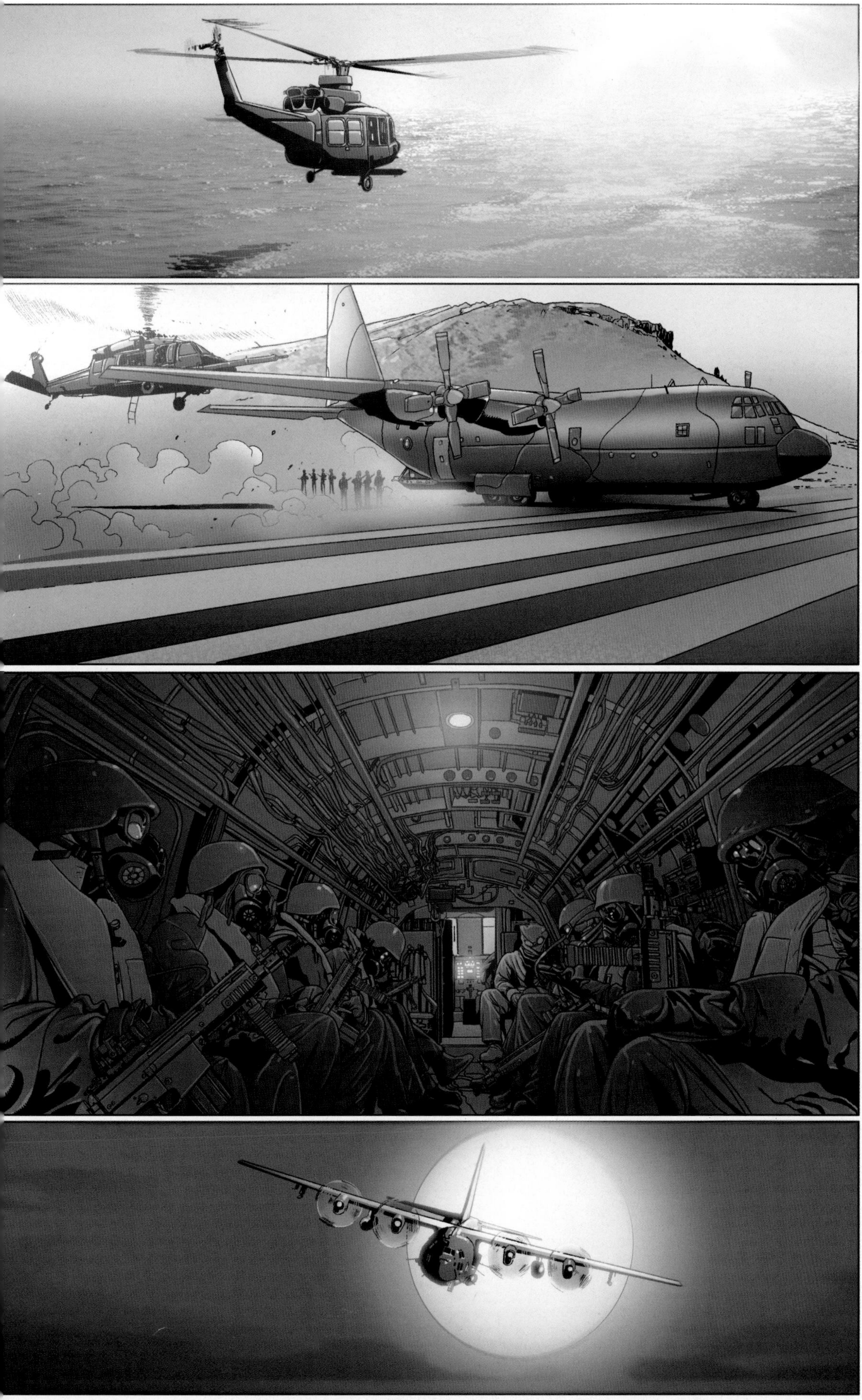

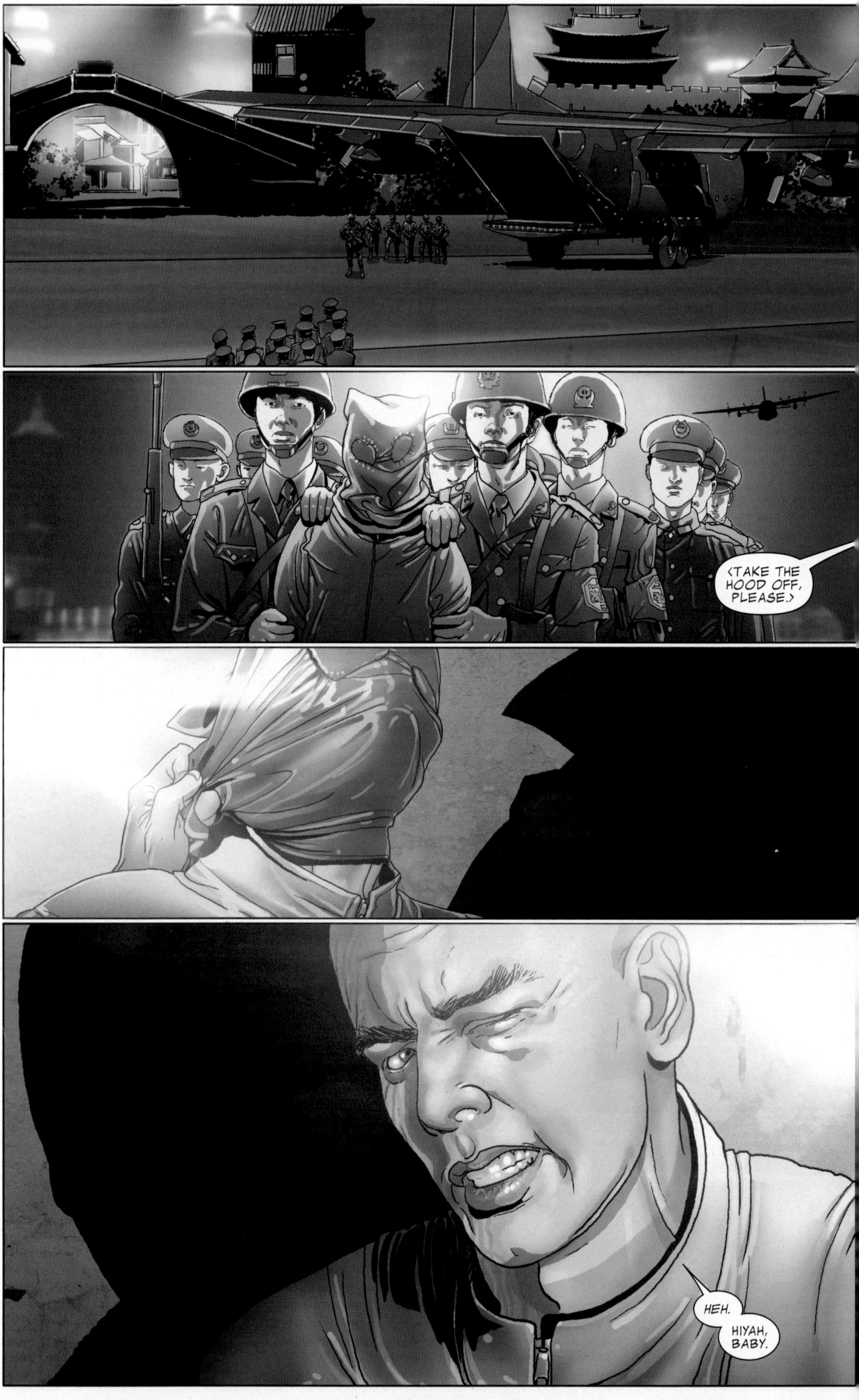
<TAKE THE HOOD OFF, PLEASE.>
HEH.
HIYAH, BABY.

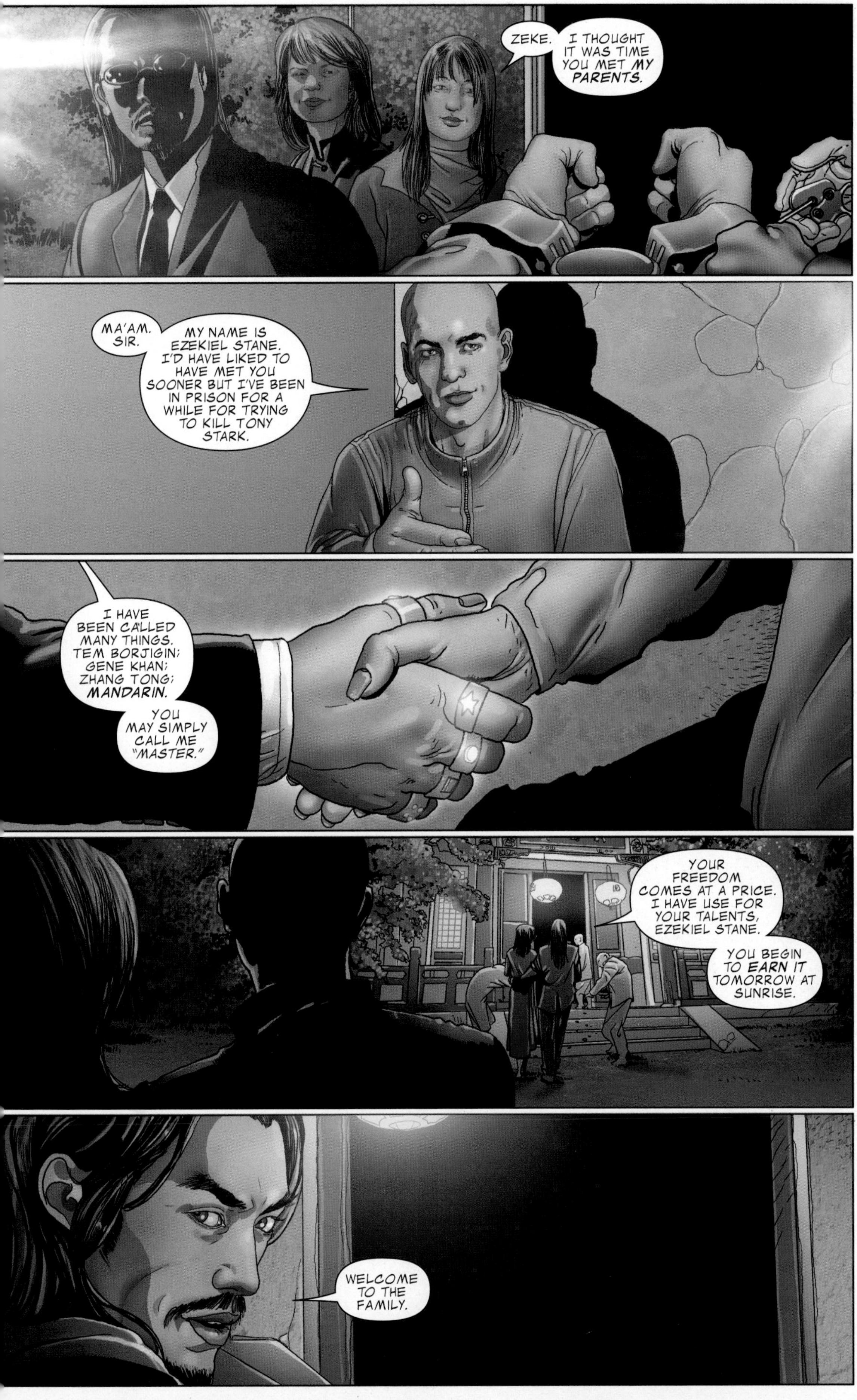

ZEKE.
I THOUGHT IT WAS TIME YOU MET MY PARENTS.
MA'AM. SIR.
MY NAME IS EZEKIEL STANE. I'D HAVE LIKED TO HAVE MET YOU SOONER BUT I'VE BEEN IN PRISON FOR A WHILE FOR TRYING TO KILL TONY STARK.
I HAVE BEEN CALLED MANY THINGS. TEM BORJIGIN; GENE KHAN; ZHANG TONG; MANDARIN.
YOU MAY SIMPLY CALL ME "MASTER."
YOUR FREEDOM COMES AT A PRICE. I HAVE USE FOR YOUR TALENTS, EZEKIEL STANE.
YOU BEGIN TO EARN IT TOMORROW AT SUNRISE.
WELCOME TO THE FAMILY.

WHEN I HAD TO DEPEND ON A CAR TO SAVE MY LIFE...

IT WAS THE *STARK RESILIENT.*

POWERED BY GROUNDBREAKING *REPULSOR BATTERIES,* IT'S THE WORLD'S FIRST ENTIRELY ELECTRIC *CONSUMER GRADE* CAR THAT CAN *PERFORM* AT THIS LEVEL.

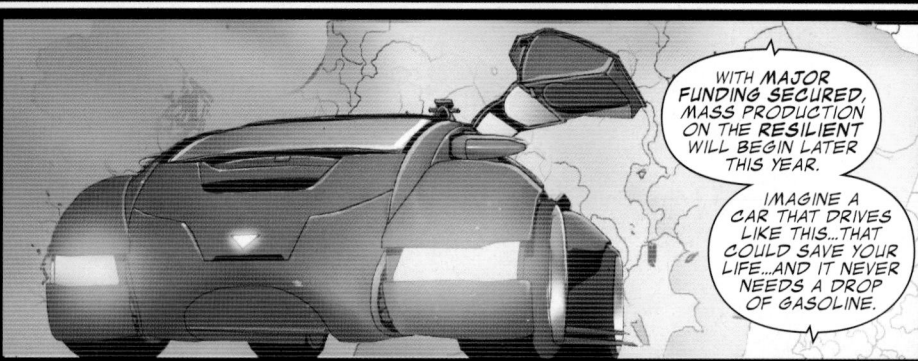

WITH *MAJOR FUNDING SECURED,* MASS PRODUCTION ON THE *RESILIENT* WILL BEGIN LATER THIS YEAR.

IMAGINE A CAR THAT DRIVES LIKE THIS...THAT COULD SAVE YOUR LIFE...AND IT NEVER NEEDS A DROP OF GASOLINE.

IMAGINE A FUTURE FREE OF FOSSIL FUELS. AND THEN IMAGINE WHAT COULD COME *NEXT.*

I'M TONY STARK. AND I AM *RESILIENT.*

FAN*TASTIC* COMMERCIAL, BOSS.

LADIES AND GENTLEMEN, PRODUCTION ON THE *STARK RESILIENT* BEGINS AS SOON AS WE GET THIS DAMN PLACE REPAIRED.

WE HAVE A *LOT* TO DO.

LET'S GET TO WORK.

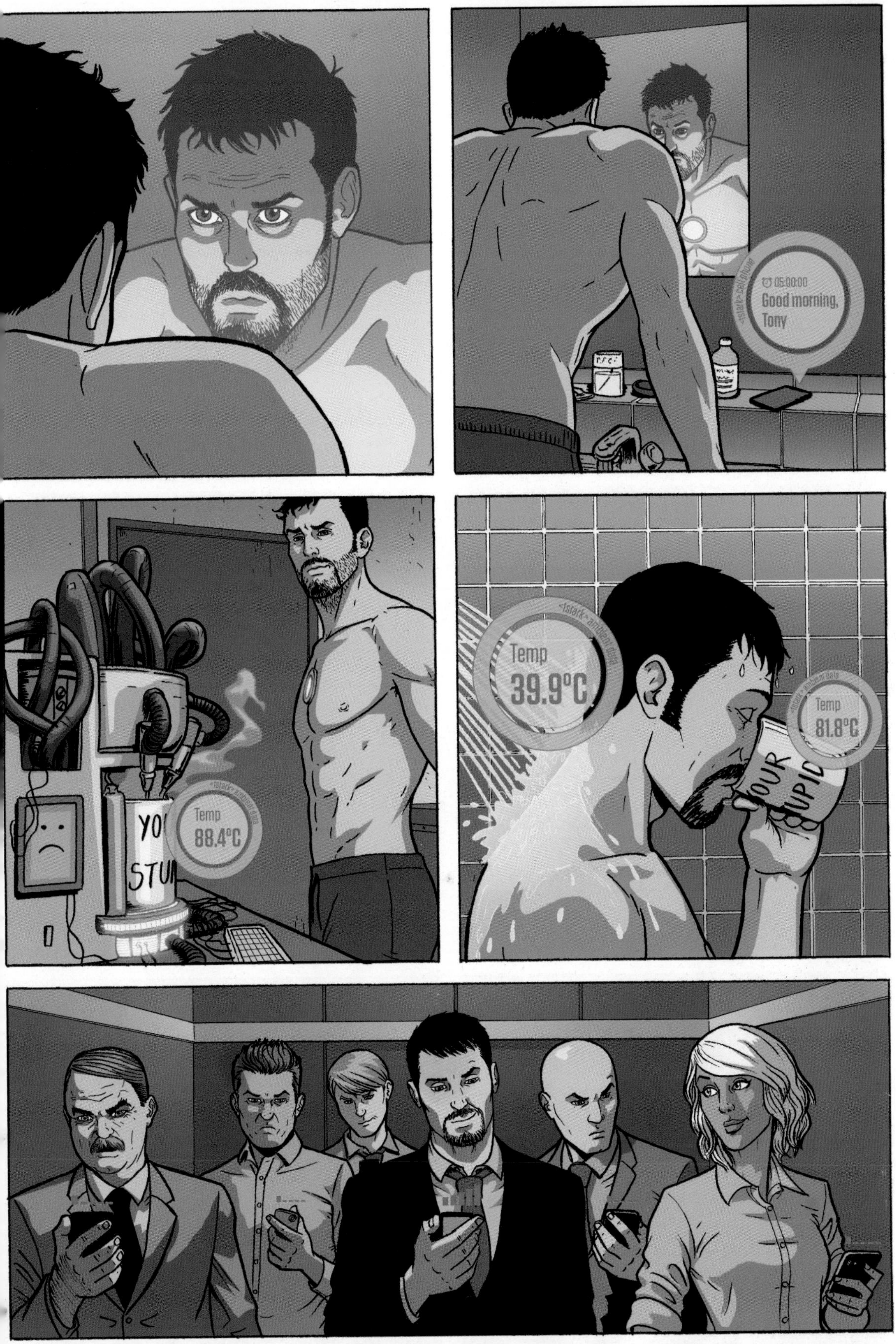
<tstark> cell phone
05:00:00
Good morning, Tony
<tstark> ambient data
Temp
88.4°C
<tstark> ambient data
Temp
39.9°C
<tstark> ambient data
Temp
81.8°C

GOOD MORNING, TONY

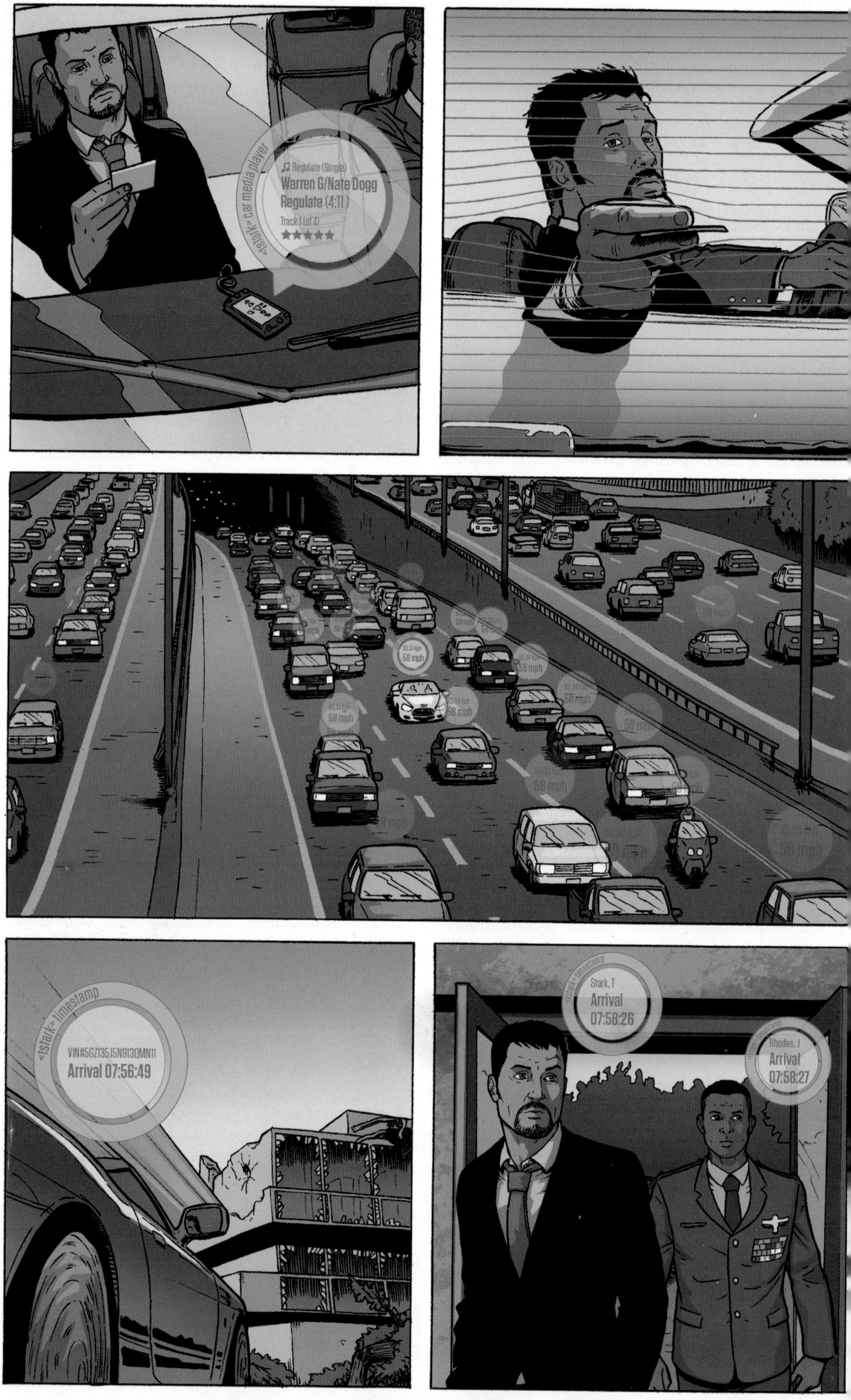
<stark> car media player
Regulate (Single)
Warren G/Nate Dogg
Regulate (4:11)
Track 1 (of 4)
93.34 kph
58 mph
<stark> timestamp
VIN#5GZ135J5N913QMN11
Arrival 07:56:49
<stark> timestamp
Stark, T
Arrival
07:58:26
Rhodes, J
Arrival
07:58:27

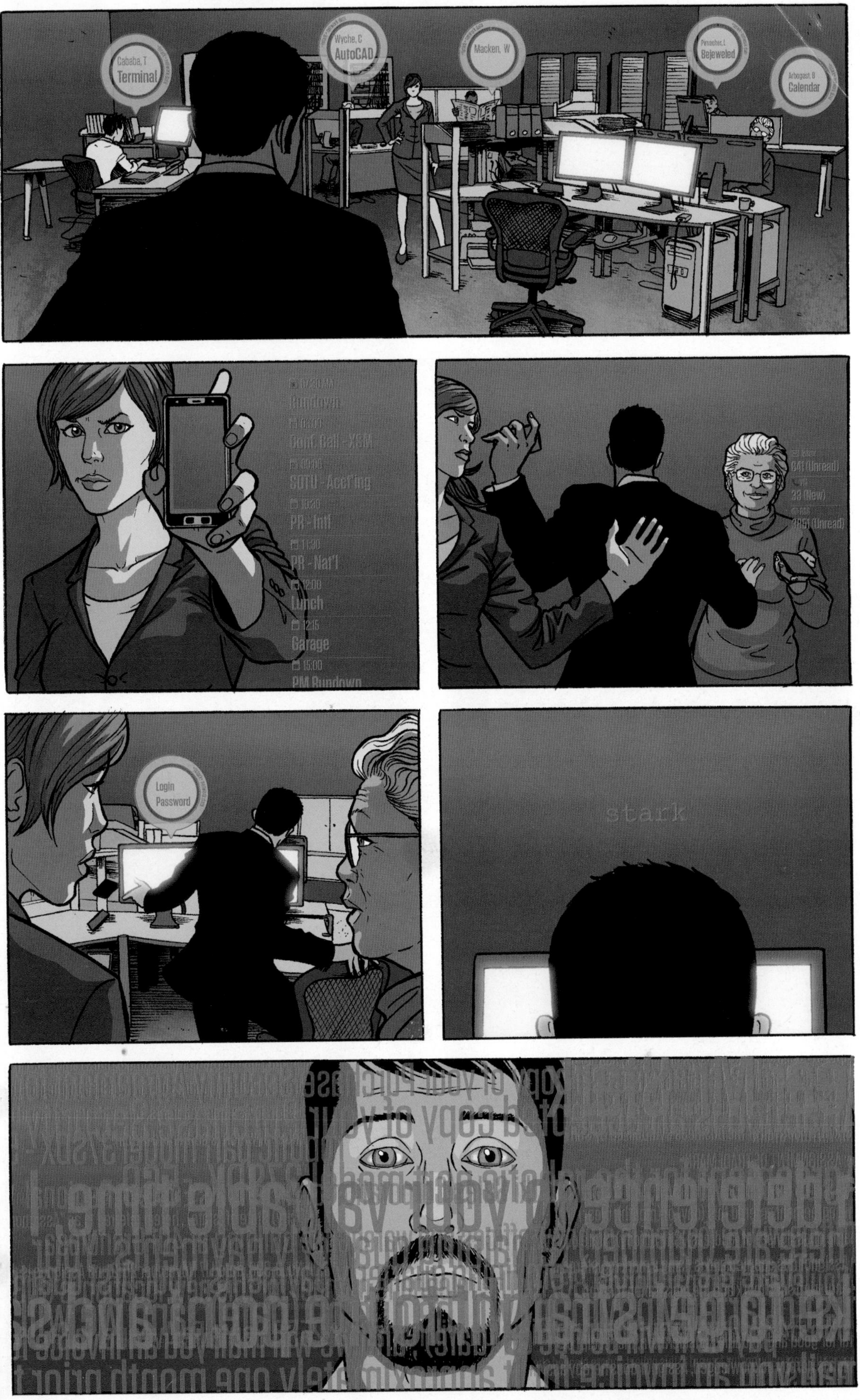

Cababa, T
Terminal
Wyche, C
AutoCAD
Macken, W
Pinochet, L
Bejeweled
Arbogast, B
Calendar
07:30 AM
Rundown
Conf. Call - XSM
PR - Int'l
11:30
PR - Nat'l
12:00
Lunch
12:15
Garage
15:00
PM Rundown
641 (Unread)
33 (New)
3851 (Unread)
Login
Password
stark

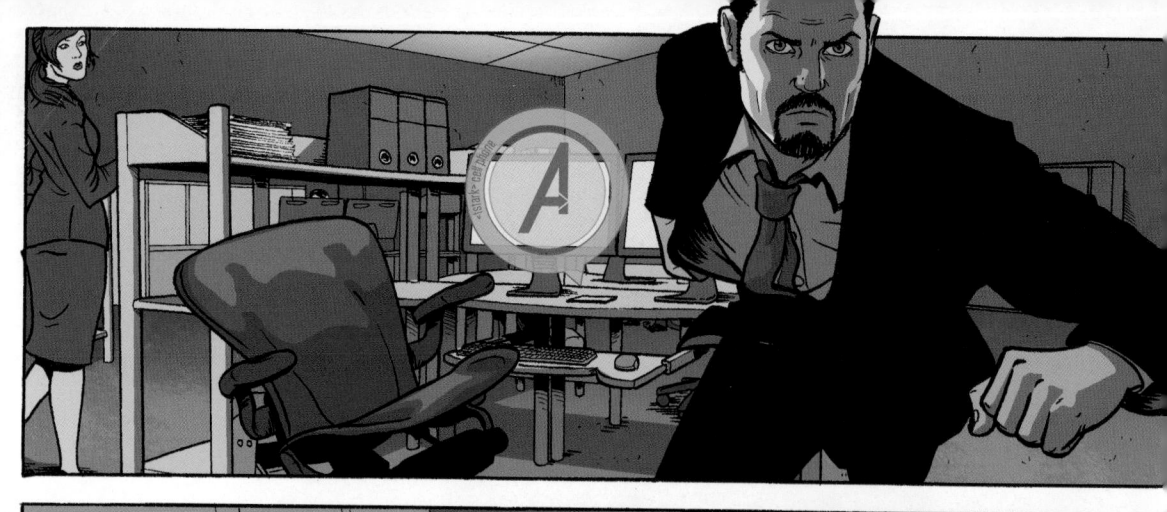

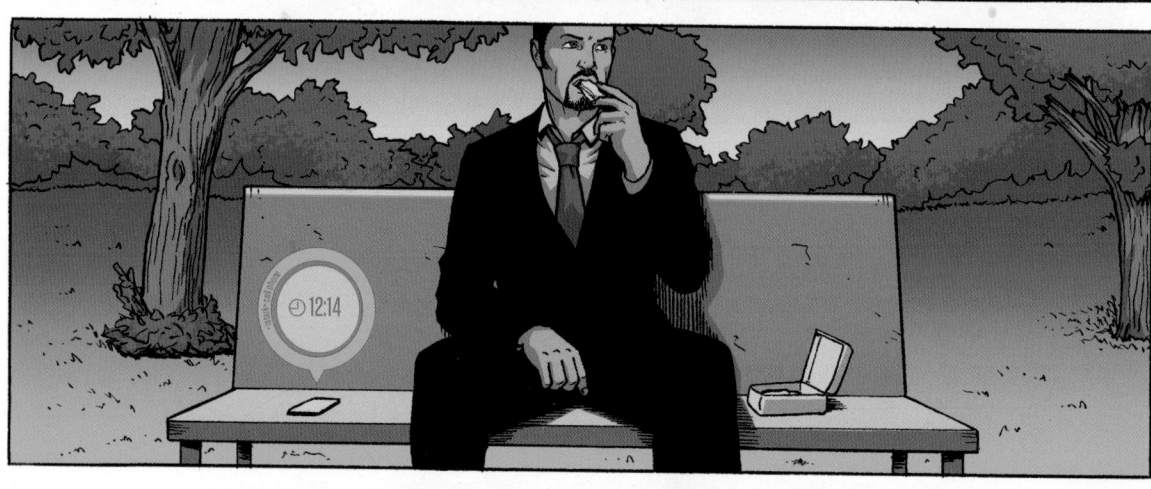

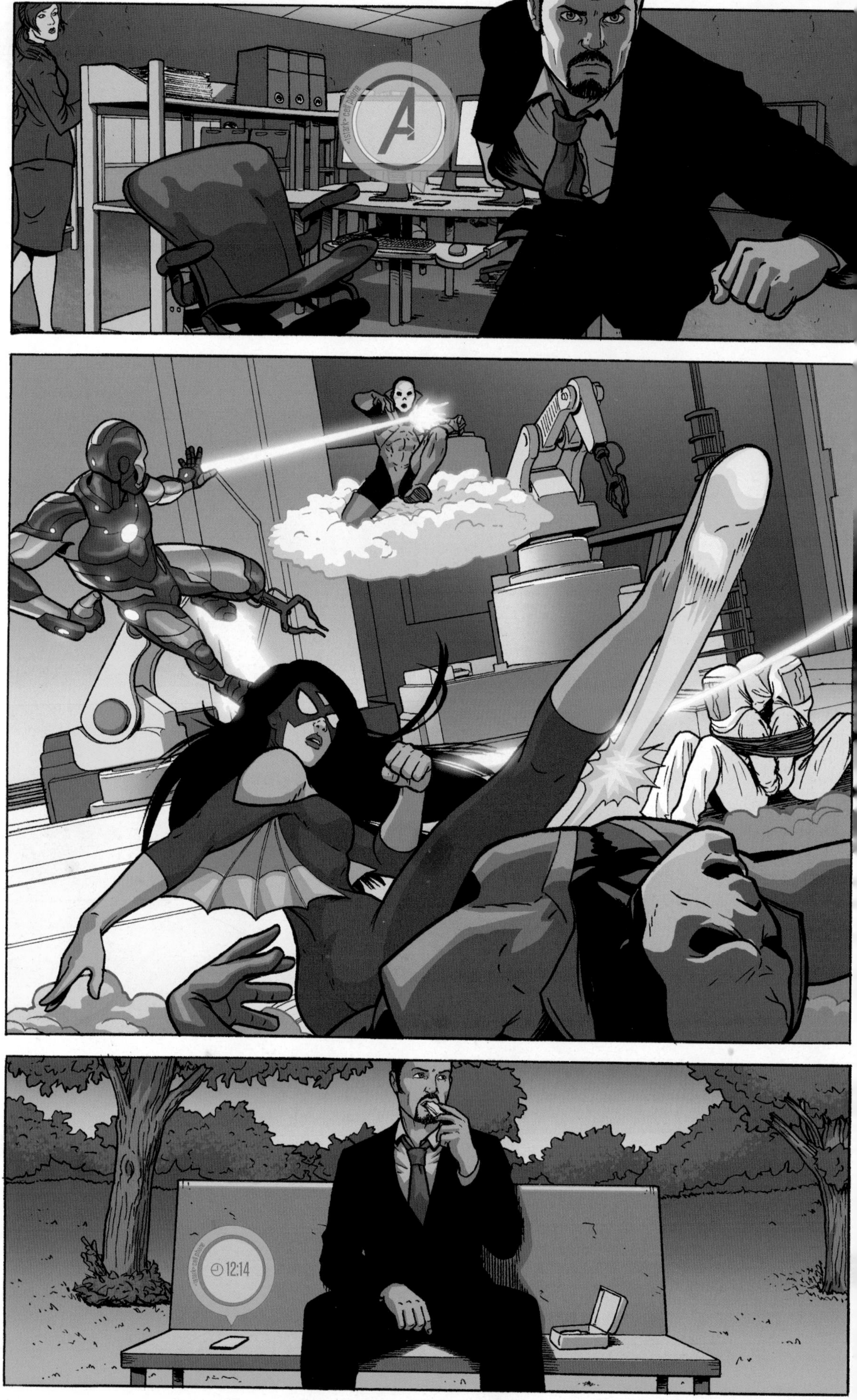
<stark> cell phone
12:14

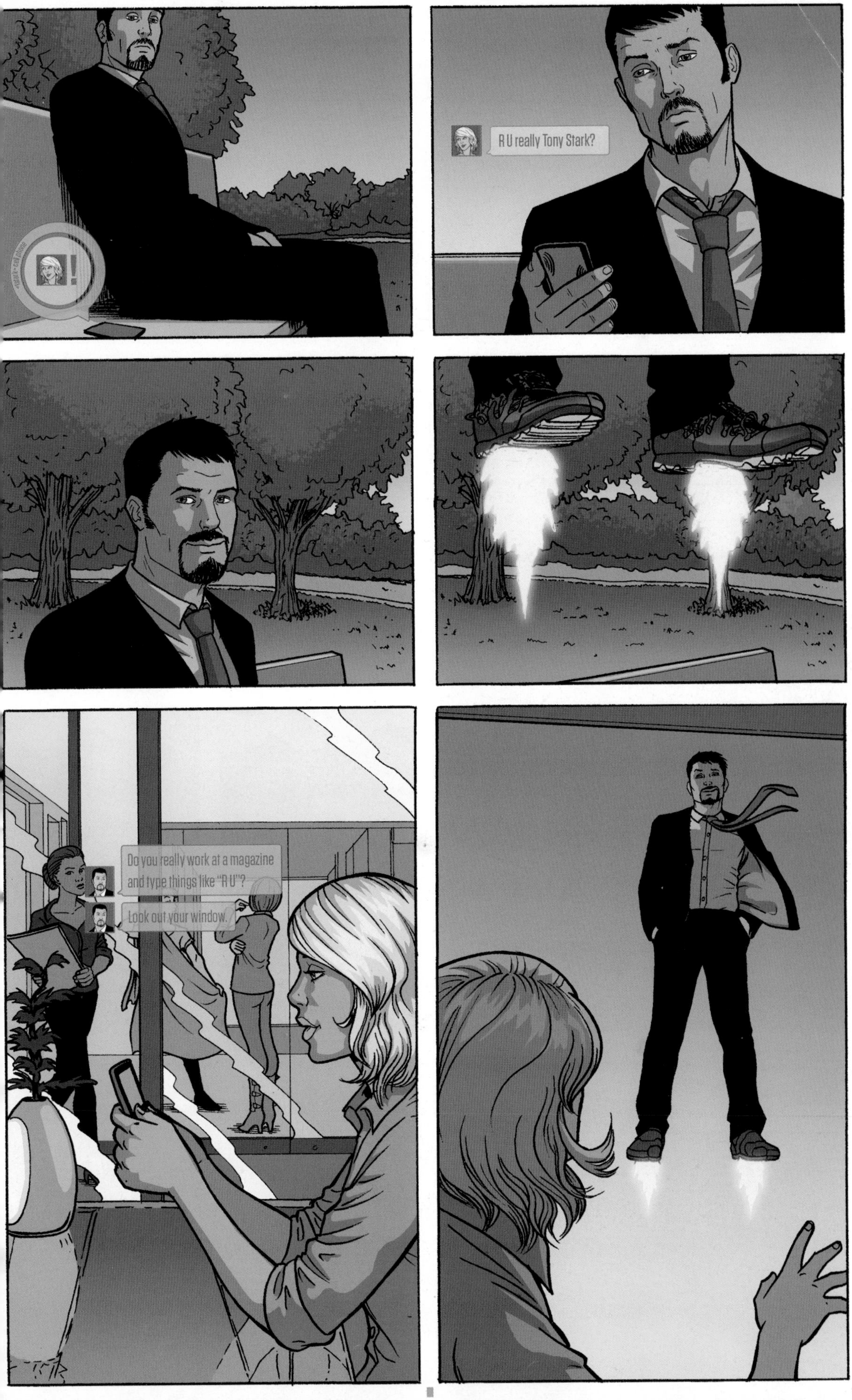
<stark> cell phone
R U really Tony Stark?
Do you really work at a magazine and type things like "R U"?
Look out your window.

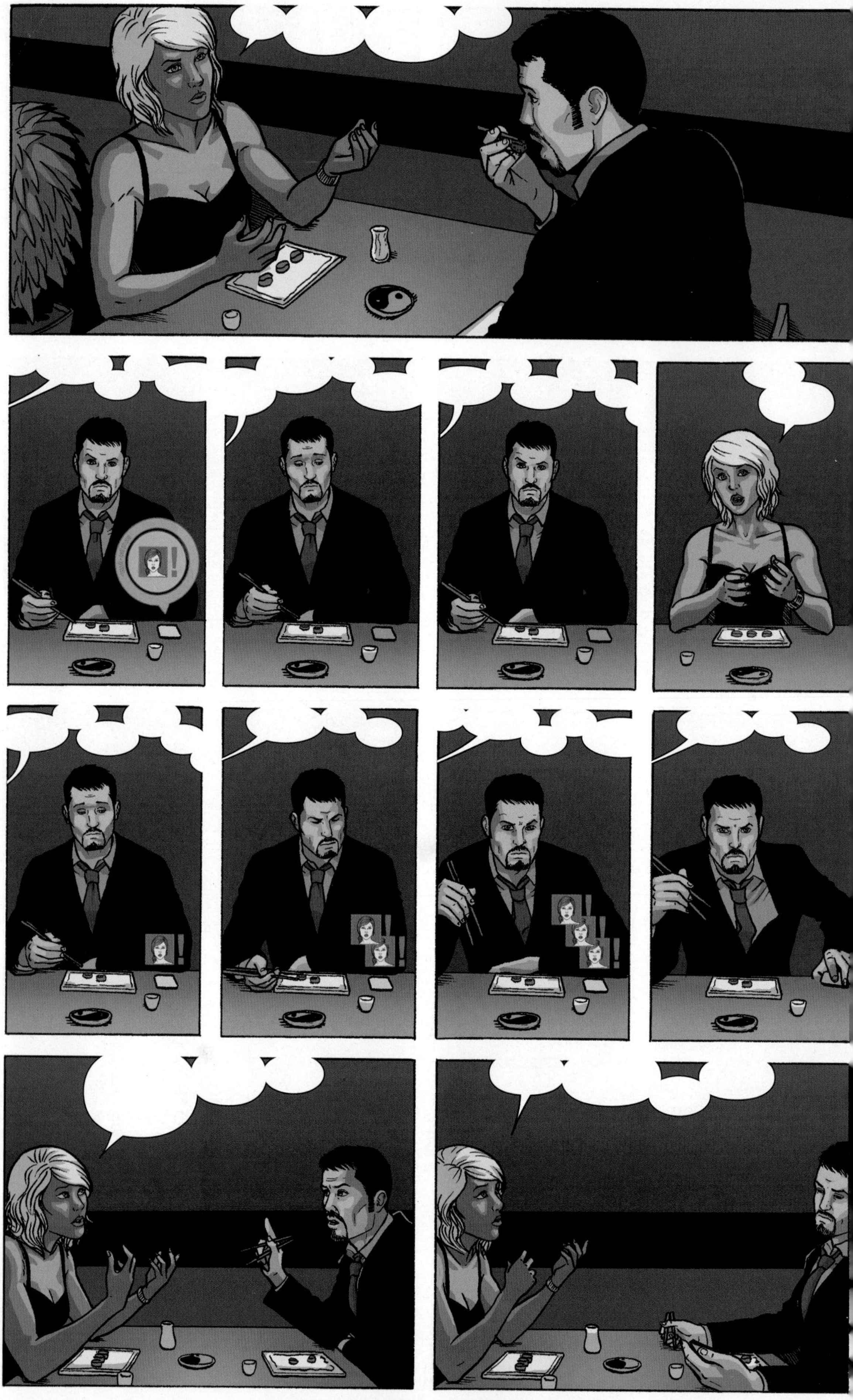

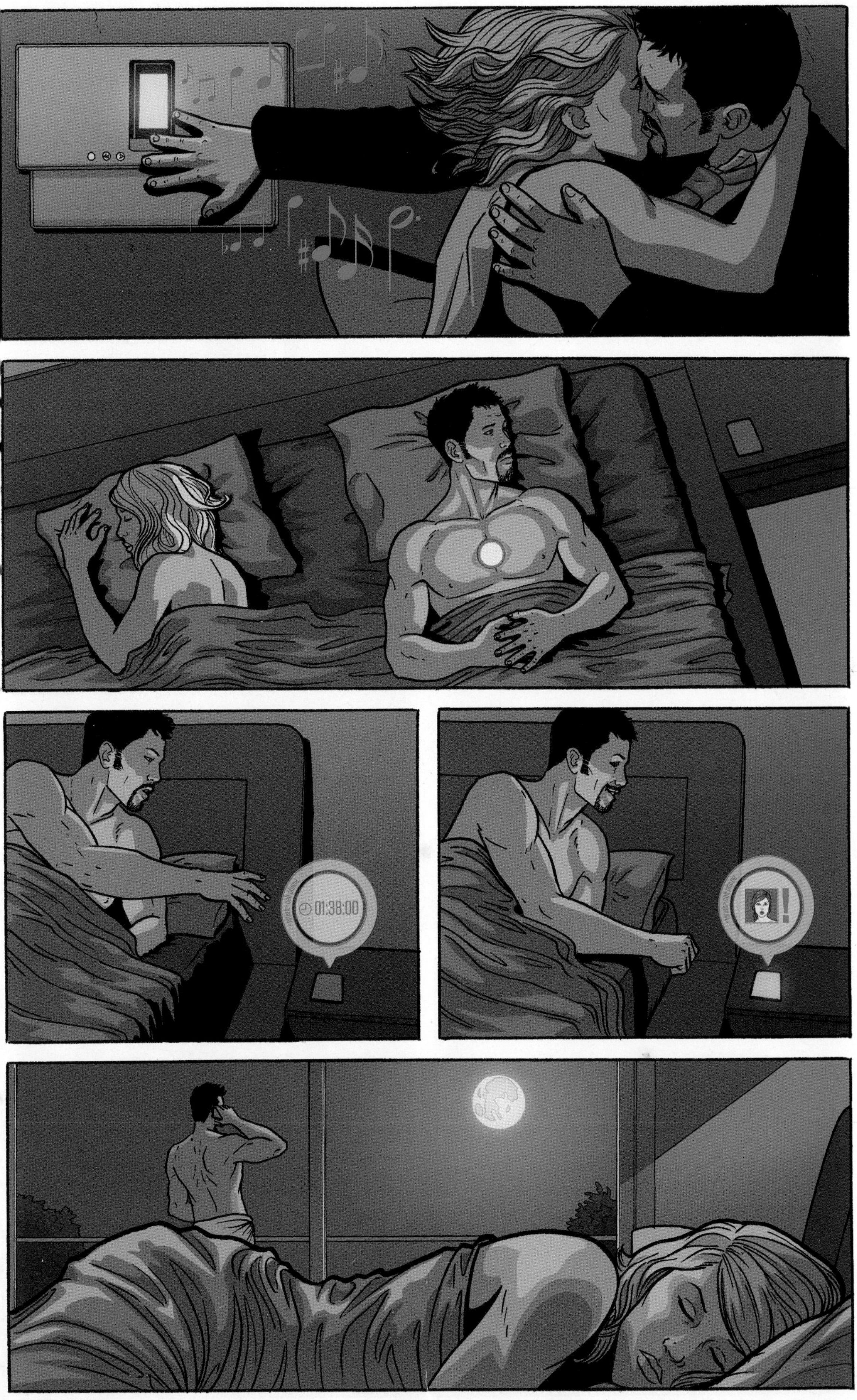
01:38:00
!

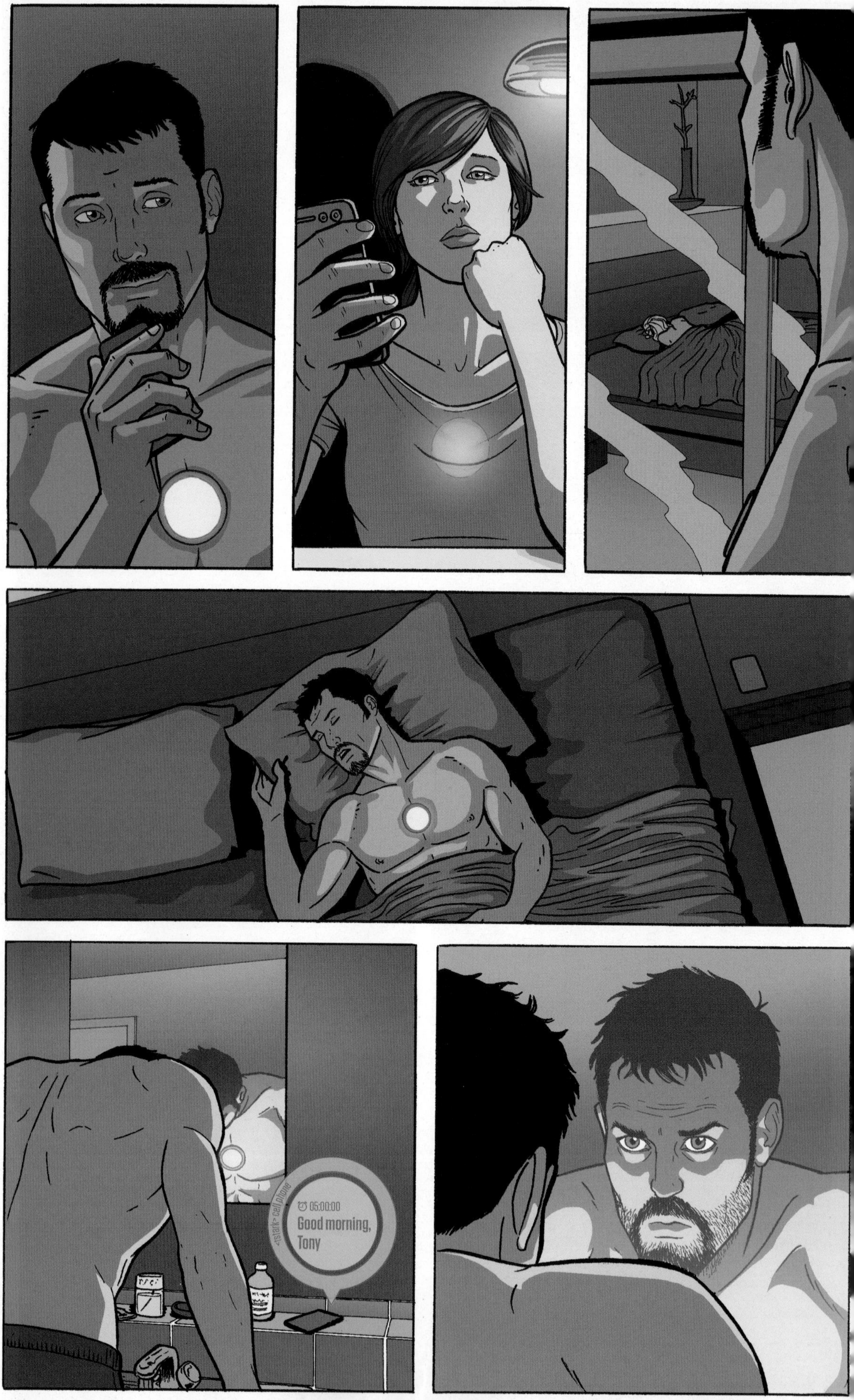
<istark> cell phone
05:00:00
Good morning, Tony

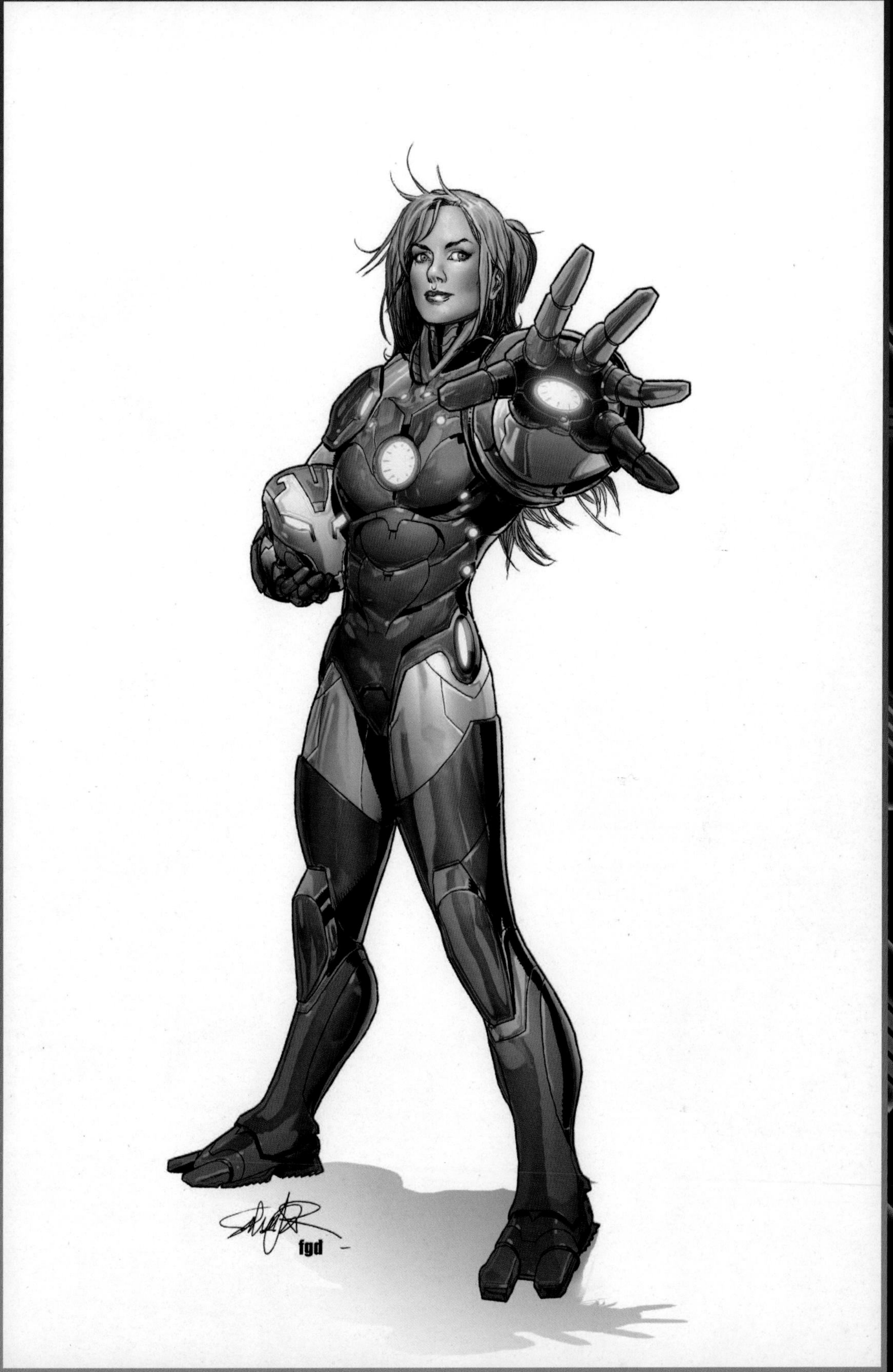
fgd

#29 WOMEN OF MARVEL FRAME VARIANT
BY SALVADOR LARROCA & FRANK D'ARMATA

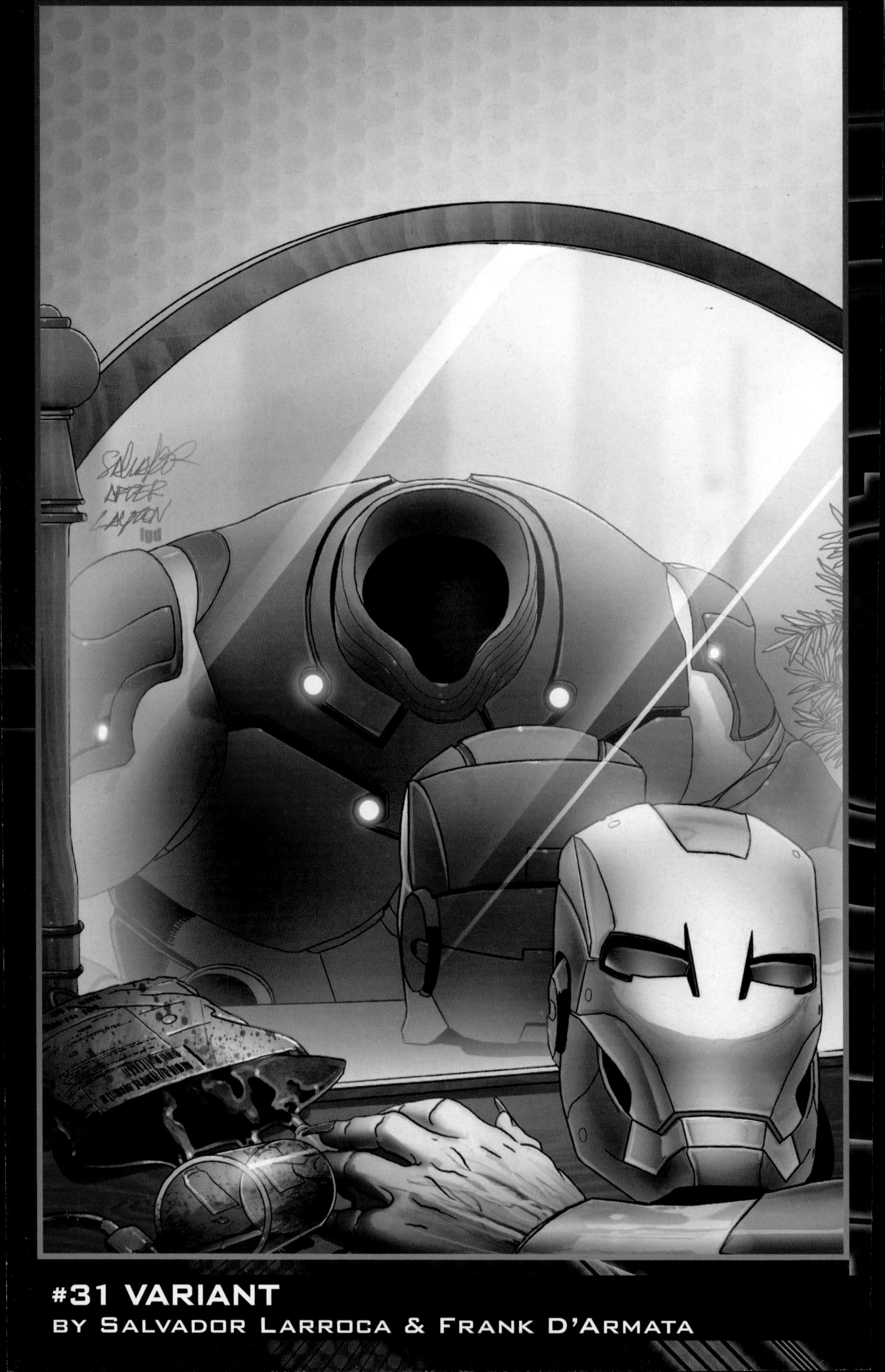

#31 VARIANT
BY SALVADOR LARROCA & FRANK D'ARMATA

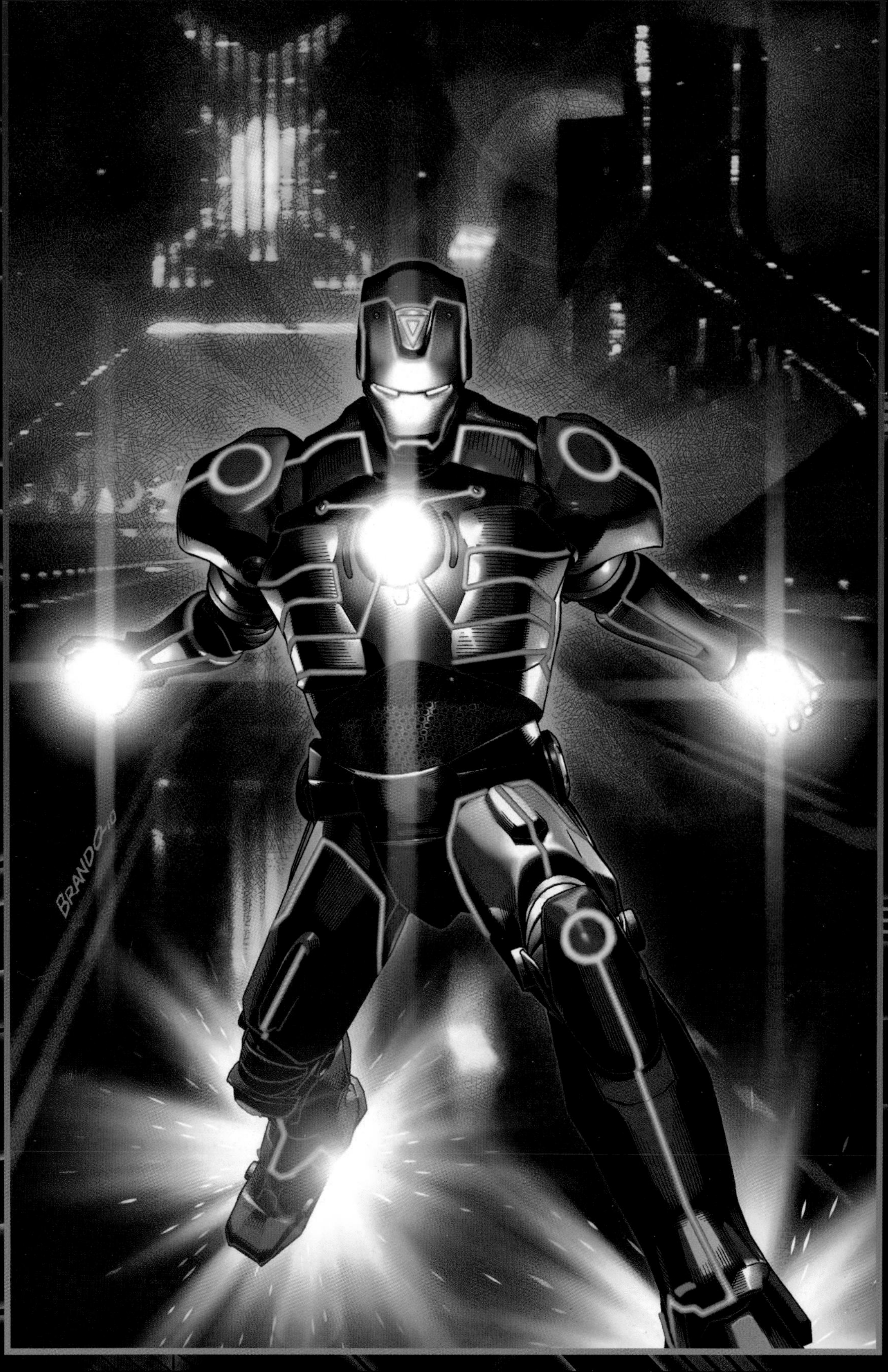

#33 TRON VARIANT

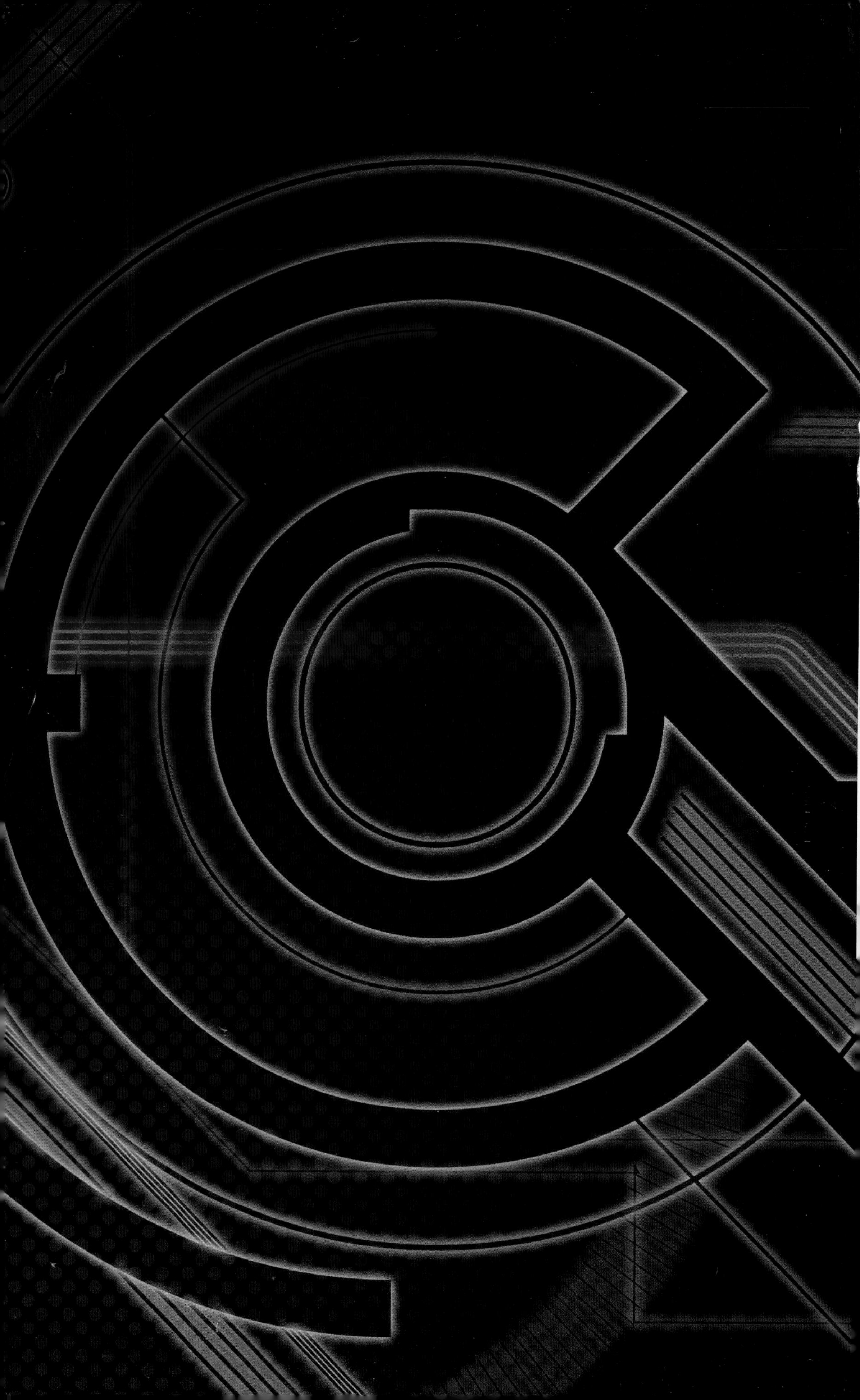